Global
Servant-Leadership

Global
Servant-Leadership

Wisdom, Love, and Legitimate Power in the Age of Chaos

Edited by
Philip Mathew
Jiying Song
Shann Ray Ferch
Larry C. Spears

LEXINGTON BOOKS
Lanham • Boulder • New York • London

Published by Lexington Books
An imprint of The Rowman & Littlefield Publishing Group, Inc.
4501 Forbes Boulevard, Suite 200, Lanham, Maryland 20706
www.rowman.com

6 Tinworth Street, London SE11 5AL, United Kingdom

British Library Cataloguing in Publication Information Available

Library of Congress Control Number: 2020945867

ISBN 978-1-7936-2186-3 (cloth: alk. paper)
ISBN 978-1-7936-2187-0 (electronic)

∞™ The paper used in this publication meets the minimum requirements of American
National Standard for Information Sciences—Permanence of Paper for Printed Library
Materials, ANSI/NISO Z39.48-1992.

Contents

Preface

A Thirty-Year Global Journey in Servant-Leadership

Larry C. Spears

This collection of essays, *Global Servant-Leadership: Wisdom, Love, and Legitimate Power in the Age of Chaos*, represents a compelling look at servant-leadership from an international perspective. The chapters in this compilation offer up deep wisdom, powerful questions, and helpful practices for those of us who desire to grow as aspiring servant-leaders who also understand that servant-leadership has been influenced by the deep insights and perspectives of many cultures around the world.

The term servant-leadership was first coined in a 1970 essay by Robert K. Greenleaf (1904–1990), entitled *The Servant as Leader*. Greenleaf spent most of his organizational life in the field of management research, development, and education at AT&T. Following a forty-year career there, he founded the Center for Applied Ethics in 1964 and enjoyed a second career that lasted another twenty-five years. In 1985, the Center for Applied Ethics was renamed The Robert K. Greenleaf Center, where I served as President & CEO from 1990–2007. Since 2008, I have divided my time between Gonzaga University (Spokane), where I serve as servant-leadership scholar, and The Larry Spears Center for Servant-Leadership (Indianapolis).

During those early years, I edited or co-edited five volumes of writings by Robert Greenleaf: *On Becoming a Servant-Leader* (1996), *Seeker and Servant* (1996), *The Power of Servant-Leadership* (1998), *Servant Leadership: 25ᵗʰ Anniversary Edition* (2002), and *The Servant-Leader Within* (2003). Working together with many others, both then and since, I have also co-produced an ongoing series of servant-leadership anthologies, including *Reflections on Leadership* (1995), *Insights on Leadership* (1998), *Focus on Leadership* (2002), *Practicing Servant-Leadership* (2004), *The Spirit of Servant-Leadership* (2011), *Conversations on Servant-Leadership* (2015),

Servant-Leadership and Forgiveness (2020), and this latest volume, *Global Servant-Leadership*.

Since 1970, more than a half-million copies of Robert Greenleaf's books and essays have been sold worldwide. Slowly but surely, his writings on servant-leadership have helped to transform both people and organizations around the world. In many ways, it may be said that the times are only now beginning to catch up with Robert Greenleaf's visionary call to servant-leadership. The idea of servant-leadership, now in its sixth decade as a concept bearing that name, continues to create a quiet revolution around the world.

But what does servant-leadership entail? Who *is* a servant-leader? Greenleaf said that the servant-leader is one who is a servant first and a leader second. In *The Servant as Leader,* Greenleaf (1977) writes,

> The servant-leader is servant first. It begins with the natural feeling that one wants to serve first. Then conscious choice brings one to aspire to lead. The difference manifests itself in the care taken by the servant—first to make sure that other people's highest priority needs are being served. The best test is: Do those served grow as persons; do they, while being served, become healthier, wiser, freer, more autonomous, more likely themselves to become servants? And, what is the effect on the least privileged in society? Will they benefit or at least not be further deprived? (pp. 13–14)

The words servant and leader are usually thought of as being opposites. In deliberately bringing those two words together in a meaningful way, Robert Greenleaf gave birth to the paradoxical term "servant-leader." His writings on the subject of servant-leadership helped to get this global movement started, and his views have had a profound and growing effect on many organizations and thought-leaders. Organizations like AFLAC, Chick-fil-A, The Container Store, Starbucks, Southwest Airlines, Synovus Financial Corporation, TDIndustries, and many more are recognized today for nurturing servant-led cultures. These institutions and many more have been encouraged and supported by a long list of servant-leadership thought-leaders such as James Autry, Cheryl Bachelder, Warren Bennis, Ken Blanchard, Peter Block, John Carver, Stephen Covey, Max DePree, Shann Ferch, Don Frick, John Horsman, James Kouzes, Parker Palmer, M. Scott Peck, Peter Senge, Margaret Wheatley, and Danah Zohar, to name but a handful of today's cutting-edge authors and advocates of servant-leadership.

In 1992, I conducted a study of Robert Greenleaf's writings. From that analysis, I was able to codify a set of ten characteristics that Greenleaf wrote about in various writings, which he considered as being central to the development of servant-leaders. These include listening, empathy, healing, awareness, persuasion, conceptualization, foresight, stewardship, commitment to the growth of people, and building community. My analysis showed these to be the ones that Greenleaf mentioned most often in his writings, which led me to codify them into a list and to begin to write about them. While these ten characteristics of servant-leadership are by no means exhaustive, they do serve to communicate the power and promise that this concept offers to servant-leaders who are open to its invitation and challenge. Like Robert Greenleaf, I am convinced that it is possible to become an increasingly authentic servant-leader through the conscious development of these and other characteristics.

It is helpful to understand that servant-leadership starts within each one of us and that it is first-and-foremost a personal philosophy and commitment that we can choose to practice in any environment. If we understand Greenleaf's best test as the fundamental understanding of servant-leadership, then it becomes clear that the choice to seek to practice servant-leadership is ours to make. Our personal embracing of servant-leadership does not require the approval of our supervisor or our organization's chief executive. We don't need anyone's permission to personally do our best to act as a servant-leader. It is our choice.

Since 1990, my work has included a strong focus on encouraging a global understanding and practice of servant-leadership. During my years with the Greenleaf Center, I worked to encourage the translation and publication of various servant-leadership essays and books into Arabic, Bahasa Indonesian, Czech, Dutch, French, German, Japanese, Korean, Mandarin Chinese, Portuguese, Russian, Spanish, Swedish, and Turkish language editions. In 2005, Shann Ferch and I launched *The International Journal of Servant-Leadership*, which is a joint publication of Gonzaga University and The Spears Center for Servant-Leadership. We have taken great care over the years to cultivate content contributions to the journal from a wide-ranging global perspective.

For thirty years, I have travelled internationally to meet with others in sharing ideas and inspiration around the servant-as-leader philosophy. While I have visited a dozen countries, the internet has allowed me to be in touch with people from many more countries who are interested in servant-leadership. Today, I maintain a strong-and-growing correspondence with many who have been impacted by their own understanding-and-practices of servant-leadership, and who are also helping to shape the future legacy of servant-leadership in the world.

Global Servant-Leadership: Wisdom, Love, and Legitimate Power in the Age of Chaos reveals many pathways available to people, institutions, and countries desiring a better way of working together through serving first, and then leading. This book also shows how servant-leadership attributes of healing, listening, awareness, community-building, and others can be used as an antidote for an increasingly fractured and divisive world. So many caring people are working across the globe to build strong relationships, grounded in the belief that serving and leading one another is yet another important expression of love in the world.

REFERENCE

Greenleaf, R. (1977). *Servant leadership: A journey into the nature of legitimate power and greatness.* New Jersey, NJ: Paulist Press.

Foreword

Serving the World with Love

Philip Mathew and Shann Ray Ferch

As practitioners and scholars of servant-leadership, we are honored to present *Global Servant-Leadership: Wisdom, Love, and Legitimate Power in the Age of Chaos*, a book we hope will engage the complexity and courage required for a more globally minded, interculturally grounded, and personally relevant conception of servant-leadership. We are grateful to Lexington Books, their editors, and our contributing authors for their support in publishing this anthology. We've divided this introductory essay into two sections, the first and foundational section written by Philip and the second section by Shann.

PHILIP ON SERVANT-LEADERSHIP

In his groundbreaking 1970 essay *"The Servant as Leader,"* Robert Greenleaf, the architect of the modern-day servant-leadership movement, began by asking if the notions of *servant* and *leader* could be fused into the same person and whether such a person could be effective in the real world. Greenleaf's presence in the world of leadership studies would have no small impact in the years that followed. Indeed, his words and work would waken worldwide interest in servant-leadership, launch the contemporary servant-leadership movement, and influence the development of servant-leaders around the globe for generations.

Looking back, it seems that Greenleaf's questions served really as an opening salvo in the direction of a leadership landscape dominated by traditional autocratic and hierarchical assumptions about the true nature of leading. In the years since the publication of his essay, our current generation of leaders are running head-on into the challenges and complexities of what many are calling the first truly "global century." In doing so, they are finding the value of such models of leadership limited in facing new realities.

Today, forces both breathtaking and challenging are dramatically reshaping the world around us. A growing tilt in geopolitical power, the rapid rise of the digital economy, and work that extends beyond time, space, and geography are converging with realities, such as economic and social insecurity, intractable conflict, political gridlock, and growing inequality. Those who assess the state of the world acknowledge that our present age seems more multifaceted, more interdependent, and yet more broken than in any other time in recent history. These transformations hold promise and peril—with some describing our world as a VUCA world: volatile, uncertain, complex, and ambiguous.

Amidst this backdrop, and given the complexity and interconnectedness of today's world, the "leader-as-hero" model, based on competition, control, and coercion, has proven insufficient. In light of VUCA realities, management scholar Meg Wheatley (2010) offered sage advice in suggesting a move from *leader-as-hero* to *leader-as-host*—calling for a servant-leadership way of leading based on collaboration, engagement, and persuasion.

Greenleaf (1977), spurred by a resilient hope and a deep faith, answered the questions he posed in his essay affirmatively by stating, "My sense of the present leads me to say yes to both questions" (p. 7). The "present" Greenleaf sensed was not entirely dissimilar to ours. Greenleaf (1977) observed, "I concluded that we in this country were in a leadership crisis" (p. 8). Much like today, he saw a society fragmented by tension and conflict, pervasive injustice, struggling with issues of power and authority (p. 9). Today, numerous polls and surveys continue to signal a long and steady decline in leadership confidence, exacerbated by leader behavior at all levels that undermine trust. The misuse of power, coercive in its expression, heightens suspicion of legitimate authority and position, particularly in our young people. Greenleaf didn't focus his assessment exclusively on the outer world, however.

Instructively, he also saved some room to reveal interior tendencies within each of us that contribute to this state of affairs. Greenleaf (1977) laid bare his own difficulty in discerning the "prophetic voices" of his age that called for a different, more effective way of leading. He confessed, "I became painfully aware of how dull my sense of contemporary prophecy had been. And I have reflected much on why we do not hear and heed the prophetic voices in our midst" (p. 8). Greenleaf asserted that the real issue for contemporary society was not in the lack of men and women, present in every age, that call us to a higher way leading, but rather in the interest, level of seeking, and responsiveness of the hearers; in essence, our own ability to listen to the still small voices of our age.

In presenting to us the foundational principles of servant-leadership, Greenleaf mapped out an anchored and authentic way of leading—a leadership path that has the potential to help address the vexing problems of our times and achieve a vision of a global community living more fully and serenely. Such great transformations are usually sparked by a personal encounter with a transcendent idea and a great dream which, when distributed to the larger system, builds a collective capacity for change.

My personal encounter with servant-leadership came about in perhaps the same way many of us experienced it: unforeseen, and then profoundly life changing. In my case, it was during my doctoral studies at Gonzaga University. I was working as a licensed mental health therapist, experiencing the rare and rewarding privilege of coming alongside persons affected by mental illnesses, psychological trauma, substance abuse, and incarceration; my role was to offer therapy, education, support, and most importantly, hope for change. I would soon realize that many of the qualities in the best counselors and therapists are also the characteristics of servant-leaders.

My awakening to the path of servant-leadership began in a class entitled "Leadership & Psychology," my first of many with Dr. Shann Ferch. In his classes, Dr. Ferch introduced me to the foundations of servant-leadership in a scholarly and compelling way. Backed by a growing body of literature and research, I learned how servant-leadership offered a way of leading different from the conventional models of leadership I had studied, experienced, and practiced. I saw how it upends the traditional leadership pyramid and that servant-leaders initiate change by focusing on the growth and well-being of others, forgiveness, healing, and serving the highest needs of others. I also learned that servant-leadership begins simply with a desire to serve.

Dr. Ferch introduced me to the servant-leadership of Mahatma Gandhi, Dr. Martin Luther King, Mother Teresa, and other world-changers in a new and evocative way.

One of my most enduring memories is Dr. Ferch commencing our first class by reciting from memory Robert Greenleaf's powerful "best test" of servant-leadership,

> Do those served grow as persons? Do they, while being served, become healthier, wiser, freer, more autonomous, more likely themselves to become servants? (1991, pp. 4)

Those words lifted my head and heart toward a higher vision of leadership and challenged me to exchange a leader-first model for a servant-leader approach.

Interestingly, MIT professor Otto Scharmer (2009) noted that the Indo-European root word for leadership, *leith*, means "to go forth," "to cross a threshold," or "to die." The original word, said Scharmer, suggests the experience of "letting go and then going forth into another world" (p. 467). Scharmer quoted the German poet Johan Wolfgang von Goethe who said, "And if you don't know this dying and birth, you are merely a dreary guest on Earth."

Servant-leaders "let go" of the egocentric spirit of our age, and in its stead, recognize and meet the needs of others, promote their growth, and thus build a better world.

It was also early in my doctoral studies that I encountered the profound work of Larry Spears, a world-renowned servant-leadership scholar, who has carried the mantle of servant-leadership since the passing of Robert Greenleaf, much like Elisha after the days of Elijah. Spears' (1995) seminal essay on the *Ten Characteristics of Servant Leadership*, along with his other writings and yeoman's work in the field of servant-leadership, crystallized for me the essence of Greenleaf's philosophy with a clarity and accessibility for which I am grateful. After graduation, I continued my association with other thought leaders in the contemporary servant-leadership movement as a professor of leadership studies and as a peer reviewer for the *International Journal of Servant-Leadership*, edited by Dr. Ferch and Dr. Jiying Song.

Greenleaf's stirring vision for the world remains just as vital today as it did in his time. He believed that servant-leaders are called to achieve constructive change as "affirmative builders of a better society" and that the flow and direction of the modern-day servant-leadership movement would largely be determined by how we meet this challenge as a global community (1977, p. 10). So how does one realize Greenleaf's great dream? How do we proceed?

The anthology presented here offers compelling answers to these questions. Indeed, it speaks directly to Greenleaf's (1970) original query: "Servant and leader—can these two roles be fused in one real person, in all levels of status or calling? If so, can that person live and be productive in the real world of the present?" (p. 7).

Because twenty-first century leaders engage in unprecedented ways with the world community, developing the global perspective this volume offers is critical. As noted by leadership scholar Richard Daft (2017), succeeding in the present environment requires more than just a desire to "go global" or acquire another set of tools and techniques. Rather, successful leaders cultivate a global mindset. Leaders who *globalize* their thinking appreciate the influence of individuals, groups, organizations, and systems that represent different social, cultural, political, institutional, intellectual, and psychological characteristics; they embrace diversity and difference, practice intercultural empathy, and see people and issues holistically. They also maintain a curiosity that spans regions, cultures, and contexts, while remaining open to different ways of seeing and doing (p.109). Leaders who cultivate such depth of mind and heart hold tremendous potential to harness the global and cultural intelligence necessary to effectively address the challenges of our age. The roots of servant-leadership philosophy go back millennia; no single country or culture can claim exclusivity to their principles.

I'm enthusiastic about this book because it provides flesh-and-blood examples of a globally distributed community of servant-leaders who are successfully fusing the idea of "servant and leader" together and being productive in the real world. In this book, you'll travel the globe and be inspired by essays, theory, and research from thought-leaders representing a variety of countries, cultures, and communities at the forefront of servant-leadership. In doing so, they show us the way forward.

SHANN ON SERVANT-LEADERSHIP

Philip Mathew is a man of rare intellect and profound engagement with servant-leadership internationally, nationally, and locally. His approach, spanning the cultures of India and America, based in the strength and depth of his family, his cultural heritage, and his will to serve the highest priority needs of others make him the ideal editor, in my opinion, for this book on global servant-leadership.

Global Servant-Leadership: Wisdom, Love, and Legitimate Power in the Age of Chaos forms a bridge to better understand, listen to, and be influenced by servant-leadership cultures around the world. I'm reminded of my close friend, Makoto Fujimura, a Japanese-American artist concerned with the intricacies of how the world is too often characterized by violence. Mako, like the authors of the chapters in this book, consistently pursues intercultural dialogue through beauty as a language of peace. His paintings, such as "Walking on Water-Azurite" which uses mineral pigments on polished gesso, are expansive, "Walking on Water-Azurite" being a seven-foot by eleven-foot work of remarkable elegance and meaning dedicated to survivors of natural and nuclear disaster.

Having visited genocide sites in Africa, Asia, Europe, and North America, I have been influenced by people like Philip and Mako to change my view of the Divine. Rilke posits a God who is beautiful, and intimate, but who is also a God of abandonment. Kenyans, Czechs, Germans, South Africans, Northern Cheyennes, Nez Perce, Blackfeet, Canadians, Americans, Indians, Japanese, Chinese, and Filipinos—exquisite men and women I've had the honor to know and be known by—have taken me to some of the most ultimate places of human brokenness, compassion, and existence. In that nexus where ultimate violence is committed and somehow also reconciled, I'm struck by the presence of our collective loneliness alongside the gravity of our collective love. At the same time, my wife has drawn me into a more contemplative life, and in our shared sense of silence, of listening and action, we began having conversations about space and time, touch, and intentional regard for the dignity of the beloved. In contemplating the Anima Christi (notably the Latin term for the soul of Christ takes the feminine form), we studied genocide and person-to-person violence differently, through a lens of atomic theory not at odds with fracture but understanding fracture or fission in the context of fusion. Fusion generates light, and life force, and in a certain sense, I think fusion also embodies love. The chapters in this book, *Global Servant-Leadership*, helps form dialogue not only around the nature of people and the nature of leadership but also around the nature of love and the nature of God. I believe they also help reconcile us with the unforeseen reality of how humility and perseverance generate more holistic leadership, authentic intimacy, and grace.

Servant-leadership is concurrently international and deeply personal. My mother grew up in Cohagen, Montana, a town of eight people. My father in Circle, Montana, a town of 300. My father is of mixed immigrant heritage, some German, some Irish, the rest spread throughout Europe. My mother's line is less dispersed. In fact, her parents were married in New York in the 1940s during World War II, her father of German lineage, her mother Czechoslovakian. Significant in its implications for peace and harmony among people, her parents' marriage, filled of square dancing and ranching, card playing and good conversation, began during the very time period in Europe when Germany invaded Czechoslovakia.

My parents remain in Montana, in Bozeman now, having moved first from Billings (where my father coached the Crow basketball players at Plenty Coups) to the Northern Cheyenne reservation at St. Labre, and from there to Livingston during my high-school years, then on to Bozeman when my brother and I attended college. Some time back, on a visit to see them in Bozeman, I was seated on the couch with my mother. Arched ceilings and oak beams lead to high, wide windows that look out on the Bridger Mountains and the Spanish Peaks, the view itself a reminder of the vast wilderness that is Montana and how thankful I am to have a good mother, a good father. We had grown up in trailers, three of them in three different towns. My parents had struggled with each other, and through some weighty decisions reconciled with one another after time apart, and from there they went on to make deep sacrifices toward my brother's and my college education. I was happy for them, the life they had given us and the life they had built for themselves.

My mom was asking me about some of my research on forgiveness and touch, and I was telling her the stories of people—how they had hurt one another deeply, how they were seeking forgiveness, and trying to return to a loving connection. South Africa, Colombia, the Philippines, Northern Ireland, the Native American reservations in Montana and throughout the

United States, so many places of human atrocity, and how even in the face of such desolation, forgiveness would rise, and sometimes move to heal the human heart. I was thanking my mother for the forgiveness she gave my father some twenty or so years earlier, for how graceful she had been. Even my choice of vocation was in large part due to the integrity she and my father brought to our family. Not surprisingly, that day as we sat on the couch, the natural, true way she carried herself shone through.

After a pause in our conversation, she looked at me and said, "You know, I'd like to get together with you and ask your forgiveness for the harms I caused you growing up." She said the words openly, with a pleasant look in her eyes, a look of confidence and assurance. I have always loved that look, the way she carries herself with sincerity and hope when dealing with things that are daunting, or cumbersome. Her power as a person is gracious and subtle.

"That would be good," I said, "but I've harmed you too, Mom. I'd also like to ask forgiveness." On my next visit to Montana, we ate dinner together and had an evening of forgiveness-asking.

From the personal to the global, servant-leadership helps people formulate culturally transformative ideas and take action to make these ideas a reality. Robert Greenleaf put forth a leadership ethos in total opposition to the traditional command and control model. He proposed the revolutionary notion that people, organizations, and nations are designed to be servants first and that their servanthood succeeds in generating greater personal, communal, and global well-being. This is not servant as slave or subordinate. Rather, it is the will and action involved in serving the highest priority needs of those around us, the stranger, the marginalized, the beloved other, the world. Greater health, wisdom, freedom, and autonomy, as well as greater individual and collective servant-leadership is the natural result.

Larry Spears, one of the foremost scholars in servant-leadership, helped name the ten characteristics of servant-leadership through an in-depth and systematic content analysis of Greenleaf's work. Spears' and Greenleaf's work continues to influence leaders worldwide. The ten characteristics of servant-leadership are: listening, empathy, healing, awareness, persuasion, conceptualization, foresight, stewardship, commitment to the growth of people, and building community.

As former CEO of the Greenleaf Center for Servant-leadership, Spears was given access to Greenleaf's writings. Spears devoted himself to a precise and discerning look at Greenleaf's vision of servant-leadership. In the early 1990s, in what became truly a labor of love, Spears named the ten characteristics of servant-leadership by meticulously going through manuscript after manuscript and placing check marks next to Greenleaf's most often mentioned and most significant ideas. Of more than forty characteristics, Spears narrowed the list to ten, which resulted in a profound contribution to leadership literature and practice. Today, the ten characteristics provide the most well-known, widely used, and profoundly accessible definition of the essence of servant-leadership.

A closer look at each of the ten characteristics is warranted. *Listening*, a contemplative and active attitude toward serving the highest priority needs of others, was Greenleaf's most ultimate and dearly held conception. For Greenleaf, the other nine characteristics, each one crucial and far-reaching, required deep listening in order to influence the heart of the world with the healing and legitimate power he envisioned. Greenleaf was known for listening to, rather than rejecting, the critiques leveled against American leadership by his global counterparts from various countries, acknowledging America's long shadow of inappropriate use of power, embeddedness in egocentrism, and failure to serve other countries under duress. Certainly, America has often shown wisdom and helped usher in greater freedoms within and in conjunction with other countries. But Greenleaf wanted to be sure to listen to leaders from diverse international perspectives in order for American leaders to be given the grace to grow individually and communally in relation to their international counterparts.

Empathy is the heartfelt expression of leaders who identify with the humanity of others. Servant-leaders not only laud the victories of others but also share in their sufferings and the immensity of their losses. *Healing*, the most rare and perhaps the most needed characteristic of leaders today, requires self-healing, great wisdom, and modesty. This is also required for a nation to heal its own wounds, to face its shadow, and make atonement with its cultures and with the cultures of the world. Few leaders in this or any age have had a true understanding of what it takes to be a healer. Healing provides the cure for injustice, oppression, wounding, and fear, and remains for leaders an element of tremendous import and gravity. People, organizations, and nations are infinitely plagued by the mediocrity and atrocity so often perpetrated by leaders who are blind to their responsibility to be healers. *Awareness* is directly linked to healing and involves an opening of one's eyes to a greater sense of the world. Greenleaf saw awareness not as something that gives peace, but a powerful entity that disturbs and awakens—a solace, and a lightning strike in the international landscape.

Poor leaders coerce others. Great leaders persuade, through a way of being that involves humility, grace, common sense, and good direction. *Persuasion* engages others in dialogue that leads to the greater good of humanity. *Conceptualization* is the ability to build the most effective and meaningful response to the complexities of personal, family, national, and international life in the context of an ever more complex, connected, and power-imbalanced world. *Foresight* then is the ability to see, with clarity and acuity, what needs to be seen before undesired elements of small or great impact come to pass. Though both conceptualization and foresight may be somewhat bound to the intuitive mind, Greenleaf posits it as the servant-leader's responsibility to purposefully develop these in order to help people, organizations, and nations avoid undue entrapment in poor thinking, mental enslavement, lack of wisdom, lack of community, and lack of autonomy.

To hold something in trust for others is to be a steward. To hold in trust for others transcendent values such as humane treatment, justice, mercy, forgiveness, and love, *stewardship* is required. A good steward is an effective guardian of the well-being of others and is generally experienced as a beloved member of the community. Stewardship has close kinship to *commitment to the growth of people*. People, even under conditions of defensiveness, self-fortification, and denial are well served by the servant-leader's robust and durable commitment to the growth of others. Under conditions of transparency and authenticity, the result is high-quality critical mass and exponential individual and community potential. *Building community* requires staying in power and having emotional, mental, and spiritual capacities that match community challenges with creatively imagined and morally persuasive resolutions. Servant-leaders build a community that is responsible, loving, sustainable, and just.

These characteristics, seen worldwide in different contexts, under different guises, uniquely and imaginatively developed and embodied, make up the essential essence of the essays in this book.

In conclusion, from Philip and Shann, thank you for engaging servant-leadership in your own context and in the context of the learnings contained in this book. *Global Servant-Leadership: Wisdom, Love, and Legitimate Power in the Age of Chaos* approaches some of the most significant leadership challenges of our time to reveal an uncommon and life-affirming path toward more healthy and sustainable individuals, families, organizations, and nations. The book challenges not only the rigidly held assumptions of traditional, hierarchical leadership approaches but provides an antidote to the cynicism so often present within workplaces, political struggles, and individual and family crises of contemporary polarized nation states.

Our hope is that this collection will further enrich the study of servant-leadership around the world, encourage leaders to become more globally aware and socially conscious, and ultimately inspire leadership that helps heal the heart of humanity.

REFERENCES

Daft, R. L. (2011). *The Leadership Experience* (6th edition). Stamford, CT: Cengage.

Greenleaf, R. K. (1970). *The servant as leader*. Cambridge, MA: Center for Applied Studies.

———. (1977). *Servant leadership: A journey into the nature of Legitimate Power and greatness*. New York, NY: Paulist Press.

————. (1991). *The Servant as leader*. Indianapolis, IN: The Robert K. Greenleaf Center.

Scharmer, C. O. (2009). *Theory U: Leading from the future as it emerges: the social technology of presencing*. San Francisco, CA: Berrett-Koehler Publishers.

Spears, L. C. (ed.). (1995). *Reflections on leadership: How Robert K. Greenleaf's theory of servant-leadership influenced today's top management thinkers*. New York, NY: John Wiley & Sons.

Wheatley, M., & Frieze, D. (2011). Leadership in the age of complexity: From hero to host. *Resurgence Magazine*. Retrieved from https://margaretwheatley.com/library/articles/leadership-in-age-of-complexity/

Introduction

The Highest Good Is Like Water

Jiying Song

Servant-leadership is not a new idea. In ancient China, the best leader was regarded as the least visible and least wordy. As Lao Tzu (2005) said, "The highest type of ruler is one of whose existence the people are barely aware. . . . self-effacing and scanty of words. When his task is accomplished and things have been completed, all the people say, 'We ourselves have achieved it!'" (p. 35). Two-and-a-half millennia later, Sun Yat-sen (孙中山, 1866-1925)—the forerunner of the Democratic Revolution in China and the founding father of the Republic of China—proposed the concept of *public servants* (公仆) (Sun, 1927), which is still widely used in China today. Sun claimed that "The State officials, beginning with the President and ending with an ordinary sentry, are all *public servants*" (pp. 136-137, emphasis added).

Beginning at the dawn of the twenty-first century, Greenleaf's theory of servant-leadership has gained the increasing attention of China. His *The Servant as Leader* (Greenleaf, 1991) and *The Servant Leader Within* (Greenleaf, 2003) have both been translated into Chinese. The number of Chinese publications of articles and research in the servant-leadership field has tripled during 2013–2018 comparing to 2007–2012 (China National Knowledge Infrastructure, 2019; Wanfang Data, 2019). Servant-leadership research has been widely conducted in China and the results are being published in English, contributing to the fields of K-12 schools (Chan, 2017), banks (Hu & Liden, 2011; Wang, Xu, & Liu, 2018; Yang, Zhang, Kwan, & Chen, 2018), hospitality industries (Ling, Lin, & Wu, 2016; Ling, Liu, & Wu, 2017; Wu, Tse, Fu, Kwan, & Liu, 2013), public sectors (Han, Kakabadse, & Kakabadse, 2010; Miao, Newman, Schwarz, & Xu, 2014), insurance companies (Wang, Kwan, & Zhou, 2017), and manufacturing enterprises (Zhang, Kwan, Everett, & Jian, 2012).

In the last several years, my perspective of servant-leadership has been broadened, not only by the studies in China and North America but also by the research and articles from all over the world I encountered as Associate Editor of the *International Journal of Servant-Leadership*. I was amazed by the rich tradition and wisdom from each culture, as well as the similarities of our humanness.

The fundamental shift from atomized individualism to networked interdependence in science and reality brings new understandings of leadership—"every act is inherently an act of leadership" and everyone can set off a new chain of behavior with their every act (Liu & Hanauer, 2011). The earth has become a village, metaphorically and literally. "A person is a person through other persons" (Tutu, 1998, p. 19). It may be so for nations as well. Leadership has never been put into such a broad perspective. With the hope of communicating the wisdom of servant-leaders around the world, this volume was born.

Spears (2002) identified ten characteristics of servant-leadership. Reynolds (2014) argued that six of the ten characteristics distinguish servant-leadership from other forms of leadership, whereas the other four are more in line with traditional notions of leadership. These six distinguishing characteristics—stewardship, listening, empathizing, healing, commitment to the growth of people, and building community—are more collectivist (Hofstede, 2001) and comprise the feminine-attributed aspects of leadership (Reynolds, 2014). The other four—foresight, conceptualization, awareness, and persuasion—are more individualist (Hofstede, 2001) and often associated with the more traditionally masculine aspect of leadership (Reynolds, 2014). This kind of sorting out is not to set up dividing walls among different genders or various cultures but to cleanse our doors of perception so that everything would appear as it is (Blake, 1975). Wherever the seed of servant-leadership is planted, paradigm shifts in leadership theory could occur and move organizations from hierarchy-driven, rules-based, and authoritative models to value-driven, follower-oriented, and participative models.

Servant-leaders can bring it together and make it whole—East and West, North and South, love and power. This is the wisdom for a chaotic world. This is the wisdom from Lao Tzu. This is the wisdom of servant-leadership:

The highest good is like water.
Water benefits everything without competing with them.
It stays where many people dislike.
Therefore, it is closest to the Tao.
In residing, good at choosing dwellings;
In thinking, good at peace and depth;
In interacting, good at mercy and kindness;

In speaking, good at keeping words;
In governing, good at management;
In working, good at using strengths;
In taking actions, good at timing.
Due to not contesting, free from blame.
(translated from the original by the author)

REFERENCES

Blake, W. (1975). *The marriage of Heaven and hell.* G. Keynes (ed.). London: Oxford University Press.

Chan, K. W. (2017). Learners' perceptions of servant-leadership in classrooms. *The International Journal of Servant-Leadership, 11*(1), 373–410.

China National Knowledge Infrastructure. (2019). Servant leadership. Retrieved from https://www.cnki.net/

Greenleaf, R. K. (1991). *The servant as leader.* Indianapolis, IN: The Robert K. Greenleaf Center.

———. (2003). *The Servant-Leader within: A transformative path.* H. Beazley, J. Beggs, & L. C. Spears (eds.). New York, NY: Paulist Press.

Han, Y., Kakabadse, N. K., & Kakabadse, A. (2010). Servant leadership in the People's Republic of China: A case study of the public sector. *Journal of Management Development, 29*(3), 265–281.

Hofstede, G. H. (2001). *Culture's consequences: Comparing values, behaviors, institutions, and organizations across nations* (2nd edition). Thousand Oaks, CA: Sage.

Hu, J., & Liden, R. C. (2011). Antecedents of team potency and team effectiveness: An examination of goal and process clarity and servant leadership. *Journal of Applied Psychology, 96*(4), 851–862. doi:10.1037/a0022465

Ling, Q., Lin, M., & Wu, X. (2016). The trickle-down effect of servant leadership on frontline employee service behaviors and performance: A multilevel study of Chinese hotels. *Tourism Management, 52*, 341–368.

Ling, Q., Liu, F., & Wu, X. (2017). Servant versus authentic leadership: Assessing effectiveness in China's hospitality industry. *Cornell Hospitality Quarterly, 58*(1), 53–68.

Liu, E, & Hanauer, N. (2011). *The gardens of democracy: A new American story of citizenship, the economy, and the role of government.* Seattle, WA: Sasquatch Books.

Miao, Q., Newman, A., Schwarz, G., & Xu, L. (2014). Servant leadership, trust, and the organizational commitment of public sector employees in China. *Public Administration, 92*(3), 727–743. doi:10.1111/padm.12091

Reynolds, K. (2014). Servant-leadership: A feminist perspective. *The International Journal of Servant-Leadership, 10*(1), 35–63.

Spears, L. C. (2002). Introduction: Tracing the past, present, and future of servant-leadership. In L. C. Spears & M. Lawrence (eds.), *Focus on leadership: Servant-leadership for the Twenty-First Century* (pp. 1–16). New York, NY: Wiley.

Sun, Y. (1927). *Memories of a Chinese revolutionary: A programme of national reconstruction for China.* Philadelphia, PA: David McKay Company.

Tutu, D. (1998). Desmond Tutu (Z. Jaffrey, Interviewer). *The Progressive, 62,* 18–21.

Wanfang Data. (2019). Servant leadership. Retrieved from www.wanfangdata.com.cn

Wang, M., Kwan, H. K., & Zhou, A. (2017). Effects of servant leadership on work–family balance in China. *Asia Pacific Journal of Human Resources, 55,* 387–407. doi:10.1111/1744-7941.12122

Wang, Z., Xu, H., & Liu, Y. (2018). Servant leadership as a driver of employee service performance: Test of a trickle-down model and its boundary conditions. *Human Relations, 71*(9), 1179–1203.

Wu, L. Z., Tse, E. C. Y., Fu, P., Kwan, H. K., & Liu, J. (2013). The impact of Servant leadership on hotel employees' "servant behavior." *Cornell Hospitality Quarterly, 54*(4), 383–395.

Yang, Z., Zhang, H., Kwan, H. K., & Chen, S. (2018). Crossover effects of servant leadership and job social support on employee spouses: The mediating role of employee organizational-based self-esteem. *Journal of Business Ethics, 147,* 595–604. doi:10.1007/s10551-015-2943-3

Zhang, H. N., Kwan, H. K., Everett, A. M., & Jian, Z. Q. (2012). Servant leadership, organizational identification and work-to-family enrichment: The moderating role of work climate for sharing family concerns. *Human Resource Management, 51*(5), 747–768. doi:10.1002/hrm.21498

Chapter 1

Re-Imagining Power in Leadership

Reflection, Integration, and Servant-Leadership

Karel San Juan

Leadership[1] is imbued with the idea of power. Think about leadership and soon after you will think of power as well. This is because power is a compelling aspect of leadership. Think about power—and you evoke several images. Power is a different and an independent phenomenon. It surrounds our everyday life in a ubiquitous and pervasive way—physical power, solar power, social power, spiritual power, and so on. It elicits impressions of greatness and grandeur, strength and stamina, energy and engagement. It evokes ideas like force, control, persuasion, authority, influence, impact, and charisma.

It is, therefore, not surprising to see that power is perhaps one of the most studied phenomena in the world. There is a preponderance of literature on power from several disciplines, such as philosophy, psychology, sociology, political science, and organizational studies. Power is defined by a multiplicity of perspectives, making it a concept that is idiosyncratic, "essentially-contested" (Wrong, 1995), and highly "privileged" (Wartenberg, 1990). The several theories that explain power indicate a variety of usages of the term, each usage carrying its own unique "language game" (from the philosopher Wittgenstein), making the search for a single concept of power elusive and "intrinsically illusory" (Haugaard, 2002).

Power is thus defined in ways differing in complexity and scope. Pfeffer (1997) notes that we are "profoundly ambivalent about power, and that ambivalence has led to recurrent questioning of the concept and its definition" (p. 137). The simplest definitions I found most acceptable are the following: "Power is the potential one individual has to change the thinking and behavior of other people" (Zaleznik & Kets de Vries, 1985, p. xiii) and Bertrand

Russell's definition of power as "the capacity of some persons to produce intended and foreseen effects on others" (Wrong, 1995, p. 10). These definitions allow us to see power generically in the diversity of its applications, like political power or mental power, social or organizational power.

How has the field of leadership studies framed the phenomenon of power? Taking Rost's (1993) definition of leadership as "an influence relationship among leaders and followers who intend real changes that reflect their mutual purposes" (p. 102), power becomes part of the process of influence that is integral to leadership (Bass & Stogdill, 1990; Yukl, 2002). Power is involved in the relationship of leader and follower, primarily in terms of the power of the leader over the follower. According to the often-quoted French and Raven's 1959 study (Yukl, 2002), the leader's power is mainly derived from and based on the leader's position (legitimate authority, reward, coercion, information, environment) as well as the leader's very person (referent, expertise).

Power is also seen as a psychological orientation, need, or motivation that drives leaders toward its use and misuse (Bass & Stogdill, 1990; Burns, 1978; Kets de Vries, 1993; Zaleznik & Kets de Vries, 1985). The problem and potential power of leaders in different settings such as politics and business have intensified interest in rethinking and recasting leadership power in terms of follower and organizational empowerment (Appelbaum, Hebert, & Leroux, 1999; Hardy & Clegg, 1996; Gordon, 2002), sharing and distribution (Hollander & Offerman, 1990; Bass & Stogdill, 1990), stewardship (Block, 1996), and transformation (Burns, 1978).

SERVANT-LEADERSHIP AND THE QUESTION OF POWER

Robert K. Greenleaf's (1977) servant-leadership proposes a new paradigm of power in leadership. As early as the 1970s, Greenleaf discerned an emerging trend toward a rethinking of the idea and practice of power in leadership and in institutions. Power is reinvented from its highly pervasive, coercive nature toward the servant-leader's power of persuasion and example. This "legitimized" form of power has become an ethical imperative in our times (pp. 5, 41). It challenges the traditional conception of power as status, manipulation, control, and domination. It re-appropriates the concept of power as a moral principle that can imbue a leader with a deeply respectable "servant stature." Greenleaf (1977) observed that not only are people learning to relate to one another in less coercive ways, they are increasingly choosing leaders who are servants first, and as this trend grows, the most sustainable organizations in the future will be servant-led.

Addressing the Gap

Scholars have pointed out the insufficiency of research and literature on power in the social sciences, in general (Pfeffer, 1997), and in the field of organizational studies, in particular (Pfeffer, 1997; Hardy & Clegg, 1996; Mumby, 2001). There has also been recognition of limited research on power in leadership studies, particularly in terms of in-depth exploration of the dynamics of power in leadership processes (Yukl, 2002; Bass & Stogdill, 1990; Hollander & Offermann, 1990). Gordon (2002), in a major leadership journal, observes that leadership theories have largely failed to address the phenomenon of power, particularly at the level of what he calls "deep structures." He describes "deep structures" as codes of behavioral order that are typically covert and implicit, but have profound influence in organizational relationships and outcomes. Such deep structures may be manifested in perceptions and actions of participants in the diverse settings of leadership—organization, community, society, and culture. How these participants in these settings experience and understand the phenomenon of power in leadership situations presents an important area of development—a gap—in leadership studies (Gordon, 2002; Bass & Stogdill, 1990; Ryan, 1984).

I would like to address this gap in leadership research and reflection. I notice the breadth and depth of thought given to power in socio-political and psychological theories. Very little, however, has been done in terms of integrating them with the phenomenon of leadership. In light of this, an exploration into socio-political and psychological conceptions of power can be useful to leadership. The chapter presents a re-imagining of conceptions of power in the following ways: one, by looking at the context of leadership from the prism of socio-political understanding of power; two, by looking at the leader's self and person from the prism of psychological and philosophical understanding of power; and three, by integrating these perspectives through the challenge of reflection, integration, and servant-leadership.

"Power Without": The Power Dynamics of Leadership

The phenomenon of leadership does not exist in a vacuum; it operates in different domains, settings, or contexts. It may be the group, organization, society, environment, or culture. It embraces realities like relationships, structures, systems, and institutions. Power is embedded in these contexts and realities. Leadership, through the aid of social theory, is challenged to understand the dynamics of power at work in the diversity of settings and contexts in which it finds itself. These social realities constitute the external environment of leadership. Thus, leadership needs a "power without" perspective.

Power as Understood in Context

How can leadership develop this perspective of looking at the dynamics of power in settings and contexts? Perhaps a fundamental step is to ask an ontological question: How do we look at social reality? Berger and Luckmann (1966) provide us with a classic thought in contemporary sociological theory. Their theory of social construction looks at social reality as a human product. Social order is not derived from "laws of nature." The social order is a product of human activity through a process called "externalization." This theory explains how institutions arise. Human activity repeated frequently is cast into a pattern of actions and decisions, which Berger and Luckmann call "habitualization." For example, habitualization of the activity of learning results in institutions of learning—the educational system. Habitualization of the activity of decision-making results in political institutions. The world of institutions then becomes experienced as an objective social reality:

> The institutions, as historical and objective facticities, confront the individual as undeniable facts. The institutions are there, external to him, persistent in their reality, whether he likes it or not. He cannot wish them away. They resist his attempts to change or evade them. They have coercive power over him . . . The objective reality of institutions is not diminished if the individual does not understand their purpose or their mode of operation. He may experience large sectors of the social world as incomprehensible, perhaps oppressive in their opaqueness, but real nonetheless. Since institutions exist as external reality the individual cannot understand them by introspection. He must "go out" and learn about them, just as he must to learn about nature. (Berger and Luckmann, 1966, p. 60)

This ontological understanding of social reality frames our first fundamental perspective: leadership needs to "go out and learn" about its setting. Focusing on human activities connected with power, a purposeful discernment accompanies leadership and creates an opportunity to more fully understand institutions, systems, and structures of power. Leadership needs to be sensitive to the dynamics of power in its environment.

Power as Situated

Discerning leadership imagines power as existing in what Wartenberg (1990) describes as a "social field." Wartenberg imagines this social field as constituted not merely by a dyadic power relationship between two agents (the power wielder and the one affected by power) but also by a "broad social context" consisting of a "vast field of social forces" of structures and processes of power. Conceiving power in terms of persons A and B, in an equation like: "power of A over B is equal to maximum force which A can induce on B minus the maximum resisting force which B can mobilize in the opposite direction" is criticized by Burns (1978) as a formula that is "more physics than power" (p. 12).

Wartenberg (1990) gives an example of the power relationship that characterizes the teacher and student in a small classroom setting. While the exercise of power may be localized in the dyad, the whole power dynamic extends beyond it: into the broader social field consisting of power structures in the grading system, into the academic profession, and into the school environment as a whole. Hence, educational leadership confronting the issue of power becomes aware of this picture of power as situated in a broader social matrix of power relationships at different levels of social reality.

Power as Heterogeneous

With this view of power as situated in a social field, the next level of imagination is to see the heterogeneity and diversity of these power relationships and institutions existing in this field:

> Situated power does not reside exclusively in a single site or institution of society. The situated conception of power shows that social power is a heterogeneous presence that spreads across an entire set of agents and practices, although its exercise depends upon the actions of the dominant agent. Such heterogeneity is constituted by a complex coordination among agents located in diverse sites and institutions, all of whose presence in a social alignment is necessary to constitute a situated power relationship. (Wartenberg, 1990, p. 151)

This view can be used in analyzing the power behind the act of grading that exists in Wartenberg's (1990) example of the dyadic relationship of teacher and student. The teacher's power over the student through the power of grading affects and is affected by diverse social forces surrounding this central dyadic relationship of teacher and student. These include not only the students' parents, who might be expecting high grades from their child, but also the principal, an honor society, an athletic club, or a fraternity. Poor grades will affect prospects of entrance into law, business, or medical schools, as well as future careers. Even a romantic relationship may affect or be affected by the power of the grade.

Leadership is challenged to see the diversity of these settings and the diversity of the power dynamic in each of these settings. Diversity of power dynamics may come in many forms, depending on the peculiarity of the leadership context. Diversity may be in terms of type or nature of organizations.

There are power dynamics inherent in groups or "tribes" within an organization (Schmookler, 1994). There are power dynamics in family systems. The organization is a vast arena for the exercise of power, and the leader or executive in an organization is always challenged to see the inherent and inescapable power dynamics in organizational life (Kotter, 1985; Morgan, 1997; Pfeffer, 1981, 1992). In a business organization, for example, executive power relates with other power centers like the board, labor, suppliers, customers, and other stakeholders, through influence and power strategies like negotiations, conflict management, alliances, and networks (Greenleaf, 1977; Morgan, 1997; Pfeffer, 1997).

Power in different organizational forms is studied by different academic disciplines: political science tends to focus on government and political organizations, management studies on business organizations, and sociology on community and other social organizations (e.g., family, church, indigenous groups).

Aside from understanding the diversity of power in different organizational forms, leadership must also see the dynamics of power framed in specific terms by interest or cause-oriented groups. A great deal of thought has been given to looking at power from the perspective of marginalized and oppressed social classes, and specific disciplines focus on issues of power as expressed by specific sectors in society. Feminist theory focuses on gender relations and the power of women. Marxist and critical theory focuses on empowering marginalized social classes and transforming power structures of economic and political domination. Cultural studies explore the dynamics of power among African-Americans and other race-based and ethnic societies or cultures. Liberation theology reflects on the power of the poor and their struggle for freedom. The discourse on power is as diverse as the sectoral groups who grapple with it in their lives in two ways: one, as the recipients of power that is exercised as coercion and domination through structures of hierarchy and control and two, as wielders of power exercised for transformation through structures of empowerment. The first function of power has been imagined as "power over" and the second one, as "power to" (Hinze, 1995; Wrong, 1995).

Greenleaf (1977) speaks of essentially two types of power embedded in institutions: coercive power and the power of persuasion and example. The former represents a preset path based on domination and manipulation, ultimately resulting in less autonomy; the latter provides opportunities and choices that enhance personal agency. Greenleaf's vision of servant-leadership encompasses a deep concern for institutional quality and integrity. Caring for institutions includes sensitivity to the dynamics of power within them, the potential to abuse it, and a balance of power (Greenleaf, 1977). A new basis of trust among stakeholders in the institution can be founded on this renewed vision of power that is shared, a power that is nurtured by persuasion and example. As Greenleaf said, "No one should be powerless!" (p. 98).

"Power Within": The Inner Dynamics of Power in Leadership

We now shift our attention from the external environment of the leader toward the interiority of the leader. Just as power can be situated in the complex setting of leadership, power can also be located in the inner life of leaders. The need, desire, craving for power—a human tendency that is all too familiar to us—resides within the interior life of the individual leader. Psychology helps us understand this phenomenon, as well as the motives that drive it. It helps us imagine how individuals can be oriented or disposed toward power. Leadership has to be informed by this process of imagining power as a motive and as a capacity of individual leaders.

Power as Desire

Leadership can benefit from empirical research done on personal power, particularly on the phenomenon of power as a need or motive. Early studies by Adler in 1927 and Homey in 1942 developed the concept of the "will to power," a craving, almost neurotic need for power due to one's feeling of inferiority and anxiety (Lips, 1981). The striving for power is central to Alfred Adler's (1966) psychology:

> To be big! To be powerful! This is and has always been the longing of those who are little or feel they are little . . .Whatever men are striving for originates from their urgent attempts to overcome the impression of deficiency, insecurity, weakness . . . Our guiding ideal is concretized as power over others . . . The striving for personal power is a disastrous delusion and poisons man's living together. (pp. 168–169)

In his book *The Power Motive*, Winter (1973) argues for recognition of this powerful driving force in people. He speaks of the tendency of individuals, especially those in public life, to mask their desire for power with more noble virtues like "service," "duty," and "responsibility." To acknowledge the existence of the power motive is essential in today's power-preoccupied world. Some psychologists have concluded that "just as sexuality was repressed and denied during the nineteenth century, so today power strivings are repressed and achieve only disguised expression through defense mechanisms such as distortion, displacement, projection, and rationalization" (p. 3).

How is the power motive manifested in action? Through projective tests that Winter (1973) developed to measure a person's level of need for power, or *n* Power, he drew out themes and imagery that indicate powerful actions and dispositions. Lips (1981) summarizes these themes and imagery as including:

> forceful behavior such as assaults, threats, or insults; sexual exploitation; taking advantage of another's weakness; giving unsolicited help, support, or protection; trying to control another person by regulating behavior or living conditions or by seeking information; trying to influence or persuade another; and trying to impress some other person or the world at large. (p. 27)

David McClelland (1975, pp. 10–12) builds on Winter's (1973) work by identifying four main actions correlated to men with high power motivation. These actions include: (1) power-oriented reading, or reading about sex, sports, and aggression; (2) accumulating prestige possessions like guns, cars, and credit cards; (3) participation in competitive sports; and (4) belonging to organizations and holding office in them. Men get power in different ways, but the same effect holds: a feeling of power.

McClelland (1975) further proposes a classification of these power actions into "power orientations." He makes the following distinctions: (1) the source of power as one's self or others and (2) the object of power as one's self (to feel stronger) or others (to influence). He then identifies four stages in power orientation, which are synchronized with the psycho-sexual and psycho-social development framework originally proposed by Freud and Erikson. McClelland describes the four stages as follows: Stage I: "I strengthen, control, direct myself"; Stage II: "Others (God, my mother, my leader, food, etc.) strengthen me"; Stage III: "I have an impact on others"; and Stage IV: "It (religion, laws, my group) moves me to serve and influence others" (pp. 13–21).

McClelland (1975) frames the power motive within a continuum that describes levels of personal maturity and development. Stage I–Stage II moves the individual from external control to internal control. Stage III–Stage IV moves the person from self-assertion to selfless service to an ideal. The desire for power, therefore, exists at these different stages of psychological growth from self-centeredness to selflessness. Maturity, however, is seen not much in terms of progressing through the stages, but in terms of the "ability to use whatever mode is appropriate to the situation" (p. 24). McClelland continues:

> The developmental model we have in mind is not like the Freudian one in which early learnings are left behind or, if they persist, are viewed as immature abnormal fixations. Rather, the modes of experiencing power are learned in succession, more or less in the order given, each depending on the successful

experiencing of the earlier ones. Yet the earlier modes should remain available to provide the opportunity for a richer, more varied life. (p. 24)

He gives the example of a young man who appropriately develops Stage II behavior to break his dependence on his mother, then gets married and develops a new sense of personal power in a Stage I manner. When he plays tennis and talks politics, he assumes Stage III competitive behavior and in church he lives out the service orientation of Stage IV (p. 24).

These empirical studies on the power motive in the mid-1970s still have relevance today in terms of reflecting on the extent to which a leader needs and desires power. New studies may be needed to re-contextualize these questions on the power motive to the exigencies of the contemporary situation. New modes of power orientation and action need to be observed. One such observation is that of imagining power as a potential pathology among leaders.

Power as Pathology

Organization specialists Abraham Zaleznik and Manfred Kets de Vries (1985) wrote about the psychodynamics of leadership and power in organizations. They studied the phenomenon of leaders' using power not only constructively but destructively as well. Unconscious motivation determines the actions and dispositions of leaders, and their positions can be used "as a stage for acting out their personal conflicts and insecurities" (p. xi). To study this unconscious motivation of leaders is to look into what Kets de Vries (1993) calls the leader's "intrapsychic theater." Clinical, psychoanalytical perspectives are used here:

> People who aspire to power frequently operate on a borrowed ego, a corporate mind in place of a cohesive self and an awareness of who one is in the flow of history and time. Busily reaching for power, the individual attempts to cast off unacceptable self-images and remains divided and ill at ease. The orientation to power then becomes defensive, as a means for uniting a divided self and as a substitute for a sustaining ego ideal. (Zaleznik & Kets de Vries, 1985, p. vii)

The psychoanalytical lens can help in understanding how and why leaders deal with power. Early childhood experiences, relationships with parents and family, defining moments of identity and individuation—these and other factors influencing individual growth and development can assist in understanding the power dynamics within a leader's interior life. One factor that influences a leader's disposition toward power is the sense of individual potency, which is an attribute of leadership (Kets de Vries, 1993, p. 16). This

feeling of individual potency, or personal power, is nurtured through childhood experiences:

> The degree of encouragement and frustration children experience as they grow
> up . . . has a lasting influence on their perception of themselves and others and
> the relationships they form throughout their lives. Any imbalance between their
> feelings of helplessness and the degree of protective nurturing they receive
> from their parents will be felt as a psychological injury . . . [and] will feed their
> natural sense of impotence . . . they will commonly respond with feelings of
> rage, a desire for vengeance, a hunger for personal power, and compensatory
> fantasies of omnipotence. This dynamic continues throughout life, and if it is not
> adequately resolved within individuals as they grow up, it is likely to be reacti-
> vated with devastating effect when they reach leadership positions and learn to
> play the game of power. (Kets de Vries, 1993, p. 16)

These psychological injuries render these individuals vulnerable to the
pathologies of power and leadership. They develop narcissistic, grandiose,
addictive, and compulsive patterns of behavior. They become power seekers,
entering the arena of leadership and politics "to compensate for feelings of
low self-esteem, unimportance, moral inferiority, weakness, mediocrity, and
intellectual inferiority" (Post, 2004, p. 17). Greenleaf (1995) observes that
common corruptions of power include personality distortion, arrogance, and
impairment of imagination or the sheer incapacity to form ideas and good
judgment.

Leadership roles become the stage for acting out and reinforcing these personality disorders at the expense of others. The glitter and glamour of power
and prestige blind them to their intoxication with and abuse of power. They
sink into a spiral of ego-indulgence, self-perpetuation, and power arrogation,
enacting Lord Acton's dictum of absolute power corrupting absolutely. The
world's history of war, violence, and aggression is filled with leaders who
have fallen into this pathological trap of power and leadership.

Power as Being

The inner dynamics of personal power include many other things aside
from looking at power as desire and as pathology. Power resides in the very
constitution of the person: mind, body, and spirit. Hence, to imagine power
from within is to imagine the power inherent in these faculties of a person's
being. Power has been described in such terms: power of intelligence and
imagination, power of soul and spirit, power of character and charisma,
power of emotion and empathy, power of values and vision. Extensive
research shows how emotional intelligence can unleash powerful energies

that build resonance in the practice of leadership (Goleman, Boyatzis, & McKee, 2002).

Power can thus be imagined as a reality that encompasses the totality of a person's being. Power is the ontological reality of *being* itself. Power is not nothingness. To possess power is to be. To be, or to exist, is to possess power. This metaphysical, ontological description of power has been proposed by Paul Tillich (1954), an influential twentieth-century theologian, in his classic book, *Love, Power and Justice*. For Tillich, power is most fundamental to love and justice, "since being itself is the 'power of being,' a power ultimately identifiable as God" (Hinze, 1995, p. 187; Pasewark, 1993, pp. 245–246; Tillich, 1954, pp. 35–40). Power drives the essence of being, of reality as a whole—without which love and justice cannot exist. He calls for an integrated understanding of love, power, and justice; a disconnected view of these three reduces love to pure emotion and power and justice to compulsion (Tillich, 1954, p. 12).

Greenleaf (1977) lends credence to the same inner power of the person's being. The servant-leader's power originates from within. This power resides in the servant-leader's own humanity. Because servant-leaders are close to the action, they hear, see, and know what is happening around them; their insight is extraordinary, they prove themselves reliable and trustworthy, and use their power for good.

Hence, Greenleaf shows that in the servant-leader's inner self is his or her "functional superiority" or power. This power includes distinctive qualities like intuition, empathy, acceptance, foresight, healing, creativity, and faith. The servant-leader has a "sense for the unknowable" and is able to "foresee the unforeseeable." This leader has a "feel for patterns" and is able to "listen *first*." These powers give leaders their "lead," as they are able to know with "discerning toughness" how to "go out ahead" and "show the way" to others.

INTEGRATING INNER AND OUTER POWER DYNAMICS: THE CHALLENGE OF REFLECTION, INTEGRATION, AND SERVANT-LEADERSHIP

I have explored the inner and outer dynamics of power in leadership. In the "power without" perspective, power is situated in the leader's setting, which is socially constructed, heterogeneous, and diverse in its forms and manifestations. In the "power within" perspective, power is fulfilling a desire, motivation, and need in leaders. Unmanaged and uncontrolled, it becomes a pathology that makes for dysfunctional and destructive leadership. From an ontological perspective, power can be grasped as descriptive of the very constitution of human existence, as *being* itself.

Leaders are challenged to have both of these power perspectives: "power without," or *exteriority*, and "power within," or *interiority*. The sense of exteriority challenges the leader to know and comprehend the power dynamics of his or her environment and setting. Sociological and political tools of understanding are useful here. The sense of interiority challenges the leader to grasp and grapple with power within the self through psychological, philosophical, and spiritual frames of understanding. The leader needs *both* exteriority and interiority. Not to have one or the other leads to a limited view of power and reality that is bifurcated and disjointed. A leader is called to attend to both internal and external realities, to both self and environment.

The challenge, however, goes beyond just *having* both perspectives, and also toward *integrating* both perspectives. The leader's tools and capacities are not only for awareness and analysis but also for integration and action. Leaders have to make sense of power as manifested in complex structures of organization, society, and culture and integrate it with their personal psychology and spirit, within an equally complex reality of their interior life or self. We have glimpsed the complexity of these processes, and what is called for is a leadership that has the capacity to make sense of these through a process of reflection. Such reflective leadership would have the following characteristics: a deep understanding of the self, a relational view of power, and an inclination to work for change and transformation.

A Deep Self-Understanding

The first challenge is a process of self-understanding among leaders. Leadership research has emphasized the need for self-awareness and understanding, as well as for other related themes like self-management and self-evaluation (Bass & Stogdill, 1990; Goleman, Boyatzis, & McKee, 2002; Yukl, 2002). Some leadership theories view the leader's values and principles as the very foundation of leadership (Covey, 1992; Greenleaf, 1977; O'Toole, 1996). Others call for a process of reflexive self-reflection on the very practice of leadership, a process which Heifetz (1994) calls "getting on the balcony" (p. 252). This habit of self-examination deepens self-knowledge and increases capacity for the regulation and management of leaders' "hungers" and needs for "power and control, affirmation and importance, as well as intimacy and delight" (Heifetz and Linsky, 2002, p. 164). Such processes of deep self-understanding can integrate the dimension of power within the psyche and spirit:

> As a precondition for acting on other people, the would-be leader must engage in self-reflection in order to heal the rifts within the psyche, tame the urges of power and aggression . . . There is no greater need for self-understanding today than in the people who achieve positions of power. (Zaleznik & Kets de Vries, 1985, pp. xiii, xv)

Greenleaf's (1977) servant-leader develops such self-understanding by moving through life from two levels of consciousness. On one level is the actual, real world of activity, where the leader is caring and involved. At the other level, the leader disengages from the fray and is able to see the long view—both of themselves and the present circumstance. This practice of detachment, withdrawal, and self-examination builds and clarifies values. It serves as "armor" against the stresses, uncertainties, and distractions of life situations. It safeguards the center and perspective of one's life and provides constant grounding to what matters most: "Awareness is not a giver of solace—it is just the opposite. It is a disturber and an awakener" (Greenleaf, 1991, p. 56).

A Relational View of Power

The second challenge is to have a relational view of power that integrates the internal and the external, the subjective and the objective, interiority and exteriority. According to process theologian Bernard Loomer (1976), relational power is the alternative to what he calls "unilateral or linear power":

> Linear power is the capacity to influence, guide, adjust, manipulate, shape, control, or transform the human or natural environment in order to advance one's purposes. This kind of power is essentially one-directional in its working . . . [Relational power] is the ability both to produce and to undergo an effect. It is the capacity both to influence and be influenced by others. Relational power involves both a giving and a receiving. (Loomer, 1976, pp. 8, 17)

According to Loomer, linear power negates the relational context of power. Linear power has dominated Western thought and culture and its effect is dominance, competition, curtailment of power over the other and inequality in the relationship. Relational power affirms the communal dimension of power, along with its values of mutuality, accountability, equality, and interdependence. These values imbue relational power with a stature of integrity, strength, of character—it is, then, a power that redefines the notion of "size." Loomer, as cited in Keller (1986), says,

> By size I mean the stature of a person's soul, the range and depth of his love, his capacity for relationships. I mean the volume of life you can take into your being and still maintain your integrity and individuality, the intensity and variety of outlook you can entertain in the unity of your being without feeling defensive or insecure. I mean the strength of your spirit to encourage others to become freer in the development of their diversity and uniqueness. I mean the power to sustain more complex and enriching tensions. I mean the magnanimity of concern to provide conditions that enable others to increase in stature. (p. 143)

The "stature" noted here might very well be the same servant stature Greenleaf (1977) envisions in leadership. The power of servant-leaders is gauged in terms of their overall influence on our lives. The influence may be neutral, or it may be one of enrichment, or one of diminishment. The servant stature enriches, rather than diminishing or depleting our lives. Servant-leaders enrich us by their sheer presence. This is where the relational power of the servant-leader comes from.

Leaders are thus challenged to reflect on power and re-imagine it in terms of relationships and community. To conceive of power this way is to see one's self as deeply connected to one's matrix of relationships. To imagine power this way is to see one's self as integrated with, and accountable to, one's environment, thereby magnified in spirit and love. Part of this integration and accountability is the openness to work for change and transformation, the third challenge.

A Consciousness for Change

A leader who reflects on her self and her environment realizes the necessity of change occurring both in her self or consciousness, and in her environment and culture. The process of change happens internally, within one's self and consciousness. Leaders can sort out their personal "power issues" (Homer, 1995)—their motives and desires for power, their psychological dispositions for potential misuse and abuse of it. Reflective leaders then become aware that power can be both a problem and a potential to them, an energy that can be both corruptive and constructive. Such awareness is the foundation for changing their consciousness toward power.

Externally, leaders reflect on their setting and see how power can be used as an instrument for domination and oppression, and also as a means for transformation and empowerment. In this aspect, leaders are called to take the role of change agents, aware of and acting for necessary changes in the structures and systems of power that govern their environment at different levels: relationships, groups, organizations, societies, and cultures.

A type of change that is called for is that of moving from compulsion to "centeredness" in power, as proposed by Tillich (1954). Leaders with power, as we have seen, are prone to compulsion and corruption. This downfall, however, can be avoided through the discipline of being centered in power as being, as integral to the self. Concretely, this idea entails a process of "self-integration, self-creativity, and self-transcendence" (p. 339). Leadership facilitates this process of achieving centeredness:

> For without the centeredness given by leadership, no self-integration and self-creation of a group would be possible . . . .The leader represents not only the power and justice of the group but also himself, his power of being, and the justice implied in it. (Tillich, 1963, p. 82)

The challenge of changing both consciousness and culture is the ethical imperative of power in leadership. It inspires leaders to integrate not just their sense of power but also their entire selves consisting of mind, body, and spirit. It commits them to the work of transforming culture and society toward building relationships and communities of justice and love. These are the strivings that nurture a new, spiritual, and transformative sense of power among reflective leaders.

The Vision of Servant-Leadership

This picture of the reflective leader is integral to Greenleaf's (1977) vision of the servant-leader. The servant-leader embodies and integrates the aforementioned challenges of deep self-understanding, relational view of power, and consciousness for change. We can discern from this vision the essence and core of servant-leadership: leaders with the capacity for both interiority and exteriority, leaders who embrace the phenomenon of power as responsibility and service, and leaders who have the courage to face the imperative of personal and social transformation.

With these qualities, leaders not only will internalize the "servant stature" but also will be encouraged and empowered to actually *lead*. This is the imperative of our times. As Greenleaf (1977) concludes in his seminal essay on servant-leadership, the real danger occurs when strong, natural servants fail to lead or choose to follow a non-servant; as a result, both the individual and society suffer. With a re-imagined, reinvented understanding of power in leadership, these leaders will choose to lead. They will be motivated, strengthened, and inspired to take on the cudgels of servant-leadership. They will lead from a platform that comes from within and flows toward the demands of change and transformation around us. These leaders will lead with integrity, authenticity, and spirituality.

NOTE

1. This chapter was previously published as San Juan, K. S. (2005). Re-imagining power in leadership: Reflection, integration, and servant-leadership. *The International Journal of Servant-Leadership. 1*(1), 187–209.

REFERENCES

Adler, A. (1966). The psychology of power. *Journal of Individual Psychology (22)*2, 166–172.

Appelbaum, S. H., Hebert, D., & Leroux, S. (1999). Empowerment: Power, culture and leadership-A strategy or fad for the millennium? *Journal of Workplace Learning: Employee Counselling Today, 11*(7), 233–254.

Bass, B. M. (1990). *Bass and Stogdill's handbook of leadership: Theory, research, and managerial applications* (3rd edition). New York, NY: The Free Press.

Berger, P. L., & Luckmann, T. (1966, 1967). *The social construction of reality: A treatise in the sociology of knowledge.* New York, NY: Anchor Books.

Block, P. (1996). *Stewardship: Choosing service over self-interest.* San Francisco, CA: Berrett-Koehler Publishers, Inc.

Burns, J. M. (1978). *Leadership.* New York, NY: Harper & Row.

Covey, S. R. (1992). *Principle-Centered Leadership: Strategies for personal and Professional Effectiveness.* New York, NY: Simon and Schuster.

Goleman, D., Boyatzis, R., & McKee, A. (2002). *Primal leadership: Realizing the power of emotional intelligence.* Boston, MA: Harvard Business School Press.

Gordon, R. D. (2002). Conceptualizing leadership with respect to its historical contextual antecedents to power. *The Leadership Quarterly, 13*, 151–167.

Greenleaf, R. K. (1977). *Servant-leadership: A journey into the nature of legitimate power and greatness.* Mahwah, NJ: Paulist Press.

———. (1991). *The Servant as leader.* Indianapolis, IN: The Robert K. Greenleaf Center.

———. (1995). Reflections from experience. In L.C. Spears (ed.), *Reflections on leadership: How Robert K. Greenleaf's theory of servant leadership influenced today's top management thinkers* (pp. 22–36). New York, NY: John Wiley and Sons, Inc.

Hardy, C., & Clegg, S. R. (1996). Some dare call it power. In S.R. Clegg, C. Hardy, & W.R. Nord (eds.), *Handbook of Organization Studies* (pp. 622–641). London, UK: Sage Publication Ltd.

Haugaard, M. (ed.). (2002). *Power: A reader.* Manchester, UK: Manchester University Press.

Heifetz, R. A. (1994). *Leadership without Easy Answers.* Cambridge, MA: The Belknap Press of Harvard University Press.

Heifetz, R. A., & Linsky, M. (2002). *Leadership on the line: Staying alive through the dangers of leading.* Boston, MA: Harvard Business School Press.

Hinze, C. F. (1995). *Comprehending power in Christian Social Ethics.* Atlanta, GA: Scholars Press.

Hollander, E. P., & Offermann, L. R. (1990). Power and leadership in organizations: Relationships in transition. *American Psychologist, 45*(2), 179–189.

Homer, A. J. (1995). *The wish for power and the fear of having it.* Northvale, NJ: Jason Aronson Inc.

Keller, J. A. (1986). Niebuhr, Tillich, and Whitehead on the ethics of power. *American Journal of Theology and Philosophy, 7*(3), 132–148.

Kets de Vries, M. F. R. (1993, 2003). *Leaders, fools and impostors: Essays on the psychology of leadership.* Lincoln, NE: iUniverse, Inc.

Kotter, J. P. (1985). *Power and influence.* New York, NY: The Free Press.

Lips, H. M. (1981). *Women, men, and the psychology of power.* Englewood Cliffs, NJ: Prentice Hall, Inc.

Loomer, B. (1976). Two conceptions on power. *Process Studies, 6*(1), 5–32.

McClelland, D.C. (1975). *Power: The Inner Experience.* New York, NY: Irvington Publishers, Inc.

Morgan, G. (1997). *Images of organization* (2nd edition). Thousand Oaks, CA: Sage Publications, Inc.

Mumby, D. K. (2001). Power and politics. In F. M. Jablin & L. L. Putnam (eds.), *The new handbook of Organizational Communication: Advances in theory, research, and methods.* Thousand Oaks, CA: Sage Publications, Inc.

O'Toole, J. (1995, 1996). *Leading change: The argument for Values-Based Leadership.* San Francisco, CA: Jossey-Bass.

Pasewark, K. A. (1993). *A theology of power: Being Beyond Domination.* Minneapolis, MN: Augsburg Fortress.

Pfeffer, J. (1981). *Power in organizations.* Marshfield, MA: Pitman Publishing.

———. (1992). *Managing with power: Politics and influence in organizations.* Boston, MA: Harvard Business School Press.

———. (1997). *New directions for Organization Theory: Problems and prospects.* New York, NY: Oxford University Press.

Post, J. M. (2004). *Leaders and Their Followers in a Dangerous World: The psychology of Political Behavior.* Ithaca, NY: Cornell University Press.

Rost, J. C. (1991, 1993). *Leadership for the Twenty-First Century.* Westport, CT: Praeger.

Ryan, M. (1984). Theories of power. In A. Kakabadse & C. Parker (eds.), *Power, politics, and organizations: A Behavioural Science View* (pp. 3–20). Chichester, UK: John Wiley &Sons Ltd.

Schmookler, A. B. (1994). *The parable of the tribes: The problem of power in social evolution* (2nd edition). Albany, NY: State University of New York Press.

Tillich, P. (1954). *Love, power and justice.* Oxford, UK: Oxford University Press.

———. (1963). *Systematic theology, Volume III: Life and the spirit: History and the kingdom of God.* Chicago, IL: University of Chicago Press.

Wartenberg, T. E. (1990). *The forms of power. From domination to transformation.* Philadelphia, PA: Temple University Press.

Winter, D. G. (1973). *The Power Motive.* New York, NY: The Free Press.

Wrong, D. H. (1979, 1995). *Power: Its forms, bases, and uses.* New Brunswick, NJ: Transaction Publishers.

Yukl, G. (2002). *Leadership in organizations* (5th edition). Upper Saddle River, NJ: Prentice Hall.

Zaleznik, A., & Kets de Vries, M. F. R. (1985). *Power and the corporate mind: How to use rather than misuse leadership.* Chicago, IL: Bonus Books.

Chapter 2

Servant-Leadership

Sustaining Democratic Schools

Carolyn Crippen

Fullan (2003) writes[1] that a strong education system is the cornerstone of a civil, prosperous, and democratic society, and Glickman, Gordon, and Ross-Gordon (2005) state, "In a democratic society, it is vital that students learn to think reflectively, function at high stages of moral reasoning, and be autonomous decision makers" (p. 156). Hence, the role of school leader and/ or teacher becomes critical in providing the example and environment to foster such democratic ethos. Today, many of our schools are moving toward a more collegial, cooperative, transformative, service approach in the learning community. Murphy and Seashore-Louis (1999) state the changes reflected in present-day educational institutions:

> In these new postindustrial educational organizations, there are important shifts in roles, relationships, and responsibilities; traditional patterns of relationships are altered; authority flows are less hierarchical; role definitions are both more general and more flexible; leadership is connected to competence for needed tasks rather than to formal position; and independence and isolation are replaced by cooperative work. (p. xxii)

Such understandings affect how we see ourselves as educational leaders. Bennis and Goldsmith (1997) state that "In order to transform ourselves as leaders, we must recognize and shift the paradigm through which we view leadership itself" (p. 71). The present chapter introduces readers to such a paradigm shift, toward servant-leadership, a concept that helps foster the development of democratic schools. This essay will provide: (1) the theoretical framework for servant-leadership, a leadership concept identified by Robert K. Greenleaf in his seminal work, *The Servant as Leader* (1970/1991); (2) a summary of the Manitoba educational stakeholders who have been introduced to servant-leadership and how these groups have integrated the concept within their educational environment; and (3) recommendations for future research.

SERVANT-LEADERSHIP

The old leadership paradigm of the nineteenth and early twentieth centuries suggested three particular beliefs: (1) leaders were born and not made (your lineage or pedigree class endowed you with the look and personality of a leader—a hierarchical position); (2) good management made successful organizations; and (3) one should avoid failure at all costs, a belief that promoted risk-avoidance and fear (Block, 1996; Hickman, 1998). Leadership was defined in the literature as being hierarchical, patriarchal, coercive, and related to wealth and influence (Bennis, 1997; Block, 1993; Hickman, 1998; Sergiovanni, 1992).

The paradoxical term *servant-leadership* is inclusive of personal service to society regardless of position (Block, 1996). This premise of a leadership-service combination was in direct opposition to the hierarchical model of leadership. In hierarchical leadership, the power of the leader was visible and obeyed by those lower in the organization (Hesselbein, Goldsmith, Beckhard, & Schubert, 1998; Senge, 1990), whereas in servant-leadership, it was through strategies of service and stewardship that a leader was identified by the people to be first among equals or *primus inter pares* (DePree, 1989, 1992; Greenleaf, 1976).

Robert Kiefner Greenleaf (1904–1990) introduced the term *servant-leadership*, a new leadership paradigm, in his first essay, titled "The Servant as Leader," which he wrote in 1970 at the age of sixty-six. Greenleaf worked first as a lineman and eventually moved into organizational management at AT&T between the mid-1920s and 1960s. He lectured at Massachusetts Institute of Technology (M.I.T.), Dartmouth, and the Harvard Business School. Greenleaf (Spears, 1998a) described how he discovered the concept of servant-leadership through reading a small book titled *Journey to the East* by Herman Hesse (1956). The book tells the story of a band of men who set out on a long journey. Accompanying the men was a fellow named Leo; his job was to care for the band of men by doing all of the menial chores and providing for their comfort. The journey progressed well until Leo disappeared. At this point, the travelers aborted the journey when they fell into disarray without Leo.

Many years later, the narrator of the story encountered Leo. It was at this point that the narrator realized Leo was the titular head of the order that sponsored the journey. He was the leader, but his nature was that of a servant. His leadership was bestowed upon him and could be taken away by the band of men. His desire to serve the group of men came from his heart and reflected the real person. Leo wanted to be of service to the band of men. Leo was a servant first, by taking care of their basic needs each day while on the journey. Greenleaf believed the message of the story was that one has to first serve society and through one's service one is recognized as a leader. Leadership must be about service (Spears, 1998a). Greenleaf (1970/1991) states,

> The Servant-Leader is servant first. It begins with the natural feeling that one wants to serve. Then conscious choice brings one to aspire to lead. The difference manifests itself in the care taken by the servant-first, to make sure that other people's highest priority needs are being served. The best test is: do those served grow as persons; do they, while being served, become healthier, wiser, freer, more autonomous, more likely themselves to become servants? And what is the effect on the least privileged in society; will they benefit, or at least, not be further deprived? (p. 7)

Greenleaf, a Quaker, believed strongly in the equality of all human beings, and he worked with educational, business, and industrial organizations (Spears, 1998a) with the goal of developing strong, effective, caring communities in all segments of our society (Greenleaf, 1976; Spears, 1998b). Greenleaf (2002) identifies an important realization. He tells of the subtleness of the servant-leader in action and how he or she is viewed by others, "They do not see the servant-leadership in action as you saw it. And that may be the fundamental key. Effective servant-leaders can be so subtle about it that all anybody is likely to see is the result. They don't see the cause" (p. 151).

Within the servant-leadership paradigm, the voices of educational leadership may be heard: Nel Noddings (2003) and her ethic of care; William Purkey and Betty Siegel's (2002) invitational leader; Thomas Sergiovanni (1992) and his moral leadership; Robert Starrat (2003) and the cultivation of meaning, community, and responsibility; and Michael Fullan (2003) and building sustainability and democratic schools through collaborative cultures.

Ten Characteristics

Autry (2001) states that the transition to a culture of servant-leadership requires time for the development of necessary features or qualities for a servant-leader. Spears (1998b), CEO of the Greenleaf Center for Servant-Leadership, identified ten characteristics of servant-leadership: (1) listening, (2) empathy, (3) healing, (4) awareness, (5) persuasion, (6) conceptualization, (7) foresight, (8) stewardship, (9) commitment to the growth of others, and (10) building community. These qualities are in a connected field that begins with the internal action of listening. A description of each of the ten characteristics follows:

1. *Listening*—This refers to a deep commitment of listening to others. Autry (2001), Bennis and Goldsmith (1997), Frick and Spears (1996), and Greenleaf (1970/1991) emphasize the need for silence, reflection, meditation, active listening, and actually "hearing" what is said and unsaid. The best communication forces you to listen (DePree, 1989). Effective educational leaders are great communicators and must be good listeners, to themselves (through their inner voice), as well as to students, parents, teachers, and other members of the learning community.

2. *Empathy*—A good servant-leader strives to understand and empathizes with others, but this understanding should be supportive as opposed to patronizing. "It is a misuse of our power (as leaders) to take responsibility for solving problems that belong to others" (Block, 1993, p. 72). Greenleaf (cited in Spears, 1998a) wrote that trust could be developed through the use of empathy when he stated,

> Individuals grow taller when those who lead them empathize and when they are accepted for what they are, even though their performance may be judged critically in terms of what they are capable of doing. Leaders who empathize and who fully accept those who go with them on this basis are more likely to be trusted. (p. 81)

3. *Healing*—The servant-leader has the potential to heal him-or herself and others. Sturnick (1998) writes extensively about six stages of healing leadership. One must first have an understanding about personal and/or institutional health. She describes the six stages as: (1) consciousness of health or being honestly aware of one's state of health, which is often triggered by an event, for instance, a heart attack; (2) willingness to change and realizing that one must do certain things to achieve improved health; (3) a teachable moment or a time when one seeks information or advice; (4) healthy support systems, which are needed to change behavior and may include one person, a group or an organization; (5) immersion in the duality of our inner lives and the realization of the good and bad or the strengths and weaknesses we each have; and (6) eventually the return to service in leadership through seeking honest answers from friends and colleagues. Stumick warns that it is not always possible as a healthy leader to find followers, and she believes that "sick organizations really do contaminate" (p. 191). Gardiner (1998, p. 122) suggests that healing can come through just quietly being and that a "quiet presence is an act of renewal," and Greenleaf, a lifelong meditator, tells us that he

views the action of meditation as a service because one is taking time to think about things, to reflect, and he writes, "I prefer to meditate; I have come to view my meditating as serving" (Gardiner, p. 123).

4. *Awareness*—The servant-leader has a general awareness, especially self-awareness. One develops awareness through self-reflection, through listening to what others tell us about ourselves, through being continually open to learning, and by making the connection from what we know and believe to what we say or do. This is called in the vernacular "walking your talk" (Bennis & Goldsmith, 1997, pp. 70–71).

5. *Persuasion*—The servant-leader seeks to convince others, rather than coerce compliance. Greenleaf speaks in Frick and Spears (1996) about persuasion:

> One is persuaded upon arriving at a feeling of rightness about a belief or action through one's own intuitive sense; persuasion is usually too undramatic to be newsworthy. Significant instances of persuasion may be known to only one or a few and they are rarely noted in history. Simply put, consensus is a method of using persuasion in a group. (pp. 139–140)

6. *Conceptualization*—The servant-leader seeks to nurture his or her own abilities to dream great dreams. Greenleaf describes conceptual talent in Frick and Spears (1998) as having,

> the ability to see the whole in the perspective of history—past and future—to state and adjust goals, to evaluate, to analyze, and to foresee contingencies a long way ahead. Leadership, in the sense of going out ahead to show the way, is more conceptual than operating. The conceptualizer, at his or her best, is a persuader and a relation builder. (p. 217)

7. *Foresight*—This is the ability to foresee or know the likely outcome of a situation. Greenleaf (1991) says it is a better than average guess about what is going to happen when in the future. He says it is "the lead that a leader has" (p. 18), and goes on to state:

> Foresight is seen as a wholly rational process, the product of a constantly running internal computer that deals with intersecting series and random inputs and is vastly more complicated than anything technology has yet produced. Foresight means regarding the events of the instant moment and constantly comparing them with a series of projections made in the past and at the same time projecting future events—with diminishing certainty as projected time runs out into the indefinite future. (p. 18)

8. *Stewardship*—Greenleaf believed all members of an institution or organization play significant roles in holding their institutions in trust (caring

for the well-being of the institution and serving the needs of others in the institution) for the greater good of society. Fullan (2003) suggests that school principals and teachers must be mindful that "changing context is the key to deeper change" (p. 21) and they must ask, "What is my role in making a difference in the school as a whole?" (p. 21). De Pree (1989) emphasizes the need for us to make a contribution to society: "The art of leadership requires us to think about the leader-as-steward in terms of relationships: of assets and legacy, of momentum and effectiveness, of civility and values" (p. 13). Sergiovanni (1992) explains that steward-ship "involves the leader's personal responsibility to manage her or his life and affairs with proper regard for the rights of other people and for the common welfare" (p. 139). Greenleaf speaks of *primus inter pares* or the "first among equals" where the leader is among the people, not above.

9. *Commitment to the growth of people*—The servant-leader is committed to the individual growth of human beings and will do everything she or he can to nurture others. "The signs of outstanding leadership appear pri-marily among the followers. Are the followers reaching their potential? Are they learning? Serving?" (De Pree, 1989, p. 12). Sergiovanni (2001) puts this in a school perspective:

> The leader serves as head follower by leading the discussion about what is worth following, and by modeling, teaching, and helping others to become better followers. When this happens, the emphasis changes from direct leadership based on rules and personality, to a different kind of leadership based on stewardship and service. (p. 34)

10. *Building Community*—The servant-leader seeks to identify some means for building community. There are several approaches to build-ing community outlined in the literature; three approaches mentioned include giving back through service to the community, investing finan-cially into the community, and caring about one's community. When Pinchot (cited in Hesselbein, Goldsmith, Beckhard & Schubert, 1998) considers the concept of community, he suggests that the person who gives or contributes or invests the most to a community has the high-est status; in other words, "giving it away, rather than keeping it, earns status" (p. 126). Sergiovanni (1994) believes that caring is an integral part of shared community. Wheatley and Kellner-Rogers (cited in Hes-selbein et al., 1998) emphasize the sense of belonging defined by a shared sense of purpose that does not eliminate one's uniqueness but focuses all energies into a resilient community. Starrat (2003) states, "In appealing to their sense of community, we invite youngsters to work toward it" (p. 95).

MANITOBA EDUCATIONAL STAKEHOLDERS

During the past eight years, over 1,500 people in Manitoba have received in-service, heard, and studied the writings of Robert K. Greenleaf (1970/1991, 1992, 2002) and the philosophy of servant-leadership. This group included the following participants/members:

a) *Parkland Leadership Academy*: With financial support from the provincial government, five superintendents in the Parkland region of rural Manitoba formed an academy for all school principals within their school divisions (districts) that met several times as a group each year. Greenleaf's writing (*Servant as Leader*, 1970/1991) was studied. Principals discussed ways in which they could implement the philosophy of servant-leadership into their schools. The group continues today.

b) *Clear Lake Summer Leadership Course*: Each summer for a full week the Manitoba Council for Leadership in Education sponsors in-service sessions in educational leadership at the Manitoba resort. During three successive summers, the writer facilitated full-day sessions on servant-leadership. These sessions created a ripple effect whereby participants requested courses on the subject.

c) *Manitoba Teachers Society (MTS)*: This is the teachers' union for all elementary and secondary school teachers in the province. In response to specific in-service requests, a servant-leadership session was provided by the writer to accommodate teachers and administrators in Winnipeg. As well, the Manitoba Teachers' Society named *Servant Leadership: A Journey into the Nature of Legitimate Power and Greatness* (Greenleaf, 1977) one of their top ten books to read for educators in the province.

d) *Manitoba Association of School Trustees*: Recently, the number of school divisions (districts) in Manitoba was reduced by government legislation. More than fifty divisions became thirty-six divisions. The anxiety, anger, and resentment that resulted were palpable. A few months prior to the formal amalgamation, I was invited to speak to 450 trustees about servant-leadership. It was a tense and bleak environment, but the message seemed well received. Once amalgamation had become a reality, I was invited to return several times to work with table groups of trustees to problem solve and focus on the future. The journey of understanding and healing continues today.

e) *University of Manitoba, Faculty of Education*: Beginning in 1998, the writer integrated the concept of servant-leadership into several university leadership courses, as formal lessons, with specific course texts, and as in-service for teacher candidates. Over 120 Special Education Resource teachers (129.567, Strategies for Inclusionary Schools and Classrooms) have studied *The Servant as Leader* and applied it to their work environment. The ten characteristics of servant-leadership provided a framework for the teachers to focus on their attitude of service and behavior in their schools. Two classes of post-baccalaureate students and practicing teachers have studied *Servant-leadership and the Art of Teaching* (Powers and Moore, 2004) as required reading for their Instructional Supervision Course. Several hundred graduate and post-baccalaureate students have studied servant-leadership through a variety of texts in Courses 129.508 and 129.509—Issues in Educational Administration (Parts I & II) during the past five years: *On Becoming a Servant Leader* (Greenleaf, 1996); *Teacher as Servant* (Greenleaf, 1979/1987); *The Servant-Leader Within: A Transformative Path* (Greenleaf, 1977/2002); *Insights on Leadership* (Spears, 1998).

f) *Winnipeg School Division School Administrators:* This is the largest school division in the province and often sets direction for the rest. The topic of servant-leadership was introduced early in 2005 during a retreat of school administrators and superintendents. The day involved case studies and the application of servant-leadership in problem solving. Louis Riel School Division followed recently with a three-part series on servant-leadership and school democracy for administrators.

These educational organizations have integrated servant-leadership in various ways: (1) as study groups analyzing Greenleaf's writing; (2) using the ten characteristics as a guide for developing a positive learning environment and integrating it into school plans; (3) as a modus operandi for school administrators; (4) as a healing and basis for discussion during the school division amalgamation process; (5) as professional development for teacher candidates going into the field; (6) as a foundation and responsive action for special education resource teachers; (7) as a means for building shared leadership within schools; and (8) as a component of university educational administration course readings. Greenleaf (1986) states,

> This is not a bandwagon idea; it is not a best-seller kind of thing; but nevertheless, these people (servant-leaders) do exist, and some of them have become very important to me. (p. 343)

And,

> The difference between organizations is how people relate and how they actually function, which may not bear a whole lot of relationship to how the thing is sketched out on paper. (p. 347)

EARLY OUTCOMES OF SERVANT-LEADERSHIP

Servant-leadership is a collaborative, empowering, serving way to build democratic learning communities. Noddings (2003) believes democracy produces freedom for individual and collective action while supporting equality and satisfying human needs. Servant-leadership is built upon the premise of individual respect, stewardship, and service to one's community and is useful as a foundation for building a democratic school culture. A sense of equality, regardless of position, permeates a school that embeds servant-leadership as its raison d'être. Noddings (2003) would say, "What is required is a sincere and meaningful respect for all positive human capacities" (p. 232). Custodian, principal, student, teacher, secretary, bus driver, all are valued members of the school community. Staff meetings and school plans invite participation and input from all the various stakeholders. Planning and meetings are transparent and build trust. The school is enriched by the presence of each member. Children need to feel wanted, and today the democratic school often becomes an inviting and safe haven for many children. Decisions are made through collaboration, on-going dialogue, and sensitive and open listening, through caring and respect for individual opinions. Children absorb this type of environment and perhaps will transfer some of these skills into their daily lives. At present, this process is being put into action in two Manitoba school divisions as part of school plans. These plans are reviewed in the late spring for outcomes related to issues of attendance, suspensions, staff development, contribution to the learning community, and student achievement. Noddings (2003) suggests that interest in service learning seems to be on the rise and states, "Active participation in community life may also be a direct source of happiness" (p. 236).

Kowalski (citing Burns, 2006) describes democratic leaders as collaborative (working toward mutual goals), while Greenleaf would suggest "*primus inter pares.*" Sergiovanni would suggest "that everyone gets a chance to be quarterback and is free to call the play; if it is a good call, then the team runs with it" (p. 134). Teachers are often the genesis for creative ideas and through encouragement and valuing of input may lead the way for effective change in a school. Democratic leaders have been granted authority (which may be withdrawn) by those within the school organization. These "leaders have a moral responsibility to fulfill social contracts with the organization's members" (Kowalski, 2006, p. 211). In addition, Sergiovanni stresses the importance of moral authority: "Such ideas as servant-leadership bring with them a different kind of strength—one based on moral authority. When one places one's leadership practice in service to ideas, and to others who also seek to serve these ideas, issues of leadership role and leadership style become far less important" (pp. 128–129).

CONCLUSION

Initially, most information about servant-leadership came from the world of business, from the work of researchers such as Autry (2001); Block (1993); Bennis (1997); De Pree (1989, 1992); Pinchot (1998); Senge (1990); and Sturnick (1998). Today, the Greenleaf Center lists many doctoral dissertations in education related to servant-leadership, and the educational research base is growing. Is servant-leadership a viable model for present-day schools? Greenleaf (1977) spoke directly to educators, encouraging them to nurture servant-leadership among their students, thus imbuing them with renewed meaning and purpose. Consider how this leadership paradigm could be implemented, for instance, in the areas of speakers, study groups, mentors, service activities to help the community, student and parent council partnerships, pilot projects, and action research. What outcomes could be expected? What are the obvious visible changes? Has productivity improved within the school? Is the school reaching outward and inward? Surveys and questionnaires could measure the pulse of the servant-leader initiative. The simple concept of working on the ten characteristics over a school year, and helping students and staff to focus upon one at a time, can increase the awareness and understanding of the ripple effect created in the learning environment. Analysis of leadership styles for evidence of servant-leadership traits in teacher candidates and senior administrators could prove interesting. Much research needs to be done to uncover the potential of servant-leadership in our schools.

Senge (1990) reminds us that systems that change require a variety of leadership types at different times in organizational development. Thus, it appears as our schools move toward democratization that servant-leadership may be a vehicle for major systems change at every level in educational organizations. In conclusion, we are encouraged by Sergiovanni (1999) to consider servant-leadership as an approach for present-day schools and our raison d'être:

> What matters are issues of substance. What are we about? Why? Are students being served? Is the school as learning community being served? What are our obligations to this community? With these questions in mind, how can we best get the job done? (p. 61)

NOTE

1. This chapter was previously published as Crippen, C. (2006). Servant-leadership: Sustaining democratic schools. *The International Journal of Servant-Leadership.* 2(1), 319–333.

REFERENCES

Autry, J. (2001). *The Servant Leader*. Roseville, CA: Prima Publishing.

Bennis, W. (1997). *Managing people is Like Herding Cats*. Provo, UT: Executive Excellence.

Bennis, W., & Goldsmith, J. (1997). *Learning to lead*. Reading, MA: Perseus Books.

Block, P. (1993). *Stewardship: Choosing service Over Self-Interest*. San Francisco, cA: Berrett-Koehler Publishers.

De Pree, M. (1989). *Leadership is An Art*. New York, NY: Dell Publishing Group.

———. (1992). *Leadership jazz*. New York, NY: Dell Publishing Group.

Frick, D., & Spears, L. (eds.). (1996). *The Private Writings of Robert K. Greenleaf: On becoming a Servant Leader*. San Francisco, CA: Jossey-Bass.

Fullan, M. (2003). *The Moral Imperative of School Leadership*. Thousand Oaks, CA: Corwin Press.

Gardiner, J. (1998). Quiet presence: The holy ground of leadership. In L. Spears (ed.), *Insights on leadership: Service, stewardship, spirit, and Servant Leadership*. New York, NY: John Wiley & Sons, Inc.

Glickman, C., Gordon, S., & Ross-Gordon, J. (2005). *The Basic Guide to supervision and Instructional Leadership*. Boston, MA: Pearson.

Greenleaf, R. (1970/1991). *The servant as leader*. Indianapolis. IN: The Robert K. Greenleaf Center.

———. (1976). *The institution as servant*. Indianapolis IN: The Robert K. Greenleaf Center.

———. (1977). *Servant Leadership: A journey into the nature of legitimate power and greatness*. New York, NY: Paulist Press.

———. (1986). *On becoming a Servant-Leader*. Indianapolis, IN: Robert K. Greenleaf Center.

———. (2002). *Teacher as servant: A parable*. Indianapolis, IN: The Robert K. Greenleaf Center.

Hesse, H. (1956/2000). *The journey to the east*. New York, NY: Farrar, Straus and Giroux.

Hesselbein, F., Goldsmith, M., Beckhard, R., & Schubert, R. (eds.). (1998). *The community for the future*. New York, NY: The Peter F. Drucker Foundation.

Hickman, G. (ed.). (1998). *Leading organizations: Perspectives for a New Era*. London: Sage Publications.

Kowalski, T. (2006). *The School Superintendent: Theory, practice, and cases* (2nd edition).Thousand Oaks, CA: Sage Publications.

Murphy, J., & Seashore-Louis, K. (1992). Framing the project: Introduction. In *Handbook of research on Educational Administration* (2nd edition). American Educational Research Association.

Noddings, N. (2003). *Happiness and education*. Cambridge University Press.

Pinchot, G. (1998). Building community in the workplace. In F. Hesselbein, M. Goldsmith, R. Beckhard & R. Schubert (Eds.), *The community of the future*. San Francisco, ca: Jossey-Bass Publishers.

Purkey, W., & Siegel, B. (2002). *Becoming an Invitational Leader*. Atlanta, ga: Humanics Trade Group.

Senge, P. (1990). *The Fifth Discipline: The art & practice of the Learning Organization*. New York, NY: Doubleday/Currency Publishing.

Sergiovanni, T. (1992). *Moral leadership*. San Francisco, CA: Jossey-Bass.

———. (1994). *Building community in schools*. San Francisco, CA: Jossey-Bass.

———. (1999). *Rethinking leadership*. Arlington Heights, IL: Skylight Professional Development.

———. (2001). *Leadership: What's in it for schools?* London: Routledge-Falmer.

Spears, L. (ed.). (1998a). *Insights on leadership: Service, stewardship, spirit, and servant leadership*. Toronto. ON: John Wiley & Sons, Inc.

———. (ed.). (1998b). *The power of Servant-Leadership*. San Francisco, CA: Berrett-Koehler Publishers, Inc.

Starratt, R. (2003). *Centering Educational Administration*. Mahwah, NJ: Lawrence Erlbaum Associates, Inc., Publishers.

Stumick, J. (1998). Healing leadership. In L. Spears (ed.), *Insights on Leadership: Service, stewardship, spirit, and Servant-Leadership*. New York, NY: John Wiley & Sons, Inc.

Wheatley, M., & Kellner-Rogers, M. (1998). The paradox and promise of community. In F. Hesselbein, M. Goldsmith, R. Beckhard & R. Schubert (eds.), *The community of the future*. San Francisco, CA: Jossey-Bass Publishers.

Chapter 3

Leadership Development for Today's Ktunaxa Youth

Command Structure versus the Crazydog Society

Christopher Horsethief

Block (2008) opened[1] his book on the structure of belonging with the statement "social fabric of community is formed from an expanding shared sense of belonging . . . shaped by the idea that only when we are connected and care for the well-being of the whole that a civil and democratic society is created" (p. 9). The concept of belonging has been studied directly in servant-leadership studies, including belonging to community or organization (Banutu-Gomez, 2004), belonging and resiliency (Wheatley & Kellner-Rogers, 1998), belonging through a sharing of humanity with followership (Birkenmeier, Carson, & Carson, 2003).

Belonging has also been examined indirectly through the examination of characteristics associated with belonging; followership perceptions of justice (Mayer, Bardes, & Piccolo, 2008; Ehrhart, 2004), community building and commitment (Spears, 1998; Laub, 1999), love and empowerment (Patterson, 2003) and development of high-quality dyadic relationships (van Dierendonck & Patterson, 2010). Sipe and Frick's (2009) theme of belonging is located in a synergistic culture of collaboration, where the servant-leader facilitates belonging by "honoring each individual contribution *and* molding them into solutions that serve a common good" (p. 80). Sipe and Frick noted the emergence of co-labor or a sense of working together that transcends the individual leader or the individual follower—such community building requires a cooperative gravity that pulls leadership and followership into an intentionally designed enterprise. But what happens when a community has had many of its internal collaborating mechanisms replaced with colonial replacements?

31

Elsewhere I have shown that the process of colonization has resulted in indigenous membership being separated from their traditional sense of purpose, and therefore from the historical contexts of many of the social systems related to belonging. The contexts supporting belonging included maintenance of oral histories (Horsethief, 2011b), traditional notions of vocational purpose (KNC, 2010), and sociocultural/sociolinguistic discourse related to word creation processes (Horsethief, 2011a). In this chapter, I assert the same process in the context of leadership development. The approach I adopt is to shift the units of analysis from Canadian structures of oppression (often built on common Western/non-indigenous ideas) to indigenous resilience.

Stated another way, I will move the discussion of leadership development away from the establishment of new Western approaches, back to the qualitative interactions that previously linked members of indigenous communities to their own culture, its histories and traditions. Doing so honors Greenleaf's (1977) theory where "leadership emerges from those whose primary motivation is a deep desire to help others" (p. 4) and pursues leadership goals described by Laub (1999) that promote the value of people, building community and honoring authenticity.

A BRIEF HISTORY OF THE KTUNAXA

To discuss family in the context of indigenous North American people is to simultaneously learn about the primary social organization of their communities, as well as the colonial impacts of North American federal governments on the cultural systems that empowered hundreds of politically distinct indigenous cultural groups to live a sense of purpose, to be connected or to exist relationally (see Horsethief 2015, 2016, 2018). According to the National Collaborating Center for Aboriginal Health (2009), most legislation has deteriorated community cohesion and belonging by advancing a range of "policies designed to assimilate Aboriginal peoples, which involved cultural and linguistic suppression, forced relocation onto reserve lands, alienation from traditional territories and ways of life, and perhaps most devastatingly, the creation of residential schools" (p. 2).

Recent Canadian efforts to reconcile the 150-year federal approach to indigenous assimilation inextricably link the Canadian Indian Residential School System (CIRSS) with indigenous child and family welfare. Justice Rene Dussault (2005) of the Quebec Court of Appeal cited the schools as detrimental to "feelings of self-worth, family connectedness, the intergenerational transfer of skills and traditions and the essential core trust in and respect for others from which all people must draw in order to build loving relationships and healthy communities" (p. 2). Similarly, Cyr (2009) linked indigenous missionary education to the loss of language and culture, of connections to family and community, of cultural identity and parenting skills (para. 4).

Other brutally honest research describes the legacy as a fundamentally "genocidal occurrence" (Tinker, 1993), "soul damaging" (Zelmer, 2010), "soul wounding" (Duran, 2004), "crushing individual energies" (Tousignant & Sioui, 2009), depleting the "collective immune systems" of indigenous communities (Abadian, 1999, p. 203), an attempted "conversion of the heart" (Petersen & Peers, 1993), "legislative genocide" (Shahram, 2017), and a process of "dis-memberment leaving us to be re-membered" (Jimmie, 2019). The indigenous response, typified by the Ktunaxa, has been a range of health research and wellness programs to re-create post-genocide, community building, soul healing, and energizing capacities.

As a participant in the British Columbia Treaty Process, the Ktunaxa Nation Council (KNC) is faced with massive systemic change: movement away from federally defined Status Indians subject to governmental mandates for education and welfare, to Nation Members capable of matching cultural values to contemporary tribal structures. According to the Ktunaxa Nation Regional Governance Outline (KNC, 2009), this historic undertaking allows Ktunaxa leaders, managers, and administrators to implement new methods of delivering social, political, and economic services to address the disparity between Canadian and indigenous determinants of health. Key in this process is re-establishing Ktunaxa social mechanisms supplanted by the federally funded and church-mandated programs at St. Eugene's Mission School, especially initiatives targeting the development of Ktunaxa children.

According to Ktunaxa community elders, a Ktunaxa's journey from childhood to adulthood includes a critical cognitive threshold (Anonymous Ktunaxa Elders, personal communication, February 2010).[2] This mechanism delineates two distinct developmental stages in the Ktunaxa culture; it is the difference between ʔiⱡkiⱡwiynam (wise-thinking) and kⱡitiⱡwiynam (thinking without wisdom). They claimed this threshold marked the ability of Ktunaxa to be self-directed by critical thought and concrete experience rather than legends, morals, or parent's warnings. Ktunaxa community discussion inspired by the Indian Residential Schools Settlement Agreement (NCTR, 2006) and Canada's Truth and Reconciliation Commission (TRC, 2016) have largely focused on the dissipation of these traditional milestones and their effects on Residential School survivors but less so for survivor's children or grandchildren. Younging, Dewar, and Degagne (2009) argued that the Settlement Agreement's financial compensation for direct survivors lacks a meaningful and comprehensive source of human capital development for their descendants.

The two Ktunaxa Elders viewed a more comprehensive settlement includ-ing means for reinstating the ʔiłkiłwiyniskił (onset of adult or wise-thinking for all). The thesis of this chapter is that contemporary military training may be used to reinvent the threshold in question. A new training program focus-ing on traditional decision-making would need a strong cultural foundation to succeed where previous youth programs have struggled. Community members with Royal Canadian Armed Forces and United States Armed Forces military experience suggested seating training goals in the traditions of the Crazy Dogs.

THE CRAZY DOG SOCIETY

Turney-High's (1941) detailed ethnography described the Ktunaxa as having a strict comprehensive social structure due to the close proximity of surround-ing tribal groups. He noted most daily behavior was oriented to the stability of the society and credited this strict tradition with a reduced need for inter-nal policing within Ktunaxa communities. Weydermeyer-Johnson (1969) supported this notion, citing the absence of "child-scarers" or "policemen" commonly found in neighboring Salish communities. Rather, the Ktunaxa maintained a rigid and disciplined military society to fend off neighboring tribes often considered to be a threat to community resources. Louie (2008) maintained the crucial component of this force was the Crazy Dog Society. Turney-High noted if survival of the camp was in jeopardy, word was sent to the Crazy Dog chief and Crazy Dog driver leadership dyad who rallied, organized, and deployed the Dogs with a no-retreat order. This society was a supplement to commonplace hunting and warfare roles and held in regard when called upon. The Dogs were ordinary camp members with extraordi-nary dedication in times of community endangerment.

Unfortunately for Ktunaxa families, the relationship between the Crazy Dogs and the Ktunaxa community was one of the earliest victims of St. Eugene's Residential School's attack on Ktunaxa family dynamics. A Ktunaxa elder spoke about the severing of these ties:

> In our earliest days at St. Eugene's we were told that our grandfathers, our fathers and our uncles were drunks. We were told not to trust them. We were told not to listen to them. We were told not to follow them. The (Anglican) fathers would say, "I saw your father in town . . . he was drinking as usual." They always made sure they told me that in front of the other kids. Those men were (military) veterans . . . and we were told to be ashamed of them. (Anonymous Ktunaxa Elder, personal communication, 2009)

Many community members' relationships to the men that comprised the trusted society became tainted. Louie supported this notion, asserting the role of elder men as reliable servants and role models dissipated as memories of the Crazy Dogs faded. The society had been an appropriate mechanism for defining the role of Ktunaxa men as providers, servants, and warriors. Its existence was a functional embodiment of the ʔiⱡkiⱡwiynam decision-making process.

When KNC staff consulted Ktunaxa veterans to explore possible strategies for developing the decision-making skills of Ktunaxa youth common themes emerged. While most interviewees agreed there was a general direction of the collective missions, the most beneficial strategies were personal in nature. Several Ktunaxa veterans credited their military service as key in the development of self-discipline, strong business practices, developing strong work ethics and timeliness, dedication to community, and understanding the uniform as a tool for unit discipline that remained long after a term of service ended (Anonymous Ktunaxa Veterans, personal communications, July 2008). These testimonials are echoed by the core values espoused by the Royal Canadian Armed Forces and the U.S. Army; duty, integrity, courage, and professionalism for the Canadian Forces (Capstick, 2008) and the LDRSHP acronym (Loyalty, Duty, Respect, Selfless Service, Honor, Integrity, and Personal courage) for the U.S. Army (US Army, 2011).

Other community members have speculated that military service allows contemporary Ktunaxa to live out the social responsibility of the Crazy Dogs. One community support worker whose husband was serving in the Canadian Forces and whose daughter was serving in the U.S. Air Force added:

> Our men had a job. Our men had a role 500 years ago. They were protectors, they were providers, and when the reservation or reserve system came in it took that role away. It took a piece of them away. It crippled them. When they had that opportunity to go to war, to be that warrior again, they took it . . . It was about trying to reclaim a piece of their role . . . I think it's a way for our young men especially to learn that role to be a man because their fathers haven't been in their lives to do that. (Anonymous Ktunaxa Cultural Person, personal communication, October 2010)

Personal dedication to individual and collective values translated well for Ktunaxa veterans. Even though it is not completely accurate to refer to contemporary military veterans as Crazy Dogs, many traditional Ktunaxa practitioners speak of their veterans in terms associated with the historic society.

THE ALPHA BOOT CAMPS

In 2009, KNC administrators sought a new direction to address troublesome collective group self-identity exhibited by younger Ktunaxa community members. One proposal submitted by Louie and Horsethief (2009) cited an overall objective to "introduce and instill key values in the participants: leadership, responsibility, duty, and respect" (p. 1). The KNC Child and Family Services Society agreed to fund an initial "Alpha Camp" with a corps training cadre assembled from Royal Canadian Forces, Royal Canadian Mounted Police, and United States Armed Forces military personnel and prior service veterans.

Training cadre agreed that the key to success was an authenticity in "booting" the individual participants. This term denotes a transformation similar to those in Canadian Basic Military Qualification, American Basic Combat Training, and One Station Unit Training programs. Generally, training cadre's job in the military is to orient a recruit's attitude to "self-discipline, sacrifice, loyalty, obedience" (Powers, 2010). The key to success involves removing the "individual" character traits that preclude effective teamwork.

For post-Residential School era indigenous youth these problematic traits reflect Sztompka's (2004) symptoms of cultural trauma, including collective distrust, pessimistic outlook, nostalgic romanticizing of the past, and apathy toward authority. Addressing these obstacles under a lens of social development is key in transforming young Ktunaxa women and men into competent community members—and ultimately confident Ktunaxa leaders. While the physical demands of the Alpha Camp were less severe than basic military training, they would emphasize punitive aspects of negative reinforcement and positive reinforcement through encouragement required to build unit cohesion.

THE LEADERSHIP IMPERATIVE

Grooming a leadership cadre is key in the development of human capital capacity. Such a body has been shown empirically to have significant impacts on military management (Yukl & Van Fleet, 1982), to be significant in increasing organizational effectiveness (Roberts & Bradley, 1988) and to be significant in political stability (Benhabib & Speigal, 1992). Qualitatively, Stanford, Oates, and Flores (1995) demonstrated the effectiveness of leadership training on participation and team-based management, Roderick (2008) linked leadership to economic development, and in the context of Native North American peoples, Becker (1997) called for a leadership corps of "capable and respected persons" (p. 3) to coordinate community or group actions. The Alpha participants were asked to envision themselves as such.

While leadership has been studied in a number of settings, the dynamic I am concerned with in this chapter is the act of focusing energies for the purpose of common achievements. Stogdill (1950) offered a concise definition where leadership is "the process of influencing the activities of an organized group in its efforts toward goal setting and goal achievement" (p. 3). Similar to this, Northouse (2007) asserted "leadership is a process whereby an individual influence a group of individuals to achieve a common goal" (p. 3). Yet another definition was offered by Wren, Hicks, and Price (2004), declaring leadership is "the process that facilitates the achievement of societal objectives" (p. xv).

Finally, reconsider Block's (2009) community building requirement of "a leader who creates experiences for others—experiences that in themselves are examples of our desired future" (p. 86). Common to leadership by these approaches are two important themes: first, there is a sense of influence where potential leaders facilitate actions and second, these actions address common social means or outcomes the leader is pursuing. Considering these definitions, the Alpha Camp appeared appropriate for countering colonial trajectories imparted by the Residential Schools and subsequent generations of Indian Child Welfare adoption.

EMERGING LEADERSHIP STYLES

In this chapter, I further refine leadership theory by differentiating emerging leadership theory from traditional or classic leadership. Beginning in the 1980s studies began to define the transformational (Bass, 1990; Bass & Avolio, 1994), charismatic (Shamir, House & Arthur, 1993; Conger, 1999), visionary (Sashkin, 1996), or meaningful management (Calas & Smircich, 2003) aspects of leadership. Another camp was based on Greenleaf's altruistic and ethical foundations: servant-leadership. Key in these emerging leadership styles are relationships; the relationship between old states of followership to new capacities, relationships of followership to charismatic attractors, relationships to visualization abilities and meaningfulness and serving purpose.

In emerging leadership dialogues, followers are changed in some meaningful way; often the change is associated with an ethical or spiritual development of the followers. This moral center provides a great deal of inertia for new leadership change initiatives. More recently, Northouse (2007) linked emerging leadership's popularity with its emphasis on "intrinsic motivation and follower development" (p. 175). Taken together, these ideas form a paradigm of leadership applied by training cadre to inspire the Alpha Camp participants to navigate the transactional management strategies inherent in top-down training structures. In the following section, I will review emerging leadership styles and provide examples of training exercises reinforcing these goals.

Relational

Like other forms of new leadership, relational leadership is grounded in empowerment, purpose, and inclusion. What makes this style "relational" is its focus on the process of change, the context of initiative, and the relationships between community members. Here, process refers to the manner by which a community accomplishes its goals. Komives, Lucas, and McMahon (2007) explain the process component as leaders and followers participating to accomplish change. They note "the process creates energy, synergy and momentum" (p. 103). Context refers to the environment surrounding a change initiative that a leader must consider. According to Wheatley (1992), "leadership is always dependent on the context, but the context is established by the relationships we value" (p. 144).

Finally, the relationships can refer to the interactions between leaders and followers. From this perspective, Uhl-Bien (2006) contributed the notion that leadership effectiveness has to do with the ability of the leader to create positive relationships within the context of a network of leaders and followers to accomplish objectives. Komives et al. (2007) summarized relational qualities between individuals and group members, noting "goals are exchanged between leaders and followers, and vice versa." According to Jackson and Parry (2008), "these [new] approaches seemed to signal a new way of conceptualizing and researching leadership" (p. 28).

The Alpha Camp facilitators, also referred to as cadre, had unique perspectives of boot camp participants as their teachers, law enforcement officers, and wellness administrators. Several Alphas had pre-existing relationships as family members, some were adversaries and some had influence over others based on social positions in their home communities. At the onset of the camp, two boys with a history of physical altercation were paired up as a team. They were informed that all personal grudges were to be set aside and that bickering would not be tolerated. Their relationship was clarified to the other participants:

> If you two bitch and moan, everyone can push (do push-ups) till your arms fall off. We can do this all day. Just let us know by your actions. We'll be watching . . . there aren't enough relationships in the Nation to waste even one. (Cadre statement to Alpha Camp participants)

This tone is very true to form for basic military training. Another instructor added:

> You have a choice every day, with every action. When you wear green there's a saying: do the right thing even when you don't want to, even when you don't

have to, even when no one else is looking. It's easier to do the right thing than it is to hate someone. (Cadre statement to Alpha Camp participants)

The participants were spoken to privately and told that their behavior was a resource that could benefit younger participants in a positive way. They were challenged to question their past and demonstrate reconciliation and cooperation. Finally, in a discussion regarding the participants' graduation dinner, training cadre asked the youth which of their family members would be attending to "accept you home." This reflected the Ktunaxa cultural value of a caretaker giving the "cared for" back to their family as a celebration of belonging. One participant indicated no one would be there to celebrate for them, and before they could finish their statement, one cadre member offered a relational bond:

Negative. Negative, that's not going to happen. I'll stand for you. I'll stand at your side when we give you your certificate. I'll welcome you back as a family member, and I'll drive you home. I want your family to know how well you did, and if I can celebrate with you that's what we're going to do, because that's how we hold each other up. (Cadre statement to Alpha Camp participants)

Transformational

Northouse (2007) explained the namesake for this style informed us of its focus—transformation of followers with respect to idealized influence, inspirational motivation, intellectual stimulation, and individualized consideration. Dubinski, Yammarino, and Jolson (1995) carried these to the management realm, noting that the transformations of subordinate employees' motivation and self-confidence were to be enhanced (p. 317). In the context of transformation and individual job performance, Walumbwa, Avolio, and Zhu (2008) noted "this body of research has shown that the effects of transformational leadership are woven and mediated through processes such as efficacy, empowerment, trust, and identification" (p. 794). Further, Jung and Avolio (2000) include a trust component where leaders "engage the emotional involvement of their followers to build higher levels of trust in the leader and his or her mission" (p. 950).

One basic transformation was to incorporate avenues of communication between participants and their families, peers, and community members. Participants were instructed to conduct conversations with each other and record details about teammates. By humanizing fellow Alphas with personal details, they were transformed into more than teammates; they were sisters, brothers, cousins, and friends. The usefulness of details in transformation were addressed:

You will keep your composition notebooks at all times . . . you will write down thoughts regularly. You will also interview each other in 5 question interviews. The purpose is to get you into the rhythm of interaction. You have to write every day, every session, anytime you want to. We will not read it, we will not criticize you or check your grammar. We will check periodically to make sure you communicate your thoughts. Most Indigenous youth that have suicidal thoughts feel that they have no one to talk to. That is not the case here . . . you will have each other once you leave. (Cadre statement to Alpha Camp participants)

Another transformation was offered to the participants. They were given the chance to listen to cadre discuss, exchange, and offer cultural knowledge. Many of the participants admitted they had no one to talk to about Ktunaxa traditional knowledge. This was partly due to the collective distrust of openly discussing culture—for the fear of the Indian Agent or that the priest would be notified and practitioners would be punished—and partly due to the practice of protecting youth by shielding them from cultural information. The belief was children free of Ktunaxa culture would be punished less at the Residential School. For a discussion of this practice, sometimes referred to as the Delayed Boarding School Effect, see Crawford (1995) and AHF (2003).

Despite these century-old tendencies to be restrictive regarding spiritual knowledge and ceremonial understandings, training cadre sought the transformation of participants from "kids not knowing and afraid to ask" to "young women and young men comfortable with discussion of culture." This compliments Becker's (1997) assertion that learner interaction with elders and community cultural consultants "may serve future generations by recording information about their unique traditional leadership" (p. 12). However, this would require a group to recognize the impacts of missionary education that caused the disconnect, develop objective awareness of the resulting anxieties, and develop strategies to re-connect learners to teachers. The following counseling (a term used in the military to denote a motivational lecture) was offered to explore transformation:

Our elders have been deceived, lied to, beaten and abused. They have watched the bits and pieces of our way of life erode and fall away. Despite their efforts to hold on many of our very important ideas have been forgotten. The result is a reluctance to talk about them for fear they will continue to be lost. . . . If you ask the old ones, be patient. . . . Don't be ashamed if they don't tell you what you want to know; they may not remember and that makes them feel shame. Tell them that it is alright. Forgive them . . .do not take it personally. Some of them were made to hate themselves and our ways when they were just scared children . . . they were told it would keep them out of Hell. Forgive them, keep your chin up, persevere. (Cadre statement to Alpha Camp participants)

Transformation of participants into more culturally knowledgeable individuals was a direct result of the cadre selected to conduct training exercises: they routinely participated in cultural gatherings, war dances, and traditional ceremonies. Each had been through military or paramilitary training while holding on to and practicing cultural values. Each had been through the physical and emotional hardships of the military training experience. Cadre relayed stories of relying on traditional songs, pictures of family members, and memories of the old ones that helped them to "drink water and drive on." These motivations were described as the true values that survived the training experience, as individual traits were sheared away, the true values remained. This allowed cadre to return home and lead in their communities.

Servant-Leadership

The final topic is servant-leadership, which generally involves an individual that leads by serving. Greenleaf (2002) declared that the leader motivates followers in an ethical manner, toward an inclusive objective, resulting in the betterment of a community (p. 27). This leader is more than a role model, though. She or he is actively concerned with the belief system of their community. Greenleaf prefaced a more just and loving society as "one that provides greater creative opportunities for its people, then the most open course is to raise both the capacity to serve and the very performance as servant of existing major institutions by new regenerative forces operating within them" (p. 62).

Elsewhere, Smith, Montagna, and Kuzmenko (2004) credit the servant-leader with placing the interest of the followers above the interests of the leader by emphasizing personal development and empowerment of followers. In the context of management, Munson, St. John, and Buchbaum-Greif (2007) argue that this has more to do with serving associates' needs than directing (p. 10). Other associations are concerned with the role of influence in leading. For instance, Nehr (2004) clarifies that this style of leadership "fosters growth, autonomy, stewardship, freedom and wisdom in those being led, as opposed to stifling, controlling and criticizing their every action" (para. 2).

Community service was illustrated as a traditional theme throughout Alpha Camp activities. Traditional stories relayed the actions of women and men that had taken a stand for the Ktunaxa way of life against neighboring tribes, with frontier soldiers, overseas campaigns and skirmishes with American and Canadian federal governments into the 1970s. The common theme was a dedication to community. Cadre members had served or were still serving their respective countries. In addition to military service, however, each had also served by volunteering for traditional events, learning the Ktunaxa language, carrying the ceremonial songs and offering to pass them on. They often do so without seeking or receiving recognition. This particular aspect of traditional indigenous leadership is noted by Munson et al. (2007) noting, "emphasis on service to others was the foundation of their belief system. The involvement of all members of the community in the leadership of the tribes and their leadership participation in the community were steadfast elements" (p. 10). Cadre addressed the connotation of the word:

> The term servant sounds like you are being submissive. But what about serving those that cannot serve themselves? What if an Elder cannot hunt, shop, cook, or take care of themselves? What if you are in a position to help someone? What if you turn your back on them? That is being a slave to your own greed or comfort. That is submissive. Do the right thing. Creator knows when you do his work, build the fire, hunt for the people and remember the songs. Those are acts of serving, and it doesn't matter if they thank you. That is not important. That is your job. (Cadre statement to Alpha Camp participants)

Daily training activities embodied community service themes, including archaeological site monitoring and reporting, patrolling tribal hunting grounds and wetlands for poaching activities, and giving food to Ktunaxa food donation programs. These acts of service were modeled as ways to establish safe communication environments and engage in basic trust building which support Absalon and Willet's (2004) indigenous community development goals of "asserting and being proud of yourself; trusting in your traditions and cultural identity to inform and guide your process of sharing and creating knowledge" (p. 15). For some, participants training exercises were the first time they were recognized for doing a good thing. For many of the participants, it was the first time they were recognized for not engaging in wrongdoing. For all of the participants, it was the first time they had been recognized for finishing a program.

CONCLUSION

In closing, consider Greenleaf's (1974) often-cited criteria for judging the actions of prioritizing people's needs through a servant-leadership lens:

> The best test, and difficult to administer, is this: Do those served grow as persons? Do they, while being served, become healthier, wiser, freer, more autonomous, more likely themselves to become servants? And, what is the effect on the least privileged in society? (p. 27)

While the immediate goal of the Alpha experience was to strengthen Ktunaxa youth self-identity, it offered a host of culturally appropriate tools for other areas of empowerment. The participants were consistently reminded of their ties to the Ktunaxa cultural network, providing access to new sources of information regarding indigenous health and wellness. Training cadre were able to take tried-and-true, top-down, centralized command-and-control military structures to introduce new and emerging leadership techniques.

While no explicit orders were given that addressed decision-making, the implicit directives were for Alphas to develop the relationships and identities to make better traditional Ktunaxa decisions. These were appeals to the heart rather than the head. Worth noting is the terms *ktitiłwiy, ʔiłkiłwiy* and *ʔat kniłwiytiyatin* (to concentrate) all have the same Ktunaxa root word: */ʔakiłwi/*. This is the Ktunaxa word for the heart. The Alphas were taught that learning was a function of the heart and that the Crazy Dogs were motivated by their love for their families, communities, and each other. Alphas were asked to make more critical and authentic self-directed decisions "with their hearts."

Since the emergence of a leadership corps cannot be assessed at the time of training, I present several observed post-training outcomes from the perspectives of cadre, KNC administration, and Ktunaxa community leaders. First, post-mission debriefings and After Action Reviews (AAR) were incorporated into everyday activities to regularly conduct constructive criticism. Senge (1999) offered military AARs are typically conducted to review what worked and what didn't. The first observation is that Alpha Camps review discussions allowed for immediate self-reflection for the participants as students, relatives, cultural beings and servants, and cadre as teachers, mentors, and program administrators. Since many of the participants were not accustomed to regular constructive criticism, regular AARs provided a sense of normalcy to both criticism and support.

Next, participants were constantly painted into the Ktunaxa community picture, regardless of their family status or living situation. Cadre offered on-going contact, cultural counseling, and support outside the training environment. This resulted in several Alphas requesting Ktunaxa Indian names. These names have traditionally been used to honor family traditions or to bring disenfranchised individuals into cultural alignment. Accepting a name requires the holder to take care of the name and the history that accompanies it (Red Horse, 1980). According to Duran (2006), "naming ceremonies are a part of Native traditions and are used to assign spiritual identities to those receiving a name" (p. 31). Seeking a name is a source of both pride and responsibility. Three individuals received names that were no longer in use, effectively serving the community by preserving the names and the cultural properties associated with them.

As a final outcome, several of the participants displayed uncommon dedication to serving at community cultural events. These actions included hunting to feed attendees at community funerals and wakes, providing elk meat for community elders, providing maintenance for community cultural structures, and participating in ceremonial flag-raising activities. These interests demonstrate Munson et al.'s (2007) component of indigenous leadership where tribal affiliation "proudly promotes participation in their culture. It is a theory of belief in preservation for the future with an emphasis on education and learning through observing others" (p. 10). Further, by participating in cultural activities, the Alphas themselves took on leadership roles, providing resources to those in need. From my perspective, this is the emergence of Sipe and Frick's (2009) collaborative co-labor transcending the efforts of either the individual leader or follower. Such an embodiment implies not only an increased sense of belonging for participants but also an indication that the Alphas are actively participating in community.

Other important conclusions related to healing should be drawn in addition to these mechanical outcomes. The nature of cultural trauma, as typified by the experiences of indigenous populations, is fundamentally different from individual trauma. When an individual is subjected to experiences beyond their capacity to internalize traumatogenic acts, their social network helps to recreate a coherent narrative by offering social stability, filling in gaps in time, and aligning disordered/de-ordered memories. However, when the trauma is experienced by the collective, the social fabric becomes frayed—there are no unaffected stable peers, so the probability of having a social network to pick you up, dust you off, and tell you that they love you diminishes. In effect, collective trauma leaves entire communities in a state of vulnerability because it's harder to identify resources and the communication pathways to foster resilience. These wounds focus on the individual's heart, the family's soul, and communities' immune systems. The ever-present context is that every single Ktunaxa person has either lost at least a generation of parents and grandparents OR a generation of children or grandchildren. Every single Ktunaxa family has been subjected to the horrific experiences of missionary education that were well beyond the community's ability to cope. These horrors were exacerbated by the degradation of intergenerational mechanisms for instilling values, information, decision-making tools, and leadership styles.

The path forward for the Ktunaxa, based on a decade of healing workshops and boot camps since this chapter was originally published, is for trauma carriers to develop objective awareness of Ktunaxa community trauma, self-identify their own anxieties, create stable resources that can exist separate from individuals and find strategies that disarm the distrust community members feel after a century of colonization. The path requires individuals to serve by sacrificing cultural knowledge, confronting the tensions of lateral violence, and investing time and effort into relationships with people that may completely reject your service. This notion is defined by the common Ktunaxa ceremonial mantra you serve by "sacrificing your sweat, giving your voice to others as songs and being hungry."

The Alpha Camp and subsequent boot camps and Ktunaxa culture camps used a similar approach to promote these outcomes, often for small budgets and significant personal investment of current, retired, and disabled military and paramilitary law enforcement personnel—many of whom are themselves PTSD trauma carriers. The camps, which totaled seven in the span of four years, never sought to create soldiers; the goal was never to break individuals down to create military units though the format was extremely effective way of setting a baseline for cooperation, small group communication, and collective problem-solving. The capacity challenges participants faced were well reflected in emerging leadership schools. The challenges were well served by leadership theories that sought to transform trauma carriers into potential stable peers, better able to identify the beautiful parts of the culture preserved by their grandparents, many of whom never met their grandchildren.

Solutions to the problems were effectively modeled by cadre willing to expose emotional vulnerabilities, personal stories of disconnection and disenfranchisement in order to become "relational." For many people in the Ktunaxa community, the ability to relate to others has been compromised, and the true purpose of the Alpha Camps was to show young people how the next generation or two could begin to relate to one another, creating stronger, more redundant, and robust relationships in the process. All of the strategies needed to solve the problems facing trauma carriers were offered in service—by Crazy Dogs that previously watched their training sergeants, drill sergeants, and drill instructors offer proven strategies under duress . . . after all the context of military training is always stress-inducing. But in the Ktunaxa camps, the stress isn't overseas deployment or targets shaped like human combatants—the stress is from cultural trauma (Alexander, 2004), unresolved historical grief (Yellow Horse Brave Heart, 2003), and the oft-perceived intractability of colonization (Sam, 2019).

Challenges were facilitated by those that have been through rigorous training to serve by imparting the only true benefit of the format: echoes of strategies that helped one-time trainees to become Crazy Dogs. In subsequent camps, issues of equality and equity were explored in domains of gender identity, age and ability, access to identity resources, post-modernist, non-binary, non-traditional, LGBTQ, and other dialogues related to indigenous resilience. It is in the exchanging of these resources, which can be thought of as new transactions in post-transactional leadership strategies, that the fundamental ideals of the leadership models discussed above can be available for empowerment.

Moving forward in the manner described in this chapter has led to Ktunaxa leadership outcomes that echo Block's (2008) "sense of belonging" where Ktunaxa see a stable network of resources which may fill in cultural gaps or anneal social tensions. Such a shift refocuses emphasis from colonial notions of power to Wren et al.'s (2004) achievement of societal objectives and Bass's (1990) transformation from transactional recipients to more capable and meaningful decision makers. Other results continue to point to a future Ktunaxa leadership regime capable of Birkenmeier et al.'s (2003) increased humanity for followership and Sipe and Frick's (2009) solutions that serve a greater common good.

By funding these capacity development camps, current Ktunaxa leadership—the Chiefs and Councils that see cultural gaps among their own corps—are ensuring critical indigenous capacities leading to Benhabib & Speigal's (1992) political stability, Stanford et al.'s (1995) effective team-based management and other desired leadership outcomes complementary to Northouse's (2007) intrinsic motivation and follower development. This shift from top-down, centralized, power-attaining/power-maintaining values to bubble-up, decentralized and empowering strategies transforms rule-rejecting and discipline-evasive Ktunaxa youth to Dubinski et al.'s (1995) empowered, motivated, and self-confident agents. These agents are groomed to see themselves in Wheatley's (1992) relationships of value, capable of cultivating Nehr's (2004) critical growth, autonomy, and stewardship in society. This character arc of recent Ktunaxa youth training provides one possible narrative for identifying resources that can transform grandchildren of Residential School survivors into stable peers armed with robust communication methods to preserve order in the face of chaos.

NOTES

1. This chapter was previously published as Horsethief, C. (2006). Leadership development for today's Ktunaxa youth: Command structure versus the crazy dog society. *The International Journal of Servant Leadership. 7*(1), 105–122.

2. All interviewee names have been anonymized and oral consent was provided for the use of their words in this chapter.

REFERENCES

Abadian, S. (1999). From wasteland to homeland: Trauma and the renewal of Indigenous peoples and their communities (Unpublished doctoral dissertation). Harvard University, Cambridge, MA.

Absolon, K., & Willett, C. (2004). Aboriginal research: Berry picking and hunting in the 21st century. *First Peoples Child and Family Review, 1*(1), 5–17.

Aboriginal Healing Foundation. (2003). *Indigenous People, Resilience and the residential School Legacy.* Ottawa, ON: Author.

Alexander, J. C. (2004). *Cultural trauma and Collective Identity.* Berkeley, CA: University of California Press.

Banutu-Gomez, M. B. (2004). Great leaders teach exemplary followership and serve as servant leaders. *Journal of American Academy of Business, 4(*1/2), 143–150.

Bass, B. M. (1990). From transactional to transformational leadership: Learning to share the vision. *Organizational Dynamics* (Winter), *18*(3), 19–31.

Bass, B. M., & Avolio, B. J. (1994). *Improving Organizational Effectiveness Through Transformational Leadership.* Thousand Oaks, CA: Sage.

Becker, T. (1997) *Traditional American Indian leadership: A comparison with U.S. governance.* St. Paul, MN: American Indian Research and Policy Institute.

Benhabib, J., & Spiegel, M. (1992). The role of human capital and political instability in economic development. C. V. Starr Center for Applied Economics, New York University, Working Paper 92–24.

Birkenmeier, B. J., Carson, P. P., & Carson, K. D. (2003). The father of Europe: An analysis of the supranational leadership of Jean Monnet. *International Journal of Organization Theory* and *Behavior, 01, 6*(3), 374–401.

Block, P. (2009) *Community: The structure of belonging.* San Francisco, CA: Berrett-Koehler.

Calas, M. B., & Smircich, L. (2003). To be done with progress and other heretical thoughts for organization and management studies. In Locke, E. (ed.), *Postmodernism and management: Pros, cons, and the alternative* (pp. 29–56). Amsterdam: Research in the Sociology of Organizations.

Capstick, M. D. (2008). *Defining the Culture: The Canadian army in the 21st century.* http://www.joumal.forces.gc.ca/vo4/nol/military-militair-eng.asp

Conger, J. A. (1999). Charismatic and transformational leadership in organizations: An insider's perspective on these developing streams of research. *The Leadership Quarterly, 10*(2), 145–179.

Crawford, J. (1995). Endangered Native American languages: What is to be done, and why? *The Bilingual Research Journal, 19*(1), 17–38.

Cyr, A. (2009). The residential school experience: Societal and individual impacts. http://www.suite10l.com/content/dark-legacy-of-residential-schools-a99906

Dubinsky, A. J., Yammarino, F. J., & Jolson, M. A. (1995). An examination of linkages and characteristics between personal characteristics and dimensions of transformational leadership. *Journal of Business and Psychology, 9*(3), 315–335.

Duran, E. (2006). *Healing the Soul Would: Counseling with American Indians and Other Native Peoples.* New York, NY: Teachers College Press.

Dussault, R. (2005). Indigenous peoples and child welfare: The path to reconciliation. Keynote address, Reconciliation: Looking back, reaching forward. Indigenous Peoples and Child Welfare Conference, White Oaks Resort, Niagara Falls, Canada.

Ehrhart, M. G. (2004). Leadership and procedural justice climate as antecedents of unit-level organizational citizenship behavior. *Personnel Psychology, 57,* 61–94.

Greenleaf, R. K. (1974). *Trustees as Servants.* Indianapolis, IN: The Greenleaf Center.

———. (1977). *The servant as leader.* South Orange, NJ: Greenleaf Center for Servant Leadership.

————. (2002). *Servant-leadership: A journey into the nature of legitimate power and greatness.* Mahwah, NJ: Paulist Press.

Horsethief, C. P. (2011a). *New words and Old Values: Discourse and neologism in the Ktunaxa language.* Paper presented at the annual meeting of International Journal of Language Studies, Oranjenstad, Aruba.

————. (2011b). What's in a baptismal name? ...if you're First Nations? ...and not Christian? Paper presented at the annual meeting of the Pacific Ancient Modern Language Association, Claremont, CA.

————. (2015). Visualizing structure & agency through social network analysis: A postcolonial case study. Featured research presentation, Center for Excellence in Indigenous Health, March 2015, University of British Columbia. Vancouver, BC.

————. (2016). Culture, stability and change: From colonization to resilience. Grand Ronde Culture and History Summit, October 2016, Grand Ronde, OR.

————. (2018). Reconciliation in the age of reconciliation: Promoting resilience in rural communities. Keynote presentation, Building Intersections: 2018 Rural Health Services Research Conference, May 31, 2018, Nelson, BC.

Jackson, B., & Parry, K. (2008). *A Very Short, Fairly Interesting and Reasonably Cheap Book About Studying Leadership.* Thousand Oaks, CA: Sage.

Jimmie, A. (2019). Regional perspectives: Ktunaxa education and reconciliation. Guest lecture at Selkirk College, May 10, 2019.

Jung, D. I., & Avolio, B. J. (2000). Opening the black box: An experimental investigation of the mediating effects of trust and value congruence on transformational and transactional leadership. *Journal of Organizational Behavior, 2*(8), 949–964.

Komives, S. R., Lucas, N., & McMahon, T. R. (2007). *Exploring leadership* (2nd edition). San Francisco, CA: Jossey-Bass. Chapter 3 found online October IO, 2010.

Ktunaxa Nation Council. (2009). *Ktunaxa Nation Regional Governance Outline.* Cranbrook, BC: Ktunaxa Nation Council.

Ktunaxa Nation Council. (2010). *Ktunaxa Nation Indicators and Outcomes Final Report.* Cranbrook, BC: Ktunaxa Nation Council.

Laub, J. A. (1999). Assessing the servant organization: Development of the servant organizational leadership (SOLA) instrument. Unpublished doctoral dissertation, Florida Atlantic University.

Louie, M. J., & Horsethief, C. P. (2009). *Ktunaxa Young Men's Boot Camp Proposal.* Cranbrook, BC: Ktunaxa Nation Council.

Louie, R. (2008). *Crazy Dog Society: Ktunaxa warrior Emergency Response.* Cranbrook, BC: Ktunaxa Nation Council.

Mayer, D. M., Bardes, M., & Piccolo, R. F. (2008). Do servant-leaders help satisfy follower Needs? An organizational justice perspective. *European Journal of Work and Organizational Psychology, 17*(2), 180–197.

Munson, T. E., St John, L., & Buchsbaum-Greif, T. (2007). A native perspective on leadership. *Review of Business Research.* http://findarticles.com/p/articles/ mi_6776/is_6_7 /ai_n28514256/

National Centre for Truth and Reconciliation (2006). Indian Residential Schools Settlement - Official Court Website. Found http://www.residentialschoolsettlem ent.ca/English.html

National Collaborating Center for Aboriginal Health (2009) *Culture and language as social determinants of First Nations, Inuit, and Metis health: Fact sheet.* Ottawa, ON: Public Health Agency of Canada.

Nehr, Jerry. (2004). Servant leadership: The importance of trading power for influence. Retrieved from https://www.thefreelibrary.com/Servant+leadership%3a+th e+ importance+of+trading+power+for+influence.-a0133220215

Northouse, P. G. (2007). *Leadership: Theory and practice.* Thousand Oaks, CA: Sage.

Patterson, K. A. (2003). Servant leadership: A theoretical model. Doctoral dissertation, Regent University (UMI No. 3082719).

Peterson, J., & Peers, L. (1993). *Sacred encounters: Father De Smet and the Indians of the Rocky Mountain West.* Norman, OK: University of Oklahoma.

Powers, R. (2010). How to survive military basic training. http://usmilitary.about.com/od/joiningthemilitary/a/basictraining.htm.

Red Horse, J. G. (1980). Family structure and value orientation in American Indians. *Social Casework, 61*(8), 462–467.

Roberts, N. C., & Bradley, R. T. (1988). Limits of charisma. In J.A. Conger & R. N. Kanungo (eds.), *Charismatic leadership: The Elusive Factor in Organizational Effectiveness* (pp. 253–275). San Francisco, CA: Jossey-Bass.

Rodrick, D. (2008). *The New Development Economics: We Shall Experiment, But How Shall We Learn?* Harvard University Working Paper 2008-0142. Cambridge, MA: Weatherhead Center for International Affairs.

Sam, M. A. (2019). Contextualizing approaches to Indigenous peoples' experiences of intractable conflict. *New England Journal of Public Policy, 31*(1) 1–17.

Sashkin, M., & Rosenbach, W. E. (1998). *Visionary Leadership Theory: A Current Overview of Models, Measures, and research.* Working Paper 9-114. Washington, DC: George Washington University.

Senge, P. (1999). *The dance of change: The challenges of Sustaining Momentum in Learning Organizations.* New York, NY: Doubleday.

Shahram, S. Z. (2017). The historical, political and social contexts of substance use during pregnancy. In H. Tait Neufeld & J. Cidro (eds.), *Indigenous experiences of pregnancy and birth.* Bradford, ON: Demeter Press.

Shamir, B., House, R. J., & Arthur, M. B. (1993). The motivational effects of charismatic leadership: A self-concept based theory. *Organization Science, 4*(4), 577–594.

Sipe, J. W., & Frick, D. M. (2009). *Seven pillars of Servant Leadership: Practicing the wisdom of leading by serving.* Mahwah, NJ: Paulist Press.

Smith, B. N., Montagna, R. V., & Kuzmenko, T. N. (2004). Transformational and servant leadership: Content and contextual comparisons. *The Journal of Leadership and Organizational Studies, 10*(4), 80–92.

Spears, L. C. (1998). *Insights on leadership: Service, stewardship, spirit, and servant-leadership.* New York, NY: Wiley.

Stanford, J. H., Oates, B. R., & Flores, D. (1995). Women's leadership styles: A heuristic analysis. *Women in Management Review, 10*(2), 9–16.

Stogdill, R. M. (1950) Leadership, membership, and organization. *Psychological Bulletin, 47,* 1–14.

Sztompka, P. (2004). The trauma of social change: A case of postcommunist societies. In J. C. Alexander (ed.), *Cultural trauma and Collective Identity*. Berkeley, CA: University of California Press.

Tinker, G. (1993). *Missionary conquest: The gospel and Native American Cultural Genocide*. Minneapolis, MN: Fortress Press.

Truth and Reconciliation Commission of Canada. (2016). *The Truth and Reconciliation Commission's Final Report*. Found: https://www.rcaanc-cirnac.gc.ca/eng/1450124405592/1529106060525

Tousignant, M., & Sioui, N. (2009). Resilience and aboriginal communities in crisis: Theory and interventions. *Journal of Aboriginal Health*, 5(1), 43–61.

Tumey-High, H. H. (1941). *Ethnography of the Kutenai*. Menasha, WI: American Anthropological Association, Memoir 56.

Uhl-Bien, M. (2006). Relational leadership theory: Exploring the social processes of leadership and organizing. *The Leadership Quarterly, 17,* 654–676.

United States Army. (2011). Living the Army Values: It means you live up to a higher standard. *Soldier Life*. Found. http://www.goarmy.com/soldier-life/being-asoldier/living-the-army-values.html

van Dierendonck, D., & Patterson, K. (2010). *Servant leadership. Developments in theory and research*. Hampshire: Palgrave Macmillan.

Walumbwa, F. O., Avolio, B. J., & Zhu, W. (2008). How transformational leadership weaves its influence on individual job performance: The role of identification and efficacy beliefs. *Personnel Psychology, 61*(4), 793–825.

Weydermeyer-Johnson, O. (1969) *Flathead and Kootenay: The rivers, the tribes, and the Region's Traders*. Washington, DC: The Arthur C. Clarke Company.

Wheatley, M. J. (1992). *Leadership and the New Science: Learning About Organization from an Orderly Universe*. San Francisco, CA: Berrett-Koehler.

Wheatley, M. J., & Kellner-Rogers, M. (1998). The paradox of promise of community. In P. Drucker (ed.), *The Community of the Future*. Hoboken, NJ: Jossey Bass.

Wren, J. T., Hicks, D. A., & Price, T. L. (2004). *Traditional Leadership Classics*. Northampton, MA: Edward Elgar.

Yellow Horse Brave Heart, M. (2003). The historical trauma response among natives and its relationship with substance abuse: A Lakota illustration. *Journal of Psychoactive Drugs, 35*(1), 7–13.

Younging, G., Dewar, J., & DeGagne, M. (2009). *Response, responsibility, and renewal: Canada's truth and Reconciliation Journey*. Ottawa, ON: Aboriginal Healing Foundation Research Series.

Yukl, G., & Van Fleet, D. (1982). Cross-situational, multi-method research on military leader effectiveness. *Organizational Behavior and Human Performance, 30,* 87–108.

Zelmer, J. (2010). PTSD spirituality: Healing souls wounded by PTSD. Retrieved form http://www.ptsdspirituality.com/2010/02/06/ptsd-spirituality-identity-damagecauses-ptsd-soul-wound/

Chapter 4

Art and Literature in a Servant-Leadership Curriculum for Undergraduate Female Students Who Are from Mexican Migrant Farm Worker Backgrounds

Patricia Valdés

This chapter[1] proposes a university leadership curriculum for undergraduate female students who are from Mexican migrant farm worker backgrounds. The curriculum incorporates the philosophy of servant-leadership and utilizes literature and art to provide media that are congruent with the cultural background of the students. The curriculum's intent is three-fold: (a) improve the capacity of Latina migrant students to be leaders and fulfill leadership roles in organizations and communities; (b) contribute to the understanding of servant-leadership and its possible congruency with the culture of female Mexican migrant students; and (c) add to the current knowledge of leadership in order to continue to develop and restructure curricula that are gender-specific and that integrate the values, traditions, and knowledge of other cultures.

Universities have an important responsibility in the development of future leaders who will impact the public and private sectors both in the United States and abroad (Skolnikoff, 1993). Therefore, it is important that university students develop leadership abilities that can be utilized as they contribute to society (Hackman, Olive, Guzman, & Brunson, 1999). Having the opportunity for leadership development may be particularly important for Latina/o students because of their increasing numbers in the United States and their traditionally limited access to formal leadership positions and educational opportunities (Castellanos & Jones, 2003). Being exposed to a leadership curriculum could increase the leadership potential for Latina students. If a leadership curriculum for Latina students is to be as effective as possible, it will need to provide a model as well as be presented in a context that is congruent with the students' gender and culture. Servant-leadership is a philosophy that can prove congruent with the cultural paradigm of most Latina students due to the similarities between the concepts and ideals of servant-leadership and the cultural norms and values of the students' cultural background.

The chapter is organized into the following sections: (a) Historical Overview of Latina/os in Higher Education; (b) Women from Mexican Migrant Backgrounds; (c) Servant-Leadership for Latinas; (d) General Description of a Servant-Leadership Curriculum for Latinas; (e) Conclusion.

HISTORICAL OVERVIEW OF LATINA/ OS IN HIGHER EDUCATION

According to Kelly (2005), the United States has lost its leadership role as the most highly educated nation in the world: "We are losing ground to several countries, particularly with respect to our younger population which represents the future workforce" (p. 1). In losing these young people's potential, society loses a portion of the individuals who could constitute the future leadership capacity of this country. One reason for losing ground, Kelly postulated, is the failure of the United States to raise the educational attainment of the minority populations to the rate of whites. Kelly noted that from 1980 to 2000, the educational attainment gaps between whites and Latinas/os widened and that "if these educational disparities are not addressed, anticipated demographic shifts will have a major impact on the educational attainment of the United States' population" (p. 1).

Latina/o students are a significant part of the university population. However, despite projections that Latina/o populations will be the largest minority group in the United States, making up 13.8 percent of the population (Hernandez, 2000), their numbers in four-year institutions is still small; Latina/o students remain seriously underrepresented in higher education. Of all the racial and ethnic minorities in the United States, Latina/os are the least likely to complete a college degree (Hernandez, 2000). In addition, for the past three decades, Latina/o students have been the least likely to take a direct path to obtaining a baccalaureate degree. These statistics pose a serious problem "because it is estimated that the work force will increasingly consist of people of color, with a large percent being Latina/os. Without a change in the educational system, the future work force will largely be illiterate and marginal" (Perez & De La Rosa, 1993, para. 4). These figures have implications for institutions of higher education in regard to recruiting, providing access, financial aid, assisting students in their transition to college, and retention (Hurtado & Kamimura, 2004). They also have implications for providing students with knowledge, values, and skills that will prepare them to fulfill positions of leadership to impact the social, educational, economic, and political spheres of society.

Women also comprise part of the student population in higher education, and in recent years, Latinas have entered institutions of higher education in larger numbers. Kelly (2005) reports that between 1980 and 2000, in nearly all racial/ethnic populations ages 25–64 with a bachelor's degree or higher, females have met or surpassed the educational attainment of males.

Gloria, Castellanos, and Orozco (2005) found that women who were of second-generation Mexican heritage, many of them of migrant farm worker background, were highly motivated to pursue advanced graduate training. In addition, their findings "challenge stereotypes of Latina students in higher education, as they valued higher education, believed they could overcome any barriers to achieve their educational goals, and used active coping responses which informed their positive and healthy functioning" (para. 1). Latinas' strengths, coupled with their resilience and their desire to serve their communities, place many of these women in a position to seek leadership roles.

Due to the smaller number of Latinas in higher education compared with women in other ethnic groups and the Caucasian population (Hernandez, 2000), it is imperative to ensure that Latina students succeed in their chosen majors and obtain the tools that will allow them to participate in leadership positions (Bordas, 2001) should they choose to do so throughout their lives. It is through various leadership roles that Latinas can make unique contributions in an increasingly diverse society.

WOMEN FROM MEXICAN MIGRANT BACKGROUNDS

Statistics show that Mexicans constitute the largest group of new immigrants to the United States, making up 64 percent of the total U.S. Latino/a population (Guranaccia, 1997). A sub-group of immigrants is migrant farm workers; 94 percent of this group has been identified as Mexican or Mexican-American (Menchaca & Ruiz-Escalante, 1995). Some individuals from the Mexican migrant farm worker population will become part of the student body in institutions of higher education.

By the time students from migrant farm worker backgrounds enter a university, their lives have been ones of continual movement and disruption. They have made and recreated their lives as they followed the crops and their hopes for a better future. Some of the issues that impact these students' lives and education are poverty, isolation, lack of English language proficiency, partial acculturation, disrupted education, lack of educational opportunity with resulting incompetence, and economic, cultural, and social discrimination (Chavkin, 1991).

Additional barriers encountered by some female students from traditional Mexican backgrounds include external expectations such as assumptions that they will be responsible for "caring for younger siblings, and pressure from boyfriends or fiancés who expect their girlfriends and future wives not to be 'too educated,' as well as from peers who accuse them of 'acting White' when they attempt to become better educated" (Anonymous, 2001, para. 7). In addition, some parents are hesitant to allow their daughters to travel away from home to attend a university. Other issues faced by female students include "an inhospitable campus climate, few mentors, cultural stereotypes and a sense of cultural misfit which influence their college navigation" (Gloria, Castellanos, & Orozco, 2005, para. 5). The women who navigate these obstacles exhibit resilience, great courage in challenging traditional norms, and ability to navigate and/or reconcile conflicting cultural values.

For many of these students, the idea that "farm workers learn early on that their bodies are worker's bodies and nothing else" (Castaneda, 2001, para. 3) had to be challenged by the belief that they were not only bodies but also minds that could achieve an education that would present them with better opportunities than their parents had. "These students' experiences of working the land alongside their parents, as well as the hardships of migrant life seems to provide them with a sense of accomplishment and competence that is difficult to obtain through school" (Mores, 1999, p. 2). For many of these students, this sense of accomplishment and competence will assist them in persevering through their academic careers by providing a strong work ethic. In addition, Garza (1998) points to the success of migrant students, asserting, "In spite of their lifestyles that label them as at risk, it is their migrant life background which also gave them the skills to become resilient and academically invulnerable" (p. ix). These qualities of resilience, courage, and strength are, in part, what provides these students with the possibility of realizing their leadership potential.

SERVANT-LEADERSHIP FOR LATINAS

For many Latina students from migrant farm worker backgrounds, higher education has become a reality more often than was true in the past. These women have unique qualities and skills due, in part, to their cultural background. For example, many migrant students are bicultural and bilingual. This way of being and skills learned in becoming bicultural and bilingual can provide a unique advantage when living in an increasingly diverse society. Latinas will have an opportunity to fulfill leadership roles, yet many of them will not have been exposed to ideas and knowledge regarding leadership. As the findings of Hackman, Olive, Guzman, and Brunson (1999) showed, many leadership programs were designed to meet the needs of unique and limited student populations. Latinas, in many instances, have not been part of these groups, and therefore many of them will not have been exposed to ideas and knowledge regarding leadership. It is to these women's advantage, as well as society's, to provide them with a leadership curriculum that prepares them for the possibility of leadership in their lives.

Offerman (1998) suggested that leadership scholars have not devoted much time to carefully rethinking the traditional leadership theories and models to accommodate leadership styles of diverse populations. In addition, Murphy and Rigiio (2003) suggested that there is a need to explore the relationship between culture and leadership in order to develop descriptive typologies that can offer a guiding framework to members of diverse cultures for implementing coherent leadership development efforts. In addition, many leadership theories were developed without regard to women. It has been generally assumed that whatever is said about leadership applies equally well to both men and women. It is time to look at leadership theories with women's experiences, contributions, and strengths in mind.

Institutions of higher education have the opportunity and the challenge to educate the next generation of leaders, and more specifically to provide women with leadership curricula and activities that are congruent with their gender and culture. Studies have shown that because women of color are discriminated against regarding gender and race, their academic experiences, in many instances, are characterized by exclusion and alienation (Nieves-Squires, 1991; Washington & Newman, 1991). Given that there is evidence of women of color feeling excluded and alienated during their academic experience, there might be a need to explore whether a curriculum designed specifically for women of migrant farm worker backgrounds could alleviate the sense of exclusion and alienation. This curriculum would utilize traditions, knowledge, and values from their cultural backgrounds as a positive tool that could enhance learning and cultural pride.

The proposed curriculum makes the assumption that culture works interdependently regarding the beliefs of leadership (Del Castillo & Torres, 1988). The curriculum provides Latinas with a model of servant-leadership to explore how, and whether, this model is congruent with their cultural background. Understanding whether certain styles are preferred by Latinas is critical in identifying leadership theories that are more congruent with their culture of origin. In addition, this understanding can assist in developing or enhancing theories that are more consonant with this population's culture.

This curriculum utilizes the philosophy of servant-leadership in the belief that this philosophy has elements that are congruent with, and have been exhibited by, leaders within the Latina/o culture of these students. In addition, it makes use of the students' familiarity with stories and art, which are very much a part of their culture of origin, in order to enhance their understanding of servant-leadership.

Robert Greenleaf (1970/1991) proposed the philosophy of servant-leadership. He stated that leadership was bestowed upon individuals who were willing to be servants first. In addition, he explained:

> The difference manifests itself in the care taken by the servant-first, to make sure that other people's highest priority needs are being served. The best test is: do those served grow as persons; do they, while being served, become healthier, wiser, freer, more autonomous, more likely themselves to become servants? And what is the effect on the least privileged in society; will they benefit, or at least, not be further deprived? (p. 7)

Servant-leadership offers much to migrant students and is congruent with some of the values of Latina culture, which embraces the idea of service. The idea of service is reflected in the language that contains phrases such as a *sus ordenes*, or *mande*, which, loosely translated, means "at your service." The idea of service is also reflected in the way people relate to each other. For example, according to Bordas (2001), "This tendency toward group benefit is rooted in the indigenous background from which many Latinos spring and is evident when noting the following: in the Nahuatl language of the Mexican Indians there is no concept for the word 'I'" (para. 33). She added, "Their sense of relatedness and helping others was the basis of their world view" (para. 33). In addition, Bordas described the Mayan Indian version of the Golden Rule: "'I am another yourself,' which reflected their belief that human beings are one people and what one does to another affects oneself" (para. 33).

The idea of service is also embedded in the spirituality of many traditional Latinas/os. Bordas (2001) explained that "spirituality is a mixture of indigenous beliefs and the influence of the Catholic Church; 80 percent identify as Catholics" (Bordas, 2001). According to Rodriguez (2004), "Latina/o culture, religion and spirituality are so integrated that to try to define spirituality separated from culture creates a false dichotomy and does a disservice to the Latina community" (par. 6). The teachings in the Judeo-Christian tradition espouse the ideas of justice, human dignity, and service (Rodriguez, 2004). The Judeo-Christian teachings combined with the inherited cultural traditions from indigenous people seem to be congruent with the philosophy of servant-leadership. Bordas (2001) postulated that through compassion, service, and strong spiritual roots, Latina and Latino leaders such as César Chávez have practiced the essence of servant-leadership (para. 35).

Spears (1995) added that servant-leadership is leadership that includes "shared decision-making power" (p. 4). Covey (1998) described servant-leadership as an approach that emphasizes "increased service to others, a holistic ecological approach to work, promoting a sense of community, of togetherness, of connection" (p. xv). This model of leadership can bring people together as equals, a desired goal for many Latina students who want to bring equality to all spheres of society, promote social justice, and create a sense of community familiar to many of them (Rodriguez, 2004).

Some may argue that the idea of a servant in relation to the historical background of women, and more specifically Latina women, might continue to promote the idea of women in a subservient role. However, when the idea of servant is examined and juxtaposed with the idea of women as leaders who are in positions to make changes in their lives and the lives of their communities, the understanding of service from a historical, political, and cultural point of view becomes clear, and Greenleaf's definition of the role of the servant can be understood in a different light. These ideas will be discussed in the curriculum, and critical thinking will be encouraged during the class discussions that deal with the concepts of servant, service, and leadership.

Lopez (1995) proposed that the idea of a servant-leader challenges us with a paradox and that "this paradox confuses us because it asks us to live with simultaneous opposites" (p. 150). Latina individuals, due to their history, cultural beliefs, and life conditions, are perhaps more comfortable living with paradoxes than are peoples of more industrialized countries. The idea of servant-leadership may not be a foreign one, especially for many of those who historically have lived a life of service with or without power.

GENERAL DESCRIPTION OF A SERVANT-LEADERSHIP CURRICULUM FOR LATINAS

This section describes the framework, goals, and objectives of the curriculum. In addition, it describes the methods and activities used for teaching servant-leadership. Finally, it provides an example of a session.

Framework of the Curriculum

Spears (2005) distilled from Greenleaf's philosophy of leadership ten characteristics that he believed were of great importance for the development of servant-leaders. These characteristics, "listening, empathy, healing, awareness, persuasion, conceptualization, foresight, stewardship, commitment to the growth of people and building community" (pp. 32-36), serve as the framework for this curriculum. However, the focus of the curriculum will be to provide students not only with the development of these characteristics and the skills that may aid in obtaining them but also with the idea that "at its core, servant-leadership is a long-term transformational approach to life and work, in essence, a way of being that has the potential for creating positive change throughout our society" (Spears, 2005, p. 30). Powers and Moore (2005) identify five of the ten characteristics described by Spears as being the "inner components of the servant-leader's character. These are: building community, commitment to the growth of people, foresight, conceptualization, and awareness" (p. 125). The separation of characteristics will be followed by, and the five characteristics will be employed in, an exploration of the idea of the servant-leader as one of *being* a leader.

The idea of servant-leadership as a way of being will also be examined through the readings about women's lives that exemplify the idea of servant-leadership in their personal and communal lives. In addition, through the engagement in dialogue, the students will have an opportunity to voice their understanding of the readings, as well as the opportunity to identify people in their lives and communities who exemplify the servant-leader. Students will also reflect about their lives and themselves in relation to the idea of servant-leadership.

The remaining characteristics will be presented throughout the sessions in order for students to conceptualize, learn, and identify these characteristics in the readings. Students also will reflect on their own personal characteristics and explore ways in which they might want to enhance or develop their own capacities as servant-leaders.

In addition to utilizing the ten characteristics of a servant-leader and the idea of servant-leadership as a way of being, the framework is conceptualized as one that pays particular attention to the gender and culture of the students. Within this framework there is an inclusion of the ideas of leadership and, more specifically, of servant-leadership in relation to the cultural experience of bicultural women from farm worker backgrounds.

Goal and Objectives of the Curriculum

The goal of the proposed curriculum is to provide students with an understanding of the philosophy of servant-leadership, which encourages leaders to live a life of service. In addition, students will examine the philosophy of servant-leadership in the context of their gender and their culture of origin and will articulate a vision of leadership that is congruent with their lives.

The learning objectives are as follows: (a) express an understanding of servant-leadership as a way of life through identifying the importance of the personal characteristics of a servant-leader (as proposed by Spears, 2005) that flow naturally from deeply held beliefs about the worth of persons; (b) demonstrate understanding of the impact of biculturalism in the conceptualization of the ideas of leadership; and (c) develop and express a personal vision of leadership and demonstrate understanding of the idea of servant-leadership in relation to their own leadership stance.

These objectives will be measured by the students' understanding of the readings as demonstrated through their engagement in dialogue, their writings, and their application of the concepts in case examples and discussions. In addition, art and the articulation of the meaning of their art will be employed to assess the students' learning.

Use of Literature and Art in the Curriculum

The use of literature is familiar to students from migrant backgrounds who belong to a culture in which stories and storytelling are an integral part of everyday living. By reviewing ancestral and current stories of Latinas, students can realize that they are connected to the historical processes occurring throughout the history of their culture of origin. Through poems, stories, and "dichos" (sayings), women can find resemblances of their experiences in the written word and thereby, perhaps for the first time, read in a book that their struggles and triumphs are similar to the experiences of other women. The selected literature will include stories of women who can be described as servant-leaders due to the way they lived their lives and because of their commitment to serving others in their communities, even at the expense of placing their lives, and those of their families, in jeopardy. Books to be included are: *I, Rigoberta Menchu: An Indian Woman in Guatemala and Let Me Speak! Testimony of Domitila, a Woman of the Bolivian Mines* and other short stories. These stories will provide students with an opportunity to reflect upon and engage in dialogue about the idea of servant-leadership as a way of being in the world. Personal stories shared among the women can provide social support and solidarity within a private sphere (the classroom), which may encourage them to make their claims within the public sphere in the future (Ramirez, 2002).

In the book *Twenty Centuries of Mexican Art: Veinte Siglos de Arte Mexicano* (Museum of Modern Art, 1940), art in the Mexican culture is conceptualized as follows:

Mexican people possess extraordinary genius for plastic invention and formal beauty. It will not be difficult to discover in our arts that the finest works are those with a religious or social conviction. The Mexican, although capable of imitating reality, uses it for the most part symbolically; that he enjoys the free play of elaborate decoration and conveys messages contained in forms charged with meaning; that he understands monumentality and also takes delight in

minuteness; that the rich profusion he loves obeys a secret discipline; that he is
delicate even to softness and violent to imprecation; and that in him a profound
and ancient sorrow nourishes the flowers of laughter and irony. (p. 17)

In many instances, it is in the contradictions that one finds the essence of
Mexican art and the soul of its people. It is the familiarity with the art used
in everyday life in the culture of these students that makes the paradox of
servant-leadership an idea that might be easily understood by Latina students.

To create art, an individual engages in a process. Throughout this process,
elements such as awareness, construction of meaning for the self and others, suspension of the known, thinking and creating together, reconstruction
of stories, and creativity are present. These elements are also present when
engaging in the process of leadership. Preble (1973) asserted, "The production of art will reveal, clarify and extend experience by providing ways of
perceiving things directly and intensely, as well as giving form to such experiences. Through these processes, the artist makes personal vision accessible
and emphasizes our shared concerns" (p. 22). In creating art, the students
find an avenue whereby their vision of leadership can be crystallized for
themselves and others.

The group process of art-making also encourages a sense of community. In
creating a sense of community in the classroom and opening a space where
art can be created, students might come to know themselves by introspection
and by communal sharing. Fassel (1998) describes how Greenleaf "knew the
value of stepping back, taking stock, retreating so as to nurture the vision
then engaging again. His always probing question is, 'How can I use myself
to serve best?'" (p. 228). In order to use oneself, one must learn about the
self. It is hoped that the classroom might be a space where students can have
the opportunity to come to know themselves better. It is in this space that the
unfolding of self to others might come to be realized through the sharing of
their art. Throughout the process of creating and engaging in community with
others, the students can discover parts of themselves previously unknown
to them. In doing so, they might come to know how creative and powerful
their collective and individual voices can be. This self-knowledge and the
experience of mutual discovery in the classroom can provide students with
a powerful milieu for developing the attitudes and tools of a servant-leader.

Methods and Activities Used in the Sessions

The curriculum will be presented from the perspective of a learning paradigm described by Powers and Moore (2005) as one in which "faculty create
environments and experiences that bring students together to discover and
construct knowledge for themselves as active members of communities of

learners" (p. 126). To create this environment, the instructor takes the stance of one who facilitates and assists in the creation of a community of learners. The ideas of servant-leadership will be presented through short lectures, and emphasis will be on allowing students to engage in reflection, critical thinking, collaborative learning, and dialogue.

In creating this environment, particular attention will be given to incorporating the culture of the students. One aspect to be considered is language. Since language is such an essential part of how individuals view and express their reality of the world, students whose primary language is Spanish might feel they can better express certain concepts, feelings, or ideas in their primary language or by mixing the Spanish and English languages. If all students in a class are bilingual, consideration might be given to conducting the class in both languages.

Some of the learning activities include readings, discussions, and writings. Students will read books about Latina women whose lives embody the idea of servant-leadership. The women will also contribute to the learning community by presenting and recommending short readings. The students and instructor will discuss the readings and identify the concepts and characteristics of a servant-leader, as well as issues of gender and culture in a leadership setting. Students will also engage in dialogue about leadership case scenarios that will allow for further exploration of the concepts presented. In addition, students will write about their learning and make connections to their lived experiences.

Another learning activity is the creation of art. After the presentation of concepts regarding leadership, the readings, and dialogue, the women will create pieces of art such as collages, masks, drawings, and sculpture. Toward the end of the class, the women will create *nuestro mural* (our mural). This activity will allow for further understanding of Greenleaf's (1977) idea of having a common vision and shared purpose as the first step in creating community. Through the mural, students will operationalize ideas of servant-leadership, as well as of self as a leader, and self in community. The mural will be gifted to the university in the last session, during which a *fiesta* or celebration will take place to acknowledge the learning and community that students created. During the last session the students' art will be on display throughout the room. At the conclusion of the class students will be invited to evaluate the class as an instrument for learning the philosophy of servant-leadership and assessing its congruence with the students' culture.

Example of a Session

In the third session, an overview of the ten characteristics of the servant-leader will be presented. The objectives of the session are for students to (a) understand these characteristics and (b) explore how these characteristics might apply to themselves. Students will also identify the characteristics in relation to Domitila, the woman from the assigned book: *Let Me Speak! Testimony of Domitila, a Woman of the Bolivian Mines* (1978). They will consider not only Domitila's characteristics but also how her way of being exemplifies the idea of a servant-leader. The students will accomplish the objectives by writing their own characteristics and areas they might want to develop and improve; they will then come together in small groups and discuss the book and their writing. A class discussion will follow.

Finally, students will create a piece of art. Students will be encouraged to find images and symbols that connote servant-leadership. They will be encouraged to think of these pieces as reminders of ideals they might want to espouse. These pieces can later be used as personal "amuletos" (amulets). After the art is completed, students will engage in dialogue about the process of the creation of their art and the meaning of their piece.

CONCLUSION

Greenleaf (1977) addressed his ideas of servant-leadership in relationship to higher education. He expressed some concerns that universities colleges and universities were not preparing young people to lead. His concern is still relevant today, and universities are challenged to conceptualize leadership curricula that prepare students to contribute to society through their leadership. This preparation also needs to be expanded to consider the needs of an increasingly diverse student population on university campuses.

Greenleaf (1977) also wrote about the idea that natural leaders from disadvantaged groups would find ways to orchestrate their efforts. He believed that the best service a school could offer to these students was not to homogenize them, but rather to develop their ability to lead their people to secure a better life for the members of their community and the community at large. His idea is relevant to many Latina students who are committed to improving the lives of others in their specific community and for universities who want to enhance society.

The intention of learning is to reach new understanding and, in doing so, to form a new basis from which to think and act. It is hoped that by engaging in learning about servant-leadership, students will not only acquire new knowledge but will also engage in learning that leads them to action as servant-leaders.

A curriculum rooted in the philosophy of servant-leadership, literature, and art that is congruent with the Latina's migrant farm worker background can be an instrument through which undergraduate students can learn about leadership. Having been engaged in a process in which they can reflect and learn about servant-leadership, and the self in relationship to others, each Latina student can become excited about the possibility of being a servant-leader who, as Greenleaf (1977) proposed, might be a "dreamer of great dreams" (p. 16).

NOTE

1. This chapter was previously published as Valdés, P. (2006). Art and literature in a servant-leadership curriculum for undergraduate female students who are from Mexican migrant farm worker backgrounds. *The International Journal of Servant-Leadership. 4*(1), 103–121.

REFERENCES

Anonymous. (2001). Fewer caps and gowns for Hispanic girls. *Black Issues in Higher Education, 17*(26), 12.

Barrios de Chungara, D., & Moema, V. (1978). *Let Me Speak! Testimony of Domitila, a woman of the Bolivian mines* (V. Ortiz, Trans.). New York: Monthly Review Press.

Bordas, J. (2001). Latino leadership: Building a humanistic and diverse society Liderazgo Latino: Edificando una sociedad humanistica y diversa. *Journal of Leadership Studies, 8*(2), 112–134.

Burgos-Debray, E. (ed.). (1984). *I, Rigoberta Menchu: An Indian woman in Guatemala.* New York: Courier Companies.

Castaneda, A. (2001). "Que se pudieran defender (So you could defend yourselves)": Chicanas, regional history, and national discourses. *Frontiers, 22*(3), 116–144.

Castellanos, J., & Jones, L. (eds.). (2003). *The majority in the minority.* Sterling, VI: Stylus Publishing.

Chavkin, N. F. (1991). *Family lives and parental involvement in migrant students' education.* Charleston, WV: ERIC Clearinghouse on Rural Education and Small Schools. (ERIC Document Reproduction Service No. ED 335 174)

Covey, S. R. (1998). Servant leadership from the inside out. In L.C. Spears (ed.), *Insights on leadership: Service, stewardship, spirit, and Servant Leadership* (p. xv). New York: John Wiley & Sons.

Del Castillo, A., & Torres, M. (1988). The interdependency of educational institutions and cultural norms: The Hispana experience. In T. McKenna & F. Ortiz (eds.), *The broken web: The educational experience of Hispanic American women* (pp. 39–60). Encino, CA: Floricanto Press.

Frick, D. (1998). Understanding Robert K. Greenleaf and servant-leadership. In L.C. Spears (ed.), *Insights on leadership: Service, stewardship, spirit, and Servant-Leadership* (pp. 216–229). New York: John Wiley & Sons.

Garza, E. (1998). *Life histories of academically successful Migrant Students*. Austin, TX: University of Texas.

Gloria, A. M., Castellanos, J., & Orozco, V. (2005). Perceived educational barriers, cultural fit, coping responses, and psychological well-being of Latina undergraduates. *Hispanic Journal of Behavioral Sciences, 27*(2), 161–183.

Greenleaf, R. K. (1974). *Trustees as Servants*. Indianapolis, IN: The Greenleaf Center.

———. (1970/1991). *The servant as leader*. Indianapolis, IN: The Robert K. Greenleaf Center.

———. (1997). *Servant leadership: A journey into the nature of Legitimate Power and greatness*. Mahwah, NJ: Paulist Press.

Grieco, E. M. & Cassidy, R. C. (2001). *Overview of race and Hispanic origin*. Washington, D.C.: US Census Bureau (No. C2KBR/01-1).

Guranaccia, P. J. (1997). Social stress and psychological distress among Latinos in the United States. In I. All-Issa & M. Tousignant (eds.), *Ethnicity, immigration, and psychopathology* (pp. 71–94). New York: Plenum Press.

Hackman, M., Olive, T., Guzman N., & Brunson, D. (1999). Ethical considerations in the development of the interdisciplinary leadership studies program. *Journal of Leadership Studies, 6,* 36–48.

Hernandez, J. C. (2000). Understanding the retention of Latino college students. *Journal of College Student Development, 41*(6), 575–588.

Hurtado, S., & Kamimura, M. (2003). Latina/o retention in four-year institutions. In J. Castellanos & L. Jones (eds.), *The majority in the minority: Expanding the representation of Latina/o faculty, administrators and students in higher education* (pp. 139–152). Sterling, VA: Stylus Publications.

Kelly, P. J. (2005). *As America becomes More Diverse: The impact of State Higher Education Inequality*. Boulder, CO: National Center for Higher Education Management Systems. Retrieved November 13, 2006, from the NCHEMS Information Center Web site: http://www.higheredinfo.org/raceethnicity/InequalityPaperNov2005.pdf

Lopez, I. (1995). Becoming a servant-leader: The personal development path. In L.C. Spears (ed.), *Reflections on leadership* (pp. 149–161). New York: John Wiley & Sons.

Mores, M. L. (1999). *Perceived experiences Which Facilitated and motivated Mexican Americans from a migrant background to obtain a Graduate Degree*. Greeley, CO: University of Northern Colorado.

Murphy, S. E., & Riggio, R. E. (eds.). (2003). *The future of Leadership Development*. Mahwah, NY: Lawrence Erlbaum Associates.

Museum of Modem Art. (1940). *Twenty centuries of Mexican art: Veinte siglos de arte Mexicano*. New York: Insitituto de Antropologia e Historia.

Nieves-Squires, S. (1991). *Hispanic women: Making Their Presence on campus Less Tenuous*. Washington, D.C.: Association of American Colleges

Offerman, L., & Phan, L. U. (2002). Culturally intelligent leadership for a diverse world. In R. E. Riggio, S. E. Murphy, & F. J. Pirozzolo (eds.), *Multiple intelligences & leadership* (pp. 187–214). Mahwah, NY: Lawrence Erlbaum Associates.

Perez, S., & De La Rosa, S. (1993). Economic, labor force, and social implications of Latino educational population trends [Electronic version]. *Hispanic Journal of Behavioral Sciences, 15*, 188–229.

Powers, J., & Moore, J. (2005). Servant-leadership and the art of teaching. *The International Journal of Servant-Leadership, 1*(1), 123–153.

Preble, D. (1973). *Artforms*. New York: Harper & Row.

Ramirez, R. (2002). Julia Sanchez's story: An indigenous woman between nations [Electronic version]. *Frontiers, 23*(2), 65–83.

Rodriguez, J. (2004). Mestiza spirituality: Community, ritual, and justice. *Theological Studies, 65*(2), 317–340.

Skolnikoff, E. (1993). Knowledge without borders? Internationalization of the research universities. *Daedalus, 122*(4), 225.

Spears, L.C. (2005). The understanding and practice of servant-leadership. The *International Journal of Servant-Leadership, 1*(1), 29–45.

―――. (ed.). (1995). *Reflections on leadership*. New York: John Wiley & Sons.

Washington, V., & Newman, J. (1991). Setting our own agenda: Exploring the meaning of gender disparities among blacks in higher education. *Journal of Negro Education, 60*(1), 19–35.

Chapter 5

Servant-Leadership in a Changing Culture

Reflections on the Brazilian Context

Robson Marinho and Josmar Arrais

As[1] in any other society, the principles of servant-leadership have an incontestable appeal to the Brazilian social and corporate environment, but the term *servant* may not sound terribly attractive to people from the Brazilian culture. In fact, this has been one of the struggles we face when spreading the servant-leadership philosophy among business corporations and Brazilian society at large. Recently, in a class on Leadership Teamwork for Master's students at University of Santo Amaro, in São Paulo, we strategically decided to explore the servant-leadership concept as the foundation of the course, so we outlined the topic on the course syllabus. As we introduced the concept for discussion among the students (most of whom came from different business corporations), we could feel three different consecutive reactions: first, they were shocked by the idea of leading different levels of the company without the traditional, heavily controlled style they are used to; second, as the class continued, they were amazed by the idea of giving priority to people and their potential as persons and professionals; and third, they raised the concern of how difficult it is to accept the idea of *servant* in the Brazilian corporate environment.

Astonished by the students' reactions, we decided to ask the following two interview questions of the twenty-eight students:

1. What does the term *servant* mean to you?
2. Which factors do you think may have influenced your conception of *servant?*

Although it was a very short research inquiry, a few preliminary conclusions or suppositions came out of this conversation with the students. As the students reported, the main reason for the reluctance to use the term *servant* may be found in part in the roots of the Brazilian culture. According to the students, two main issues may play a significant role in creating this context: the popular religious culture and the historical background, which I comment on briefly below.

INFLUENCE OF RELIGIOUS AND
HISTORICAL BACKGROUND

Brazilian society is characterized by multiculturalism, miscegenation of ethnicities, and religious pluralism. As a result, the popular religious culture in Brazil has been mostly influenced by three main religious groups among others. First, the Catholic culture as the dominant popular religion in the country, with its strong beliefs and traditions. In fact, Brazil is today the country with the largest number of Catholics around the world, with 123 million followers, which has been declining in the last few years. Second, the increasing Evangelical population has been climbing in the last few decades, rising from 26 million (15 percent) in 2000 to 42 million (22 percent) in 2010. Third, spiritualism, including African-derived religions in Brazil, spiritist movements, and global religions, such as Buddhism and Islam, has grown in 2010, to 10 million (5 percent), according to data from the Pew Research Center (2013), as shown in table 5.1.

The implication of the popular religious culture in Brazil for the concept of servant-leadership seems to be a distorted perception of the term. In contrast to the Judeo-Christian concept of *servant as follower* (Hirsch, 2019), the popular religious culture in Brazil tends to see no clear distinction between the concept of *servant,* which implies the idea of belonging and dedication, and the concept of *slave,* more related to the idea of passive submission and an object of exploitation. The concept of *servant-first,* implying the idea of serving people's highest-priority needs (Greenleaf, 1977; Spears, 1995), is

Table 5.1   Religious Background of the Brazilian Population

	Religious Background of the Brazilian Population							
	Catholics		*Evangelicals*		*Spiritualists*		*No Religion*	
Year	*%*	*Million People*	*%*	*Million People*	*%*	*Million People*	*%*	*Million People*
2000	74	125	15	26	4	6	7	12
2010	65	123	22	42	5	10	8	15

Note: Table by Robson Marinho, PhD, based on data from the Pew Research Center (2013).

not echoed by the term *slave,* which is strongly tied to the idea of blind obedience and having no choice or initiative. So, the semantic confusion between the terms *servant* and *slave* in the Brazilian culture presents a significant challenge to engaging in servant-leadership as a way of life in familial, as well as corporate culture.

From a historical point of view, like many other Western cultures, Brazilian culture was strongly influenced by a long period of slavery in the colonial society. This slavery background favors the same semantic confusion between the images of servant and slave. Adding to this context, another ingredient that emerged in recent Brazilian history is the 20-year military dictatorship from 1964 to 1984, when Congress was responsible for assigning the president of the country, and there was no popular vote at all. At that time, Brazil faced terrorism of the right and the left, and the military police responded to guerrilla attacks with widespread torture and the formation of death squads to eradicate dissidents. This background of violence made people somewhat uncomfortable with anything that sounded like submission, which may be easily associated with the confused distinction between servant and slave in the Brazilian culture.

Despite the repression and authoritarianism though, the military dictatorship was confronted by the brave influence of servant-leadership and the determination of a few leaders who committed their lives in favor of the underprivileged people of society who were marginalized and whose needs were forgotten and ignored by the government and authorities. One of the icons of servant-leadership in that period in Brazil was Paulo Freire, whose life and career were dedicated to the poor and uneducated people of Brazil. His story is briefly described below.

THE CONTRIBUTION OF PAULO FREIRE

Paulo Freire, known worldwide for the dozens of books he published on educational philosophy, stands out as one of the early supporters of altruistic leadership in Brazil. His leadership project began in the 1960s with a program and a campaign to end adult illiteracy in one of the poorest and most illiterate regions in Latin America: the Brazilian region named Northeast, where he was born and raised (Marinho, 2018). Paulo Freire's method was revolutionary in its goal to teach adults to read in a record forty hours of classroom time, teaching the basics of reading based on concepts of democracy and citizenship. In fact, the attraction of his method "was the promise of providing 'basic literacy in forty hours using minimal resources'" (Kirkendall, 2010, p. 30).

The illiteracy rate in Brazil was alarming, especially in rural areas and the northeast of the country, with indices comparable with the poorest countries in Asia and Africa, where illiteracy rates hovered around 80 percent of the population. It's estimated that in 1960, nearly 20 million Brazilians were illiterate, in a population of around 70 million (Kirkendall, 2010). In the northeastern and rural parts of the country, the illiteracy rate was as high as two-thirds of the population, depending on the area. "With 15 percent of Brazil's territory and one-third of its population, the region 'had the lowest per capita income in Latin America' and a significant portion of the nation's illiterates (Kirkendall, 2010, p. 25)."

With support from the Federal University of Pernambuco, which named him to lead the Department of Extension at the university, Paulo Freire started his adult education program, soon expanding it throughout Northeast. In 1962, Freire officially began his first large-scale experiment. He selected the city of Angicos in the state of Rio Grande do Norte, "where three hundred rural farm workers were taught how to read and write in forty-five days. The following year, Paulo Freire was invited by President João Goulart and by the Minister of Education, Paulo de Tarso Santos, to rethink the literacy schemes for adults on a national basis (Gadotti, 1994, p. 15)."

With help from the president of the republic, the program that was Paulo Freire's brainchild won a place and support in several governments in northeastern states, seeking to help reduce the illiteracy rates in the region with an intense mass education campaign. In fact, in February 1963, the state government set a plan "to use the Freire method to teach 100,000 in the state to read and write. By January 1964, plans were launched to teach 200,000, including many in the rural interior (Kirkendall, 2010, p. 33)."

At a time when the world was waking up to the need to fight illiteracy, Paulo Freire stands out as a leader who was concerned about the ignorance and misery that the majority of his contemporaries lived in, oppressed by misinformation and a lack of opportunities for education and attaining the dignity of being active citizens in society. In fact, Paulo Freire's servant-leadership flourished in the context of a group of social, educational, economic, and political factors, at a time when Brazil and the world were passing through a critical ideological phase in the struggle between capitalism and socialism. In the big context, the time of Paulo Freire coincided with an international movement of several countries toward fighting illiteracy on a large scale. "The first half of the twentieth century saw a variety of attempts to achieve mass literacy. In its first two decades of existence, the Soviet Union made eliminating illiteracy a central component of its attempt to transform Russian society (Kirkendall, 2010, p. 4)."

In that context, Paulo Freire's adult literacy program received financial and logistical support directly from then U.S. President John Kennedy, who, concerned with Communism's implementation in Cuba and the threat of Communist expansion in Latin America, adopted an international policy of financial aid to needy Latin American regions. The intent was to strengthen democratic support for elected governments in the region, especially in Brazil because of its size and tendency toward leftist politics.

At that occasion, the United States wanted to impress the governments of local states in Brazil with large programs to improve people's lifestyle, such as economic cooperation between the United States and Latin America fostering the promise of democracy. Freire's influence was increasing in the Northeast, where nationalist politicians "made mass literacy campaigns important components in their political projects. At the same time, as part of the Alliance for Progress, a 'Special Northeast Agreement' was signed on the 13 April 1962. In a letter to President Goulart, President Kennedy promised that this agreement would 'change the face of Northeast Brazil (Kirkendall, 2010, p. 30).'"

Providing food, clothing, and educational funds, the Alliance for Progress was part of the American government's project to neutralize Cuba's influence and the repercussions of the Cuban proposal of a government that prioritized poverty reduction and sought to elevate the level of education of the population. Paradoxically, in spite of the American support for the literacy program, some of the state governments that most supported and adopted Freire's program in the Northeast were the governments with leftist tendencies.

Paulo Freire ended up being criticized by both sides of the political spectrum at the same time. The far right said that his teaching methods were subversive and planted ideas in favor of Communist ideology. The far left criticized him for accepting financial support from the American government, accusing him of submitting to American imperialism and favoring American influence in Brazil. With his vision as an educator, Freire explained that his objective was to educate the populace, independent of any ideological influence from one side or another. As a matter of fact, Freire openly explained his position and said, "Where the money is coming from does not matter if I can work independently for the political dream to which I am committed" (Freire, 2016, p. 15).

MILITARY COUP AND DICTATORSHIP

The government's political instability led the military to plan a coup to take power, which finally occurred on March 31, 1964, with the support of the United States and other "Brazil's foreign allies (Gadotti, 1994, p. 30)." With the rise of the new regime, Brazil submitted to military dictatorship, with Marshal Humberto de Alencar Castelo Branco as president, unleashing a ferocious persecution of anyone who was suspected of opposition. The dictatorship would last twenty years, until 1985, when Tancredo Neves would be named the first civil president since 1964. Throughout the long military dictatorship, in spite of apparent political stability and national growth, many civilians were violently tortured and killed under the smallest suspicion that they might be in opposition to the government. From one day to another, countless people would just vanish and never be found again. Many were held prisoner without any right to a trial.

The coup came as a complete surprise to most people associated with the literacy programs in the Northeast, who didn't expect a right-wing coup. In fact, many of them were imprisoned or forced to flee. "The University of Recife and its rector were accused of subversion. Literacy program materials were destroyed, and even some of the school buildings themselves were burned (Kirkendall, 2010, p. 54)."

Hundreds of politicians, intellectuals, and artists left the country to escape the military persecution, and many of them were imprisoned and lost their political rights. Even the teachers who helped with the literacy program went to prison, including Paulo Freire, who was one of the first victims to be arrested by the military dictatorship. No matter how much he explained his independent educational vision, Paulo Freire had his literacy program abruptly interrupted when he was taken to prison.

Freire was in prison for seventy-two days, in a small cell with no comforts. After that time, he was released, and in the face of the constant threat that he would be arrested again, he decided to leave the country and negotiated his move to Chile, where he received political asylum and where his project was finally expanded into a national educational campaign.

FREIRE'S LEGACY TO THE WORLD

Paulo Freire lamented seeing his project destroyed and reduced to ashes. Upon leaving Brazil, he would remain in exile for a decade and a half. Unable to see the future, Paulo Freire couldn't imagine that the exile was the beginning of a new stage in his life that, in reality, would open the doors of the world for him to expand his adult education project and his global leadership in education.

In Chile, Paulo Freire began the most productive phase of his career, broadening his research and publishing his first works. After publishing his first book, *Education: The Practice of Freedom*, in 1968, Paulo Freire was invited to Harvard University to lecture as a visiting professor at the Center for Studies in Development and Social Change, during which time he published his second book, *Cultural Action for Freedom*. Soon after, he also published his most famous work, *Pedagogy of the Oppressed*, disseminating the concepts he had developed in his work in Brazil and Chile. And with this book,

Freire would revolutionize the concept of education in the world. In fact, the "publication of *Pedagogy of the Oppressed* in English in 1970 opened many doors for him, and in the following four years, editions of the book were published in Italian, French, German, Dutch, and Swedish. The English edition circulated widely in Africa and Asia (Kirkendall, 2010, p. 96)."

After lecturing and doing research at Harvard, Paulo Freire accepted an invitation by the World Council of Churches (WCC) and moved to Geneva, Switzerland, as a consultant for the education department. At that time, the WCC played an important role in the liberation of the African colonies, and Paulo Freire traveled extensively through the African continent promoting adult education campaigns in various countries. Paulo Freire's educational leadership was not limited to any political or geographical territory but rather came from an internal principle of helping those ignored by society wherever they might be. Although his initial dream had been to serve his own country, no kind of political pressure or restrictions could contain his educational vision. On the contrary, local pressures merely compelled him to exercise his educational leadership on new horizons, wherever needs and opportunities presented themselves.

Paulo Freire's leadership had a focus on helping disadvantaged people all over the world. It was that attitude that made him a servant-leader in the global context. His disposition toward serving citizens of any part of the globe made him a citizen of the world, especially in developing countries, to which he dedicated himself all of his life through his adult education programs.

After a long sixteen-year exile, Paulo Freire finally returned to Brazil in 1980 and served as a professor at the State University of Campinas and the Pontifical Catholic University of São Paulo. In spite of the frustration of having seen his educational project interrupted at the beginning of his career, it was gratifying to see that his efforts were not totally in vain, as other educational programs were inspired by his initial project, including a major literacy project during the military dictatorship.

Paulo Freire's work goes way beyond mere political activism for the Third World. Through the philosophy of education proposed in his writing, Paulo Freire stands apart from the temporal context of popular movements for adult literacy, and his name joins the list of other great educators and educational philosophers like John Dewey, Carl Rogers, and Lev Vygotsky, whose theories developed the concepts of critical thinking, active learning, and student-centered pedagogy.

Paulo Freire left his life of solidarity with the poor and humanity's social problems, as well as his philosophy of critical pedagogy, as a legacy in favor of an active education centered on the student as a free and thoughtful being. His contribution, recognized worldwide, impacted the history of educational thinking, influencing generations of educators.

Throughout his life, Paulo Freire received recognition and awards from various entities and institutions around the world. Among the prizes he was given are the UNESCO Prize for Education for Peace in 1986, the Equator Prize from the Organization of American States in 1992, and the King Baudouin International Development Prize from Belgium in 1980. He received the title of doctor honoris causa from more than thirty universities around the world, such as the London Open University, the University of Michigan, the University of Barcelona, the University of Geneva, and the University of Bologna (Marinho, 2018).

THE CONTRIBUTION OF POLITICS AND DEMOCRACY

In the early 1980s, an extensive popular movement toward democracy, known as *Diretas já* (meaning "electoral votes now"), took place throughout the country, demanding political change that would allow people to elect the president of the country. Finally, a civilian government was restored in 1985 when all citizens were given the right to vote.

Now things have changed and are still changing in Brazil. The political, economic, and social panorama is in the middle of a dynamic change. Along with this changing context, Brazilian society and its corporate world is beginning to welcome the revolutionary new concept of servant-leadership.

One of the most influential persons in consolidating this process of political, economic, and social change in Brazil was sociologist Fernando Henrique Cardoso, who became the twenty-fifth president in Brazilian history, and the third president of Brazil elected by popular vote after the military dictatorship.

In 1995, Cardoso was elected to his first term as president of Brazil, and then in 1999 he was elected to a second term—the first president ever democratically re-elected in Brazil. During his presidency from January 1995 to January 2003, Seidman (2004) states, Cardoso strengthened political institutions, increased economic stability and growth, and expanded educational opportunities for all Brazilians while promoting human rights and development. In addition, high school enrollments increased more than one-third, and the number of students entering college doubled. Cardoso's emphasis on improving health care in poor rural areas resulted in a 25 percent decrease in infant mortality. The United Nations Development Program recognized his work with the inaugural Mahbub ul Haq Award for Outstanding Contribution to Human Development. In 1986, he was selected as the Fulbright Program's 40th anniversary distinguished fellow and lectured at Columbia University on democracy in Brazil.

According to Seidman (2004), "After two terms as Brazil's president, Cardoso is surely the most public sociologist in the world, a global figure who is currently advising the United Nations on how to incorporate global civil society into international deliberations" (para. 3). Formerly president of the International Sociological Association, Cardoso was professor-at-large at Brown University's Watson Institute for International Studies. His research, including his early work on Brazilian racial inequality and later research on the political economy of Latin America, opened new lines of inquiry for scholars around the world.

Cardoso's lecture during a recent fellowship at the Library of Congress reflects a remarkable dual career. As Seidman (2004) comments, "Simultaneously sociologist and elder statesman, he is as likely to invoke Keynes, Habermas, or Marx as he is to mention a recent conversation with Bill Clinton, Nelson Mandela, or Kofi Annan" (para. 8).

On October of 2003, the Fulbright Association announced that the 2003 J. William Fulbright Prize for International Understanding was awarded to Fernando Henrique Cardoso, the former president of Brazil, who consolidated his country's democracy, curbed inflation, and invested in health, education, and human development programs recognized by the United Nations as international models (Fulbright Association, 2019). According to Cardoso,

> Leadership demands flexibility, capacity to listen to the next person, due to the relational, democratic character of today's world. At the same time, leadership demands a vision to be presented, based on the values that may bind the relationship between leaders and followers, and the drive to seek objectives. It is not so much about charisma as it is about capacity, the competence, in complex societies, to point direction, motivate, accept divergence and convince. Etymologically, to convince means to "win together." The leader, therefore, has to make others feel they are a companion (etymologically, "he who breaks bread together" or "eats the same bread"). (Marinho & Oliveira, 2005)

THE CORPORATE JUMP-START IN BRAZIL

Little by little, changes in the political and social environment in Brazil began to be reflected in the corporate world as well. More traditional leaders showed skepticism about an approach that reversed the hierarchical, pyramidal, and autocratic structure of organizations. In recent decades, however, some publications have had a positive impact and inspired a real jump-start in the Brazilian corporate thinking. An example of a pioneer organization with the most participative form of management was Ricardo Semler's company. Heir to the company SemCo, a company that in the 1980s equipped 70 percent of the Brazilian naval fleet, he started a corporate revolution. With approaches known as "industrial democracy," Semler saw the company grow from $4 million to $212 million in twenty-one years, increasing its staff from

90 to 3,000 employees, a pioneering case of servant-leadership with expressive results. His differentiated ideas were disclosed in the book *Maverick* (1988) (*"Turning Your Own Desk Upside Down,"* in Brazil), among other publications.

Soon after, another publication became an editorial phenomenon in Brazil. Translated and edited under the title *The monk and the Executive*, the book *The Servant* (1989), by James Hunter, had a highly positive impact on the Brazilian corporate world. Debated by business consultants and discussed in workshops across the country, the book has become highly popular in Brazil and its content has inspired a new mindset among executives in the country, producing a positive image on the subject of servant-leadership in corporate language. For the first time, the concept ceased to be viewed with prejudice or in a pejorative (servant) way and began to be paradoxically elitist as the result of great illumination. With almost 4 million copies sold since its publication in 2004, the book is among the top ten bestsellers in Brazil. Recently, other publications have broadened this positive view of segregating leadership, including Kouzes & Posner's *New Leadership Challenge* (2013). For years, it was a top bestseller in the area.

These changes in corporate thinking were consolidated in the relationship between the areas of internal training and professional development in large organizations and consulting companies, such as Blanchard, Covey, VitalSmarts, CCL, AfferoLab, HSM, AmanaKey, DDI, Dale Carnegie, among others, which leveled modern concepts of leadership (including servant) in structured training. Topics such as trust, employee engagement, decision-making and delegation, and respectful communication became present in the daily corporate life. Initially, these concepts were mixed with philosophical and oriental approaches, such as anthroposophy, integral theory, and Buddhism. Little by little, however, they were incorporated into organizations as corporate strategies aimed at the well-being of the human person as a complete and holistic being.

A CORPORATE CASE: MSD INTERVIEW

One typical example of corporate servant-leadership in Brazil is the experience of one of the largest animal health pharmaceutical companies in the world, very prestigious in research, production, and sale of medications: MSD Animal Health. Edival Santos, fifty-four, is the vice president of the company for all Latin America. With a degree in veterinary medicine, Santos began his meteoric career shortly after twenty years of age as new product development coordinator and responsible for the company's experimental farm, dealing with peasants and simple people. Subsequently expatriated to Holland and later to Spain, he learned about the research literature on the topic and confirmed what he had practiced throughout his empirical period.

Since 2013 when he returned to Brazil, he has been particularly impacted by the concepts of Ken Jennings and John Stahl-Wert. As a result, this new paradigm has crystallized into the practice of making a difference starting with top leadership. Since then, he has adopted many of the ideas of Jim Collins, Patrick Lencioni, Howard Schultz, Bill George, Shawn Achor, Jon Gordon, among others, and became even more convinced and passionate about the development of people and the organization.

We (authors) had the privilege of advising MSD Animal Health in Brazil while teaching Servant-Leadership for a corporate Executive MBA Program in Leadership and Human Potential Development. We spoke personally with Edival Santos, who kindly gave us the following interview:

Authors: At MSD, what were the most significant steps in the transition from traditional leadership to servant-leadership?

Santos: Awareness raising, role modeling, intentionality, discipline, and celebration. I have known the term servant-leadership by some references to working and leading by purpose. I have always observed that the best managers who deliver the greatest results are precisely those who can influence with dignity and authority, but without using the power of the position. In our case, an important step, and one of the turning points for the walk-the-talk demonstration was the distribution of Bill George's book *Authentic Leadership: Rediscovering the Secrets to Creating Lasting Value* to all of our executives. At board meetings, we emphasized and revised the concepts and their importance for everyone to focus on: (1) Living by purpose, (2) Raising the bar, (3) Breaking new ground, (4) Building strength, and (5) Building strong teams. In other words, as servant-leaders it was important that all directors knew what they did and why, so to develop a strong sense of purpose, practice values, lead with and from the heart, build relationships that connect them with others and others with each other, and discipline themselves.

Authors: What were the biggest obstacles facing this change process?

Santos: Reality has shown that the implementation of servant-leadership in the company was not an easy task and is not "soft" at all, as some mistakenly delude themselves. In fact, it was the result of intentional discipline. As with all change processes, we did not have full support. Several executives were fired and others left on their own. But after the initial changes, when we had the "right people" for a new culture, the acceptance and adherence became very high. People were somehow eager for it.

Authors: What strategies would you recommend for dealing with the resistance of the most conservative team members?

Santos: We used an innovative and symbolic strategy at a traditional event of the company as a step to break resistance. At the 2014 annual convention, for example, at the get-together dinner, the top executives and directors dressed in typical waitress attire and cheerfully served the tables of employees. To this day, we are thrilled to remember. This symbol broke resistance and became a turning point in the implementation of the new culture. Every company lives a paradox in implementing the concepts of servant-leadership while at the same time seeking superior and sustainable results (raising the bar). Support comes when you implement and develop a mindset of a people-oriented culture at all levels. In order to demonstrate that they are serious about the change and to break resistance, leaders must provide a free environment for honest, relevant, and open conversation and encourage actions to increase personal, interpersonal, and organizational trust. Confidence is the foundation of leadership, especially of a strong team.

Authors: What characteristics of servant-leadership do you think most influenced positive results and increased productivity?

Santos: In my career, I have always noticed that managers who adopted the egocentric stance of distant kings isolated in their rooms quickly lost their moral credibility, which prevented them from getting the best of their employees. For a decade, as a field technician and living closely with farm workers, I observed that dealing with people, speaking their language, being close, listening, and being available to help touched people's hearts and motivated them. I decided to invest in relationships, using the resources of emotional intelligence and empathy, and realized that this combination of professional and personal aspects had positive effects. This experiential phase prepared me for my career. Humility, listening, being present, engaging, and giving opportunities are key. But it always has to be from the heart, otherwise it gets worse by the lack of authenticity.

Authors: To what extent do you think the positive results are sustainable and tend to continue in the long run?

Santos: In this period, MSD Animal Health of Brazil (with the merged company Vallée) jumped from third to first place in the market. The strategic goals were achieved with a positive and consistent increase in profitability. In a short time, we were already distancing ourselves from the average growth compared to competitors in the sector and we stood out in the market. For five consecutive years, we received the award for being among the 150 best companies to work for, according to the Brazilian business magazine Você S/A, and among those best companies, the number one in our segment of activity. Recently the company experienced some changes with a new president and replacement of some top executives in Brazil. Unsurprisingly, we continue growing in profitability and being the first in the segment, now for the sixth consecutive year, which shows that the results are being sustainable and promise to be long-term. More than the economic results, what brings me real joy is seeing the high engagement of the team. People develop and deliver "voluntary energy" reflected in the Gross National Happiness scale, an index used to measure the collective happiness and well-being of a population or team (80.8 points, the highest in the sector in the 2019 survey). An engaged team makes an impact on customer relations and adds value to the products sold. In addition, the changes that occurred in Brazil were recognized and valued by the executives of the global headquarters. A visible example was the acquisition of Vallée, recommended by the Brazilian team.

Authors: What advice would you give to a traditional company that wants to implement server leadership today?

Santos: For those who are in the right place for transformation, I would say that they could start with awareness. I suggest starting with the distribution of books and taking time to discuss the topics at team meetings. This will certainly sensitize the executive team and become a symbol. The example of the leaders, however, is crucial. For a cultural change, walk the talk must be the desired behavior. Make sure to give collective credit to everyone who contributes to making the project successful. In order to implement a new culture and enthusiasm, it is important to have transparent communication. As a suggestion, we implemented an action plan that had a very positive impact on MSD, which was an event we call "Chat Café", where I invited employees on a weekly basis to have coffee, talk and, mainly, for me to listen to what the employee had to say, what he thought of the environment, how the company could improve, among other topics. Finally, resolutely have the right people, with attitude and aptitude, added to the right leaders, servants and positive, who in turn implement right strategies and generate the right culture, which ultimately results in winning and satisfying the final customer. Everything is a consequence of the internal environment. We believe that a healthy environment is built with servant-leadership.

In conclusion, historical, religious, political, and sociological factors delayed the implementation of servant-leadership in Brazil and the application of its concepts to business corporations in the country. However, after a slow beginning, political changes and inspiring publications have jump-started the development and expansion of servant-leadership, and business corporations are now experiencing new excitement with the perspective of organizational growth focused on the dignity and value of people, including clients, coworkers, and society at large.

NOTE

1. This chapter was previously published as Marinho R., & Arrais, J. (2005). Servant-leadership in a changing culture: Reflections on the Brazilian context. *The International Journal of Servant-Leadership. 1*(1), 115–122.

REFERENCES

Achor, S. (2013). *Before happiness: the 5 Hidden Keys to Achieving Success, Spreading Happiness, and Sustaining Positive Change.* New York: Currency.

———. (2018). *The Happiness Advantage: How a Positive Brain Fuels Success in work and life.* New York: Currency.

Antoniazzi, A. (2003). As religiões no Brasil segundo o censo de 2000. *Revista de Estudos da Religião, 2,* 75–80. Retrieved February 20, 2020, from http://www.pucs p.br/rever/rv2_2003/p_antoni.pdf.

Cardoso, F. H. (2003). *Leadership today.* CBEL: Centro Brasileiro de Estudos em Liderança, *1.* São Paulo: Unisa, 1.

Collins, J. (2001). *Good to great: Why Some Companies Make the leap and others don't.* New York, NY: Harper Business.

Collins, J. and Porras, J. (2004). *Built to last: Successful habits of Visionary Companies.* New York, NY: Harper Business.

Freire, P. (2016). *Letters to Cristina: Reflection on my life and work.* New York: Routledge. Kindle edition.

Fulbright Association. (2019). J. William Fulbright prize for international understanding. Retrieved December 15, 2019, from https://fulbright.org/wpcontent/uploads/2019/01/2018-Fulbright-Prize-Program-Jan-28-2019.pdf.

Gadotti, M. (1994). *Reading Paulo Freire: His life and work.* Albany, NY: State University of New York Press.

George, B. (2004). *Authentic leadership: Rediscovering the secrets to Creating Lasting Value.* Francisco, CA: Jossey-Bass.

———. (2015). *Discover Your True North.* Francisco, CA: Jossey-Bass.

Gordon, J. (2007). *The Energy Bus: 10 rules to fuel Your Life, Work, and team with Positive Energy.* Hoboken, NJ: Wiley.

———. (2018). *The Power of a Positive team: Proven principles and practices that make Great Teams Great.* Wiley.

Greenleaf, R. K. (1977). *Servant-leadership: A journey into the nature of Legitimate Power and greatness.* New York: Paulist Press.

Hirsch, E. Jewish encyclopedia. Retrieved December 15, 2019, from: http://www .jewishencyclopedia.com/articles/13444-servant-of-god

Jennings, K. and Stahl-Wert, J. (2016). *The Serving Leader: Five Powerful Actions to transform Your Team, Business, and community.* San Francisco, CA: Berrett-Koehler Publishers.

Kirkendall, A. (2010). *Paulo Freire and the Cold War Politics of literacy.* Chapel Hill, NC: University of North Carolina Press. Kindle edition.

Lencioni, P. (2002). *The Five Dysfunctions of a team: A Leadership Fable.* Francisco, CA: Jossey-Bass.

Marinho, Robson. (2018). *Leadership legacy—Chance or choice: Stories and ideas to develop Your Own Legacy.* Dowagiac, MI: Global Learning Publishing.

Marinho, Robson M. and Oliveira, J. F. (2005). *Liderança: Uma questão de competência* (Leadership: A matter of competency). São Paulo: Saraiva.

Pew Research Center. (2013). Retrieved December 15, 2019, from: https://www.pew forum.org/2013/07/18/brazils-changing-religious-landscape/

Schultz, H. and Gordon, J. (2012). *Onward: How Starbucks fought for its life without losing its soul.* Emmaus, PA: Rodale Books.

Seidman, G. (2004). Former President of Brazil: Fernando Henrique Cardoso: A most public sociologist. *Footnotes: Newsletter of the American Sociological Association, 32*(3). Retrieved October 27, 2004, from: http://www.asanet.org/foo tnotes/mar04/index.html.

Spears, L. C. (1995). *Reflections on leadership.* New York: John Wiley & Sons, Inc.

Chapter 6

What Can Hunter-Gatherers Teach Us about Servant-Leadership?

Richard Leider and Larry C. Spears

For[1] most humans living today, it is hard to imagine life without mobile phones and tablets. Every day we all face endless choice points. As our technologies accelerate the speed and frequency of choices coming at us, the faster we feel compelled to respond to each choice. We can be overwhelmed by the emails, tweets, phone calls, text messages, voice mails, all piled on top of the basic life we live each day.

On the scale of human history, however, the Internet and mobile devices are recent inventions. Until just 10,000 years ago, we lived in small groups, hunting and gathering. While that life might seem to be ancient, it is also the life for which our bodies and brains are adapted. We have something to learn from people who still live as we did for most of our evolutionary history.

THE ORIGINAL SERVANT-LEADERS

The early origins of the Hadzabe hunter-gatherer tribe qualify them as one of the oldest peoples on Earth, and perhaps as the original servant-leaders. They have been living in the Lake Eyasi basin in northern Tanzania for thousands of years.

What can the Hadzabe teach us about servant-leadership? We are not suggesting that we romanticize the lives of hunter-gatherers or shape our lives like them. We couldn't do that even if we tried. We are suggesting, however, that we can learn from them. They have thrived—and they still survive—by living their lives with a servant-leader mindset. The Hadzabe provide a living glimpse of the evolution of servant-leadership.

SHARING CULTURE

Interestingly, the Hadzabe "sharing culture" with its leaderless structure is at odds with the power required to maintain control of their land rights in the face of increasing external pressures. With their strong cultural ethos, which requires sharing for the common good, they find it difficult to find leaders among them who will lead publicly.

Perhaps this is the conundrum of leadership today. Progress requires power, and also sharing for the common good. How do we blend the two? Servant first, leader second may be the answer. The Hadzabe are a living example of that blend.

Robert Greenleaf (1970/1991), the father of servant-leadership, defined servant-leadership in this way:

> The servant-leader is servant first. It begins with the natural feeling that one wants to serve. Then conscious choice brings one to aspire to lead. The difference manifests itself in the care taken by the servant-first, to make sure that other people's highest priority needs are being served. The best test is: do those served grow as persons; do they, while being served, become healthier, wiser, freer, more autonomous, more likely themselves to become servants? (p. 7)

The Hazdabe embody the notion that "the servant-leader is servant first." In fact, they consider it bad for anyone to try to control others or to have more power or higher status than others. Although camps may be named after a well-known and respected elder, that individual has no more authority than anyone else in that camp.

ANCIENT WISDOM

The hunter-gatherer exists in all of us. For 90 percent of human history we were almost exclusively hunter-gatherers. Living in our technology-dependent world does not mean that we have totally severed our hunter-gatherer roots and lost the wisdom learned from all those millennia of survival. One does not erase the souls of one's ancestors. Even if we no longer actively use those skills for daily survival, the untapped wisdom remains within us. Could it be that we could reclaim the things we have forgotten and need to relearn today?

Hadzabe wisdom is grounded in a worldview that requires "sharing" as the essential path to surviving. The Hadzabe don't recognize any leaders or any one person as having more power or influence than others. And even though they have clearly defined gender roles, men and women in their society participate equally in decision-making. Their traditional "immediate return" economy supports this equality, because all people from an early age have the skills and knowledge to get what they need each day. To be a Hadza means that if someone asks for something, they have no option but to share. It is considered bad to hoard or accumulate more than what one needs. Everyone shares. Everyone serves. Everyone leads. Everyone is a servant-leader.

EVOLUTION OF SERVANT-LEADERSHIP

While our focus in this chapter is on servant-leadership and the hunter-gatherer Hadzabe tribe of Tanzania, other significant concepts and people serve as important links in the evolution of servant-first, leader-second. Chief among these influences are *ubuntu* and *harambee*.

Ubuntu and South Africa

The African social philosophy of *ubuntu* is reflected in the saying, "Your pain is my pain, my wealth is your wealth, and your salvation is my salvation" (Afolayan & Falola, 2017b, p. 648). The South African word *ubuntu* means that a person is a person through his or her interaction with others. *Ubuntu* expresses mutuality, compassion, and a desire to build communities that are just and caring. *Ubuntu* is an idea that goes deep in African culture. It conveys the importance of interdependence. Respect for differences among people is an important part of *ubuntu*.

Harambee and East Africa

Like *ubuntu*, *harambee* is deeply grounded in African beliefs about the importance of helping one another and building community. Many East Africans view *harambee* as a way of life, much as we view servant-leadership as a way of life, a way of being. It is the embracing of *harambee* that has helped to hasten development in Kenya in recent decades. *Harambee* self-help projects have inspired the building of hundreds of schools, health centers, nursery centers, and bridges, as well as hundreds of miles of rural roads.

Nelson Mandela and the Xhosa tribe are examples of *ubuntu* in practice in South Africa. Mandela's living testament as a powerful African servant-leader has resulted in a growing interest in *ubuntu* and servant-leadership. In a similar vein, Bishop Desmond Tutu is well known for his emphasis on being a servant first, a leader second. We view these and other African leaders as exemplary servant-leaders. Whether we call it *ubuntu*, *harambee*, or *servant-leadership* matters less than the fact that those who embrace these beliefs have much to teach us about life and leadership today.

BACK TO THE FUTURE

In the Pulitzer Prize-winning book *Guns, Germs, and Steel*, Jared Diamond (2005) writes that after thirty-three years of working with hunter-gatherers, "They impressed me as being on the average more *intelligent*, more *alert*, more *expressive*, and more *interested* in things and people around them than the average European or American is" (p. 20).

Who among us would not like to be more intelligent, more alert, more expressive, and more curious? Let's consider that sentence, one word at a time.

"Intelligent"

Why are they smarter? Diamond writes that part of it is the combined result of their lifestyle and the process of natural selection, which would promote genes for intelligence by weeding out those not quite savvy enough to make sense of what was going on in the world around them.

First, they are "walking encyclopedias" of natural history. Observations by close observers of the Hadzabe, such as David (Daudi) Peterson of Dorobo Safaris in Tanzania, show that they know the names and have detailed knowledge of hundreds of plants, birds, and animals and their characteristics, distribution, and potential uses. In his seminal book, *Hadzabe: By the Light of a Million Fires*, Peterson (2012) details this wisdom and intelligence. Your observational skills mean living or dying. You live in the now, since today's survival is the primary focus of your day.

Second, they live a sustainable lifestyle. Because they know with certainty that each day will provide them with food from their natural environment, they don't need to store food for tomorrow. They share whatever they have today with everyone. But to ensure that they have enough for tomorrow, they live a seminomadic life that allows the land to recover in their wake. When they return, they find the land healthy and plentiful once again. They serve each other and they serve the land around them. Each person is significant to the survival of all. Robert Greenleaf (1998) writes,

> [T]his takes a special view of the self. The sustaining feeling of personal signifi-
> cance is important. It comes from the inside. I am not a piece of dust on the way
> to becoming another piece of dust. I am an instrument of creation, unlike any
> that has ever been or ever will be. So is each of you. No matter how badly you

may be shaken, no matter how serious the failure or how ignominious the fall from grace, by accepting and learning you can be restored with greater strength. Don't lose this basic view of who you are. (p. 63)

"Alert"

The Hadzabe wake up every day alert to the reality that time is precious and limited; they live close to life and death. They live in the present moment. Richard notes in his many visits with the Hadzabe that they appear to experience more joy in a day than some of us do in a lifetime. Living in the present brings forth an infectious presence that is passed on to the children, who become equally alert. They are fulfilling time, not filling time.

"Expressive"

The Hadzabe are the "original affluent society." They are satisfied with few possessions in the material sense. They spend time gathering what is needed today. Such a worldview leaves time for creative expression and for community. To be a Hadzabe is to serve the tribe and the survival of the community through sharing. Servant-leadership is in their DNA.

Greenleaf (1998) once gave a talk about expressiveness before the faculty and students of Barnard College. Years later, his talk was turned into an essay titled "Education and Maturity" in which he wrote about a time when the famous architect Frank Lloyd Wright was invited by a woman's club in Madison, Wisconsin to speak on the subject, "What is art?" After the kind introduction, he pulled out of his pocket a book with Hans Christian Anderson's fairy tales and proceeded, in his fine voice, to read the story of the little mermaid. Greenleaf shared, "He read it beautifully and it took about fifteen minutes. When he finished he closed the book, looked intently at his audience, and said, 'That, my friends, is art,' and sat down" (p. 62). Implicit in his actions was the idea that storytelling is a powerful means of expressiveness, for understanding one another. We need to relearn the power and art of storytelling and its relevance for thriving and, ultimately, surviving. The Hadzabe are great storytellers. They make sense of the world through storytelling. With no alphabet or writing, the upside is that you develop a better memory and you do more storytelling; you become a keener listener and you speak from the heart of experience.

"Curious"

Curiosity is a constant in Hadzabe life. Hourly, daily, weekly, monthly, and yearly changes powerfully modify Hadzabe lives, as do the wind and waves on the earth's surface. The seasonal nature of resources requires and encourages curiosity. Survival itself forces constant scouting and curiosity.

In *Education and Maturity*, Greenleaf (1998) talks about what he called his long "wilderness" period in which he sought resources outside of himself. He wrote about how he searched fruitlessly, for a number of years, for solutions to the daily frustrations of life. Eventually, he found what he'd been seeking within himself,

> It took a long time for me to discover that the only real answer to frustration is to concern myself with the drawing forth of what is uniquely me. Only as what is uniquely me emerges do I experience moments of true creativity; moments which, when deeply felt, temper the pain of long periods of frustration that are the common lot of most of us and give me the impulse and the courage to act constructively in the outside world. (pp. 62–63)

Curiosity may seem ordinary, but it is an extraordinary thing. A curious mindset shifts the way we see, the way we choose, and ultimately, the way we live. That's something we can definitely learn from.

THE BEST TEST

Intelligence. Alertness. Expressiveness. Curiosity. These four traits of hunter-gatherer life resonate deeply with Robert Greenleaf's insights into what it takes to become a mature human being, and ultimately a servant-leader. The Hadzabe embody "the best test" in the way that they honor servant first, leader second.

Greenleaf (1998) concluded his talk at Barnard College and his essay on *Education and Maturity* by sharing the following story:

> I had a dream—a big dream. I've only had four or five big dreams in which I came sharply awake realizing that something important had happened and remembering enough so that I could reconstruct it in detail.
>
> It is a beautiful day and I am in a lovely woods on level ground in which there is a labyrinth of paths.
>
> I am riding a bicycle through these paths. In my left hand I hold a map of these paths by which I am guiding my journey. I am riding rapidly and buoyantly as I follow my map. There is a delightful certainty about it.
>
> Suddenly there is a gust of wind and my map blows out of my hand. As I come to a stop, I look back and see it flutter to the ground. It is picked up by an old man who stands there holding it for me. I walk back to get my map.
>
> When I arrive at the old man he hands me, not my map, but a small round tray of earth in which are growing fresh grass seedlings. (p. 59)

WISDOM CAUGHT, NOT TAUGHT

All Hadzabe children are "seedlings." They are given attention and cared for from birth by all members of a bush camp. The Hadzabe never punish young children and rarely punish older children; rather, they let them learn by experiencing. Because they give children much freedom, and because they participate in all activities from an early age, their children are independent choice-makers much earlier than in most societies. They become mature— intelligent, alert, expressive, and curious—at a very early age.

The wisdom of both Robert Greenleaf and our hunter-gatherer ancestors teaches us much about servant-leadership today. The wisdom exists so deeply in our memories and psyches that it cannot always be taught. But it can be "caught." We need to recall more of our ancestral intelligence, alertness, expressiveness, and curiosity to survive and thrive. The Hadzabe, and Robert Greenleaf, continue to have much to teach us about servant-leadership and about surviving and thriving in the twenty-first century.

SOME QUESTIONS FOR REFLECTION

The late Stephen Covey (2004) spoke of "sharpening the saw" as one of the seven habits of highly effective people. If we apply the idea of sharpening one's saw to that of developing our intelligence, what are some things that you might do to develop your intelligence (intellectual, emotional, spiritual)?

For the Hadzabe, *alertness* has a lot to do with living in the present moment. Do you live in the present moment or do you tend to spend considerable time either dwelling on the past or contemplating the future? What steps could you take to center yourself more often in the present moment?

Allowing time for creative *expressiveness* and building community is also key to the Hadzabe way of life. Do you allow time for building community and for your own creative expression? If you think that is also important for you, what might you do to make or increase time for your own self- expression and spending time with others?

Curiosity shifts the way we see, the way we choose, and ultimately, the way we live. Are you curious about your world and the larger world? What simple things might you do to make curiosity more of a focal point in your life?

NOTE

1. This chapter was previously published as Leider, R., & Spears, L. C. (2014). What can hunter-gatherers teach us about servant-leadership? *The International Journal of Servant-Leadership. 10*(1), 23–31.

REFERENCES

Covey, S. R. (2004). *The 7 habits of Highly Effective People: Powerful lessons in personal change*. New York: Free Press.

Diamond, J. M. (1999). *Guns, germs, and steel: The fates of Human Societies*. New York: W.W. Norton & Co.

Etieyibo, E. (2017b). Ubuntu and the environment. In Afolayan, A. & Falola, T. (eds.), *The Palgrave Handbook of African Philosophy* (pp. 633–657). New York: Palgrave Macmillan.

Greenleaf, R. (1970/1991). *The servant as leader*. Indianapolis, IN: The Robert K. Greenleaf Center.

Greenleaf, R. K. (1974). *Trustees as Servants*. Indianapolis, IN: The Greenleaf Center.

———. (1997). *Servant leadership: A journey into the nature of Legitimate Power and greatness*. Mahwah, NJ: Paulist Press.

Greenleaf, R. K., & Spears, L. C. (1998). *The power of Servant-Leadership: Essays*. San Francisco, CA: Berrett-Koehler Publishers.

Peterson, D., Baalow, R., Cox, J., & Woodburn, J. (2012). *Hadzabe: By the light of a million fires*. Dar es Salaam: Mkuki na Nyota.

Chapter 7

The Anchor of Servant-Leadership

Julius Nyerere and the Virtue of Humility

Peter Mulinge

The[1] emergence of the concept of servant-leadership initiated a new era of moral emphasis in the field of leadership, which was and still is dominated by self-serving models of leadership. When Robert Greenleaf (1970) conceived servant-leadership as a philosophy and practical model of leadership, he highlighted the need for a better approach to leadership, one that embraces the notion of serving others as the number one priority. He visualized leaders who would "take a more a holistic approach to work, promote a sense of community, and to share power in decision making" (SanFacon & Spears 2011, p. 115). Fundamentally, servant-leadership "is long-term, transformational approach to life and work-in essence, is a way of being that has potential for creating a positive change throughout our society" (Spears, 2003, p. 16). In this process, a servant-leader acts with humility to engage himself or herself with others and create a connection that raises the level of motivation and morality in both the leader and follower (Northouse, 2016, p. 162). Leaders enable others to act not by holding on to the power they have but by giving it away (Fairholm, 1998; Kouzes & Posner, 1987; Melrose, 1995). Thus, the fervent power of servant-leadership is communicated by sharing power and involving followers in planning and decision-making (Bass, 1990). According to Maxwell (1998), "only secure leaders give power to others" (p. 121).

The essence of servant-leadership is to bring out the best in others by meeting their needs. To accomplish moral purpose, servant-leaders are called upon to clothe themselves with the virtue of humility. This style requires the humbling of one's self in order to lead others (Hayes & Comer, 2010; Patterson, 2003). The notion of humbling does not mean that the one leading is weaker or becomes less of a leader; rather, it is a way of stating, "I am not into me. I am into serving you and other people. And I know for me to be a servant, I have to be a model or I will lose the spirit servant" (Covey, 2002, p. 31). For example, Julius Mwalimu Nyerere, the founding leader and the first president of Tanzania, led a simple life even as president, and today, he is eulogized as an exemplar of humility (Magesa, 2011). According to Vinokurov, Shlyonskaya, and Dyachkova (2005), "Julius Nyerere belonged to those few statesmen and political leaders of Africa whose names are becoming mightier with time, and whose meaningful contribution to the continent's history is still waiting for appropriate recognition" (p. 167). On this, Ferch (2011) expounded that servant-leadership does better than other leadership models, in that it:

> calls people towards a communal effort with others that both revitalizes the individual person and draws the community toward moral clarity; therefore, it requires a sustained effort at both personal and spiritual formation, the disciplined pursuit to understand the interior. (p. 41)

The aim of this chapter is to demonstrate that humility is the characteristic upon which servant-leadership is anchored. A critical analysis of the ten characteristics of servant-leadership demonstrates a consistent motif of humility. In fact, humility has been identified by scholars as a "primary aspect of servant leadership" (Focht & Ponton, 2015, p. 52). It is a quality that has recently emerged in the discourse of leadership due to its remarkable emphasis on encouraging the success of followers ahead of a leader's personal gain. In contrast to traditional assumptions that portray humility with a sense of unworthiness and low self-regard, Tangney (2000) viewed humility as a rich, multifaceted construct that entails an accurate assessment of one's characteristics, an ability to acknowledge limitations, and a forgetting of the self.

The idea of servant-leadership is not about the weakening of leaders and subduing their legitimacy, but rather strengthening their role through their service (Greenleaf, 2002), humility (Hayes & Comer, 2010), and empathy (Spears, 2010). As a philosophy and practice of service, servant-leadership gives meaning to a leader's life. Servant-leadership in this chapter is emphasized as a philosophy of leadership that carries with it the responsibility to serve others with humility. It is argued in this chapter that servant-leadership as a practical model is anchored upon humility. As a virtue of morality that energizes the effectiveness of practical-centered leadership, the practitioner ought to be a humble servant-leader, one who is concerned with the well-being of others. Since its conceptual inception, servant-leadership has been espoused by researchers such as Russel and Stone (2002) and Chin and Smith (2006) as a modeling theory with many potential effects upon an organization. To further examine humility as the anchor of servant-leadership, this chapter defines humility as a construct, explores its essence and dimensions, and concludes by presenting an exemplar of humility with respect to servant-leadership, Julius Mwalimu Nyerere.

HUMILITY DEFINED

Humility in servant-leadership serves various purposes. Morris, Brotheridge, and Urbanski (2005) suggested that "humility may influence leaders to behave in a manner that is primarily other enhancing, rather than self-enhancing" (p. 1325). Vera and Lopez (2004) argued that "humility as a leadership trait may contribute to organizational performance through its impact on organizational learning and organizational resilience" (p. 356). Thus, humility is an intrinsic moral virtue that marks the innate character of a servant-leader. It is a magnet that, when applied, makes servant-leadership a people-centered and people-driven form of leadership. The servant-leader leads with a moral reasoning, and in this capacity, Northouse (2016) emphasized that it enables servant-leaders to make decisions that transcend individual differences and align individuals toward a common goal. This ability also enables a leader to promote justice and achieve what is right for a community (Luthan & Avolio, 2003).

Patterson (2003) identified humility as one of the pillars upon which servant-leadership is built, and Russel and Stone (2002) viewed humility as an essential backbone of the servant-leader. As humility is diversely defined as "the ability to put one's accomplishments and talents in perspective" (Patterson, 2003, p. 36), it is also a "relatively stable trait that is grounded in self-view that something greater that self exists" (Ou et al., 2014, p. 37). According to Morris et al. (2005), humility "fosters a broader understanding of the small role one plays in a vast universe" (p. 1331). I agree with Morris et al.'s (2005) view that humility is a personal orientation founded on a willingness to see the self accurately and a propensity to put oneself in perspective. This view displays three distinct dimensions of a leader: awareness, openness, and foresightedness. First, Greenleaf (1970) posited that leaders' self-awareness is a key element in understanding oneself and the impact one has on others. Second, leaders' sense of openness is the "tendency to be informed, creative, insightful and curious" (Northouse, 2016, p. 27). This suggests that to be humble is to be open to learn new ideas and listen to others. Finally, foresightedness encompasses a leader's ability to predict what is coming based on what is occurring in the present and what has happened in the past. Spears (2010) pointed out that foresight is a characteristic that "enables the servant leader to understand the lessons from the past, the realities of the present, and the likely consequence of a decision for the future" (p. 28). Thus, humility encompasses leaders' ability to be accountable for deeds and words.

Greenleaf's vision for a transformative leadership that is selfless and effective with the potential for creating positive change throughout society expounded the concept of humility. In his thoughts, Greenleaf (1998) expressed that the servant-leader is a servant first:

> It begins with the natural feeling that one wants to serve, to serve first. Then conscious choice brings one to aspire to lead. The difference manifests itself in the care taken by the servant—first to make sure other people's highest priority needs are being served The best test is: Do those served grow as persons? Do they, while being served, become healthier, wiser, freer, more autonomous, more likely themselves to become servants? (p. 4)

The effectiveness of servant-leadership depends on a leader's character. For example, when followers receive caring and empowerment from a servant-leader, then they, in turn, will likely begin treating others the same way. Mother Teresa is a great example, as her years of service for the hungry, homeless, and unwanted resulted in the creation of a new religious order—the Missionaries of Charity. This order now has more than one million workers serving in hospitals, schools, and hospices for the poor. Northouse (2016) wrote that "Mother Teresa's servant-leadership has had an extraordinary impact on society throughout the world" (p. 238). From this example, I view the trait of humility as conscientious behavior that can be inherited or passed on to other generations.

The idea of serving and putting the needs of others before a leader exemplifies courage driven by the spirit of humility. On the idea of serving in humility, Williams (2002) pointed, "Servant-leaders avoid the limelight and work behind the scenes, where the needs are greatest and rewards, when they come, are most gratifying" (p. 67). This means that the attitude of serving others is an intrinsic motivator, at the heart of servant-leadership, and thus humility regulates the leader's effectiveness in motivating others.

THE ESSENCE OF HUMILITY

Humility has been recognized and appreciated as a supreme virtue manifested in the lives of humble leaders from every tradition and culture, who chose to lead selfless lives dedicated to helping others. Humility is a practice of servanthood that enables leaders to achieve good internal acts (MacIntyre, 1984, p. 291). Thus, cultivating humility binds leaders and followers, and servant-leaders do not value themselves as better than those who follow them. Many philosophical and religious teachings and writings have humility as a consistent theme. Three of the world's major religions—Judaism, Christianity, and Islam—all promote humility as a foundational virtue, upon which the practice of other virtues relies (Bollinger & Hill, 2012). In Judaism, the Torah portrays humility as a high value and one among the greatest virtues. Jacobs (1995), a rabbi scholar, viewed humility as one of the most expansive and life-enhancing of all the virtues. According to Rabbi Kook (1978), humility strengthens the memory of a person, for it is impossible to achieve any clear perception except through humility. On leadership, Kook stated that "humility makes sincere genuine leadership possible" (p. 34). Most rabbi scholars suggest that humility aims at placing others first to appreciate others' worth (Dunner, 2001; Sacks, 2002; Schimmel, 1992). Spiegel (2003) argued that humility is the avenue to glory.

In Christianity, humility is exhorted in the teaching of Jesus Christ; for example, Jesus taught "those who exalts themselves will be humbled, and those who humble themselves will be exalted" (Matt. 23:12, New International Version). In the Bible, humility is viewed as it fits to be a recipient of grace: "God opposes the proud but gives grace to the humble" (Prov. 3:34). In Catholicism, humility is viewed as annexed to the cardinal virtue of temperance; for example, humility was extolled by Francis Assisi, and the Franciscan piety led to the development of the Madonna of humility, which they used first for contemplation (Schiller, 1971, p. 112). Thomas Aquinas noted that "humility consists in keeping oneself within one's bounds, thereby not reaching out to things above one but submitting to one's superiors" (Nelson, 1992, p. 189). McInerney (2016) paraphrased St. Augustine's assertion that "humility is not only a significant virtue; it is the indispensable foundation of human greatness" (p. 46). In his confession, St. Augustine asked, "Do you wish to be great? Then begin by being. Do you desire to construct a vast and lofty fabric? Think first about the foundations of humility. The higher your structure is to be, deeper must be its foundation" (Augustine, 1940/1949, p. 43). Patterson (2003) clarified that, "humility forms the essential backbone of the servant-leaders" (p. 15).

In Islam, the Koran teaches that, "The servants of the Most Merciful are those who walk upon the earth in humility, and when the ignorant address them, they say words of peace" (Al-Furgan 25:63). Thus, in Islam, humility is described as a way of humbling in worship to God and service to mankind. Muslims advocate that true piety is not achievable without cultivating a sense of humility.

In Hinduism, humility is an essential virtue that must exist in a person for other virtues to emerge (McInerney, 2016). As cited in Merton (2007), Gandhi pointed that, "truth can be cultivated as well as love, but humility cannot be cultivated because humility has to be the starting point" (p. 530). Thus, humility in Hinduism is the nonjudgmental state of mind when we are best to learn, contemplate, and understand everyone and everything else.

Philosophers such as Immanuel Kant paid homage to humility "as a meta-attitude which constitutes the moral agent's proper perspective on himself that underlies other virtues such as courage, wisdom, and compassion" (Grenberg, 2005, p. 194). Reginster (2006) cited Nietzsche's argument that the "essence of humility is one's ability to estimate himself or herself according to the truth" (p. 157). Elliot (2014), in an analysis of Nietzsche, pointed out the humble person does not fawn or grovel but forthrightly acknowledges his or her abilities and standing. The humble person, moreover, will not suppress the truth out of fear but speaks the truth modestly even in the most dangerous environments, that is, environments that the weaker person would not be able to handle (Kupfer, 2003). This argument concludes that humble people have an abiding awareness of their indebtedness to other individuals and to social institutions; they naturally feel and express their gratitude. Chambliss (1987) postulated that Dewey believed the essence of humility is for one to prize the opportunity to grow for the sake of others. In this regard, humility demonstrates its ability to establish effective leadership.

In comparing the effectiveness of humility with the ten characteristics of servant-leadership, empirical studies by Focht and Ponton (2015), Collins (2001), Irving and Longbotham (2007), Sendjaya, Sarros, and Santora (2008), and Sandage and Wiens (2001) established that humility is a critical and foundational dimension in servant-leadership, the driving force of servant-leaders, and the intrinsic virtue that makes a servant-leader value others above self. These studies affirm that humility is a quintessential anchor upon which servant-leadership holds.

The root word of humility is derived from the Latin "*humilitas* or from humus, it has a connotation from earth, which is beneath us" (Online Etymology Dictionary, n.d.). Therefore, humility makes one to bend or to break down to the earth. In African tradition, bending before a person is a demonstration of respect and honor, and in some African cultures, the act of bending or prostrating on the floor in front of an elder or a person by the one paying homage simply means, "Here I am to serve you in humility." When a servant-leader displays humility, he or she is telling those being served "I respect and honor you." In accordance, Ferch (2012) highlighted humility as a "sense of self-transcendence, a way of living that engages humanity's greatness" (p. 48). Furthermore, Morris et al. (2005) defined humility "as a personal orientation founded on a willingness to see the self accurately and a propensity to put oneself in perspective" (p. 1324). From this background, one is able to conclude that humility is a measure to address moral issues, as well as a virtue that can help influence others' lives.

HUMILITY DIMENSIONS

The supremacy of humility can be analyzed in four dimensions. First, modeling is an essential element to adding value to others. A leader reinvents himself or herself in his or her followers' lives through a unique behavior. He or she models service through his or her behavior thus cultivating a culture of service that inspires and motivates others (Patterson, 2003). According to Covey and Merrill (2008), "empowerment is an inclusivity of modeling; thus, it constitutes modeling and mentorship for those being led" (p. 7). The test of servant-leadership is modeling. Thus, the challenge of servant-leaders is whether or not those they lead are equipped to be themselves servant-leaders. Servant-leaders must, in effect, multiply themselves (Poon, 2006).

The second dimension is emptying. This concept is clearly captured in one of Greenleaf's quotes, "The servant-leader is servant first . . . It begins with the natural feeling that one wants to serve" (Greenleaf, 2002, p. 27). Beazley (2003) noted "serving assumes a larger role in our whole lives" (p. 7). Thus, the concept of emptying means giving out personal life, knowledge, experiences of life accumulated over time, and personal devotion for the sake of others' well-being. The term emptying in this chapter implies the willful acceptance to put aside one's dignity, power, and honor for the sake of others. Emptying is not a change of physical structure but is about emptying oneself of selfishness and living for the benefit of others. Emptying is compelled by love; therefore, it is love for others that would prompt a leader to conquer his or her leadership ego to accept the role of a servant. As a leader expresses the acts of love "they become healthier, wiser, freer, more autonomous, and more likely themselves to become servants" (Greenleaf, 2002, p. 27). The concept of emptying is about leaders' depositing their personal experiences and knowledge into others. Emptying of a leader is an intrinsic commitment to the growth of people. A servant-leader believes that people have an inherent value beyond their tangible contributions as workers, and once these intrinsic values are reenergized, people become wiser, healthier, and focused. The humble responsibility of a servant-leader is to model his or her behaviors to others and do everything possible to nurture the growth of those he or she serves (Greenleaf, 2003).

Greenleaf (2002) emphasized that a servant-leader's task is to serve the needs and legitimate interest of others. Moreover, a leader and followers should "raise one another to higher levels of motivation and morality" (Burns, 1978, p. 20). Though servant-leadership has an idea of servicing beyond self-interest, the servant-leader does not only pursue "self-sacrificial servanthood, just for the sake of serving followers but also for his or her own personal growth" (Sendjaya & Sarros, 2002, p. 405). Greenleaf (2002) believed that a servant-leader's success within an organization is seen in the growth of followers as individuals and their own service for others. The impact a servant-leader has in an organization, to his or her followers, is supposed to be lasting and positive. Leadership through service is not merely a way to move toward a goal or vision but is a way of life for a servant-leader.

In view of this, humility is one of the most essential motivators that character-ize the true nature of a servant-leader.

The third dimension is identifying with others. This dimension is grounded in a leader's ability to strive to understand and empathize with others. People need to be accepted and recognized for their special and unique spirits. In a working environment, the leader intensifies himself or herself with the good intentions of coworkers and does not reject them as people, even if one finds it necessary to refuse to accept their behavior or performance. The leader's act of identifying himself or herself with others involves promises or com-mitments that are rooted in exchangeable values, such as respect and trust. According to Russel and Stone (2002), "leaders identify with others as they take the position of a servant to his or her followers and aim to fulfill the needs of others" (p. 146). Identifying with others helps the leader to know the prevailing issues affecting followers. The leader subjectively identifies with others from a vantage point to actively understand their feeling and empathize with them.

Fourth, immersion is an effective way of knowing and understanding peoples' needs, as it is a vital way for one to find acceptance and establish a relationship. According to Spears (2004a), "People need to be accepted and recognized for their special and unique spirits. Many people have broken spirits and have suffered from a variety of emotional hurts" (p. 13). As a servant-leader immerses himself or herself in recognizing peoples' needs and commits to helping them in the process of transformation, he or she identifies with them in their deepest sense by infusing in them feelings of self-worth. Identifying with others is important for healing one's self and others. On this, Spears (2004b) noted that, "There is something subtle communicated to one who is being served and led if implicit in the compact between servant-leader and led is the understanding that the search for wholeness is something they share" (p. 3). The notion of identifying with others is a characteristic of extraordinary individuals whose egos have been humbled.

HUMILITY AS A STRENGTH

The term humility is sometimes wrongly associated with self-abasement and as a form of weakness. In actual sense, humility is an acknowledgment of one's talents and abilities in a noble manner. Being humble is not a sign of weakness; it is a sign that one knows where his or her strength lies. Humility contributes to moral strength by fostering charity and intellectual strength. It gives one power to own, rather than to deny or cover up one's cognitive limitations. Humility simply requires a leader to think of his or her abilities and actions as no greater and no lesser than they are. In essence, humility presupposes to lead an authentic life and serve naturally. As Grenberg (2005) stated, "the humble person is one who has achieved a balance of appreciation of self-worth and limit, and thereby avoids despair" (p. 181). A humble person takes his or her awareness of limit as an impetus to action instead of a warrant for despairing inaction.

The strength of humility is a reflection of neither weakness nor self-doubt. Instead, it implies a reverential gratitude of the strengths of others, a lack of self-importance, and a sense of self-confidence. Humility does not mean ignoring the problem or admitting defeat; instead, it demonstrates understanding one's limitations and reveals one's resolve to do something about the problem by enlisting the help of others (Baldoni, 2004). Humility, therefore, is the leader's strength to put the interests of others before his or her interests to influence others toward a purposeful course as they maximize their full potential. Baldoni (2010) noted that the "strength of humility is about motivating others to stand in the limelight, knowing that the ultimate achievement of a servant-leader is to develop others to lead successfully as servant-leaders" (p. 65). It gives a leader consent to accept and recognize his or her own limitations, to learn from them and continue to grow. In fact, humility is not only an intrinsic value but also an external strength.

THE EXEMPLAR OF HUMILITY

Julius Mwalimu Nyerere, the former President of Tanzania and one of Africa's most revered twentieth-century leaders, is eulogized as an exemplar of humility. According to Magesa (2011), Nyerere's humility is like a sense of profound self-knowledge and acceptance of personal fallibility. Nyerere was distinguished as a politician of principle and intelligence. According to Tanzanians, he was an honorable *Mwalimu* (teacher); he never called himself *Mwalimu*, but people referred to him as a teacher because, as a role model, he emulated and taught what he believed was helpful for his people and country. As visionary leader, Nyerere envisioned *Ujamaa* (familyhood), a philosophy that was motivated by the desire to bring about some sort of egalitarianism in the social structures and situation of the Tanzanian people. Carney and Masabo (2016) noted that:

> Nyerere attempted to marry the ideals of modern Catholic social teaching, the communitarian ethos of traditional African society, and socialist economic theory. Through binding these three ideals together, he hoped to avoid the gaping socio-economic divisions that plagued much of Africa. He encouraged and led the entire Tanzanian population to start from the bottom and work their way to the top together. (p. 86)

He refused to condone the idea of huge economic differentials among people, where a few were ostentatiously rich while the majority of the population was impoverished.

Julius Nyerere grew from a young hunter with bow and arrows to be commander-in-chief in Tanzania (Kaufman, 1999, para. 13). He came from a small tribe to become a leader of over 100 tribes. At the age of 12, he would walk 26 miles to school from Monday to Friday. He metamorphosed from a polygamous family of twenty-two stepmothers to a monogamous devout Christian family. He transformed from traditional faith belief to a staunch Catholic and from unenlightened folk to a learned scholar. In this case, a humble background validates humility as the narrow path to greatness.

Nyerere's sense of humility is noted at the quest for Tanzania's independence from British rule. While many African countries gained independence through bloody struggle from their colonists, "Nyerere won independence for Tanganyika and ascended to power without bloodshed and a single shot being shot. He kept clear from confrontation with British and was always a step ahead of them" (Ismail, 1999, p. 516). As President, Nyerere exemplified ties between humility and other pro-social qualities that could increase relational well-being. He encouraged *Ujamaa*-socialism sense of familyhood or extended family in Tanzania to build a society:

> In which all members have equal rights and equal opportunities; in which all can live in peace with their neighbors without suffering or imposing injustice, being exploited, or exploiting; and in which all have a gradually increasing basic level of material welfare before any individual lives in luxury. (Nyerere, 1968, p. 340)

He believed in people-centered leadership and social cooperation in an economic game rather than capitalism, which seeks to build a happy society on the basis of the exploitation of man by man. According to Keregero (2005), Nyerere believed socialism was an attitude of mind that countered discrimination and entailed equality of all human beings. He embraced the *Ujamaa* socioeconomic lifestyle to build a happy society on the philosophy of caring leadership, which embodies humility (Assensoh, 1998). Nyerere, unlike many other African leaders and politicians, did not amass a large fortune by means of exploitation.

Nyerere's humility is demonstrated with his repudiation of the affluent lifestyle many African leaders enjoy. He "never received more than $8,000 annual salary as President. He rarely wore western expensive dressings both abroad and at home; he put on gray or black safari shirt over his trousers" (Kaufman, 1999, para. 4). In contrast to many African leaders, whose motorcades are heavily guarded, Nyerere had a simple motorcade with a handful of security personnel that often obeyed traffic rules.

Devenish-Meares (2016) noted that "humility is the sensible self-awareness and recognition of a leader's frailty and that such sound self-awareness and realistic thinking does not abolish true self-respect" (p. 69). Thus, when his socialist philosophy of *Ujamaa* failed to deliver prosperity to his people and inspire the Tanzanian economy, Nyerere was quick to admit that his government was unable to implement *Ujamaa* policies. Thus, to his credit he stepped down peacefully and voluntarily, long before it became fashionable for Africa's self-appointed life presidents to subject themselves to the verdict of their peoples in multi-party elections (Mazrui, 2013). Nyerere joined Maurice Yaméogo of Burkina Faso and Ahmadou Ahidjo of Cameroon to relinquish power voluntarily as sitting presidents (Kaufman, 1999). After handing over power, Nyerere lived peacefully at his farm in Butiama, his home village, near the shore of Lake Victoria. Nyerere was credited for unifying local dialects and promoted the Kiswahili language as a vehicle of expression and education in Tanzania, as well in East Africa. While many people in Africa are aligned along tribal lines, Tanzanians are exceptional; they embrace brotherhood, which gives them a sense of national identity.

Upon his death in 1999, Keregero (2005) and Brennan (2014) noted that many world leaders eulogized Nyerere as a servant-leader who exemplified integrity and humility. He was one of Africa's greatest patriots, and Nelson Mandela may have been the only Africa leader to surpass him. He was a shining example not only to Tanzanians but also to Africans all over the world. Among many renowned world leaders, Elnur (1999) noted:

> Former US president Bill Clinton described Nyerere "as a pioneering leader for freedom and self-government in Africa." Jimmy Carter, a personal friend of Nyerere, described him "as a visionary and principled leader who will be remembered as one of the greatest leaders of this century." French president Jacques Chirac said, "Nyerere was a tireless champion of the emancipation and unity for of the Africa continent." Queen Elizabeth of England described Nyerere "as one of her most favorite leaders in the commonwealth who will be missed not only by Tanzanians but also by the international community." British Prime Minister Tony Blair said, "Mwalimu Nyerere was a leading African statesman of his time." Nelson Mandela said "the passing away of Julius Nyerere is a sad event that took away one of mankind's greatest sons, but left us intact with the ideals, inspiration, fortitude, courage and vision, that he stood for shall forever remain in this world." World Bank President Wolfensohn was full of admiration for Nyerere's integrity. (p. 514)

Nyerere's servant-leadership attitude to put his country and people of Tanzania above his personal interest accorded him an indelible legacy of a sense of nationalism, pride, and dignity instilled in the people of Tanzania.

Today a Tanzanian is proud to say, "I have a sense of belonging. I speak freely, fluently, and with a lot of pride in Swahili." This confession is rarely heard in many African countries as many people are attached to their tribal languages. I note that Nyerere clearly understood that it is the people left behind that will carry on his legacy.

Nyerere's leadership style demonstrated a measure of likeability one of the most ignored factors of being a servant-leader. His humility emerged from his humble social background, even while serving in an office that afforded him all the glamour and glory a sitting president enjoys; he chose to be a servant-leader. Nyerere's attitude toward leadership depicted a self-relentless effort for seeking the good of others. His ability not to abandon his purpose and vision for Africa's liberation distinguished him from other African leaders of his time.

BEATIFICATION INQUIRY FOR JULIUS NYERERE

Julius Mwalimu Nyerere's legacy of humility and servanthood was honored by Pope Benedict XVI on May 13, 2005, by declaring him the servant of God. This declaration initiated a process of Nyerere's beatification and finally canonization to sainthood. The process of declaring him a saint was initiated because of the way he conducted his public life as a politician, thinker, and writer. In 2006, Tanzanian hierarchy introduced his cause for sainthood, seeing him as an African statesman model in a region known for its political dysfunction and violence. Nyerere is widely celebrated as a devout Catholic who committed himself to the national common good, Catholic social thought, and religion. He attended mass for much of his life; as a faithful Catholic, he often fasted and received Holy Communion while kneeling as a sign of respect to the Lord Christ. The Catholic Church in Tanzania embraces him as a fighter for peace and social justice, a loving father, a respected elder, and above all, a man of integrity. He earned respect for his integrity and his modest lifestyle to the point of austerity, in stark contrast to the excesses of his contemporaries.

THE ATTRIBUTES OF HUMILITY

The attributes of humility are the intrinsic values externally displayed by a humble person. Attributes are natural dispositions that distinguish humility from the ten characteristics of servant-leadership. Humble leaders can be recognized through the lens of who they are but not by their self-accomplishments. According to Clinton (2012), "effectiveness of leadership flows out of the being of a leader and not doing" (p. 34). The concept of "the being of a leader" embodies the authentic self of a leader; in fact, true leadership is leading by heart. It is a natural expression of being and acting in any leadership situation in a natural way that tells who the leader is intrinsically. The being of a leader is characterized by natural expression of the attributes of humility. Four key attributes of humility discussed here demonstrate how they complement the concept of servant-leadership.

First, a humble leader acknowledges he or she does not have it all; this is the antithesis of self-gratification that brings a leader to acknowledge "without others I am no body." Humility is a way of acknowledging that none of us stands at the center of the universe.

The second attribute is self-confidence; Northouse (2016) noted that self-confidence could be described "as the ability to be certain about one's competencies and skills. It includes a sense of self-esteem and self-assurance and the belief that one can make a difference" (p. 20). This attribute is the driving power without which a leader is vulnerable to failure. A humble leader possesses extraordinary confidence that dispels fear, insecurity, and self-doubt.

Self-confidence is necessary for a leader to take risks and accomplish high goals. Chance and Chance (2002) noted that "a self-confident leader tends to deal immediately and directly with problems and conflicts, rather than procrastinating, ignoring, or passing problems to others" (p. 86). A leader who demonstrates confidence takes a stand not because he or she thinks it is right, but because he or she is not afraid to be wrong. A confident leader does not mind being proved wrong; he or she feels finding out what is right is more important than being flattered, and when wrong, he or she is secure enough to step aside graciously.

Leadership involves influencing others, and self-confidence allows the leader to feel assured that his or her attempts to influence are appropriate and right. Self-confidence is an attribute that gives a leader courage to influence followers toward a purposeful course. It allows a leader to exercise authority, accept criticism, and open communication. The more followers perceive a leader's confidence, the more they build trust in him or her.

Self-confidence is the most essential attribute of humility each leader should desire to develop. A leader with self-confidence will make decisions without having doubt in him or her and without fear of repercussion. Templeton (1995) presupposed "self-confidence as knowing that one has personal power but not believing that he or she is omnipotent" (p. 36). This attribute gives a leader the ability to be influential, to make decisions with true conviction while admitting limitations.

Third, accountability and responsibility are rare attributes to find in many leaders. These attributes are at the heart of servant-leadership, thus compelling every leader to be accountable of his or her responsibilities and actions.

Being responsible does not imply that a leader has to conform to conventional expectations and morality of the environment. Rather, it means "taking responsibility facing any situation without switching to autopilot or sweeping problems under the rug" (Gunnarsson & Blohm, 2011, p. 82). When a leader neglects to assume responsibility, it means that he or she is failing to fulfill a trust extended in good faith and is also failing to discharge a duty, a moral accountability. Gardner (1990) argued that one of the characteristics of leadership "is the willingness, indeed eagerness, to accept responsibilities" (p. 53). Furthermore, Gardner believed that "taking of responsibility is at the heart of leadership and the impulse to exercise initiative in social situations, to bear the burden of making the decision, to step forward when no one else will" (p. 55). Being a leader is not thinking about power; rather, it is having responsibility for power to serve others and be accountable of one's responsible actions.

Accountability is key to effective leadership and essential in building strong relationships. It is the glue that binds relationships and a virtue that promotes trust between a leader and his or her followers and leadership. On accountability, Gardner (1990) concluded that, "the concept of accountability is as important as the concept of leadership" (p. xvii). To be accountable requires action from the authority holding one to answer for his or her actions or lack of actions. Evidently, a leader who is accountable ought to be responsible because accountability breeds responsibility.

Accountability promotes stewardship; discussing stewardship, Spears (1998) stated, "Servant-leadership, like Stewardship, assumes first and foremost a commitment to serving the needs of others. It also emphasizes the use of openness and persuasion rather than control" (p. 5). Further, Braye (2002) noted that, "stewardship does not just occur, it is a conscious act to care and conserve, and balanced with appropriate use" (p. 302). When a leader demonstrates humility, he or she holds followers accountable for their actions and becomes a good steward. Also, a leader who possesses these two attributes inspires confidence in his or her followers.

The last attribute discussed in this chapter is gratitude. Our world is of a "scarcity" society. So, from this perspective, it is noted that the aspect of being truly thankful is lacking. "Our dispositional and experimentally induced self-focus inhibits the attribute of gratitude" (Watkins, 2014, p. 86). On this, Comte-Sponville (2001) nicely described:

> Gratitude is a sign of being humble because it knows it is graced, graced by existence, or by life, or by all things, and gives in return, not knowing to whom or how, simply because it is good to offer thanks—to give grace—in return, to rejoice in one's own joy and love, whose causes are always beyond our comprehension but which contain us, make us live, and carry us along. (p. 133)

Empirical studies by Emmons and Crumpler (2000), McCullough and Tsang (2004), and Bartlett and Desteno (2006) concluded that gratitude drives helping behaviors, increases assistance to strangers, and builds relationships, as well as showing that gratitude is the pinnacle of virtue and a source of human strength in enhancing one's personal and relational well-being. Gratitude serves as a moral virtue that gives the joy of serving and revitalizes the confidence of those who are being served. Gratitude seems to be a core feature of servant-leadership.

CONCLUSION

This chapter examined the concept of leadership with respect to leadership moral virtues. It is noted that servant-leadership, at its core, is leading from the heart, because the constructs that bring forth the individual to serve are intrinsically formulated. On this, Stephen Covey said, "The deepest part of human nature is that which urges people—each one of us—to rise above our present circumstances and to transcend our nature" (as cited in Ferch, 2012, p. 113). Humility is the heartbeat of servant-leadership, in which resides the disposition that sustains the practice of servanthood. This practice enables leaders to achieve good internal acts and act as a key virtue found in many philosophical and religious teachings.

Patterson (2003) clarified that "humility forms the essential backbone of the servant leaders" (p. 15). The strength of *humilitas* is a reflection of neither weakness nor self-doubt. Instead, it implies a reverential gratitude of the strengths of others, a lack of self-importance, and sense of self-confidence. The term *humus* is often associated with self-abasement and a form of weakness. However, humility is an acknowledgment of one's talents and abilities in a noble manner. Being humble is not a sign of weakness; it is an indication that one knows where his or her strength lies. Humility contributes to moral strength by fostering charity and rational vitality.

In examining the characteristic of humility with respect to servant-leadership, the former president of Tanzania, Mwalimu Julius Nyerere, emerged as an iconic exemplar of humility. Nyerere's honesty and selflessness portrays the true characteristics of a servant-leader. Vinokurov et al. (2005) noted that Nyerere's humility has been widely noted which, like honesty, draws from a sense of profound self-knowledge and acceptance of personal fallibility. When leaders in humility prioritize the success of others ahead of theirs, they are provided with a tremendous opportunity for personal development. Even though humility goes against the norms of our society, embracing humility can help us transcend selfishness and serve others with relentless humility.

NOTE

1. This chapter was previously published as Mulinge, P. (2018). The anchor of servant-leadership: Julius Nyerere and the virtue of humility. *The International Journal of Servant-Leadership. 12*(1), 195–228.

REFERENCES

Assensoh, A. B. (1998). *African Political Leadership: Jomo Kenyatta, Kwame Nkrumah, and Julius K. Nyerere*. New York, NY: Krieger.

Augustine of Hippo. (1940/1949). *The confession of Saint Augustine* (E. B. Pusey, Trans.). Milton Keynes, UK: Authentic Media. (Original work published 354-430).

Beazley, H. (2003). Forward. In H. Beazley, J. Beggs, & L. Spears (eds.), *The Servant Leader Within: A Transformative Path* (pp. 1–12). Mahwah, NJ: Paulist Press.

Baldoni, J. (2004). On leadership communication: Humility. Darwin Online. Retrieved from: http://www.darwinmag.com/read/060104/baldoni.html

————. (2010). *Leading with a purpose*. New York, NY: AMACOM.

Bartlett, M.Y., & DeSteno, D. (2006). Gratitude and prosocial behavior: Helping when it costs you. *Psychological Science, 17*(4), 319–325.

Bass, M. (1990). *Bass & Stogdill's handbook of leadership: Theory, research & Management Applications*. New York, NY: The Free Press.

Bollinger, R. A., & Hill, P. C. (2012). Humility. In T. G. Plante (ed.), *Religion, spirituality and Positive Psychology: Understanding the Psychological Fruits of faith* (pp. 31–47). Santa Barbara, CA: Praeger.

Braye, R. (2002). Servant-leadership: Leading in today's military. In L. Spears, & M. Lawrence (eds.), *Focus on leadership: Servant-leadership for the 21st century* (pp. 295–304). New York, NY: John Wiley & Sons.

Brennan, J. (2014). Julius Rex: Nyerere through the eyes of his critics. *Journal of Eastern African studies, (8)*3, 459–477.

Burns, J. (1978). *Leadership*. New York, NY: Harper and Row.

Carney, J., & Masabo, K. (2016). The social legacy of (Saint?) Julius Nyerere. *Journal of Global Catholicism, 1*(1), 1–25.

Chambliss, J. J. (1987). *Educational theory as a theory of conduct: From Aristotle to Dewey*. New York, NY: SUNY Press.

Chance, P. L., & Chance, E. W. (2002). *Introduction to Educational Leadership & Organizational Behavior: Theory into practice*. New York, NY: Routledge.

Chin, D., & Smith, W. (2006). *An Inductive Model of Servant Leadership: The Considered Difference to transformational and Charismatic Leadership*. Melbourne, Australia: Monash University Department of Management.

Clinton, R. (2012). *The making of a leader: Recognizing the lessons and stages of Leadership Development*. Colorado Spring, CO: NavPress.

Collins, J. (2001). Level 5 leadership: The triumph of humility and fierce resolve. *Harvard Business Review, 79*(1), 67–77.

Comte-Sponville, A. (2001). *A Small Treatise on the Great Virtues*. New York, NY: Henry Holt & Company.

Covey, S., & Merrill, R. R. (2008). *The speed of trust: The One Thing That Changes Everything*. New York, NY: Free Press.

Covey, S. (2002). Servant-leadership and community leadership in the twenty-first century. In L. Spears, & M. Lawrence (eds.), *Focus on leadership: Servant leadership for the Twenty-First Century* (pp. 27–33). New York, NY: John Wiley & Sons, Inc.

Devenish-Meares, P. (2016). Humility as a force enhancer: Developing leaders and supporting personal resilience and recovery. Retrieved from: http://www.defence.gov.au/ADC/ADFJ/Documents/issue_200/Devenish Meares_Nov_2016.pdf

Dunner, J. (2001). An unashamed and fearless defender of ultra-orthodox Judaism. Retrieved from https://www.theguardian.com/news/2007/jul/03/guardianobituaries.religion

Elnur, I. (1999). Tributes to Mwalimu Nyerere. *Review of African Political Economy, 26*(82), 512–516.

Emmons, R. A., & Crumpler, C. A. (2000). Gratitude as a human strength: Appraising the evidence. *Journal of Social and Clinical Psychology, 19*(1). 56–69.

Elliot, R. (2014). Humility & magnanimity in Nietzsche and Christianity. Retrieved from: https://ethikapolitika.org/2014/05/29/humility-magnanimity-nietzsche-christianity/

Fairholm, G. (1998). *Perspective on leadership: From the science of management to its Spiritual Heart*. Westcot, CT: Greenwood Publishers Group Inc.

Ferch, S. (2011). Servant-leadership and the interior of the leader: Facing violence with courage and forgiveness. In S. Ferch & L. Spears (Eds.), *The spirit of servant-leadership* (pp. 21–49). Mahwah, NJ: Paulist Press.

Ferch, S. (2012). *Forgiveness and power in the age of atrocity*. Lanham, MA: Lexington Books.

Focht, A., & Ponton, M. (2015). Identifying primary characteristics of servant leadership: Delphi study. *International Journal of Leadership Studies, 9*(1), 44–61.

Gardner, W. (1990). *On leadership*. New York, NY: The Free Press.

Greenleaf, R. (1970). *The servant as a leader*. Indianapolis, IN: Greenleaf Center.

Greenleaf, R. K., & Spears, L. C. (1998). *The power of Servant-Leadership: Essays*. San Francisco, CA: Berrett-Koehler Publishers.

Greenleaf, R. (2002). *Servant leadership: A journey into the nature of legitimate power and greatness*. Mahwah, NJ: Paulist press.

———. (2003). The servant-leader within: A transformative path. In H. Beazley, J. Beggs, & L. Spears (eds.). Mahwah, NJ: Paulist press.

Grenberg, J. (2005). *Kant and the ethics of humility: A story of dependence, corruption and virtue*. Cambridge, UK: Cambridge University Press.

Gunnarsson, J., & Blohm, O. (2011). The welcoming servant-leader: The art of creating hostmanship. In S. Ferch & L. Spears (eds.), *The spirit of Servant-Leadership* (pp. 68–85). Mahwah, NJ: Paulist Press.

Hayes, M., & Comer, M. (2010). *Start with humility: Lessons from America's quiet CEOs on how to build Trust and Inspire Others*. Indianapolis, IN: Greenleaf Center for Servant-Leadership.

Humility. (n.d.). In *Online Etymology Dictionary*. Retrieved from https://www.etymonline.com/word/humility.

Irving, J. A., & Longbotham, G. J. (2007). Team effectiveness and six essential servant leadership themes: A regression model based on items in the organizational
leadership assessment. *International Journal of Leadership Studies, 2*(2), 98–113.

Ismail, A. (1999). Tributes to Mwalimu Julius Nyerere. *Review of African Political
Economy, 26*(82), 512–516.

Jacobs, L. (1995). *The Jewish religion: A companion.* Oxford, NY: Oxford University
Press.

Kaufman, M. (1999). Julius Nyerere of Tanzania dies: Preached African socialism to
the world. Retrieved from: http://www.nytimes.com/1999/10/15/world/julius-nye
rere of-tanzania dies-preached-african-socialism-to-the-world.html

Keregero, K. (2005). Mwalimu Julius Nyerere on socialism: The guardian media.
Retrieved from https://www.theguardian.com/news/1999/oct/15/guardianobituaries

Kook, A.I. (1978). *The lights of penitence, the moral principles, lights of holiness,
essays, letters, and poems.* (B. Z. Bokser, Trans.). New York, NY: Paulist Press.

Kouzes, J., & Posner, B. (1987). *The Leadership Challenge: How to Get Extraordinary
Things Done in organizations.* San Francisco, CA: Jossey-Bass.

Kupfer, J. (2003). The moral perspective of humility. *Pacific Philosophical Quarterly,
84*(3), 249–269.

Luthan, F., & Avolio, B. (2003). *Authentic leadership: A Positive Development
Approach.* San Francisco, CA: Barrett-Koehler.

MacIntyre, A. (1984). *After virtue: A study in Moral Theory.* Notre Dame, IA:
University of Notre Dame Press.

Magesa, L. (2011). *Head of state and saint? Julius Part 3* [Blog post]. Retrieved from
http://pascalbcdeng.over-blog.com/article-head-of-state-and saint-julius-nyerere
part-3-666.

Maxwell, J. (1998*). The 21 Irrefutable Laws of leadership.* Nashville, TN: Thomas
Nelson Inc.

Mazrui, A. A. (2013). *Why Nyerere failed on his socialism policy.* Retrieved from
http://dirayetu.blogspot.com/2013/05/why-nyerere-fail-on-his-socialism-it.html

McCullough, M., & Tsang, J. (2004) (eds.). *The psychology of gratitude.* New York,
NY: Oxford University Press.

Mclnerney, J. (2016). *The greatness of humility.* Eugene, OR: Pickwick Publications.

Melrose, K. (1995). *Making the Grass Greener on Your Side.* San Francisco, CA:
Berrett-Koehler Publishers, Inc.

Merton, T. (2007). *Gandhi on Non-Violence.* New York, NY: New Direction
Publishing Corporation.

Morris, J., Brotheridge, C., & Urbanski, J. (2005). Bringing humility to leadership:
Antecedents and consequences of leader humility. *Human Relations, 58*(10),
1323–1350.

Nelson, M. (1992). *The priority of prudence: Virtue and Natural Law in Thomas
Aquinas and implications of Modern Ethics.* University Park, PA: University Press.

Northouse, P. G. (2016). *Leadership: Theory and practice* (7th edition). Thousand
Oaks, CA: Sage Publications.

Nyerere, J. K. (1968). *Ujamaa: Essays on socialism.* Oxford, UK: Oxford University
Press.

Ou, A. Y., Tsui, A. S., Kinicki, A. J., Waldman, D.A., Xiao, Z., & Song, L. J. (2014). Humble chief executive officers' connections to top management team integration and middle managers' responses. *Administrative Science Quarterly, 59*, 34–72.

Patterson, K. (2003). Servant leadership: A theoretical model (Doctoral Dissertation). Available From ProQuest Dissertation and Theses Database (UMI No. 3082719).

Poon, R. (2006). A model for servant leadership, self-efficacy and mentorship. *Servant Leadership Research Roundtable.* Retrieved from http://www.regent.edu/ acad/global/publications/sl_proceedings/2006/poon.pdf

Reginster, B. (2006). *The affirmation of life: Nietzsche on overcoming nihilism.* Cambridge, MA: Harvard University Press.

Russell, R. F., & Stone, A. G. (2002). A review of servant leadership attributes: Developing a practical model. *Leadership and Organizational Development Journal, 23*(3), 145–147.

Sacks, J. (2002). *Dignity of difference: How to avoid the class of civilization.* New York, NY: Bloomsbury Publishing.

Sandage, S. J., & Wiens, T. W. (2001). Contextualizing models of humility and forgiveness: A reply to Gassin. *Journal of Psychology and Theology, 29*, 201.

SanFacon, G., & Spears, L. (2011). Holistic servant-leadership: A multidimensional approach. In S. Ferch & L. Spears (eds.), *The spirit of the servant-leadership* (pp. 113–123). Mahwah, NJ: Paulist.

Schiller, G. (1971). *Iconography of Christian art.* New York, NY: New York Graphic Society.

Schimmel, S. (1992). *The Seven Deadly Sins: Jewish, Christian, and Classical Reflections on Human Nature.* New York, NY: Free Press.

Sendjaya, S., & Sarros, J. (2002). Servant leadership: Its origin, development, and application in organizations. *Journal of Leadership and Organizational Studies, 9*(2): 57–65.

Sendjaya, S., Sarros, J. C., & Santora, J. C. (2008). Defining and measuring servant leadership behavior in organizations. *Journal of Management Studies, 45*(2), 402–424.

Spears, L. (ed.). (1998). *Insights on leadership: Service, stewardship, spirit, and servant leadership.* New York, NY: John Wiley & Sons, Inc.

———. (2003). Understanding the growing impact of servant-leadership. In H. Beazley, J. Beggs, & L. Spears (eds), *The Servant-Leader Within: A Transformative Path* (pp.13–27). Mahwah, NJ: Paulist Press.

———. (2004a). The understanding and practice of servant-leadership. In L.C. Spears & M. Lawrence (eds.), *Practicing Servant-Leadership: Succeeding through Trust, Bravery, and forgiveness* (pp. 9–24). San Francisco, CA: Jossey-Bass.

———. (2004b). Practicing servant-leadership. *Leader-Leader, 34*, 1–11.

———. (2010). Servant leadership and Robert K. Greenleaf's legacy. In K. Patterson & D. van Dierendonck (eds.), *Servant leadership: Developments in theory and research* (pp. 11–24). New York, NY: Palgrave Macmillan.

Spiegel, J. S. (2003). The moral irony of humility: Logos. *A Journal of Catholic Thought and Culture, 6*, 131–150.

Tangney, J. (2000). Humility: Theoretical perspectives, empirical findings and directions for future research. *Journal of Social and Clinical Psychology, 19*(1), 70–82.

Templeton, J. M. (1995). *The humble approach.* New York, NY: Continuum Publishing.

Vera, D., & Lopez. A. R. (2004). Humility as a source of competitive advantage. *Organizational Dynamics, 33*(4), 393–408.

Vinokurov, N., Shlyonskaya, S., & Dyachkova, Y. (eds.). (2005*). Julius Nyerere: Humanist, politician, thinker.* Dar es Salaam: Mkuki na Nyota Publishers.

Watkins, P. C. (2014). *Gratitude and the Good Life: Towards a psychology of appreciation.* New York, NY: Springer Media.

Williams, L. (2002). Fannie Lou Hammer: Servant of the people. In L. Spears & M. Lawrence (eds.), *Focus on leadership: Servant-leadership for the Twenty-First Century* (pp. 65–87). New York, NY: John Wiley & Sons, Inc.

Chapter 8

A Kenyan on Servant-Leadership

Harambee and Service

Jeremiah Ole Koshal and Kathleen Patterson

Robert K. Greenleaf (1977) offers[1] a foundational understanding of servant-leadership with this statement:

> The servant-leader is servant first . . . It begins with the natural feeling that one wants to serve first . . .Then, conscious choice brings one to aspire to lead . . . The difference manifests itself in the care taken by the servant—first to make sure that other people's highest-priority needs are being served. The best test, and the most difficult to administer, is: Do those served grow as persons? Do they, while being served, become healthier, wiser, freer, more autonomous, and more likely themselves to become servants? And what is the effect on the least privileged in society? Will they benefit, or at least not be further deprived?" (p. 27)

Greenleaf's statement offers all hope in the power of servant-leadership to transform society through service. A primary motivation for leadership should be to serve others, according to Snyder, Dowd, and Houghton (1994). Congruent with this thinking is Sarkus (1996), who notes that much of the current leadership literature supports serving and valuing people; as well, this line of thinking has been presaged by the work of Robert K. Greenleaf. Servant-leadership, which is a paradigm of leadership based on the philosophy of Greenleaf (1977), calls for leaders to be of service to others in society (e.g., employees, customers, and communities). To help create a platform for more specific research on servant-leadership, Patterson (2003) developed a working theory of servant-leadership comprising altruism, empowerment, humility, love, service, trust, and vision; such research has opened the door for empirical contextual research on the theory.

This chapter first examines the popular literature on servant-leadership theory, servant-leadership as a viable theoretical perspective as defined by Patterson (2003), leadership and service in the African context, and the Kenyan *harambee* philosophy. The chapter further presents a study and findings on twenty-five Kenyan leaders and managers of varied backgrounds who were interviewed on the construct of service and the leadership application in the Kenyan setting.[2] The findings show the connection of servant-leadership with the Kenyan concept of *harambee*. In addition, themes that have emerged are presented; these are role modeling, sacrificing for others, meeting the needs of others and developing them, service as a primary function in leadership, recognizing and rewarding employees, treating employees with respect (humility), and involving employees in the decision-making process.

SERVANT-LEADERSHIP THEORY

Snyder, Dowd, and Houghton (1994) posited that writers who study leadership suggest that one of the primary motivations of leadership should be serving others; they argued that a real customer focus requires leadership with service to others. Service to others calls for leaders who genuinely serve others' needs (Kanungo & Mendonca, 1996; Murray, 1997; Nair, 1994), meaning that a strong relationship exists between service and leadership ("A Draft," 2000; Bass, 1995; Bennis & Nanus, 1985; Bradley, 1999; Fuller, 2000; Murray; Nair; T'Shaka, 1990; Taninecz, 2002). Sarkus (1996) observed that much of the current literature that supports serving and valuing people has been presaged by the work of Robert K. Greenleaf, who is most notable in most, if not all, work in servant-leadership. In fact, servant-leadership, which is a paradigm of leadership based on the philosophy of Greenleaf (1977), calls for leaders to be of service to others (e.g., employees, customers, and communities), to give more than they take, and to serve others' needs more than their own. Though Greenleaf is the one most responsible for popularizing the theory of servant-leadership (Spears, 1996), the theory has been practiced for many years throughout all cultures (Nyabadza, 2003).

Two key notions underlie the various definitions of servant-leadership. First, servant-leadership emphasizes service (Blanchard, 2000; Farling, Stone, & Winston, 1999; Greenleaf, 1977; Lee & Zemko, 1993; Lubin, 2001; Melrose, 1995; Russell & Stone, 2002; Sarkus, 1996; Spears, 1995, 1996, 1998; Spears & Lawrence, 2002; Tatum, 1995; Wis, 2002). Second, servant-leadership is other-centered rather than leader-or self-centered (Covey, 2002; Fairholm, 1997; Greenleaf, 1997; Joseph, 1997; Kouzes & Posner, 1993; Laub, 1999; Melrose, 1995; Pollard, 1997; Spears & Lawrence, 2002;

Stone, Russell, & Patterson, 2003). Similarly, according to Saunders (1993), servant-leadership means supporting others in their growth and development. Blanchard (1997) and Yukl (2002) posited that servant-leaders listen to their people, praise them, support them, and learn about their needs. In other words, they are constantly trying to find out what their needs are in order to be successful. Some of these characteristics, including service, appear in the list of characteristics that are central to the development of servant-leaders (Spears, 1995, 1996, 1998, 2002). Thus, the emergence of servant-leadership is likely to meet the deep desire in our society for a world where people truly care for one another, where workers and customers are treated fairly, and where leaders can be trusted to serve the needs of their followers rather than their own (Spears, 1998).

Patterson's Definition of Servant-Leadership Theory

To help create a platform for more specific research on servant-leadership, Patterson (2003) developed a working theory of servant-leadership. According to Patterson:

> Servant-leaders signify those who lead an organization by focusing on their followers, such that the followers are the primary concern and the organizational concerns are peripheral. Servant-leaders lead and serve with (a) altruism, (b) empower followers, (c) act with humility, (d) exhibit love, (e) lead with service, (f) are trusting, and (g) are visionary to their followers. (p. 5)

According to Patterson (2003), servant-leadership theory provides a marked contrast to transformational leadership theory. While transformational leaders strive to align their personal interests (i.e., organizational interests and the interests of the followers) with the interests of the group, organization, or society, the primary focus of the leaders in servant-leadership theory is on serving their followers individually (Arjoon, 2000).

Though servant-leadership crosses all boundaries and is being applied by myriad organizations (Spears, 1996), the theory is mainly concentrated in North American organizations (Autry, 2001; Branch, 1999; Douglas, 2003; Galvin, 2001; Levering & Moskowitz, 2000, 2001; McLaughlin, 2001; Pollard, 1997; Rubin, Powers, Tulacz, Winston, & Krizan, 2002; Spears, 1996; Spears & Lawrence, 2002; Taninecz, 2002), where it has provided a means for companies to value their people in order to be successful (Fletcher, 1999; Lowe, 1998). Thus, Patterson's servant-leadership theory and the construct of service may be contextually constrained and needs to be researched in various contexts in order to see whether it applies in varied cultural and organizational settings, for example in Kenya.

A 2003 study by Nelson explored Patterson's (2003) servant-leadership theory (i.e., all constructs: altruism, empowerment, humility, love, service, trust, and vision) among black leaders in South Africa. These leaders' perception of service was expressed as "serving and supporting the people who serve the customers" (Nelson, p. 72). This study found that Patterson's servant-leadership theory has acceptability and applicability among black leaders in South African organizations, even though there were some contextual concerns. This is not a strange outcome, given that Nelson capitalized on *ubuntu* philosophy, which focuses on the person not living for himself or herself, but rather living for others ("An Afro-centric," 2001; Dia, 1994; Mamadou, 1991; Mazrui, 1986; Mbiti, 1969; Mibigi & Maree, 1995; Wright, 1984). *Ubuntu* serves as a metaphor embodying group solidarity in many traditional African societies (Mibigi & Maree, 1995). In other words, it focuses on the person and stresses communal support, group significance, and cooperation. It acts like a public philosophy that ties people together as a strong, united community ("An Afro-centric"). Nelson found service based on the interest and welfare of their employees to be the primary function of leadership among black leaders in South Africa. The study is limited in the sense that it can be generalized only to black leaders in South African organizations. Thus, there is need to undertake a similar study in the Kenyan context.

However, the fact that *ubuntu* and other concepts and philosophies that relate to serving others (e.g., "I am because we are: and since we are, therefore I am" (Mbiti, 1969, p. 10) are widely shared across Africa, means that servant-leadership and the construct of service might be positively received by Kenyan leaders and managers. The traditional African leadership set-up has been more intent on reaching consensus (Ayittey, 1992; Mamadou, 1991; Mersha, 2000) and has always placed the community's interests ahead of its own. Even the African communities themselves believed that the welfare of an individual means the welfare of the entire community (Bell, 2002; Gakuru, 1998; Mamadou, 1991; Waiguchu, Tiagha, & Mwaura, 1999; Wright, 1984). Furthermore, the Kenyan philosophy of *harambee*, which was adopted by Jomo Kenyatta, who was the founding president of Kenya (Chieni, 1997; Versely, 1997), is based on African traditions of community cooperation and mutual aid (Hill, 1991; Mbithi & Rasmusson, 1977; Ngau, 1987). It embodies and reflects a strong ancient value of mutual assistance and community reliance (Bailey, 1993; Chieni, 1997; Ngau, 1987; Shikuku, 2000; Yassin, 2004). The *harambee* philosophy, which is usually used in the discussion of economic and social developments (Chieni, 1997; Ngau, 1987), became a kind of voluntary movement in post-independence (after 1963) and has continued to play a cardinal role in local development initiatives and projects (Bailey, 1993; Chieni, 1997; Hill, 1991; Ndegwa, 1996; Ngau, 1987; Wilson, 1992).

LEADERSHIP AND SERVICE IN
THE AFRICAN CONTEXT

Service has come to be identified with the African concept of interdependence, which calls for individuals, including the leaders, to depend on each other; the welfare of every individual in the African communities means the welfare of the entire community (Gakuru, 1998). Nigerian novelist Chinua Achebe famously articulated this idea: "Whereas an animal scratches itself against a tree, a human being has a kinsman to scratch it for him" (cited in Gakuru, para. 11). Bell (2002) posits that Africans do not think of themselves as "discrete individuals," but rather understand themselves as part of a "community," which is often referred to as "African communalism." Many local dialects have a word for the concept of mutual responsibility and joint effort. In thinking about "African communalism," a passage from Mbiti's widely read book *African Religions and Philosophy* comes to mind:

> The individual owes his existence to other people. He is simply part of the whole. Whatever happens to the individual happens to the whole group and whatever happens to the whole group happens to the individual. The individual can only say: "I am, because we are; and since we are therefore I am." (1969, p. 10)

According to Wright (1984), Africans are people who regard each other as brothers and sisters, and the interest of the local communities takes precedence over that of those in government, organizations, or leadership positions in general.

The strong and ancient values of service and mutual assistance have always been brought to life in African societies through networks and associations. The voluntary spirit in Africa predates modern governments and Western influence. Before the advent of colonialism, African people had structures that catered to the needy among them (Gakuru, 1998). It is worth noting that the idea and practice of giving a hand (service) to others, whether one acts individually or through organization, is as old as Africa. Voluntary individual and communal activities retain deep roots among Africans. In practical terms, one helps and works with neighbors and fellow villagers as the need arises and dictates (Waiguchu et al., 1999). Furthermore, the interest of the local and ethnic communities takes precedence over whatever the leadership or government may declare as national interests (Mamadou, 1991).

Tradition places social achievement above personal achievement in most African communities. Common phrases usually exist that signal social disapproval of the individual who places himself or herself above fellow human beings (An Afro-centric Alliance, 2001). Dia (1994) said that individual achievements are much less valued than are interpersonal relations. Mamadou (1991) posits that a higher value is placed on interpersonal relations and the timely execution of certain social and religious activities than on individual achievements. The value of economic acts, for instance, is measured in terms of their capacity to reinforce the bonds of the group. Thus, efficient indigenous management practices, in which shareholding is democratized and cultural values and traditions serve as a means of stimulating productivity, can be used in today's organizations.

As part of service, consensual decisions are a critical part of African leadership. According to Ayittey (1992), the traditional African leadership from time immemorial has always placed the community's interest (service) ahead of its own. For instance, the chief did not rule, but rather served and led only by consensus. In situations where the council (governing body) failed to reach a consensus, the chief would call a village assembly (representatives) to put the issues before the people for debate. This signifies the importance of service to the people. Similarly, Mamadou (1991) observed that the traditional judge in black Africa is more intent on reaching a consensus than in litigating by the book. In legal as well as political matters, African leaders tend to seek unanimity and are generally prepared to engage in seemingly interminable discussions. Perhaps this explains why self-reliance and self-interest tend to take a back seat to group or community loyalty. According to Mersha (2000), studies based on African organizations indicate that decisions based on a consensus still have greater acceptability in African societies. Specifically, a study based on Kenyan industries showed that both workers and managers preferred a modern democratic style of leadership to build consensus and trust.

THE KENYAN *HARAMBEE* PHILOSOPHY

According to Chieni (1997), *harambee*, which is a *Bantu* (a major grouping in Africa) word, has its origins in the word *halambee*, which literally means, "let us all pull together" (para. 3). While tracing the origins of *harambee*, Yassin (2004) noted that the alternative linguistic interpretation of *harambee* is derived from the twin words *halahala* and *mbee*. While *halahala* is a Swahili (a language spoken in East Africa) word for doing things quickly and collectively, *mbee* is Swahili for forward. *Halahala/mbee* would thus signify "doing things quickly and collectively with a forward connotation" (Yassin, para. 7). However, the phrase has since been simplified, given official recognition, and coined as *harambee*. The same word is echoed by everyone when a collective effort is made for the common good, such as helping a family in need or the construction of a school or a church ("Special Feature," 2002).

The *harambee* philosophy is based on African traditions of community cooperation and mutual aid (Hill, 1991). This may refer to the institutions of work parties, which embrace a variety of forms of cooperative labor assistance. Similarly, Mbithi and Rasmusson (1977) perceived *harambee* as the collective and cooperative participation of a community in an attempt to fill perceived needs through utilization of its own resources. They further noted that the notion of self-help to which the term *harambee* seems to refer is solidly grounded in the indigenous cultures of most Kenyan communities, where different names for joint efforts can be found. Perhaps that is the reason for Chieni's (1997) assertion that *harambee* is variously described as a way of life in Kenya and as a traditional custom of Kenyans that encourages all Kenyans, along with their leaders, to give in order to complete any task at hand for community development and advancement. Thus, for the most part, the term embodies mutual assistance, joint effort, mutual social responsibility, and community self-reliance.

Though *harambee* is a traditional Kenyan principle that has always existed, it gained prominence after independence (1963). When President Kenyatta encouraged his people to help one another in the spirit of *harambee*, he placed the destiny of Kenyans in the hands of their fellow Kenyans, especially their leaders. He rallied black, white, and brown Kenyans (both ordinary people and their leaders) to launch into the twentieth century by adopting the philosophy of *harambee* (Versely, 1997). As far as Kenyatta was concerned, it was only out of everybody's efforts and toil that a new and better Kenya could be built. He stressed a continued close collaboration between the people throughout their self-help efforts, as well as with the government and the leaders, when he said: "But you must know that Kenyatta alone cannot give you everything. All things we must do together to develop our country, to get education for our children, to have doctors, to build roads, to improve or provide all day-to-day essentials" (Chieni, 1997, para. 5). Perhaps that is why some people see *harambee* as both a political slogan and a movement that developed rapidly in response to people's actions and inspirations, rather than simply as a creation of the government and its leadership (Hill, 1991). Thus, the spirit of *harambee* (i.e., we must all pull together) symbolizes the Kenyan people's attitude and effort in working together to build and strengthen themselves and their nation as a whole (Shikuku, 2000; Wilson, 1992).

According to Ngau (1987), *harambee* projects are broadly classified into social development and economic development types. The former include education, health, social welfare and recreation, and domestic projects, while the latter includes water supply, transport and communication facilities, and agricultural ventures. Chieni (1997) noted that Kenyatta realized that social development—the process by which the standards and conditions of living of the majority of the people in a community are improved—could not be accomplished without a firm cultural foundation coupled with the involvement of the majority of the people themselves. Kenyatta then decided to stress a continued close collaboration between the people (through their self-help efforts) and the government (through the provision of necessary services). According to Wilson (1992), the *harambee* philosophy has actually come to mean the provision of goods—usually social infrastructure through the voluntary cooperation of members of the community, including their leaders. The philosophy is utilized in community self-help programs to build roads, schools, medical facilities, and daycares. The shift of *harambee* to social amenity development emanates from the fact that the basic means of production (e.g., farming, industry, and mining) have come under private, family, and company or organizational ownership. As far as most people are concerned, collective effort is aimed at, above all, schools, health facilities, roads, and churches, rather than development of farms or businesses (Ngau).

Through *harambee*, the efforts of the people, non-governmental organizations (NGOs) and the government have come together in a cooperative endeavor to speed up development (Chieni, 1997). In his book *The Two Faces of Civil Society: NGOs and Politics in Africa*, Ndegwa (1996) observed that besides relative political stability and a well-developed communication network, the *harambee* philosophy has contributed to Kenya's having the highest number of both international and local NGOs in the whole of sub-Saharan Africa. In areas where the state has been unable to fully provide adequate services such as healthcare, education, and agricultural and credit extension, the NGOs have entered these fields and become indispensable partners in service provision through the *harambee* philosophy.

According to Bailey (1993), *harambee* is not just a theoretical fancy concept—it has achieved tangible results. *Harambee* has specifically brought about near miracles in the entire nation of Kenya; *Harambee* self-help projects have been responsible for the building of over 200 schools, 40 health centers, 60 dispensaries, 260 nursery centers, 42 bridges, and 500 kilometers of rural access roads throughout the country. Ngau (1987) explains that a typical *harambee* today consists of fundraising, where the local people, government officials, elected politicians, church leaders, and the general public make contributions on a voluntary basis, ranging from cash and materials to pledges for labor. Further, local and foreign business firms, foreign agencies and governments, foundations, and non-governmental organizations (NGOs) also get involved and make contributions to *harambee* projects. Hence, *harambee* has in one way or another improved the quality of life for different people and communities in Kenya.

METHOD

Description of Research Design

The study employed a qualitative in-depth interviewing technique, which is a type of interview that researchers use to elicit information in order to achieve a holistic understanding of the participant's point of view (Rubin & Rubin, 1995). It involved asking participants standardized open-ended questions and probing wherever necessary to obtain data deemed useful by the researcher (Huberman & Miles, 2002).

Research Participants

Based on theory-derived criteria for being a servant-leader, twenty-five leaders and managers from Kenyan organizations were interviewed who seem to espouse Patterson's (2003) servant-leadership theory's construct of service and the Kenyan *harambee*. The individual leaders and managers were drawn from the executive and upper management units that are charged with instituting and directing organizational vision/mission and policies. Such individual leaders and managers represented corporate organizations, governmental organizations, non-governmental organizations (NGOs), and institutions of higher learning.

The number of the leaders and managers was considered significant to identify themes and patterns that are meaningful theoretically and empirically (Bryman & Burgess, 1999; Mason, 2002), even though they may not be generalizable to a larger universe (Yin, 1994).

Data Collection

A standardized open-ended interview, which involves preparing a set of open-ended questions that are carefully worded and arranged for the purpose of minimizing variation in the questions posed to the participants, was used to collect data (Huberman & Miles, 2002). The main questions were customized according to what the researcher thinks the participant might know about servant-leadership theory's construct of service. Though the questions were open enough to encourage participants to express their own opinions and experiences, they were also narrow enough to keep them from wandering too far off from the subject at hand. Probes were used to help specify the level of depth that the researcher wanted (Rubin & Rubin, 1995).

All the interviews, which took an average of sixty minutes, were taped and transcribed verbatim; an audit trail was maintained (Merriam, 1988).

Data Analysis

Qualitative data analysis is essentially about detection, and the tasks of defining, categorizing, theorizing, explaining, exploring, and mapping are fundamental to the role of the analyst (Huberman and Miles, 2002). As per Rubin and Rubin (1995), the goal of the analysis is to find themes that both explain the research arena and fit together in a way that a reader can understand. Thus, the analysis must move from summarizing the data, to identifying related themes and patterns, to discovering relationships among the themes and patterns (coding), and to developing explanations for these relationships (interpretations) (Walsh, 2003).

Summarizing Data

After every interview, the researcher had the audiotaped interview results transcribed for qualitative data analysis. After the audiotaped interviews were transcribed, the researcher read the interview results, paragraph by paragraph and word by word, marking off the main ideas, issues, concepts, or themes mentioned during the contact (Rubin & Rubin, 1995).

Coding Data

The researcher used NUD*IST, a computer program that provides for non-numerical unstructured data indexing, searching, and theory-building. The program allowed for the coding of the transcribed data. In other words, the researcher was able to sort data into categories based on participant emphasis and frequent use of concepts, terms, or key words that are indicative of servant-leadership and the construct of service.

Interpreting Data

Once coding was completed, a cross-interview analysis (Patton, 2002) was conducted to group data into categories that allowed the researcher to compare what different leaders said, the themes that were discussed, and how concepts were understood. This involved comparing the material within the categories to look for variations and nuances in the meaning of servant-leadership theory's construct of service, as well as across the categories in order to discover connections between themes (Rubin & Rubin, 1995).

The categories that resulted were used to create overarching themes that guided the development of a theoretical model of servant-leadership theory's construct of service, in which the researcher presented a "logical chain of evidence" (Walsh, 2003, p. 69), and eventually offered the implications of the study (Rubin & Rubin, 1995).

FINDINGS

Twenty-five leaders and managers from four organizational sectors—NGOs, institutions of higher learning, corporate organizations, and governmental organizations—were interviewed; all of the interviewees hold college degrees and most of them hold an advanced degree (e.g., master's and doctorates) in addition to having been in positions of leadership for a number of years in their organizations. In total, nine CEOs, three deputy CEOs, and thirteen division heads were interviewed. Twenty-two males and three females were interviewed.

Using a text search in NUD*IST, the researchers were able to quickly pull together all material from the imported documents containing a reference to a word or group of words, phrases, or patterns of characters related to the construct of service. The analysis of the responses resulted in seven categories: (a) role modeling, (b) sacrificing for others, (c) meeting the needs of others (employees) and developing them, (d) service as a primary function of leadership, (e) recognizing and rewarding employees, (f) treating employees with respect (humility), and (g) involving others (employees) in decision-making.

Role Modeling

The participants stated that the primary way they demonstrated service to their followers was by role modeling or leading by example; they expect leadership to be the best example in any situation, as it allows others to see what is required and how it is done. The participants asserted that one of their responsibilities as leaders and managers is to influence others through their own actions; they asserted that they like leading by example because if one wants things to be done in a specific manner, that is the best way to demonstrate the precise way in which one wants something to be done.

A total of nineteen out of the twenty-five participants interviewed indicated that they demonstrate service to their followers through role modeling. Of the nineteen participants, seven indicated that role modeling signals to others (employees) what the leader perceives to be important. For instance, S. M., a legal advisor for a bank, expressed that whatever he does triggers a sense of importance and direction as far as the employees are concerned. He stated, "We like leading by example; we realize that if you want things to be done in a specific manner, you be the first person to do it" (personal communication, November 2, 2004).

Five of the nineteen participants stated that role modeling is the best way to influence others. For example, B. W., a principal consultant, believes he influences others primarily through his behavior. He stated, "A leader leads by example. It is how I treat customers here; it is how I treat other people that has more influence than what I tell them. It is more what I do, not what I say" (personal communication, September 25, 2004).

Five of the nineteen participants expressed that leaders should "walk the talk." In other words, they should not "preach water and then drink wine." Two of the nineteen participants expressed that the leader must be an example of good service to others. J. L., a general manager, explained:

> The leader must ensure that he/she is an example of good service to the guests or to the general public; then from there the workers, who are under him or her, will follow suit and take a good example from him or her. (Personal communication, October 18, 2004)

Thus, the participants strongly believed that service is about role modeling. In other words, leaders are best understood and most influential when they lead by example.

Sacrificing for Others

The participants' view of sacrificing for others is embedded in the way they give their time, resources, and even themselves for work that benefits others. The participants indicated that they have accepted low pay on many occasions in order to serve others. The idea of sacrificing for others also borders on the Kenyan *harambee* philosophy.

A total of sixteen out of the twenty-five participants interviewed indicated that they sacrifice in order to serve others, mainly their followers. Seven of the sixteen participants strongly expressed a desire to sacrifice their time, resources, and self in order to serve others. For instance, according to C. L., a departmental chairman at a university, leaders should even go to the extent of spending personal resources for the welfare of the people they are leading. He explained:

> There are some ways you spend your own money to make sure that the group you are leading or the unit you are leading actually succeeds. So to the extent that a leader even spends one's own money—personal resources in it suggests that the leader does not treat the job from a purely official standpoint, but treats it at the personal level as well, and sees personal stake in the matter. (Personal communication, November 4, 2004)

Two participants, both from government, expressed that working for the government has been an act of sacrifice due to a lack of necessary resources. An example is J. N., a principal engineer, who said that working for the government calls for endurance and great sacrifice. He explained, "I have personally worked for twenty years and have served in many areas. But I have to be honest with you that we have so many limitations" (e.g. equipment) (personal communication, October 26, 2004).

Three of the sixteen participants stated that their current jobs have been labors of love. In other words, their pay is not commensurate with their training and their contributions. For instance, C. K., a director general, felt strongly that his profession could have taken him far if he had chosen not to sacrifice for others. He explained,

> I want to believe that my being here has been because I have sacrificed to be here. Technically, my profession could have taken me elsewhere for better pay if that is what I wanted. First and foremost, I saw myself contributing to the growth of the industry in this country at various levels as I grew up in the system. I went to the extent of sacrificing, rather going for low salary for job satisfaction. You know public service in this country is not well paying, and I have been around without what I think I am worth. (Personal communication, November 3, 2004)

Four of the sixteen participants expressed that service borders on the Kenyan *harambee* philosophy, which calls for sacrificing for the benefit of others. In the following excerpt from an interview, C. L. explains his idea of the connection between service (sacrifice) and *harambee*:

> You see there are two ways in which you can look [at] or understand service. One, of course, you can look at the standpoint of the *harambee* philosophy, which is serving by sacrificing for the interests of others. So that is one, which borders on something like voluntary, probably sacrifice, dedication of your time and profession to the service of others. (Personal communication, November 4, 2004)

Thus, the participants believed that it is almost impossible to serve people (others) without sacrifice. Sacrifice borders on the Kenyan *harambee* philosophy, which calls on leaders to make a great sacrifice for the service of others.

Meeting the Needs of Others (Employees) and Developing Them

The participants expressed that leaders should sufficiently remunerate their employees (offer competitive salaries or wages, medical coverage, travel bonuses, and loan schemes), create a productive working environment (in terms of equipment and other materials), guide employees in identifying their personal and professional goals, and develop them through training. These are indicators that the participants view the employees as the greatest assets that any functional organization can have.

A total of twenty-one out of the twenty-five participants interviewed provided strong views indicating that they care about meeting the physical and the developmental needs of their employees. Eight of the twenty-one participants offered the belief that people only follow leaders who are ready to meet their needs. This was the case with G. N., a professor and vice-chancellor of a university, who said,

> You can only lead if there are followers, and people are likely to follow if they can see that their interests are being taken care of. They are more easily [able] to follow if they can identify the one they are supposed to follow, and people are identified best if they see a person who is ready to listen to them and to respond to their needs. (Personal communication, September 6, 2004)

Five of the twenty-one participants said that providing a productive working environment for the workers has always been a core agenda for them. For example, J. M., a manager, expressed the belief that giving employees the priorities they deserve will cause them to take good care of the company's clients. Six of the twenty-one participants indicated that they are attuned to helping others to achieve their goals and objectives, while four of the twenty-one participants said that they put emphasis on developing their followers through training. For instance, C. K. asserted that if employees are to be able to provide an efficient service, they need to be trained in that area of service. He explained, "They should have customer care in their portfolio. It means you have to train them to be able to appreciate the customer; they have to appreciate that they are providing a very essential service" (personal communication, November 3, 2004).

Eight of the twenty-one participants made comments suggesting that employees are the most valuable assets they have in their organizations. J. O. acknowledged this perception when he said, "Our employees, as few as they are—we must recognize that they are the most important resource that this organization has" (personal communication, September 13, 2004). Thus, the participants were ebullient about pursuing the holistic needs of their employees.

Service as a Primary Function of Leadership

The participants did not find a dichotomy between service and leadership. They said that the two concepts are so intertwined that they can be used interchangeably. They expressed that leadership is about providing a service, that leadership does not exist in the absence of service, that service delivery is possible only through leaders that model it, and that service calls for strict adherence to certain key leadership principles.

A total of eighteen out of the twenty-five participants interviewed offered incendiary views of service as the primary function of leadership. Seven of the eighteen participants perceived leadership as service first. One among them was J. O., who saw service as the main function of leadership. He explained, "A leader is out there to serve, not to be served. Anybody who occupies any position of leadership must know at the very onset that their very function as they occupy those positions is to serve, to be selfless" (personal communication, September 13, 2004).

Five of the eighteen participants expressed the belief that leadership is futile and meaningless if service is not there. The following quotation from G. M., an executive director, emphasizes the fact that leadership and service cannot be divorced from one another:

> In the absence of service or [in the event of] poor quality service, then leadership has no meaning. In our case, for example, if it transpires that the services we are offering in our clinics and the field offices are not meeting the expectations of the communities out there, that has a reflection directly on the leadership of the organization. If we are able to anticipate properly, correctly, the needs of the community members, the poor people out there, and satisfy that need through offering our services, that has a reflection on leadership. (Personal communication, September 23, 2004)

Six of the eighteen participants expressed that service is best delivered when it is modeled. For instance, K. W., a director, asserted that modeling keeps a leader from accumulating extra work because his or her employees look at him or her as a role model and emulate his or her behavior. He stated, "So in your provision of your services to the customers, the kind of leadership you show to your employees is what they will copy. If your leadership is bad, if it is crooked, your staff will be crooked" (personal communication, October 8, 2004).

Four of the eighteen participants indicated that they identify service with certain fundamental leadership principles. These include integrity and excellence, which are described as being among the most important qualities of a leader. S. S., a doctor, mentioned these principles while discussing service and leadership. He stated, "One of them is servant-leadership, another one is excellence, another one is integrity, and another one is cherishing family" (personal communication, August 3, 2004).

Hence, leadership and service cannot be divorced from one another. In other words, leaders are simply out to serve others (their constituents or followers) selflessly by giving their time and even their resources.

Recognizing and Rewarding Employees

The participants said that recognizing and rewarding employees (for their contributions) takes center stage in their organizations. They offer this recognition at various times and in a variety of ways, include putting measures and systems in place to affirm employees, using verbal and written messages when addressing them, hosting parties and get-togethers for them, and promoting divergent views as part of a learning process.

A total of sixteen out of the twenty-five participants interviewed offered the necessary support to the notion of the importance of recognizing and rewarding employees. Four of the sixteen participants said that they already have some measures and systems in place to affirm the employees in the organization. These measures and systems provide a way of granting awards and promotions to the outstanding workers while putting pressure on those who are less hardworking and committed.

In addition, seven of the sixteen participants said that they emphasize both verbal and written messages as part of recognizing and appreciating their employees for excellent performance. For instance, I. B., a director, believes people get even more energized when they are offered appreciation in public, something not many leaders do (personal communication, September 24, 2004).

Two of the sixteen participants indicated that partying, get-togethers, and common celebrations act as a precursor to recognizing and rewarding employees. One of these participants was S. S. who said that employees are rewarded and recognized through various celebrations, stating, "Everybody's birthday is celebrated in this office. Also, every now and then we come together for parties just to say thank you to the employees. Our leaders truly appreciate the employees and the employees reciprocate by giving excellent, topnotch [service]" (personal communication, August 3, 2004).

Four of the sixteen participants stated that they promote the expression of divergent views by their employees in order to encourage and motivate them. An example is M. K., a director who expressed the belief that divergent views are not necessarily negative. Thus, participants do a variety of things as part of recognizing and encouraging their employees. This encourages and motivates them a great deal.

Treating Employees with Respect (Humility)

According to the participants, leaders who adopt humility exercise great respect for others. As practitioners of this virtue, the participants reported seeing and regarding everybody as equal and important, taking the time to listen to others (having an open door policy), and handling corrections and criticisms in a manner that builds up the individual rather than destroying the individual.

A total of seventeen out of the twenty-five participants interviewed gave splendid and detailed support for the idea that treating others with respect is a sign of humility. Twelve of the seventeen leaders and managers uttered variations on the theme of valuing all and seeing them as equal and important. One among them was I. B., who said that people should be regarded equally even though they play different roles and functions:

> I would like to see everybody as a person who is created equally. To me, it does not matter if it is my deputy or a janitor; they have got the same value, they are human beings, and I try to treat them equally. They do different jobs, they have different roles, but they have a human value that is equal. (Personal communication, September 13, 2004)

Similarly, P. K., a dean of faculty at a university, emphasized the importance of humility. He stated, "Humility is important because everybody's self-worth must be allowed to show" (personal communication, November 3, 2004).

Nine of the seventeen participants stated that they understand the open door policy as a cardinal element of leadership. They stressed their belief in leaving their doors opened wide so that their employees and customers can access them without much difficulty. For instance, K. W. indicated that they operate more or less in an open system. He explained, "This door is permanently opened; anybody can walk in; there is nobody, from the lowest to the highest, who will say they need an appointment to see the boss; they just walk in" (personal communication, October 8, 2004). K. W. also observed that great ideas have come from his employees as a result of his listening to them. He explained: "I try to tell people that I have no monopoly of ideas. And whatever little project we are doing I listen to them, and some of the great ideas have come from employees, and they are very many" (personal communication, September 25, 2004).

The participants, however, observed that humility is a bit of a challenge to those who work for the government, where orders and directives must be followed to the letter. According to J. N., working for the government calls for endurance and great sacrifice. He noted:

> We are a hard industry, whereby when orders are given they must be followed to the letter. You see governments operate by orders and directives, some of which do not necessarily require humility. But I always endeavor to communicate and I always try to put a human face and touch [on situations]. (Personal communication, October 26, 2004)

Four of the seventeen participants indicated that humility calls for leaders who are ready and willing to correct and criticize others in a manner that does not destroy them but that builds them up. For instance, B. W. said that he never allows his employees to be reprimanded publicly because, as he put it,

I treat them and I listen to them and I have time for them and nobody is allowed, even my supervisors, to reprimand anybody in public. I tell them to take them aside and tell them slowly, quietly, what they have done wrong. (Personal communication, September 25, 2004)

Involving Others (Employees) in Decision-Making

The participants strongly believed they have no monopoly on ideas and that there is always need to consult others before making any decisions. They said that they consult with their staff in departmental meetings, offer them training on teamwork, accept and respect their views and opinions, and generally view consensual decisions as having a motivating impact.

A total of twenty-two out of the twenty-five participants interviewed offered a paragon of support in terms of involving others in decision-making. Eleven of the twenty-two participants said they consult with their deputies and other staff members before making most of their decisions. An example is J. M., who stressed seeking individual views and then matching them together in order to get the best solution to any problem. He stated, "We do it in the perspective of meetings of key heads of departments, where we all, the general manager, the heads of departments, will come together and say what problems, what challenges" (personal communication, October 7, 2004). Similarly, J. N. said they usually build consensus before making collective decisions on many issues. He stated:

One of the most common ways of building consensus in our organization is to meet as heads of branches to discuss various problems affecting the organization. This way we are able to take collective decisions on issues dealing with description, service, and ability to meet goals, and generally to plan and assess completed projects. (Personal communication, October 26, 2004)

Three of the twenty-two participants said they have adopted the principle of teamwork in their organizations. They argued that unlike in the past, when leadership often took the form of intimidation, employees are now receiving training on team spirit. For instance, O. P. stated, "What they are trying to do the last two years is train people on team basis, teamwork, and I believe that is the direction that the organization wants things to go" (personal communication, August 21, 2004).

Five of the twenty-two participants offered that they always take into account the opinions of others whenever they make decisions. They said that soliciting people's ideas and suggestions and then agreeing to accept and respect the popular views plays a part in good leadership.

Six of the twenty-two participants expressed that consensus has a motivating impact. They said that when decisions are reached by consensus, people get highly motivated and they will make sure that the decisions or solutions reached are fully implemented. This idea is supported by J. O., who stated:

> What we are noticing is that through consensus-building, through participation and through a review of different viewpoints, then we are likely to build the consensus, and the most important thing about consensus-building is that it has a motivating impact. When everybody feels they participated in the decisions, then they buy in; [they have] the momentum with which they will implement it and see to it that it is not the portion of the greater. (Personal communication, September 13, 2004)

DISCUSSION

The leaders and managers who participated in this study gave statements and comments that led to the emergence of themes reminiscent of Patterson's (2003) servant-leadership theory's construct of service and the Kenyan *harambee* philosophy. A brief discussion of the following themes is presented:

Role Modeling

The participants in this study stated that one of their major ways of demonstrating and practicing service is by modeling their behavior and actions. They said that role modeling signals to their followers what is important and expected of them. The Kenyan *harambee* philosophy became a success because the leaders modeled and lived it. It was the leaders, along with the help of their communities, who spearheaded *harambee* as an undertaking for collective good (Bailey, 1993).

Sacrificing for Others

The participants in this study expressed strong feelings about sacrificing for the sake of others. Their view of sacrificing is embedded in the way they give their time, their resources, and even themselves for the work of others. Those participants working for the government especially indicated that circumstances (e.g., inadequate resources—such as a lack of equipment) force them to sacrifice a great deal. The idea of sacrificing for others borders on the Kenyan *harambee* philosophy, which is guided by the principle of collective good rather than individual gain. The *harambee* philosophy for the most part embodies mutual assistance, joint effort, mutual social responsibility, and community reliance. In other words, the end product benefits the general public as opposed to an individual (Chieni, 1997). According to Hill (1991), it is African traditions of community cooperation and mutual aid that are the foundation of the *harambee* philosophy.

Meeting the Needs of Others (Employees) and Developing Them

Like the proponents of the *harambee* philosophy, the participants indicated a willingness to invest their own time, energies, and personal resources for the benefit of the employees. The participants also recognized training as a way of guiding their followers in order to identify and develop their personal as well as professional goals. All these are in line with Wright's (1984) "African communalism," in which life's means are seen to be relatively minimal and natural resources scarce, and hence every individual must depend on his or her community. According to Mibigi and Maree (1995), some of the prevalent African values (e.g., *ubuntu*) put emphasis on a person's living for others rather than for the self.

Service as a Primary Function of Leadership

The participants indicated that service is a fundamental goal in their careers. As a matter of fact, they did not find a dichotomy between leadership and service. They expressed that leadership is all about providing a service. In other words, a leader is simply out there to serve and be selfless. Such exuberance and enthusiasm about service is not a strange viewpoint, given that some of the prevalent African values (e.g., *ubuntu*) put emphasis on the person's living not for himself or herself, but rather living for others (Mibigi & Maree, 1995). Similar emphasis is found in Mbiti's (1969) often- quoted line: "I am because we are; and since we are, therefore I am" (p. 10) from his widely read book, *African Religions and Philosophy*.

The *harambee* philosophy calls on Kenyan leaders to serve their constituents by being a part of the self-help projects that are aimed at promoting the common good (Chieni, 1997). The participants' view of service as being a primary function of leadership also resembles the traditional African view of leadership, which places the community's interests (service) ahead of its own (Ayittey, 1992).

Recognizing and Rewarding Employees

According to the participants in this study, recognizing and rewarding employees takes center stage. The participants have put certain measures and systems in place (e.g., performance appraisal) that provide the criteria for promotion and awards granting. They use both verbal and written messages to express appreciation for, and recognize, excellent performance. The expression of divergent views is also promoted as part of encouraging and motivating employees.

Since individual achievements are much less valued than are interpersonal relations in African traditions (Dia, 1994), not much emphasis is given to recognizing or rewarding those who do well; rather, doing well is taken as an obligation that has to be fulfilled. Furthermore, Africans see themselves as part of a community and not as discrete individuals (Bell, 2002). Thus, even those who take part in *harambee* efforts are seen as fulfilling what society requires and expects of them and not as anything special or extraordinary. This is not to say that recognizing and rewarding those who do well is unheard of in African values and traditions; it is just that it is not overemphasized. It is more implicit than explicit.

Treating Employees with Respect (Humility)

According to the participants in this study, every employee has a right, a voice, and the same human value, even though each performs different functions and has different responsibilities. They indicated that they adopt an open door policy so that their employees and customers can access them without much difficulty. Corrections and criticisms are also handled in a manner that builds the individual up instead of destroying the individual. Humility, which allows everybody's self-worth to show, is rooted in the *harambee* philosophy, which encourages mutual sharing of resources (mutual social responsibility) for the benefit of others. It calls for people to be mindful of each other's welfare—whether rich or poor, whether black or white (Chieni, 1997).

It is, however, important to note that leaders in government acknowledged that strict adherence to orders and the public service tradition of elevating the boss above everybody else hamper the development and practice of humility. They indicated that the government still operates via orders and directives, some of which do not necessarily require humility. This is not a strange occurrence, since government officials still tend to adopt the colonial mentality of controlling employees and intimidating them instead of being humble. Since the *harambee* philosophy is a product of government legislation, we should see more government officials embrace humility in their dealings with others.

Involving Others in Decision-Making

The participants in this study strongly believed in making nearly all their decisions on a consensual basis, indicating they usually get in collective talks as heads of departments before making any key decisions. The participants stated that organizations are now inculcating a culture of teamwork and team spirit and that many of their people are receiving training in these areas. According to Ayittey (1992), plurality decisions are extrapolated from a crucial pattern of traditional African leadership, which inexorably puts the community interest (service) ahead of its own. For instance, the chief did not rule, but rather served and led by consensus. Similarly, Mamadou (1991) observed that the traditional judge in black Africa is more intent on reaching consensus than in litigating by the book. Mersha (2000) also noted that a study based on Kenyan industries showed that both workers and managers preferred a modern democratic style of leadership to build consensus and trust.

CONCLUSION

This chapter examined the construct of service in the context of Kenyan leaders and managers. In other words, it sought to determine whether Kenyan leaders and managers of varied organizational settings understand and apply the construct of service. It emerged that (a) role modeling, (b) sacrificing for others, (c) meeting the needs of others (employees) and developing them, (d) viewing service as a primary function of leadership, (e) recognizing and rewarding employees, (f) treating employees with respect (humility), and (g) involving others in decision-making were prevalent themes consistent with Patterson's (2003) construct of service. These characteristics help leaders to both lead and serve their employees. This study found that in the Kenyan context, the construct of service is understood and applied by Kenyan leaders and managers of varied organizational settings, namely government, business corporations, NGOs, and academic institutions.

NOTES

1. This chapter was previously published as Koshal J. O., & Patterson, K. (2008). A Kenyan on servant-leadership: Harambee and service. *The International Journal of Servant-Leadership.* 4(1). 245-279.

2. All interviewee names have been anonymized and oral consent was provided for the use of their words in this chapter.

REFERENCES

A draft discussion document towards a white paper on traditional leadership and institutions. (2000). Available at http://209.85.173.104/search?q= cache:VEpIZNgAV wkJ:www.thedplg.gov.za/index2.php%3Foption%3Dcm _content%26do_pdf%3D l%26id%3D285+A+DRAFT+DISCUSSION+ DOCUMENT+TOWARDS+A+W HITE+PAPER+ON+TRADITIONAL+ LEADERSHIP+INSTITUTIONS&h l=en&ct=clnk&cd=4&gl=us

An Afro-Centric Alliance (2001). Indigenizing organizational change: Localization in Tanzania and Malawi. *Journal of Managerial Psychology, 16*(1), 59–78.

Arjoon, S. (2000). Virtue theory as a dynamic theory of business. *Journal of Business Ethics, 28,* 159.

Autry, J. A. (2001). *The Servant-Leader: How to build a Creative Team, develop great morale, and Improve Bottom Line Performance.* Roseville, CA: Prima Publishing.

Ayittey, G. B. N. (1992). *Africa betrayed.* New York: A Cato Institute Book.

Bailey, J. (1993). *Kenya: The National Epic.* Nairobi, Kenya: Kenway Publications.

Bass, B. M. (1995). Concepts of leadership: The beginnings. In J. T. Wren (ed.), *The leader's companion: Insights on Leadership Through the ages* (pp. 50–69). New York: The Free Press.

Bell, R. H. (2002). *Understanding African philosophy: A Cross-Cultural Approach to classical and Contemporary Issues.* New York: Routledge.

Bennis, W., & Nanus, B. (1985). *Leaders: The strategies for Taking Charge.* New York: Harper and Row.

Blanchard, K. (1997). Situational leadership. In K. Shelton (ed.), *A New Paradigm of leadership: Visions of excellence for 21st Century Organizations* (pp. 149–153). Provo, UT: Executive Excellence Publishing.

———. (2000). Leadership by the book. *Executive Excellence, 17*(13), 4–6.

Bradley, Y. (1999). Servant-leadership: A critique of Robert Greenleaf's concept of leadership. *Journal of Christian Education, 42*(2), 44–53.

Branch, S. (1999). The 100 best companies to work for in America. *Fortune, 139,* 118.

Bryman, A., & Burgess, R. G. (eds.). (1999). *Qualitative research.* Thousand Oaks, CA: Sage Publications.

Chieni, S. N. (1997). *The harambee movement in Kenya: The role played by Kenyans and the government in the provision of education and other social services.* Retrieved July 17, 2003, from http://boleswa97.tripod.com/chieni.htm

Covey, S. (2002). Servant-leadership and community leadership in the twenty-first century. In L. Spears (ed.), *Focus on leadership: Servant-leadership for the 21st century* (pp. 27–34). New York: John Wiley & Sons, Inc.

Creswell, J. A. (1994). *Research design: Qualitative & Quantitative Approaches.* Thousand Oaks, CA: Sage.

Dia, M. (1994). Indigenous management practices: Lessons for Africa's management in the '90s. In I. Serageldin & J. Taboroff (eds.), *Culture and development in Africa* (pp. 165–191). Washington, D.C.: World Bank.

Douglas, M. E. (2003). Servant-leadership: An emerging supervisory model. *Supervision, 64*(2), 6–9. Retrieved June 11, 2003, from ABI/Inform Global.

Ellsworth, R. R. (2002). *Leading with purpose: The New Corporate Realities.* Stanford, CA: Stanford University Press.

Fairholm, G. W. (1997). *Capturing the heart of leadership: Spirituality and community in the new American workplace.* Westport, CT: Praeger.

Farling, M. L., Stone, A. G., & Winston, B. (1999). Servant-leadership: Setting the stage for empirical research. *Journal of Leadership Studies, 6*(1/2), 49–72.

Fletcher, M. (1999). The effects of internal communication, leadership and team performance on successful service quality implementation: A South African perspective. *Team Performance Management, 5,* 150.

Fuller, T. (ed.). (2000). *Leading & leadership.* Notre Dame, IN: University of Notre Dame.

Gakuru, O. (1998). Lean on me. *Orbit, 68.* Retrieved July 7, 2003, from http://www .oneworld.org/vso/pubs/orbit/68/volunt.htm

Galvin, T. (2001). A culture of the heart. *Training, 38*(3), 80–81.

Greenleaf, R. K. (1977). *Servant leadership: A journey into the nature of Legitimate Power and greatness.* New York: Paulist Press.

Hill, M. J. D. (1991). *The Harambee Movement in Kenya: Self-help, development and education among the Kamba of Kitui District.* Atlantic Highlands, NJ: The Athlone Press.

Huberman, A. M., & Miles, M. B. (2002). *The Qualitative Researcher's Companion.* Thousand Oaks, CA: Sage Publications.

International: The view from the slums: Kenyan corruption. (2002). *The Economist, 363,* 56.

Joseph, J. A. (1997). The idea of African renaissance: Myth or reality? *Vital Speeches of the Day, 64*(5), 133–135. Retrieved July 6, 2003, from ABI/Inform Global database.

Kanungo, R. N., & Mendonca, M. (1996). *Ethical dimensions of leadership.* Thousand Oaks, CA: Sage Publications.

Kouzes, J. M., & Posner, B. Z. (1993). *Credibility: How Leaders Gain and Lose It, Why People Demand It.* San Francisco, CA: Jossey-Bass.

Laub, J. A. (1999). Assessing the servant organization: Development of the Organizational Leadership Assessment (OLA) instrument. *Dissertation Abstracts Online.* Retrieved October 17, 2003. (AAT 9921922)

Lee, C., & Zemke, R. (1993). The search for spirit in the workplace. *Training, 30*(6), 21–35. Retrieved May 28, 2003, from Inform/Global database.

Levering, R., & Moskowitz, M. (2000). The 100 best companies to work for in America. Portland, OR: Plume.

Levering, R., & Moskowitz, M. (2001). The 100 best companies to work for in America. *Fortune, 143*(3), 60–61.

Lowe, J. (1998). Trust: The invaluable asset. In Spears, L. C. (ed.), *Insights on Leadership* (pp. 69–76). New York: John Wiley & Sons.

Lubin, K. A. (2001). Visionary leader behaviors and their congruency with servant leadership characteristics. *Dissertation Abstracts Online.* Retrieved January 15, 2004. (AAT 3022943)

Mamadou, D. (1991). Development and cultural values in Sub Saharan Africa. *Finance & Development, 28*(4), 10. Retrieved July 6, 2003, from ABI/ Inform Global.

Mason, J. (2002). *Qualitative researching* (2nd edition). Thousand Oaks, CA: Sage Publications.

Mbithi, P., & Rasmusson, R. (1977). *Self-reliance in Kenya: The case of harambee.* Uppsala: Scandinavian Institute of African Studies.

Mbiti, J. (1969). *African religions and philosophies.* London: Heinemann.

McLaughlin, K. (2001). A strong foundation. *Training, 38*(3), 84.

Melrose, K. (1995). *Making the Grass Greener on Your Side: A CEO's journey to leading by service.* San Francisco, CA: Berrett-Koehler Publishers.

Mersha, T. (2000). Quality, competitiveness in sub-Saharan Africa. *Industrial Management and Data Systems, 100*(3), 119-124. Retrieved June 11, 2003, from ABI/Inform Global.

Mibigi, L., & Maree, J. (1995). *Ubuntu: The spirit of African transformation management.* Johannesburg: Knowledge Resources.

Miles, M. G., & Huberman, A. M. (1994). *Qualitative Data Analysis* (2nd edition). Beverly Hills, CA: Sage Publications.

Morse, J. M., & Richards, L. (2002). *Read Me First for a User's Guide to Qualitative Methods.* Thousand Oaks, CA: Sage Publications.

Murray, M. (1997). Philanthropy: No better arena for servants and leaders. *Executive Speeches, 12*(2), 27–30.

Nair, K. (1994). *A Higher Standard of leadership: Lessons from the life of Gandhi.* San Francisco, CA: Berrett-Koehler Publishers.

Ndegwa, S. N. (1996). *The Two Faces of Civil Society: NGOs and politics in Africa.* West Hartford, CT: Kumarian Press, Inc.

Nelson, L. (2003). *An exploratory study of the application and acceptance of servant-leadership theory among black leaders in South Africa.* Regent University: Digital Dissertations. (UMI No. 3086676)

Ngau, P. M. (1987). Tensions in empowerment: The experience of the harambee (self-help) movement in Kenya. *Economic Development and Cultural Change, 35*(3), 523–538. Retrieved April 17, 2004, from ABI/Inform Global.

Nyabadza, G. W. (2003). Leadership at the peak—the 10th trait of effective leaders: Servant-leadership [Electronic version]. *Zimbabwe Independent-AAGM.* Retrieved January 20, 2004, from LexisNexis.

Patterson, K. (2003). *Servant-leadership theory: A theoretical definition and a presentation of the virtues of the servant-leader including love, humility, altruism, vision, trust, empowerment and service.* Regent University: Digital Dissertations. (UMI No. 3082719)

Patton, M. Q. (2002). *Qualitative research & Evaluation Methods* (3rd edition). Thousand Oaks, CA: Sage Publications.

Pollard, W. C. (1997). The leader who serves. *Strategy and Leadership, 25*(5), 49–51. Retrieved May 27, 2003, from ABI/Inform Global.

Rubin, D. K., Powers, M. B., Tulacz, G., Winston, S., & Krizan, W. G. (2002). Leaders come in all shapes and sizes but the great ones focus on people. *Engineering News Record, 249*(23), 34–36. Retrieved May 28, 2003, from ABI/Inform Global.

Rubin, H. J., & Rubin, I. S. (1995). *Qualitative interviewing: The art of Hearing Data*. Thousand Oaks, CA: Sage Publications.

Russell, R. F., & Stone, A. G. (2002). A review of servant-leadership attributes: Developing a practical model. *Leadership and Organization Development Journal, 23*(3), 145–157.

Sarkus, D. J. (1996). Servant-leadership in safety: Advancing the cause and practice. *Professional Safety, 41*(6), 26–32.

Saunders, V. R. (1993, February). A few good leaders. *Training and Development, 47*(2), 4–6.

Shikuku, W. (2000). Why "harambee" spirit is dying. *Daily Nation*. Retrieved July 17, 2003, from http://www.nationaudio.com/News/DailyNation/24102000/Letters/Letters4.html

Seidman, I. (1998). *Interviewing as Qualitative Research: A guide for researchers in education and the Social Sciences* (2nd edition). New York: Teachers College Press.

Snyder, N. H., Dowd, J. J., Jr., & Houghton, D. M. (1994). *Vision, values and courage: Leadership for Quality Management*. New York: Free Press.

Spears, L. C. (1995). *Reflections on leadership: How Robert K. Greenleaf's theory of Servant Leadership Influenced Today's Top Management Thinkers*. New York: John Wiley & Sons, Inc.

———. (1996). Reflections on Robert K. Greenleaf and servant-leadership. *Leadership and Organization Development Journal, 17*(7), 33–35.

———. (ed.). (1998). *The power of Servant-Leadership: Essays by Robert K. Greenleaf*. San Francisco, CA: Berrett-Koehler Publishers, Inc.

———. (2002). Tracing the past, present, and future of servant-leadership. In L. C. Spears (Ed.), *Focus on leadership: Servant-leadership for the Twenty-First Century* (pp. 1–16). New York: John Wiley & Sons.

Spears, L. C., & Lawrence, M. (eds.). (2002). *Focus on leadership: Servant leadership for the Twenty-First Century*. New York: John Wiley & Sons, Inc.

Special feature: The canonization of blessed Josemaria Escriva. (2002). *Business World*, p. 1.

Stone, A. G., Russell, R. F., & Patterson, K. A. (2003). *Transformational versus servant-leadership: A difference in leader focus*. Paper presented at the Servant Leadership Roundtable, Regent University, Virginia Beach, VA.

Taninecz, G. (2002). Healing the corporate soul. *Chief Executive,* 8–11.

Tatum, J. (1995). Meditations on servant-leadership. In Spears, L. C. (ed.), *Reflections on Servant-Leadership* (p. 308). New York: John Wiley & Sons.

T'Shaka, O. (1990). *The art of leadership*. Richmond, CA: Pan Afrikan Publications.

Versely, M. (1997). Kenya's watershed elections. *African Business, 227,* 18–21. Retrieved July 6, 2003, from ABI/Inform Global.

Waiguchu, J. M., Tiagha, E., & Mwaura, M. (1999). *Management of organizations in Africa: A handbook and reference*. Westport, CT: Quorum Books.

Walsh, K. (2003). Qualitative research: Advancing the science and practice of hospitality. *Cornell Hotel and Restaurant Administration Quarterly, 44*(2), 66–74.

Wilson, L. S. (1992). The "Harambee" movement and efficient public good provision in Kenya. *Journal of Public Economics, 48*(1), 19.

Wis, R. M. (2002). The conductor as servant-leader. *Music Educators Journal, 89*(2), 17–23.

Wright, R. A. (ed.). (1984). *African philosophy: An introduction* (3rd edition). New York: University Press of America.

Yassin, A. (2004). Rethink new law that restricts participation in harambee. *Sunday Nation*. Retrieved April 17, 2004, from http://www.nationaudio.com/News/Dai lyNation/23112003/Letters/Letters231120039.html

Yin, R. K. (1994). *Case Study Research: Design and methods* (2nd edition). Thousand Oaks, CA: Sage Publications.

Yukl, G. (2002). *Leadership in organizations* (5th edition). Upper Saddle River, NJ: Prentice Hall.

Chapter 9

A Priest Forever

The Story of Rev. Florence Li Tim-Oi

Peter L. Lim

Apart[1] from sectarian movements, the institutionalized protestant churches by and large did not provide women with opportunities for ministry in the seventeenth and eighteenth centuries (Tucker & Liefeld, 1987, pp. 243–244). Nevertheless, the issue of women in ministry has become a hot topic for discussion since the 1970s and 1980s, even in a relatively smaller denomination such as the Church of God in Anderson, Indiana (Leonard, 1989, p. xiii). The ordination of women priests in the Anglican churches officially began in 1971 (Jones, 2004, p. 20). However, the fact that the ordination of the first woman priest within the Anglican Communion actually happened during World War II in wartime China remains unknown to many within the flock and beyond.

Florence Tim-Oi Li (hereafter referred to as Rev. Florence Li), a deaconess of the Anglican Diocese of Victoria, Hong Kong and South China, was ordained by her bishop in 1944 to address the sacramental needs of a congregation in a particular situation caused by the Japanese invasion of China. She surrendered her license in 1946 when she became aware of the pressure on her bishop and of the dispute her ordination had caused within the Anglican Communion. She continued to serve faithfully for the next thirty-nine years under extremely difficult circumstances, especially during the decades of political upheavals in Communist China.

Ted Harrison (1985) recognized that the story of Rev. Florence Li is "a story of the Anglican Church . . . a story of revolutionary China . . . but above all it is the story of a rare and extraordinary person" (p. viii). A study and examination of such a leader can indeed improve our ability to lead. With understanding that a biographical study allows us to learn from the weaknesses and strong points of its subject, I will explore the life and times of Rev. Florence Li with the intent of examining whether her leadership demonstrated Greenleaf's (1977) idea of servant-leadership.

The advantage of examining the life of Rev. Florence Li against the concept of servant-leadership is twofold: (a) appraising Rev. Florence Li's experience may help Anglican and other Protestants understand a significant yet somewhat unfamiliar ministry leader who provided pastoral leadership without recognition under very challenging conditions and (b) the study might help bring insights concerning certain aspects of Greenleaf's model of the servant-leader through engaging specific examples of her essential thoughts.

The structure of this chapter provides an overview of servant-leadership and a description of the life and times of Rev. Florence Li before examining her leadership. The chapter concludes by summarizing the findings from the examination, specifically whether the leadership of Rev. Florence Li demonstrated Greenleaf's (1977) idea of servant-leadership.

SERVANT-LEADERSHIP THEORY: A BRIEF OVERVIEW

The idea of the servant-leader was first proposed by Robert Greenleaf (1977) who believed that the servant-leader is by nature a servant first, before or after holding a position of leadership. The natural feeling to serve is followed by a conscious choice to lead and care for the best interests of others. According to Greenleaf (1974),

> The best test, and difficult to administer, is: Do those served grow as persons? Do they, *while being served*, become healthier, wiser, freer, more autonomous, more likely themselves to become servants? And, what is the effect on the least privileged in society; will they benefit, or, at least, not be further deprived? (p. 27)

Greenleaf crystallized his thought on the subject in the 1960s after reading Hermann Hesse's story about a spiritual pilgrimage, *Journey to the East*. The central figure in this story happens to be a servant serving a team of people embarking on a spiritual journey, but whose real identity is the head of the order that sponsored the journey. For Greenleaf, the essential meaning of the story was that the great leader is first a servant to others. Greenleaf emphasized the importance of the motivation of a leader, to serve or to lead, as an identification of true leadership (Spears, 1998, p. 30).

Greenleaf asserted that leadership is for the most part the result of personal characteristics rather than special leadership skills. In other words, it is performed not so much by doing as by "being" (Zohar, 1997, p. 146). At the same time, Greenleaf mentioned in his writings that a servant-leader must display a number of special abilities, such as listening and persuading

(Greenleaf, 1977, pp. 16–17, 29–30). Drawing upon Greenleaf's writings, Spears (1998) listed ten central characteristics of the servant-leader that "communicate the power and promise that the concept offers to those who are open to its invitation and challenge." The ten characteristics of the servant-leader are as follows:

1. Listening: The servant-leader "listens receptively to what is being said and unsaid."
2. Empathy: The "servant-leader strives to understand and empathize with others."
3. Healing: The "servant-leaders recognize that they have an opportunity *to help make whole* those with whom they come in contact."
4. Awareness: "General awareness, and especially self-awareness, strengthens the servant-leader."
5. Persuasion: The "servant-leader seeks to convince others, rather than coerce compliance."
6. Conceptualization: The "servant-leaders seek to nurture their abilities to *dream great dreams.*"
7. Foresight: "A characteristic that enables the servant-leader to understand the lessons from the past, the realities of the present, and the likely consequence of a decision for the future."
8. Stewardship: "Servant-leadership, like stewardship, assumes first and foremost a commitment to serving the needs of others."
9. Commitment to the growth of people: The "servant-leader recognizes the tremendous responsibility to do everything in his or her power to nurture the personal and professional growth of employees and colleagues."
10. Building community: "Servant-leadership suggests that true community can be created among those who work in businesses and other institutions." (pp. 4–6).

These ten characteristics of the servant-leader will be used to examine the leadership of Rev. Florence Li after a brief description of her life and times.

THE STORY OF FLORENCE LI

Rev. Florence Li was born in Shek Pai Bay, Aberdeen, a little village in the British colony of Hong Kong, on May 5, 1907. Her father, a physician turned headmaster of a local government school, gave her an interesting name: "Tim-Oi," which means "another much beloved daughter" in Chinese. Girls were generally undervalued and "despised" in Chinese society, but her father "was determined to show that a daughter can be loved and cherished"

(MacDonald, 1999, p. 34). At medical school, Mr. Li was a classmate and roommate of Dr. Sun Yat-Sen, the physician turned revolutionary.

Rev. Florence Li joined the congregation of the Anglican Church of St. Paul in her early twenties. She chose the name "Florence" as her Christian name at her baptism in remembrance of her role model Florence Nightingale. Harrison (1985) reported her sharing, "I so much wanted to be a selfless lady like (Nightingale). I admired her and the way she had comforted the wounded soldiers, as the lady with the lamp" (p. 18).

In 1932, shortly after Rev. Li joined the Anglican Church, Bishop Ronald Hall became the bishop of the diocese in 1849. Bishop Hall would later play a very significant role in Rev. Li's life.

Rev. Florence Li (1996) described hearing the call to ministry while attending the ordination of a deaconess in 1931. She wrote that she "knelt down reverently and responded to God, 'I am here. Please send me.'" She also wrote that she asked, "Am I suitable?" She discerned God's calling reverberating in her "ears" (p. 7).

She started her theological training at Union Theological College in Guangzhou, China, in 1934. She was ordained a deaconess on May 22, 1941 by Bishop Ronald Hall. She was then assigned to serve a congregation in the Portuguese colony of Macau, where a great number of refugees had fled as a result of the Japanese invasion of China. According to Harrison (1985), Portugal was not at war with Japan and "although the Japanese made life difficult for the people of the colony, they never invaded it" (p. 28). After Japan's occupation of Hong Kong on Christmas Day of 1941, Bishop Hall could no longer get permission to send priests from Hong Kong to Macau, and there was no one to administer the Sacrament.

Harrison (1985) reported that the bishop wrote a long letter to his friend, William Temple, the Archbishop of Canterbury, concerning his intention to ordain Rev. Florence Li, the then deaconess serving in Macau, to satisfy the pastoral needs of the congregation:

> I am not an advocate for the ordination of women. I am however determined that no prejudices should prevent the congregations committed to my care having the sacraments of the church. (p. 42)

In late December 1943, Rev. Florence Li received a letter from Bishop Ronald Hall inviting her to the Anglican Church of Shaoping, Guangdong, to be ordained as priest (Li, 1996). On January 25, 1944, the Feast of the Conversion of St. Paul, she was ordained and thus became the first woman priest in the Anglican Communion (Jones, 2004, p. 20).

Harrison (1985) noted that Bishop Hall wrote to Archbishop Temple two days later, reporting the ordination and explaining his action:

Please be sure that my reason was not the theoretical views of the equality of men and women but the needs of my people and the manifest gift of the charism. (p. 49)

The Archbishop's response to Bishop Hall's first letter, which stated that he did not approve of Rev. Li's ordination, came after that ordination due to "the unreliability of the wartime postal service" (Harrison, 1985, p. 49).

After the end of World War II in 1945, the war against the ordination of women began in the Anglican Church. The bishops at the Lambeth Conference indicated their opposition to Bishop Hall's ordination of Rev. Florence Li (Harrison, 1985, pp. 57–58). Rev. Li was summoned to Hong Kong in 1946 and was told that either Bishop Hall would have to resign or that Rev. Li would have to give up her ordination as priest (Li, 1996). Rev. Joyce Bennett (cited in Harrison, 1985) reported Rev. Florence Li's response. She wrote that she was only "a very tiny person, a mere worm, and her influence was very small" in comparison to Bishop Hall and that she did not require a title to continue in ministry (p. 52). With the letter, Rev. Florence Li gave up her license as priest but continued to carry out her priestly ministry. Two years later, the Chinese Communist Party came into power in China. As a result, Rev. Li was forced to minister in extremely difficult conditions, but she persevered (Harrison, 1985, pp. 66–110).

Rev. Florence Li left China in 1983 for Canada to serve in two Anglican churches in Toronto. She was officially reinstated as a priest in 1984, the fortieth anniversary of her ordination. She died in 1992.

AN ASSESSMENT OF REV. FLORENCE LI'S LEADERSHIP

Listening

Greenleaf noted the prayer of St. Francis, *"Lord, grant that I may not seek so much to be understood as to understand"* when he discussed listening. He believed that when faced with a problem, a true servant-leader's first inclination is to listen.

Rev. Florence Li was a good listener. According to Harrison (1985), she listened to her father's problem of not being wealthy enough to provide for her education after primary school and "for seven years she lived dutifully at home, helping to raise the younger children" (p. 6). She was in her early twenties when she was finally able to attend the Belilios Public School for Girls.

Her listening skill was also evident in her response to the controversy caused by her ordination. Having been told that Bishop Hall had broken the canon law by ordaining her as priest and that either he must resign as a bishop or she must give up her title as priest, she was quite troubled. Yet after meditation, she was able to appreciate the situation. In light of her respect for Bishop Hall's office, piety, and influence in China and around the world, she willingly surrendered her title as priest (Li, 1996). This is very much in tune with Spears' comments about the servant-leader's ability to listen "receptively to what is being said and unsaid" (Spears, 1998, p. 4).

Empathy

Greenleaf believed that leaders who empathize earn trust (Greenleaf, 1977). There were many stories concerning Rev. Li's ministry in Macau that testified to her empathetic spirit. One of those involved a certain Mrs. Leung whose husband had passed away; she dreaded the process of visiting the morgue to identify her husband's body and lacked the funds to purchase a coffin. Rev. Florence Li reported that she "gathered up enough courage to walk straight into the morgue" and guaranteed the payment for the coffin (p. 16).

Healing

Greenleaf (1977) asserted that as a servant-leader extends healing to others, they are also healed. An incident during the Cultural Revolution provided evidence of Rev. Li's actions in this area:

> For two weeks we were put to work in the YMCA grounds digging. They suspected we had arms hidden, buried underground . . . They tried their best to break us, to take away our dignity. Sometimes they shouted at those who didn't do what they were told. I tried my best to be obedient. I just did the digging. We found not a thing, not even a piece of iron. I try my best to forgive everyone. God understands everything . . . it's God's will to train us. I don't blame the Red Guards. They do not know, they do not understand. One day, I comfort myself, they will know. (Harrison, 1985, p. 94)

Greenleaf (1977) suggested that in terms of healing, the process is never complete (1977).

Awareness

Greenleaf (1977) believed that effective leaders are awake and in tune with the disturbance around them. In her year of "re-education" during a political "Cleansing Movement," Rev. Florence Li was asked to explain why Bishop

Hall would break the Anglican tradition and ordain her as the first woman priest (Li, 1996, p. 41), implying sexual indiscretion between her and the bishop. The same question had been asked by the Guangdong Provincial Ministry of Public Safety in 1958. She was very much aware of the regime's intention to damage the reputation of her bishop. Her handler finally withdrew after she gave her blunt reply: "Bishop Hall was my superior. His status was holy, and his character, pure. How could he turn from God's love and holiness to take advantage of his subordinate? I am willing to undergo medical test(s) to prove that I am untainted" (p. 42).

Persuasion

Rev. Florence Li's persuading ability was seen in action during the final days of her ministry in Macau before her reassignment to Guangdong Province following the controversy over her ordination:

> Before my transfer from Macau, I pondered over the fact that the Chunghua Shungkunghui did not have its own church premise. As church members could enjoy peace and a new beginning after the war by the mercy of God, I decided to bravely suggest to each member that he or she offer a thanksgiving donation towards a permanent church building as the home of the Macau parish . . . and for days I travelled around Guangzhou, Hong Kong, and Macau without rest, visiting parishioners to invite them to participate in this thanksgiving drive. Consequently, all pitched in. (Li, 1996, p. 23)

Very much like John Woolman's example in persuading his fellow Quakers to denounce and forbid slavery as referred to by Greenleaf (1977), Rev. Florence Li's action proved that leaders who choose persuasion have more sustainable outcomes than those who attempt to coerce.

Conceptualization

When Rev. Florence Li was sent along with other pastors to work in the factory during the Cultural Revolution, it was still very dangerous for them to share their faith openly. However, they were able to look beyond day-to-day realities:

> We didn't talk while we were working. Many of us liked to work honestly, quietly, faithfully and show our Christianity by example. We didn't talk about these things but we acted quietly, patiently, happily. We tried to do our work beautifully to show our Christianity. It was a silent witness. And the authorities saw what we were doing. The results in our factory were much better than in

the other factories. They noticed it and praised us for our honesty. Sometimes leaders would come and visit us and be very friendly and say good words to us. We were quite different from other factories. We are Christians. (Harrison, 1985, p. 99)

The "delicate balance between conceptual thinking and a day-to-day operational approach" (Spears, 1998, p. 5) was sought and attained by Rev. Florence Li and her fellow pastors in that "Christian factory."

Foresight

Spears (2004) defines foresight as "a characteristic that enables the servant-leader to understand the lessons from the past, the realities of the present, and the likely consequence of a decision for the future" (p.33). English teachers were in high demand when China decided to open its doors in 1979, and Rev. Florence Li was listed as a potential teacher. She was contacted by the Army Medical School to help a group of Army personnel learn about foreign lifestyles and learn the English language before their study abroad. She declined on medical grounds, as she had just gone through an eye surgery a year earlier. The real reason behind Rev. Li declining the invitation, however, was her belief that if she followed through, she might be subject to accusations of covertly entering military institutions to engage in anti-revolutionary activities (Li, 1996).

Stewardship

Servant-leaders often regard themselves as stewards (De Pree, 1989, p. 12; Senge, 1990, p. 7). Stewardship is essentially the willingness to be held responsible for the well-being of a larger community by working in the service of those around oneself (Block, 1993, p. 41). Rev. Florence Li's commitment to serve the needs of others was evident even before her ministry days. She accepted a position teaching children of fishermen upon graduation from secondary school. She "trekked over land and sea to render service with all heart and mind" (Li, 1996, p. 6).

Commitment to the Growth of People

According to Spears (1998), "Servant-leaders believe that people have an intrinsic value beyond their tangible contributions as workers. As such, the servant-leader is deeply committed to the growth of each and every individual within his or her organization" (p. 6). When Rev. Florence Li was transferred from Macau to Guangdong Province, she also took up a teaching position at a Provincial secondary school as an English teacher. She developed deep friendships with her colleagues and students. She formed both a Chinese and an English Bible study class for youth catechism. She also organized a Friends of Christ Society "so that young people could learn to love the church through fellowship life" (Li, 1996, p. 27). She did everything in her power to nurture her parishioners.

Building Community

Spears (1998) quoted Greenleaf in summarizing building community:

> All that is needed to rebuild community as a viable life form for large numbers of people is for enough servant-leaders to show the way, not by mass movements, but by each servant-leader demonstrating his or her unlimited liability for a quite specific community-related group. (p. 6)

Rev. Florence Li's (1996) writings indicate that she chose to support the Movement for the Ordination of Women in her final years even though she didn't fight to defend her ordination in her younger years:

> As Christians, we should understand God's will. God created both male and female, and we are all His children. He surely wants His children to work with each other and support each other in making "heaven on earth" a reality. Why are there unenlightened, intransigent, and obstinate people who want to strip away women's freedom to serve the Lord, and suppress their work? Could that be in accordance with Christ's teachings? (pp. 56–57)

In essence, Rev. Florence Li was working hard in her last days to build community within the Anglican Communion.

CONCLUSION

Rev. Florence Li heard others' ideas and valued them. She understood what was happening in others' lives and how they were affected. She was resolved to heal herself and her relationships with others. She had a strong awareness of what was going on. She sought to convince rather than to coerce. She was able to attain a balance between vision and reality. She was able to foresee a likely outcome of her situation based on lessons of her past and the realities of her days. She was willing to work for the well-being of those around her. She was committed to helping others grow. She created a sense of community among the women in ministry. She was a servant-leader.

Comments made by Archbishop Ted Scott in Toronto at the golden jubilee of her ordination illustrate the depth of both her servanthood and leadership:

> I do not think Florence was ever aware of the tremendous influence she had, both on individual persons and on the church. She influenced me very deeply and I know that she also influenced many leaders of the World Council of Churches. She had a great influence upon the thinking of the church. She modeled faithfulness, and when she was given the authority to do so, she modeled priesthood at its best. Her example led many people struggling with the issue, among them Archbishop Runcie, to move to a more positive stance vis-à-vis the ordination of women. (Li, 1996, p. 94)

Christopher Hall, son of the bishop who ordained Florence Li, commented that "she was not a woman who just happened to be around at that time and place. God had prepared her for her role in His story . . . . In the warmth of God's love, 'she showed us how the Christ she talked about is living now'" (Li, 1996, p. 99).

I have selected from Rev. Florence Li's life history a tapestry of stories that help illumine the characteristics of Greenleaf's servant-leadership. I want the stories to give voice to the life and essence of Rev. Florence Li. My hope is that in the interpretation I offer here a good beginning has been made for further research into the story of Rev. Florence Li and that her story can contribute to furthering the understanding of women in ministry.

NOTE

1. This chapter was previously published as Lim, P. (2007). A priest forever: The story of Rev. Florence Li Tim-Oi. *The International Journal of Servant-Leadership. 3*(1), 189–202.

REFERENCES

Block, P. (1993). *Stewardship: Choosing service Over Self-Interest.* San Francisco CA: Berrett-Koehler.

De Pree, M. (1989). *Leadership is an Art.* New York: Dell Publishing.

General Synod of the Anglican Church of Canada. (2005). *Explanatory note/background information to the General Synod 2004 resolution on memorial of Florence Li Tim-Oi.* Retrieved February 21, 2006, from http://www.anglican.ca/faith/worshi p/documents/Propers-Li Tim-Oi.pdf

Greenleaf, R. K. (1974). *Trustees as Servants.* Indianapolis, IN: The Greenleaf Center.

————. (1977). *Servant-leadership: A journey into the nature of Legitimate Power and greatness.* New York: Paulist Press.

Harrison, T. (1985). *Much Beloved Daughter: The story of Florence Li Tim Oi.* London: Darton, Longman and Todd Ltd.

Hesse, H. (1956). *Journey to the East.* New York: Noonday.

Jones, I. (2004). *Women and priesthood in the Church of England: Ten years on.* London: Church House.

Leonard, J. E. (ed.). (1989). *Called to minister...empowered to serve: Women in ministry and missions in the Church of God reformation movement.* Anderson, IN: Warner Press.

Li, F. T. O. (1996). *Raindrops of My Life: Memoirs of the Rev. Florence Li Tim-Oi.* Toronto: Anglican Book Center.

MacDonald, L. O. (1999). *In Good Company: Women in ministry.* Glasgow: Wild Goose Publications.

Senge, P. M. (1990). The leader's new work: Building learning organizations. *Sloan Management Review, 32*(1), 7–24.

Smith, E. J. (1999). *Bearing fruit in Due Season: Feminist hermeneutics and the Bible in worship.* Collegeville, MN: Liturgical Press.

Spears, L. C. (1998). *Insights on leadership: Service, stewardship, spirit, and servant leadership.* New York: John Wiley & Sons.

Spears, L. C. (2004). Practicing servant-leadership. *Leader to Leader, 34*, 7–11.

Tucker, R. A., & Liefeld, W. (1987). *Daughters of the church: Women and ministry from New Testament times to the present.* Grand Rapids, MI: Zondervan.

.

Chapter 10

One Woman's Struggle

A Reflection on Servant-Leadership

Margaret Muchiri

Kenya[1] is a free democracy now. The British colonizers left Kenya in 1963, but they left a land devastated both in terms of a ruined ecosystem and an uprooted culture (Kemble, 2003, p. 206). In terms of an ecosystem, Kenya was reduced to a mere shell of its former self. Kenyan land had been deforested and its fertility exhausted by the colonial masters (Kenyatta, 1989; Maathai, 2006, pp. 3–8). Wangari Maathai, upon seeing the devastation, decided to do what she could to combat environmental and poverty issues arising from deforestation ("Wangari Muta Maathai," n.d., para. 2). Because of her, some thirty million trees have been planted and much of Kenya's ruined land has been reclaimed. In recognition of her efforts, she received the 2004 Nobel Peace Prize (Maathai, 2004, pp. ix–x).

How was it possible for an individual, and for that matter a woman, to bring forth such a level of leadership against such formidable odds? I attempt to answer this question herein, reflecting on Maathai's living servant-leadership attributes and the theoretical statements those attributes represent. Before answering the question raised above, it is important that I place my reader into the perspective of what the terms *leadership* and *servant-leadership* mean in the context of this chapter. Next, I will present a historical background of the environmental problems in Kenya. Finally, I will provide an account of how Maathai implicitly used her servant-leadership qualities to resolve the problem.

THE NATURE OF SERVANT-LEADERSHIP

The concept of leadership is elusive in terms of definition due to various factors that include culture, institutions, social influence, diverse processes and evolution of different societies, and so on (Wren, 1995, p. 38). According to Northouse (2004, p. 2) there are almost as many different definitions of leadership as there are people who have tried to define it. Despite the elusiveness of the term, I find Northouse's description of the term quite fair. His claim is that four components are central to the phenomenon of leadership. These are process, influence, group, and goal (2004).

Leadership in Northouse's (2004) view may be defined as a process. This means that leadership is not necessarily a trait or characteristic that resides in the leader but a transactional event that occurs between the leader and his or her followers. Process implies that the leader and the follower affect each other and that leadership is a shared responsibility among all involved. Leadership may also be defined in terms of influence that takes place between the leader and followers. It is important to note that both leaders and followers are necessary for leadership to occur. Lack of one of the two components renders leadership unnecessary (Burns, 1978) by virtue of their being like two sides of the same coin (Rost, 1991). Leadership is actually a relationship between two partners—one who leads and the other who is led (Jassy, 2001). Leadership is also regarded as a reality that occurs among a group of individuals with a common goal. It involves directing a group of individuals toward accomplishing some task or end.

The notion of servant-leadership was formulated by Robert Greenleaf (Greenleaf Centre for Servant-Leadership, 2007) in the 1970s. It is a service-oriented leadership theory based on the idea that genuine leadership is founded on a deep desire to serve others (Greenleaf, 2002). In Greenleaf's notion, one chooses to serve first and to lead as a secondary priority. The legitimate power involved in servant-leadership is not a power that dominates or controls but that which heals, restores, and reconciles. The servant-leader in this regard submits to subtle forces of life that lead away from self-embeddedness and toward the kind of transcendence that is capable of leading and healing the self and beloved others (Ferch, 2005, p. 4). Servant-leadership involves a positive transformation through personal sacrifice, example, and selfless dedication of other people's lives whose priorities stand out as paramount and preeminent.

Greenleaf (2002) believes that servant-leadership emerges from within a person as a natural state of being. Covey echoes similar understanding when he says that for a person to be defined as a servant-leader, specific aspects of that person's being must be present. Covey (2004) describes these characteristics as involving the whole person: mind, body, heart, and spirit (p. 21). In other words, to talk about a servant-leader is to talk about the identity of the whole person.

According to Greenleaf (2007), servant-leaders become leaders through their inner desire to live a life of service. Servant-leaders manifest the desire to ensure that other people's needs are served before their own. Spears (2004) claims that clear manifestations of servant-leadership are evident in the lives of people like Jesus, Martin Luther King Jr. Gandhi, and Mother Teresa. Spears believed that the leadership portrayed in these personalities was not motivated by the traditional power-driven and self-centered interests approach, but by the desire to serve others' needs.

While there are several paths to becoming a servant-leader, community building is vital (Lad & Luechauer, 1998). Through service and volunteer work within community, discovery and contribution can be realized. It is through such leadership of oneself as "separate self" that change to one self-embedded in community occurs (p. 59).

Spears (2002) identifies essential characteristics of servant-leadership. He says that while the said qualities may be found in many types of leadership, they are simply emphasized more strongly by servant-leaders. Spears claims that servant-leaders tend to see themselves as equal with and not above those led. They see others as peers to teach and learn from. They understand and speak the language of their followers. Servant-leaders encourage others to do what they do well without dictating to them.

Servant-leaders use leadership to obtain the general good and not a personal end. Listening is innate to this type of a leader and caring is a part of who they are. They start where people are but don't stop there. They help others reach their full potential as they explore new horizons. Servant-leaders inspire others to service and the realization that they cannot do it alone. So they work with, and for, others. They inspire others to be servants by their own desire to serve. Honesty, awareness, empathy, passion, ability to overcome obstacles, a sense of joyfulness, optimism, and flexibility are some of the essential components of the personality of a servant-leader. Spears (2004) concludes by likening a servant-leader to a sage. For him, a servant-leader is a sage who stays below others in order to be above; who, wishing to be before them, stays behind them. Having defined and described leadership and servant-leadership, I now turn to providing a historical background of the deforestation and general degradation of the environment in Kenya.

THE LEADERSHIP CHALLENGES
WANGARI MAATHAI FACED

Before the coming of the Europeans, Kenya's agricultural regions comprised an abundance of shrubs, creepers, ferns, and indigenous trees (Maathai, 2004, pp. 3–8; Gaily, 1970, p. 210). Some of the indigenous trees produced fruit while others provided shade, firewood, and fodder for animals. The trees also produced protection against soil erosion. The humus from the trees acted as a fertilizer to revitalize soil. Local people didn't need artificial fertilizer to grow healthy crops. Above all, trees formed forests that attracted regular rainfall.

It is important to note that Kenya is an equatorial country and is located on the east coast of Africa. It has an area of about 225,000 square miles. It has a wide range of geographical and ecological regions ranging from the tropical coastal plains on the Indian Ocean to the glaciers of Mount Kenya. More than 70 percent of the land is considered arid, receiving fewer than twenty inches of rain per year. Only 7 percent of the country is suitable for agricultural production and that is concentrated in the central and western highlands of the Rift Valley, where 85 percent of the population and most economic enterprises are concentrated (Banks, Muller, & Overstreet, 2007, p. 648; Kemble, 2003). Kenya enjoys international fame as one of the African countries with the most attractive artifacts of cultural heritage, wildlife, and natural scenic attractions.

Before the coming of the colonial period, Kenya's local peoples' religious beliefs and cultural values about the importance of natural forests led them to protect the forests rather than destroy them (Kenyatta, 1989). For example, Mount Kenya, originally known as Kirinyaga, or place of brightness, the second-highest peak in Africa, was a sacred place of worship. Everything good was believed to come from it. Abundant rains, rivers, streams, clean water, medicinal tree roots, game for meat, firewood for fuel, building material, and such were seen as originating from there. People literally believed that God dwelt on top of this mountain (Hansen & Twaddle, 1995). The natural forest surrounding this mountain, and indeed, any other natural forests within Kenya, were viewed as God's lodges as she toured the land.

Because rain fell regularly, reliably clean drinking water was easily available for the people and their animals. Soil was rich and produced abundant food. Indigenous crops such as bananas, peas, arrowroots, assortment of green vegetables, sweet potatoes, millet, sorghum, assortment of indigenous beans, pumpkins, and various fruits were produced abundantly whenever they were planted. Domestic animals such as indigenous cows, sheep, goats flourished. As long as rain fell regularly, people were assured of sustenance. Since there was enough for everybody, a major cause of war, lack of food, was allayed (Maathai, 2004).

Then came the European colonialists in 1800, and a little later, the missionaries. With them came their worldview. The Europeans' aims of occupying African land were to explore for the sake of political and material benefit (Harris, 1979, p. 148; Ochieng & Ogot, 1995); in order to gain root in Africa without much resistance, the Europeans started by colonizing the African mind (Mazrui, 1986, pp. 11–21; Rodney, 1982, p. 76). Ani (1995) expresses this idea of colonial manipulation well when he says, "If you control a man's thinking you do not have to worry about his actions. When you determine what a man shall think, you do not have to concern yourself about what he will do" (p. 429). The Europeans worked on replacing the local cultural values, political ideologies, religious beliefs, economic structures, educational systems, and medical health systems with their own (Kenyatta, 1989, p. 269). In time, the entire political and economic structure had been removed from the local population and came to be in the hands of the Europeans (Gupta, 1998).

In Kenya, the British authorities allowed the European migrants to take over the ownership of Kenyan land. The indigenous people were simply kicked off and often became paupers. For example, "[T]he Kikuyu took to migrant labor following the alienation of their land by European settlers in the first two decades of the twentieth century. Those who stayed put either became 'squatters' or remained confined to economically unviable pieces of land" (Kenyatta, 1989, p. 26).

The new settlers replaced native crops with various foreign crops such as wheat, maize, coffee, tea, and indigenous wildlife with exotic livestock (Ela, 2001, pp. 87–89; Maathai, 2006). McWilliams (1976) stated that it was in the field of agriculture that the European politico-economic dominance was most strongly marked. He further claimed that by 1960 there had been created a substantial plantation sector of tropical export crops (sisal, coffee, and tea) covering more than 350,000 acres and, more remarkably, a mixed farming sector of cereals, livestock, and other crops in which over a million acres were brought under active cultivation together with more than two million acres of paddocked natural grazing land (p. 257).

By the early 1950s, about 40,000 settlers, most of them British, had moved onto about 2,500 farms, in a region that later came to be known as the white highlands. It is to be noted that at that time only foreign settlers were allowed to grow cash crops. These cash crops included tea, coffee, cotton, pyrethrum, and exotic trees. The elimination of indigenous trees for cash crop use offered an engine of economic growth but threatened to displace both native species and rural inhabitants (Clapp, 1995).

In time, a railway line was put in place to enable easy transportation of raw material from the mainland to the coast, where the same material would then be shipped to Europe. Its construction required a lot of iron and timber. That meant planting more exotic trees, further squeezing out the local varieties, to provide quick timber.

As local crops were being replaced with exotic ones, following the dynamic described by Clapp (1995), so were local foods. For example, breakfast meal comprising millet porridge was replaced with tea. Clothes of animal skin were replaced by cotton ones. This made it necessary for the introduction of cotton growing. A nearly complete transformation of the local culture into one akin to that of Europe had taken place. The economy was monetized and that served as a final nail in the coffin of a previously thriving culture. Kenya was no longer Kenya.

Upon the exit of the British in 1963, many Kenyan people expected that the new local government would help its people retrace and reclaim some of their traditional values that had been weakened or replaced by the European ones. But this dream was never to be (Maathai, 2006, p. 125). Greed for money and other wealth commodities had invaded the local people's minds. Those that became leaders used the system to enrich themselves and their next of kin. Government-owned natural resources were used in whatever way possible for money making just as in the time of colonialists. Neither the political leadership nor the citizens were keen on restoration of the environment. Local people planted coffee, tea, cotton, pyrethrum, and exotic trees for money making. Indigenous animals were completely discarded and replaced with exotic, cash-producing ones. Interference with the natural interplay of living things led to some unforeseen long-term side effects (Harris, 1979, p. 148; Warren, 1997).

Deforestation for the sake of introducing plantations for various export crops had major negative effects with regard to shortage of rainfall. Deforestation affected the pattern of seasons. It became harder by day to anticipate rain. Though this effect may not be self-evident, ecologist Gupta (1998) explains,

> The global and long-term effects [of deforestation] are not clearly understood yet, but certain consequences are feared. The loss of the forest decreases the moisture in the soil and, if large-scale, is also expected to lead to a reduction in the rainfall of the region. Together, these would lead to changes in the flow patterns of local rivers. The surface of the deforested land reflects a greater amount of solar energy back to the atmosphere. (p. 13)

Reduced rain led to reduced production of food crops and fodder for animals. At times there were longer spells of dry seasons than usual. Maathai (2006) later observed that many local farmers had converted practically all their land into growing coffee and tea to sell in the international markets. These cash crops occupied the land previously used to grow food crops. As a consequence, families had now turned to feeding on processed foods such as white bread, maize, flour, and white rice, all of which were high in carbohydrates but relatively low in vitamins, proteins, and minerals (Maathai, 2006, p. 123). On the other hand, introduction of artificial fertilizers, insecticides, pesticides, and various processing industries (of coffee, timber, cotton, sisal, tea, and pyrethrum) caused air pollution and soil degradation. Lack of adequate forestation affected the natural equilibrium where nature creates and nourishes itself.

Although the local people, and especially women, given the advantage they had as a result of regular direct contact with the soil as they tended crops (Warren, 1997), in time were remotely aware that something needed to be done to alleviate the problem, none took any significant step toward the change required. But there arose a single person, a woman, who believed she knew a single and practical solution to the many problems bedeviling Kenyan people: degraded land, poverty, warring tribes, shortage of nutritious food, clean water, and firewood. Maathai initiated the famous Green Belt Movement (GBM) in Kenya, which would be a vehicle for dealing with the environmental issues facing the country.

MAATHAI'S LEADERSHIP

Wangari Muta Maathai is both a local and international celebrity after fighting a winning battle against all elements of environmental degradation in Kenya for over thirty-five years. The environmental concerns she fought for are the totality of the ecological and social conditions of our being. Her spirit of optimism and unbowed attitude in the midst of challenges proved to be handy tools in her life as a leader (Maathai, 2006).

Having been born in Nyeri, Kenya (Africa), in 1940, Maathai's humble beginnings as a rural Kikuyu girl, from which she rose to attain the highest level of academic achievement, is an inspiration to any young woman who might need some encouragement in overcoming cultural obstacles to realize her career dream. Maathai hails from a heavily patriarchal society that demeans education for girls. When still pursuing her elementary schooling, some of her neighbors would tell her mother, "There is no need to keep her in school. She cannot even become a clerk; she is a girl after all" (Maathai, 2006, p. 72). But as it turned out, Maathai was not distracted by such discouragements. She was the first woman in East and Central Africa to earn a doctoral degree (2006). She obtained a bachelor's degree in biological sciences in 1964, after which she attained a Master of Science degree in 1966. In 1971, she obtained a Ph.D. from the University of Nairobi, where she also taught veterinary anatomy. She became chair of the Department of Veterinary Anatomy and an associate professor in 1976 and 1977, respectively. In both cases, she was the first woman in Kenya to hold such positions. It was while still holding those positions that she received her insight of beginning a tree-planting campaign in Kenya that later came to be known as the GBM.

Why Tree Planting?

Back in 1975, Kenyan women came together under the auspices of the National Council of Women in Kenya (NCWK) to express what they regarded as issues of much concern to them as women. NCWK was/is a movement founded in 1964 to serve as an umbrella organization to unify various women's groups both large and small throughout Kenya with a membership drawn from urban and rural areas (Maathai, 2006, p. 122).

Maathai, who was already an executive member of NCWK, received her tree-planting insight after listening to the issues the rural women raised at the 1975 NCWK annual conference. Among other things, the women said their families were suffering from malnutrition and traveling long distances in search of firewood and water. They said their families suffered water-related diseases because the available water was not only insufficient, but also too polluted for human and animal consumption. The women's hope was that the leaders of NCWK would help them in one way or another to seek a quick solution to the problem. These concerns mentioned above are certainly what the World Health Organization (WHO) alludes to when it says that 85 percent of sickness and disease in countries in the southern hemisphere is attributable to inadequate water and that as many as twenty-five million deaths a year are due to water-related illnesses (Warren, 1997, p. 7).

As Maathai listened to the women, she gained an insight that the root cause of all their problems was the deforestation that had been occurring on the land for a long time—so she embarked on a tree-planting program in 1977 (Pal, 2005) that would later be named the GBM. Being the pragmatic woman that she is, Maathai integrated her education with her observation to come up with a practical solution to the women's plight. These characteristics are implicit as Maathai narrates in her memoir how the tree-planting project was born:

> I focused on what could be done. As it turned out, the idea that sprang from my roots merged with other sources of knowledge and action to form a confluence that grew bigger than I would ever have imagined. (Maathai, 2006, p. 119)

In her view, tree planting was such a simple and practical idea that, if implemented, would solve all the problems that existed. The trees would provide a supply of wood for fuel and construction work, supply shade for humans and animals, protect watersheds and bind the soil, and, if they were fruit trees, provide food. They would also heal the land by bringing back birds and small animals and regenerate the vitality of the earth.

Paths Set for Tree Planting

Having such a conviction that her idea was viable, she used the NCWK as a vehicle for implementation. Being the visionary leader that she was, Maathai decided to not only plant trees but also ideas. In her opinion, incorporating educative seminars in the tree-planting venture would empower local people with an understanding of the importance of a healthy environment. Maathai (2006) hoped that this same knowledge would eventually lead people to take personal responsibility in tree planting (p. 174). Wangari identified and incorporated into the tree-planting project relevant issues such as environmental education, civic education, human rights, gender, and power.

In June 1977, the GBM, which was initially known as 'Save the Land Harambee', marked its first tree-planting campaign by planting its first green belt, consisting of seven trees in one of the capital city parks. From then on, the movement embarked on establishing a green belt in every locality with an aim to promote the movement among locals. The planting exercise was either preceded or concluded by educational seminars.

By late 1977, news of the tree planting had spread throughout the nation and soon farmers, schools, and churches were eager to set up their own programs. That was the beginning of communities taking ownership of the movement's initiatives. Maathai's (2006) work was comprised of organizing ideas, instructing people, and even doing the actual tree planting with the people (p. 133).

OBSTACLES ON THE WAY

With the exercise now taking root and expanding day by day, Maathai was required to spend more and more of her time on the project. It became difficult for her to retain her teaching job in the university and to fully concentrate on the tree-planting exercise. After some discernment, she quit her teaching position and dedicated herself fully to the nonprofit tree-planting exercise (Maathai, 2006). The other challenging part for Mathaai was how to raise the money required for the exercise. At its initial stage, Maathai relied on her own funds to buy seedlings and distribute them all over the country (p. 128). The cost of educational tours and developing tree nurseries and distributing them all over the country was becoming overwhelming. Maathai and her team had to initiate new ways of meeting these demands. As she was concerned about the availability of seedlings, Maathai sought help from the government's chief conservator of forests.

She requested that the trained foresters give seminars to women on how to run their own nurseries. The trained foresters were reluctant to share their knowledge, claiming that they couldn't understand why Maathai was trying to teach rural women how to plant trees. According to the foresters, "You need a professional; people with diplomas to plant trees" (p. 135). To this, Maathai said, "I learned that professionals can make simple things complicated" (p. 135). According to Maathai, "[All] the women needed to know was how to put the seedling in the soil and help it grow. Anybody can dig a hole, put tree in it, water it, and nurture it" (p. 135). Since these women were farmers experienced in growing all sorts of crops, Maathai encouraged them to "use your woman sense because tree seedlings are very much like the seeds you deal with; beans and maize . . . put them in the soil. If they are good they will germinate. If they are not they won't survive" (p. 136).

With encouragement from their mentor and facilitator, the women gained self-confidence and seized the opportunity to use their informal technological know-how, and before long, the women proved incredibly resourceful. Tree nurseries sprang up on farms and public lands around the country. Maathai (2006) proudly says, "These were our 'foresters without diplomas'" (p. 136). With sufficient seedlings, the tree planting exercise intensified. The other contribution that increased the tree-planting exercise was the introduction of environmental and civic education carried out by GBM. With this education, women knew the importance of the tree-planting exercise and did it from their hearts, rather than doing it to please their mentor.

Maathai encouraged women to move on their own with their already acquired knowledge to neighboring regions, convincing others of the importance of tree planting. To this, Maathai (2006) says, "This was a breakthrough because it was now communities empowering one another for their own benefit" (p. 137). In this way, step-by-step, the process replicated itself several thousand times. As the local communities intensified their efforts, more and more green belts were established. It was due to the inspiration received from these belts that the movement at last changed its name from 'Save the Land Harambee' to the now-famous GBM.

To date, more than thirty million trees have been planted in Kenya under the umbrella of the GBM. More than 30,000 women have been trained in forestry, food processing, beekeeping, and other trades that help them earn income while preserving their lands and resources (Maathai, 2006). Ecotourism and just economic development have been incorporated into the movement's objectives. In recognition of her contribution to sustainable development, democracy, and peace, Maathai became the first African woman to receive the Nobel Prize in 2004. In her acceptance of the prize speech, Maathai said,

> The thirty million trees planted by the movement volunteers, mostly rural women, are testament to individuals' ability to change the course of environmental

history. Working together, we have proved that sustainable development is possible. I hope this realization will encourage women to raise their voices and take more space for leadership. (Maathai, 2004; Pal, 2005)

MANIFESTATIONS OF SERVANT-LEADERSHIP IN MAATHAI

By dedicating her life and energy to environmental restoration and conservation activities for the sake of eliminating poverty among the local people of Kenya, Maathai expresses the servant-leadership characteristics that Greenleaf describes when he says that the legitimate power involved in servant-leadership is not a power that dominates or controls, but that which heals, restores, and reconciles (Greenleaf, 2002). For Maathai, to have left the socially and economically dignified professor position at the University of Nairobi to dedicate her time and energy to the Greenbelt Movement is a sure sign of servant-leadership. By making this move, Maathai portrays the characteristic of servant-leadership that Spears (1998) certainly alludes to when he describes servant-leadership as a reality involving a positive transformation through personal sacrifice, example, and selfless dedication of other people's lives whose priorities stand out as paramount and preeminent.

By volunteering her life to the service of the Kenyan people through environmental preservation, Maathai manifests the characteristic of servant-leadership as described by Greenleaf. For Greenleaf (2002), a servant-leader is one whose deep desire is to ensure that other people's needs are served before his or her own (p. 29). By choosing to share her time and knowledge with the local community for their good is to have chosen the best path to servant-leadership, according to Lad and Luechauer (1998). For Lad and Luechauer (1998), service and volunteer work within one's community is the surest path to becoming a servant-leader. To have sacrificed her socially dignified status as a university professor to become a "forester," Maathai proves that what inspired and motivated her in the tree-planting project was not a search for greatness and power but a deep desire to be a servant of others. For her tree-planting insight to occur and be implemented not only required a scientific and intuitive mind (Gordon, 1996), but also a person embodying servant-leader characteristics.

In Maathai, the identified servant-leadership characteristics are present. Some of these are a deep and prompt desire to serve, intelligence, passion, optimism, flexibility, a listening and caring attitude, acceptance, valuing others' contributions, and a deep capacity to discern, perceive, and intuit. Above all, Maathai has proved her servant-leadership qualities by scoring excellently in Greenleaf's (1977) servant-leadership test: Do those who are being served flourish? Do they grow in health, wisdom, freedom, and personal agency? Are they being transformed into servant-leaders themselves? And what about the less fortunate? Are they also being served, or at least not further harmed? For Maathai, the answer to the above questions would certainly be a firm yes. She would support her answer by listing what the GBM has achieved so far. The main mission for GBM has been to raise community consciousness on self-determination, equity, improved livelihood security, and environmental conservation using trees as an entry point. The movement has helped small-scale farmers become agro-foresters through expert technology transfer, while public awareness has been broadened to understand the relationship between population, food production, and energy. The movement has literally reduced poverty and improved the self-esteem of the Kenyan people.

Note: This chapter was originally published in the *International Journal of Servant Leadership* and is reprinted here with permission.

NOTE

1. This chapter was previously published as Muchiri, M. (2011). One woman's struggle: A reflection on servant-leadership. *The International Journal of Servant-Leadership.* 7(1), 91–104.

REFERENCES

Ani, M. (1995). *Yurugu: An African-centered critique of European Cultural Thought and behavior.* Trenton, NJ: Africa World Press, Inc.

Banks, A. S., Muller, C. T., & Overstreet, W. R. (eds.). (2007). Kenya. In *Political handbook of the world* (pp. 648–662). Washington, DC: CQ Press.

Burns, J. M. (1978). *Leadership.* New York: Harper & Row.

Clapp, R. A. (1995). The unnatural history of the monterey pine. *The Geographical Review, 85,* 1–19.

Covey, S. R. (2004). *The 8th Habit: From effectiveness to greatness.* [Sound Recording]. New York: Simon & Schuster Audio.

Ela, J. M. (2001). *My faith as an African.* Nairobi: Acton Publishers.

Ferch, S. (2005). Servant-Leadership, forgiveness, and social justice. *International Journal of Servant-Leadership, 1,* 97–113.

Gaily, H. A. (1970). *History of Africa from Earliest Times to 1800.* New York: Holt, Rinehart, & Winston.

Gordon, A. A. (1996). *Transforming capitalism and patriarchy: Gender and development in Africa.* Boulder, CO: Lynne Rienner.

Greenleaf, R. K. (1974). *Trustees as Servants.* Indianapolis, IN: The Greenleaf Center.

————. (1977). *Servant-leadership: A journey into the nature of Legitimate Power and greatness.* Mahwah, NJ: Paulist Press.

Greenleaf Center for Servant-Leadership. (2007). *What Is Servant-Leadership?* Retrieved from https://www.greenleaf.org/what-is-servant-leadership/

Gupta, A. (1998). *Ecology and development in the Third World.* London: Routledge.

Hansen, H. B., & Twaddle, M. (1985). *Religion and politics in East Africa: The Period Since independence.* London: James Currey.

Harris, J. E. (1979). *Repatriates and refugees in a Colonial Society: The case of Kenya.* Washington, DC: Howard University.

Jassy, M. F. P. (2001). Leadership. *Spearhead,* nos. 153–154. Eldoret: Amecea Gaba Publications.

Kemble, R. (2003). Kenya. In *The Greenwood encyclopedia of women's issues worldwide: Sub-Saharan Africa* (pp. 201–223). London & Westport, CT: Greenwood Press.

Kenyatta, J. (1989). *Facing Mount Kenya: The traditional life of the Gikuyu.* London: Heinemann.

Lad, L. J., & Luechauer, D. (1998). On the path to servant-leadership. In L. C. Spears (ed.), *Insights on leadership: Service, stewardship, spirit, and servant-leadership* (pp. 54–67). New York: Wiley.

Maathai, W. (2004). *The Green Belt Movement: Sharing the approach & the experience.* New York: Lantern Books.

Maathai, W. (2006). *Unbowed: One Woman's Story.* London: Heinemann.

Mazrui. A. (1986). *The Africans; A Triple Heritage.* Boston, MA: Little Brown.

McWilliam, M. (1976). The managed economy: Agricultural change, development, and finance in Kenya. In *History of East Africa* (Vol. 3, pp. 251–289). London & Oxford: Clarendon Press.

Northouse, P. G. (2004). *Leadership: Theory and practice.* London: Sage.

Ochieng, W. R., & Ogot, B. A. (1995). *Decolonization and independence in Kenya,* 1940–93. London: James Currey.

Pal, A. (2005). Interview with Wangari Maathai. *The Progressive.* Retrieved from www.progressive.prg/wangari_maathai_interview_html.

Rodney, W. (2006). How Europe underdeveloped Africa. In P. Rothenberg (ed.), *Beyond borders: Thinking Critically About Global Issues* (pp. 107–125). New York: Worth.

Rost, J. C. (1991). *Leadership for the Twenty-First Century.* New York: Praeger.

Spears, L. C. (1998). *Insights on leadership: Service, stewardship, and Servant Leadership.* New York: Wiley.

————. (2002). *Quest for Caring Leadership.* Greenleaf Centre for servant-leadership: http://www.Greenleaf.Org/Leadership/Read-About-It/Article/Quest- For-Caring Leadership.html.

Spears, L. C., & Lawrence, M. (2004). *Practicing Servant-Leadership: Succeeding through Trust, Bravery, and forgiveness.* San Francisco, CA: Jossey-Bass.

Wangari Maathai. (n.d.). Biographies. Retrieved November 27, 2007, from http://www.answers.com/topic/wangari-maathai.

Warren, K. J. (1997). *Ecofeminism: Women Culture Nature.* Bloomington, IN: Indiana University Press.

Chapter 11

Waiting in Line

Muzabel Welongo

Having[1] the only choice to wait in line, I spent five hours at water tap in a long line under a hot sun so that I can get water. When there are no water taps in a village, rivers are the only hope. What happens when rivers also dry at the same time?

I visited my uncle in dry season. In Kabare, my uncle's village, people stayed five days without water. The river had muddy, non-potable water. After struggling for five days, there was somewhere to find water. Everybody in the village needs to fill their water. The servant of the tap, with a little pride, commanded us to stay on a line and that everyone fetch only 20 liters. We were served in order of first come, first served basis. I was the last in line. I had to wait in line because we had no water to prepare food at home. In my line, there was an old woman behind me who looked vulnerable. I felt the responsibility to help her get water as soon as possible to allow her go back earlier. Nobody on the front line accepted to let her pass. I left my line and went to the servant of the tap asking him to help the old woman. The woman was given a chance to fill her container without waiting. When I joined my line someone occupied my place and people in the whole line told me to restart at the end.

The time I wasted to help the woman was a grace that day. I stayed at the end of the waiting line, waiting for my turn. Touched by my kindness toward the old woman, the tap servant allowed me to fetch water immediately. I had three containers of 20 liters each; all were filled.

Honesty and patience are essential when waiting in line. With patience, people at the tap said I am kind and honest. Flexibility is also important: we all suffered of lack of water, but some of us were more vulnerable than we. I made sure my neighbors on the line are served as I wanted to be served.

NOTE

1. This chapter was previously published as Welongo, M. (2011). Waiting in line. *The International Journal of Servant-Leadership.* 3(1), 249–250.

Chapter 12

Xhosa Tribal Culture and Its Influence on the Servant-Leadership of Nelson Mandela

Mary C. Sobralske

In 1994,[1] Nelson Mandela became the first democratically elected black president of South Africa. This historical event had tremendous impact on the world. Much has been written about Mandela as a leader, but few have highlighted his cultural background, how it influenced his deep-seated cultural values and beliefs, and how his culture shaped his leadership. It is important to analyze how his cultural upbringing determined his destiny as a dignified, respected, and popular global servant-leader.

SERVANT-LEADERSHIP AND
AFRICAN TRIBAL CULTURE

There are many styles of leadership, and leadership has been studied and theorized over throughout modern history. Greenleaf (1977, 2005) challenged traditional leadership theories and practices. He believed that respect, honor, and dignity are crucially important and maintained that a great leader is seen as a servant first, and then as a leader.

Servant-leaders are committed to serving others, and the art of leading is the act of serving. One must think and act as a leader and a servant at the same time: a leader who serves and a servant who leads. Leaders must bend their efforts to serve with skill, understanding, and spirit, and followers are responsive only to able servants who lead them. Awareness is key to develop leadership and strengthen the effectiveness of a leader (Greenleaf, 1977). Servant-leaders are leaders who put other people's needs, aspirations, and interests above their own (Sendjaya & Sarros, 2002).

According to Williams (2002), servant-leaders often have "a cause . . . or a crusade . . . with humanitarian, not materialistic, goals" (p. 67). The leader works "behind the scenes" or in "the trenches" (p. 68). He or she leads even in the face of danger and adversity.

A strong trust develops between the servant-leader and followers. The servant-leader is often willing to risk personal safety and is persuasive, inspiring, personable, creditable, honest, and selfless. The servant draws strength from a strong commitment to faith and spiritual beliefs (Greenleaf, Beasley, Beggs, & Spears, 2003). The servant-leader sets an example for the group through "credibility, integrity, diligence, humility, and the spirit of servant-leadership" (Covey, 2002, p. 27).

The servant-leader values and believes in the people. The servant-leader serves the needs of others before himself, encouraging and affirming others. Servant-leaders change the system not just by doing, but more fundamentally, by being (Zohar, 1997). "Servant-leadership promotes the valuing and development of people, the building of community, the practice of authenticity, the proving of leadership for the good of those who are led, and the sharing of power and status for the common good" (Laub, 1999, p. 83).

Horsman (2001) presented a thorough and compelling review of servant-leadership literature. In some cases, servant-leaders felt they had no choice when they realized that someone must solve a problem or change the attitudes of society. Horsman (2001) investigated the characteristics of servant-leaders and surmised that the servant as leader is not new to Western or Eastern cultures. Jesus Christ as a symbol of servant-leadership evokes familiarity for many Christians (p. 43). Greenleaf's cultural and religious background of Westernized Judeo-Christianity helped form his ideas on leadership. He saw churches as one of the most influential forces for developing servant-leadership.

Greenleaf (1977) believed that natural leaders from disadvantaged groups would find ways to orchestrate their efforts and "lead their people to secure a better life for many" (p. 164). This is a long and arduous journey of being disciplined, learning to listen, and being patient.

Servant-leadership has very old roots in many indigenous cultures— cultures that are holistic, cooperative, communal, intuitive, and spiritual (Bordas, 2005). These cultures center on being "guardians of the future and respecting the ancestors who walked before them" (p. 42).

Although the model of servant-leadership has been formally recognized only since the publication of Greenleaf's first writings (1977), leaders, through compassion and personal sacrifice, enabled and empowered others to achieve their goals (Lad & Luechauer, 1998); leaders such as Nelson Mandela have long been practicing servant-leadership. Greenleaf discussed servant-leadership in a way that described actions that were the foundation of Mandela's role as a leader in changing the attitudes of an entire country and the world.

Mandela (1994) explained in his autobiography that to be African in South Africa means that one is politicized from the moment of birth, regardless of whether it is acknowledged. He had no "epiphany, no moment of truth, but a steady accumulation of a thousand slights, a thousands indignities, a thousand unremembered moments" producing "anger, a rebelliousness, and a desire to fight the system" that imprisoned his people: He simply found himself taking action and could not do otherwise (p. 95).

One can debate whether Mandela was influenced more by his tribal culture or by his religious upbringing. Perhaps the two belief systems were intertwined and integrated, reinforcing the notion that a true leader is a servant to his people. Mandela did what he did for his people—for future generations. He dreamed of making his own humble contributions to the struggle for freedom and the opportunity to serve his people (Mandela, 1994). Although Mandela was raised with a Christian morality in school, he was also raised in a tribal collective society in which the group is most important. In this regard, Mandela's tribal cultural background and upbringing laid the foundation for the type of leader he would become.

NELSON MANDELA AND XHOSA TRIBAL CULTURE

Although he was born and grew up at a time when South Africa was plagued by cultural genocide, racial aggression and separation, and political oppression by an all-white Nationalist government, Nelson Mandela's leadership was very much a product of his Xhosa tribal culture and heritage. Clearly, Mandela's cultural beliefs and background strongly dictated his commitment to his people as their leader. In his autobiography, he points out key cultural values that formed his philosophy of leadership. One does what is best for the tribe, not what is best for himself as a self-serving individual. In a tribal society, the group, the collectivist value as opposed to the individualist value, is the foundation of leadership. Obligations and responsibilities to the people take precedence over loyalty to an individual.

Mandela was born in 1918 in a small rural village near Umtata in the Xhosa Transkei of South Africa. He was a member of the Xhosa tribe, the Tembu people, and part of the Bantu-speaking group who are thought to be the original South Africans. Xhosa tribal culture was governed by loosely connected autonomous chiefdoms until the Bantu people were conquered by white Europeans (Africana.com, 2003; Hammond-Tooke, 1974). Xhosa village communities were based on grain farming and pastoralism. Xhosa society was structured around vast cattle herds that were moved from one grazing place to another, moving freely over the open pastureland. According to Mostert (1992), cattle were the focal point of Xhosa existence. Cattle bound the material and the sacred (Alberti, 1811) and formed the tribal and family bank (Soga, 1930, 1983). Xhosa life consisted of daily council meetings between the chief and his counselors, held in the *kraal* (a corral in which cattle were held), in which all aspects of people's affairs were examined (Mostert, 1992). The *kraal* was surrounded by gardens and situated in the center of the village. Xhosa people occupied the land, forests, and rivers. They operated their own government, controlled their own armies, and organized their own trade and commerce.

According to Mostert (1992), African life was an outdoor life. The huts were considered simply places to sleep. Xhosa people were generally hospitable and lived a peaceful existence in which violence between individuals was suppressed. The *kraal* was the man's domain and the place where the chief generally conducted meetings and deliberations (Alberti, 1811). There was a powerful tradition of democratic debate, and the Xhosa were acknowledged for their gift for logic. They were reported to be astute diplomats (Cape of Good Hope Commission on Native Laws and Customs, 1883; Molema, 1963). They examined all facets of people's affairs, dealing with complaints brought and misdemeanors committed. Each individual case was handled thoroughly (Cape of Good Hope Commission on Native Laws and Customs, 1883; Molema, 1963). When judging cases, the chief and counselors drew on a body of law based on a long accumulation of past experiences (Maclean, 1866).

The Xhosa lived peacefully under the democratic rule of the chiefs and counselors. In principle, everything and everyone belonged to the chief; however, the relationship between Xhosa chiefs and their subjects was finely balanced (Mostert, 1992). If a chief constantly put himself above traditional laws and customs, he was abandoned by his people, who would ally themselves with another chief (Cape of Good Hope Commission on Native Laws and Customs, 1883). The Xhosa people were extremely loyal to their chiefs, and the chief was vested with much authority based on reverence, not coercion (Kay, 1834). The chief's authority was inherited by patrilineal descent. Chiefs were considered priests of ancestral heritage (Richards, 1940) and were believed to have mystic power over the land. The main safeguard against the abuse of power by the chief was through his group of counselors, known as the *amapakati*, or the "middle ones" (Mostert, 1992). They were the chief's "Parliament and Supreme Court" (p. 200). The chief of a tribe combined executive, ritual, and judicial functions of leadership (Native Laws and Customs, 1883). Chiefs presided over democratic decision-making and judicial verdicts (Alberti, 1811).

According to Mostert (1992), prior to the 1700s, Xhosa societies probably did not change much in basic principles of customs and culture for over 300 years. However, Xhosa culture was forever changed when white Europeans settled their land in the eighteenth and nineteenth centuries.

In the early 1900s, many Xhosa migrated in search of wage work in gold and diamond mines scattered throughout South Africa (ANC, 2003). Missionaries converted them to Christianity. Some were wealthy and fortunate enough to send their children to attend missionary schools, the only schools available to black South Africans at the time.

Mandela was born of a lineage of royalty and chiefdom. He defined himself through his father, Chief Henry Mgadla Mandela, principal counselor to the Acting Paramount Chief of Thembuland, Jongintaba David Dalindyebo (Mandela, 1994). His birth name was Rolihlahla, which literally means, "pulling the branch of a tree." However, the colloquial meaning is "one who brings trouble on himself" or "stirs up trouble" (Mandela, 1994). Later in his life, it became obvious that this name fit him well.

Growing up, Mandela was captivated by the tribal elders' stories about Xhosa ancestors and their valor during the Frontier wars of resistance. He was profoundly impressed by cases he heard before the chief's court in the cattle *kraal* in his village. Later in his youth, he became determined to be a lawyer, partly because of having witnessed these tribal deliberations (Mandela, 1994), and ultimately practiced the art of sophisticated argumentation in a court of law.

In 1930, his father died and young Rolihlaha became the Paramount Chief's ward. He was carefully groomed to assume a high tribal office. According to Sampson (1999), Rolihlaha's model for "benign authority and chiefly leadership style" was instilled in him by this chief (p. 69). Mandela was reminded of his responsibility to his tribe and expected to serve as a leader to his people. This extensive training and constant modeling as a man fated to become a chief, and his predisposition to be a "troublemaker," later helped carve and determine his destiny as a committed servant-leader.

In his autobiography, Mandela (1994) clearly expresses his strong religious, moral, and cultural convictions. He was a devoted Christian. No doubt the morality of Christianity was a backdrop for some of Mandela's leadership. Mandela (1994) related that during his schooling as a child and a young man, he was haunted by historical references alluding to his *Kaffir* people as savages, barbarians, and cattle thieves. He was appalled that black Africans were constantly being humiliated and considered less than human by whites, even though many of his people were Christians too, just like the white Afrikaners who oppressed them.

In 1985, while imprisoned, he was interviewed by reporters from the *Washington Times* who asked him about his attempts to commit bloodless acts of sabotage for his cause. Mandela (1994) responded by referring to the Bible, explaining,

> I am a Christian and have always been a Christian. Even Christ, when he was left with no alternatives, used force to expel the moneylenders from the temple. I am not a man of violence, but had no choice. I had to use force against evil. (p. 520)

MANDELA'S PATH TO GLOBAL SERVANT-LEADERSHIP

The beginning of the twentieth century in South Africa was marked by a system of segregation that allowed the Afrikaners (whites of Dutch descent) to dominate and control the majority of the wealth created by exporting and manufacturing the nation's natural resources. The Afrikaners controlled the nation's agriculture, leaving the black South Africans entirely out of the nation's quest for economic development (Thompson, 2001).

In 1948, the Afrikaner National Party established the policy and laws of apartheid as a means to cement Afrikaner control over the economic, political, and social system (Thompson, 2001). Apartheid literally means, "of being on one part, aside." From the start, the theory of apartheid was laden with contradictions. The supposition of apartheid was that whites were superior to Africans, Coloreds, and Indians, and its function was to entrench white supremacy. The attitude at the time was, *"Die wit man moet altyd baas wees"*—the Dutch belief that the white man must always remain boss. Thompson (2001) explains that the apartheid system was based on four premises (a formula which made the white nation the largest in the country):

1) The population of South Africa is comprised of four racial groups: white, colored, Indian, and African, each with its own inherent culture.
2) Whites were entitled to absolute control over the state.
3) White interests should prevail over black interests; therefore, the state was not obliged to provide equal facilities for the subordinate races.
4) The white racial groups formed a single nation, with Afrikaans and English-speaking components, while Africans belonged to several distinct nations.

According to "The History of Apartheid in South Africa" (2003), with the enactment of apartheid laws, racial discrimination was institutionalized. Race laws included every aspect of social life, including a prohibition of marriage between non-whites and whites and the sanctioning of white-only jobs. Afterward, the National Party won the national election, and then conveniently removed all the government representatives of the black and colored voters. It consolidated its political power by placing its Afrikaner members, or the British who supported apartheid policies, in most influential government and important non-government positions.

For the majority of South Africans, apartheid was seen as a philosophical and political system that would insure a parallel development of white and black interests and an ultimate economic, political, social, cultural, biological, and territorial separation (Giniewski, 1961). Apartheid excluded blacks from free competition in the economy and from the white world, while whites maintained their political position and efforts to preserve their advantageous economic status. Apartheid was a selfish instinct that placed great restrictions on black Africans and colored people (South African Institute of Race Relations, 1957). It was highly effective in achieving its goal of obtaining preferential treatment for whites (*The History of Apartheid in South Africa*, 2003).

Exacerbating the matter was the 1950 Population Registration Act, which required that all South Africans be racially classified into one of three categories: white, black (African), or colored (mixed descent). The colored category included major subgroups of East Indians and Asians. Classification into these categories was based on physical appearance, social acceptance, and descent (Neame, 1962). Non-compliance with race laws was dealt with harshly.

Earlier in South African history, black Africans founded a nationwide organization that became known as the African National Congress (ANC). The group survived official obstruction and was destined to become a formidable instrument of resistance in the struggle of black African liberation, especially in the second half of the twentieth century (Thompson, 2001).

In 1941, Mandela (1994) was introduced to Walter Sisulu, who was regarded as a "trouble maker and rabble-rouser" (p. 73). Sisulu was engaged in African politics. Although Mandela was counseled by confidants to avoid Sisulu and politics in general, he nevertheless got deeply involved in the ANC.

Sisulu was to become Mandela's closest friend; he even referred to Sisulu as his "spiritual father" (Mandela, 1994). They were ultimately imprisoned together at Robben Island and Pretoria. The connection between the two men provides a beautiful image of servant-leadership. From the start, Mandela regarded Sisulu as "strong, reasonable, practical, and dedicated" (p. 95). Sisulu was Mandela's mentor. He was a "brother," and his "friendship and support never faltered" (p. 208). Sisulu was an "uncle" to Mandela's children. They were co-leaders in the political movement to organize against the "harsh realities of the African struggle" (Tambo, 1965, p. 2).

In 1944, Mandela joined the ANC and helped found the ANC Youth League. In 1952, he was elected volunteer-in-chief of the Defiance Campaign and the President of the Transvaal Branch of the ANC (Mandela, 1994). He was persuaded to become the Deputy National President of the ANC. Unfortunately, within a year, he was ordered to resign from the ANC by the Afrikaner-dominated Nationalist Government. The government prohibited him from attending ANC meetings and assemblies and from engaging in any strikes or protests. For the next decade, Mandela was an unfortunate victim of various forms of repression, bans, arrests, and charges. To remain active in the anti-apartheid movement, he eventually went underground in the early 1960s (Mandela, 1994). Despite the government's ban, he continued his anti-apartheid activity by traveling around the country, organizing resistance to discriminatory legislation, and even a labor strike. His defiance and rebellious activities eventually resulted in his being arrested and charged with treason, a serious accusation in South Africa.

Originally, Mandela advocated protest through non-violence, but over time found that non-violent protest did little to change the government and society, whereupon he became convinced that violent activity was justified. It was only when all else failed, when all channels of peaceful protest were barred, that he decided to embark on violent forms of political struggle (Mandela, 1994).

According to the ANC (2003), despite a ban on leaving the country, in January 1962 Mandela toured Africa, visiting Tanganyika, Ethiopia, Sudan, Egypt, Libya, Tunisia, Algeria, Morocco, Mail, Senegal, Guinea, Sierra Leone, Liberia, Ghana, and Nigeria, meeting the heads of state of those countries. Shortly after his return to South Africa, he was arrested and charged for leaving the country illegally and inciting a strike. To these charges he pleaded guilty, and, as an experienced lawyer, conducted his own defense. He was convicted and jailed for five years for defying the laws of apartheid. While serving this sentence, he was charged with sabotage and conspiracy. A guilty verdict meant a sentence of death by hanging.

What followed was what became known as the famous Rivonia trial: the State versus Nelson Mandela (Britannica Online, 2005). He and many of his ANC comrades were found guilty and sentenced to life in prison rather than receiving the death sentence, mainly because the judge in the case knew the rest of the world would be appalled if the death sentence were to be carried out (Mandela, 1994). Mandela's sentence ended after twenty-seven years of imprisonment, when apartheid fell.

According to Benson (1986), Mandela's imprisonment did not hamper his spirit and leadership. At Robben Island prison, a bleak, cold, island prison off South Africa's Cape Hope, Mandela continued his fight against oppression by focusing on reforming the prison system. He protested against the poor conditions in which the prisoners were forced to work. He became a symbol of resistance and hope to fellow prisoners and to the world at large. He became a martyr to his people and to the world. He protested in prison by leading hunger strikes and engaging in other forms of resistance, attracting worldwide attention. Mandela became even more powerful in changing the political and social system in South Africa after he was imprisoned (Benson, 1986).

The Robben Island prison became a center for learning. Mandela was the central figure in organizing political and academic education classes for the inmates. He was a source of strength for the prisoners. His resistance held steady despite his tribulations in dealing with prison life. After completing twenty years of his imprisonment sentence, he continued to refuse offers to have his sentence remitted. This meant that he would receive special treatment and the rest of his comrades who were in prison would not be released. He explained that he could not sell his birthright as one being entitled to all human rights that any white African enjoyed (Mandela, 1994). He would not compromise his moral, political, and cultural principles.

In the 1980s, the dominant culture of South Africa was changing along with the rest of the world, albeit later than in many Westernized countries. The Dutch Reformed Church in South Africa, the original seedbed of apartheid, was changing due to the leadership, persuasion, and the courage to defy conformity (Thompson & Prior, 1982).

Starting in 1986, Mandela engaged in secret meetings between senior National Party government officials. What followed was the decision of the Afrikaner Broederbond, or brotherhood, to abandon apartheid and initiate clandestine negotiations with the ANC (de Klerk, 1998).

AFRICAN TRIBAL VALUES

Mandela was brought up with the cultural concept of *ubuntu*, the worldview of most African societies that influence social conduct. According to Broodryk (1997), *ubuntu* is a way of life that is fundamental to one's personhood, humanity, humanness, and morality. Integral to *ubuntu* is the idea of group solidarity and the survival of communities (Goland, 2004). An individual's existence is based on and expressed through relationships with others and on the principle of caring for each other's well-being (Louw, 2005). Conformity, compassion, respect, human dignity, collective unity, and the spirit of mutual support are key to the social values of *ubuntu*.

Mandela demonstrated the *ubuntu* cultural attitude when he entered the court during the 1964 Rivonia trial wearing a traditional Xhosa leopard-skin *kaross* (cloak) instead of a suit and tie (Mandela, 1994). The sight of the *kaross* and its cultural symbolism electrified the spectators. He chose the traditional dress to emphasize that a black African was walking into a white man's court. He was literally carrying the history, culture, and heritage of his people on his back. He felt like the embodiment of African nationalism, the inheritor of Africa's difficult but noble past and her uncertain future. He knew the authorities would feel threatened by the *kaross*, as so many whites felt threatened by the true culture of Africa. This was the day on which he gave a most memorable speech about apartheid laws being immoral, unjust, and intolerable. Mandela (1994) expressed his determination to bring apartheid to an end by declaring, "We must attempt to alter it, we must protest it, we must oppose it" (p. 324).

Ubuntu was the spiritual and social foundation in the development of the ANC. The importance of the value of group solidarity was pivotal to the survival of African communities and served to undergird the moral purpose of the strategies devised and the action taken by the ANC (Liwane, 2005). These same values were held and provided the impetus to continue the struggle undertaken by the ANC while Mandela, Sisulu, and other ANC leaders were in prison.

Greenleaf's (1977) premise of servant-leadership closely matches the principles of *ubuntu*. Servant-leaders affirm the value of others while building their strength, making them more autonomous and healthier. By their stewardship, they exhibit creative insight, a strong sense of foresight, and innate intuition. Servant-leaders use persistent persuasion and trust others. They are empathic and understanding. They truly listen without judging. Servant-leaders are deeply aware of and perceive that which surrounds them. They are committed to their communities and to the idea of the healing and growth of community members.

The principles and ideals of *ubuntu* include interconnectedness and harmony while building, maintaining, and strengthening communities—communal responsiveness. *Ubuntu* stresses humility, humanness, human dignity, compassion, respect, justice, fairness, mutual affirmation, reciprocity, group solidarity, and collective unity. *Ubuntu* is imbedded with the spirit of service to others (Goland, 2004).

Like the many Xhosa chiefs before him, Mandela acknowledged that experience is the foundation of leadership (Mandela, 1994). He knew himself and he knew his enemy's shortcomings. One cannot know another completely until he or she starts ruling people and making laws. Leaders are luminaries, noteworthy, and most influential (Mindell, 1995). They wait and watch others. They follow environmental and human signals. They see beyond the moment while studying the moment. They are prudent, judicious, wise, and solemn. Vision is the essence of leadership. Leaders see ways to accomplish their goals and ideas without compromising their own values and principles. They lead by giving power and guidance to others, so that they too may lead. Leaders have a balanced view of the world and community. They are global thinkers. They think about the long-term consequences of action and inaction. They put heavy emphasis on the intangibles of vision.

As a leader, Mandela worked outside the legislative process before and during his imprisonment. He wielded considerable power and influence, motivated by feeling compelled to improve conditions for his people in South Africa. He handled setbacks and difficulties by sticking with his mission and lived to struggle for the liberation of his people. He was a freedom fighter, defying laws on the grounds that they were unjust.

Nelson Mandela knew who he was. He used persistent persuasion to change attitudes worldwide. His leadership was inspired by other leaders of freedom movements at the time and in the past, like Gandhi in Britishcolonial India and the civil rights movement in the United States led by the Reverend Dr. Martin Luther King, Jr. Events and sentiments across the world all contributed to these fights.

CONCLUSION

Great leaders and their ways of leading others depend on many factors. The legacy they leave behind is very much dependent on the environment and world surrounding them. Leadership never happens in a vacuum. Leadership theorist John Gardner (1990) points out that leaders always live with conflict, especially in a multicultural world. Gardner believes that leaders' inherent attributes and power to lead enables them to motivate others, develop organizations, renew lost hopes, and build communities.

Mandela exhibited many of the attributes that a great leader must possess: loyalty to a cause, capacity to motivate, willingness to stand alone, great courage, intelligence, adaptability, and enduring physical stamina (Gardner, 1990). Nelson Mandela was a keen networker and a logical problem solver; he was able to envision the future; he believed in human rights and prosperity for all people. As a strong leader of his people, he maintained deep, moral convictions and was proficient in political strategy and diplomatic legal debate. He was not afraid to rebel and demand political and social reform. Mandela (1994) was motivated by circumstances created by apartheid and the constant struggles of humanity surrounding him.

Mandela possessed the courage, conviction, and beliefs that many Xhosa tribal chiefs possessed before him in a long line of royal ancestry. Mandela had more than the need to serve his people. From the time he was a small child listening to the men of his tribe argue cases in the cattle *kraal*, he was destined to be a chief. This vocation surpassed the responsibility of merely being a leader to his people. His success meant the cultural survival of this tribe in modern times and gave to the world a sacred gift of healing.

NOTE

1. This chapter was previously published as Sobralske, M. C. (2008). Xhosa tribal culture and its influence on the servant-leadership of Nelson Mandela. *The International Journal of Servant-Leadership.* *4*(1), 141–157.

REFERENCES

African National Congress. (2003). Historical documents. Retrieved on March 15, 2003 from http://www.anc.org.za/ancdoes/history

Africana.com web page. Retrieved on February 1, 2003, from http://www.africana.com

Alberti, L. (1968). *The Kaffirs of the South Coast of Africa* (W. Fehr, Trans.). Cape Town: Balkema. (Original work published 1811).

Benson, M. (1986). *Nelson Mandela: The man and the movement.* New York: W.W. Norton & Co.

Bordas, J. (2005). African American leaders—Guardians of public values. *International Journal of Servant-Leadership, 1*(1), 231–254.

Britannica Online. (2005). Rivonia Trial. Retrieved on February 26, 2008, from http://www.britannica.com/eb/topic-504997/Rivonia-Trial

Broodryk, J. (1997). Ubuntuism as a doctrine for the ordering of society. Unpublished doctoral dissertation, UNISA, Pretoria, South Africa.

Cape of Good Hope Commission on Native Laws and Customs. (1883). Report and proceedings of the government commission on native laws and customs. Cape Town: W. A. Richards & Sons.

Covey, S. R. (2002). Servant-leadership and community leadership in the twenty first century. In L. C. Spears & M. Lawrence (eds.), *Focus on leadership* (pp. 27–33). New York: John Wiley & Sons.

de Klerk, F. W. (1998). *The Last Trek: A New Beginning—The autobiography.* London: Macmillan.

Gardner, J. W. (1990). *On leadership.* New York: The Free Press.

Giniewski, P. (1961). *The Two Faces of apartheid.* Chicago: Henry Regency.

Goland, Simon (2004). *Ubuntu as a concept.* Retrieved March 1, 2004, from www.simongoland.com

Greenleaf, R. K. (1977). *Servant leadership.* New York: Paulist Press.

Greenleaf, R. K. (2005). What is Servant Leadership? Retrieved July 22, 2005, from http://www.greenleaf.org

Greenleaf, R. K., Beasley, H., Beggs, J., & Spears, L. C. (eds.). (2003). *The Servant-Leader Within: A Transformative Path.* New York: Paulist Press.

Hammond-Tooke, W. D. (ed.). (1974). *The Bantu-Speaking Peoples of southern Africa*. London: Routledge & Kegan Paul.

Horsman, J. H. (2001). Perspectives of servant-leadership and spirit in organizations. Doctoral dissertation. Gonzaga University, Spokane, Washington. (UMI 3010149)

Kay, S. (1834). *Travels and researches in Caffraria*. New York: Harper & Brothers.

Lad, L. J., & Luechauer, D. (1998). On the path to servant-leadership. In: L. C. Spears (ed.), *Insights on leadership: Service, stewardship, spirit, and Servant-Leadership* (pp. 54–67). New York: John Wiley & Sons.

Laub, J. A. (1999). Assessing the servant organization: Development of the Organizational Leadership Assessment (OLA) instrument. Unpublished doctoral dissertation, Florida Atlantic University. (AAT 9921922)

Liwane, N. (2005). The significance of ubuntu in the development of the ANC cadre. Retrieved on August 17, 2005, from http://www.anc.org.za/ancdocs/pubs/umrab ulo/umrabulo 13v.html

Louw, D. J. (2005). Ubuntu: An African assessment of the religious other. *University of the North*. Retrieved on April 25, 2005 from http:www.bu.edu/wcp/Papers/Afr i/AfriLouw.htm

Maclean, J. (ed.). (1968). *Compendium of Kafir laws and customs*. Cape Town: State Library Reprint, Pretoria. (Originally published in 1858).

Mandela, N. (1994). *Long walk to freedom*. Boston: Little, Brown, and Co.

Mindell, A. (1995). *Sitting in the fire: Large Group Transformation Using Conflict and diversity*. Portland, OR: Lao Tse Press.

Molema, S. M. (1963). *The Bantu: Past and present*. Cape Town, South Africa: Struik Publishers.

Mostert, N. (1992). *Frontiers: The epic of South Africa's creation and the tragedy of the Xhosa people*. New York: Alfred A. Knopf.

Neame, L. E. (1962). *The history of apartheid: The story of the colour war in South Africa*. New York: London House & Maxwell.

Richards, A. I. (1940). The political system of the Bemba Tribe: Bantu political organization. In: M. Fortes & E. E. Evans-Pritchard (eds.), *African Political Systems* (pp. 83–120). New York: Oxford University Press.

Sampson, A. (1999). *Mandela: The Authorized Biography*. New York: Alfred A. Knopf.

Sendjaya, S., & Sarros, J. C. (2002). Servant-leadership: Its origin, development, and application in organizations. *Journal of Leadership and Organization Studies, 9*(2), 57–64.

Simon Says Consulting. (2004). Ubuntu as a concept. Retrieved on March 1, 2004, from www.simongoland.com

Soga, T. (1931). *AmaXhosa life and customs—The southeastern Bantu*. Johannesburg: Lovedale Press.

South African Institute of Race Relations. (1957). *The Native Laws amendment bill: Its effect on religious and Other Freedoms*. Cape Town

"The history of apartheid in South Africa." Web Page. Retrieved February 12, 2003, from http://www-cs-students.stanford.edu/~cale/cs201/apartheid.hist.html

Thompson, L. (2001). *A history of South Africa* (3rd ed.). New Haven: Yale University Press.

Thompson, L., & Prior, A. (1982). *South African politics*. New Haven: Yale University Press.

Williams, D. (ed.). (1983). *The journal and Selected Writings of the Reverend Tiyo Soga*. Cape Town: Balkema.

Williams, L. E. (2002). Fannie Lou Hamer: Servant of the people. In: L. C. Spears & M. Lawrence (eds.), *Focus on leadership: Servant-leadership for the Twenty First Century* (pp. 65–87). New York: John Wiley & Sons.

Zohar, D. (1997). *Rewiring the Corporate Brain: Using the New Science to rethink how we structure and Lead Organizations*. San Francisco: Berrett-Koehler.

Chapter 13

Fethullah Gülen as a Servant-Leader

Gürkan Çelik and Yusuf Alan

The[1] leadership literature enumerates different leadership types and qualities (Northouse, 2019). This chapter examines servant-leadership by using an empirical example with a coherent theoretical basis. It centers on Fethullah Gülen, the initiator of a worldwide faith-based social movement. The Turkish-born Gülen has lived in self-exile in the United States near Saylorsburg since 1999 because of Turkey's repressive political atmosphere and for health reasons (Palh, 2019). He speaks of Islam, writes mystical works, does not want to build mosques, but schools. He has been called a harmonizing leader and an Islamic intellectual scholar (*ulama*) focusing on social reforms and mentality change (Alam, 2019; Bulaç, 2005; Mercan, 2019). But Gülen also has been opposed by a number of people outside the movement. First, the Kemalist state of Turkey saw him as a danger: he would undermine the secular character of the country. He then became a figurehead of modern Turkey in which democracy and Islam can go hand in hand. But the situation has changed again: after the Gezipark protests in the summer of 2013 at Taksim Square in Istanbul, and especially in the run-up to the 2016 coup attempt, Gülen has increasingly become the subject of hatred and enmity for Turkish President Erdoğan.

The movement initiated by Gülen emerged in the late 1960s as a local group around Izmir, an Aegean province in Turkey. By the mid-1980s, it had led to the establishment of schools and spread rapidly to other parts of Turkey, transforming itself into a nationwide movement. In the 1990s, the Gülen movement, also known as *Hizmet* ("service" in Turkish), experienced its second transformation; by opening institutions internationally and gathering followers from various nationalities, it went from a national to a transnational social movement (Çelik, 2010; Çetin, 2009; Çelik, Leman, & Steenbrink, 2015; Ebaugh, 2010). Given this rapid growth, it is worth analyzing the role of Gülen's leadership in the transformation and extension processes. This chapter offers an answer to the question of which characteristics and dynamics of his leadership style have played key roles in the spread and success of his movement. A thorough analysis of his leadership can offer important insights into successful leadership approaches and help to understand his philosophical and theological anthropology and views on the human condition.

In this chapter, we discuss the concept of leadership in Islam, in general, and Gülen's leadership pattern, in particular. First, we provide a brief biography of Gülen and Hizmet to provide a broad picture of his leadership role and style. Second, we analyze his views on and practices of leadership, emphasizing both his formative and determinant leadership characteristics. In addressing these topics, we take the concept of servant-leadership as our main framework, with appropriate references made to the various dimensions of Gülen's leadership. To analyze his leadership approach, a systematic review of speeches and relevant written works by and about Gülen was carried out. Additionally, several in-depth interviews with Gülen experts, students, and followers are anonymously cited to gain additional insights into his leadership style.[2] In our analysis, we used Gülen's thoughts on this topic and examined his actions and deeds to provide a well-rounded picture of his leadership.

THE GÜLEN-INSPIRED MOVEMENT

Gülen was born in 1941 in Erzurum, a province in eastern Turkey, less than a generation after the collapse of the Ottoman Empire and the establishment of the Republic of Turkey in 1923. The Turkish War for Independence, the transition from one regime to another, World War II, and the global phenomenon of modernity versus religion had all taken a toll on Turkey and its newly emerging citizens. It was within this context that Gülen grew up and experienced the difficulty, degradation, and poverty of his country's people. Education was sporadic, materialism rampant, and civic-mindedness replaced by egocentrism. Seeing all this, Gülen embarked on a lifelong journey to make a difference by promoting education, economic activism, and a re-reading and fresh understanding of religious texts to evoke voluntarism, worldly ascetics, and a type of universalism that kept local values and customs alive (Çelik, 2010; Ünal, 2002; Valkenberg, 2015).

Fethullah Gülen has been lauded as a Muslim initiator and intellectual leader who inspired social and educational activities intended to develop a new sense of religiosity in touch with modern realities (Çelik & Alan, 2012; Pahl, 2019; Yavuz & Esposito, 2003).[3] He is also known for his contributions to world peace through dialogue activities and educational efforts around the globe (Ateş, Karakaş, & Ortaylı, 2005; Çelik, 2011; Çelik, Cobben, van Dijk, & Valkenberg, 2005; Esposito & Yilmaz, 2010).[4] In interviews, talks, and writings, Gülen continually and argumentatively underlined the importance of understanding, education, dialogue, and tolerance, in addition to moral and spiritual values (Ergene, 2008; Gülen, 2010; Sarıtoprak, 2005). Throughout his life, he has always articulated that "there is goodness in peace and peace is always good" (Mercan, 2017, p. 175).[5] People know him as an advocate for tolerance and dialogue, a man of extraordinary breadth, a scholar with a profound appreciation for Islamic sciences and contemporary thought, and a passionate activist (Carroll, 2007; Sevindi, 2008; Ünal & Williams, 2000). He obtained his license to preach in 1959 at the age of eighteen and began giving sermons at mosques, speeches at conferences, and talks at public coffeehouses in Turkey. His objective was to cultivate the "ideal individuals" who would combine spirituality with intellect, reason with revelation, and mind with heart. He wanted the new generation of Turks to have sound faith, motivated love, a balanced perception of science, and a newly re-evaluated view of the human condition. This goal was to promote free-thinking and respect for freedom of thought where collective consciousness was combined with a multi-dimensional and mathematical logic and appreciation of art (Gülen, 2005a). Many observers regard Gülen as a Muslim intellectual leader who puts people and their spiritual, ethical, and personal development at the center of everything (Alam, 2019; Mercan, 2019; Pahl, 2019; Sevindi, 2008). Gülen's (2004) particular purpose was and still is to urge a younger, "golden" generation to integrate intellectuality and modern realities with morality, wise spirituality, and caring, humane, and democratic activism. He developed a positive vision of an individual who can solve the problems of humanity in a harmonious and dialogical manner (Çelik & Steenbrink, 2015; Gülen, 2004). He believes unwaveringly that the initial step in any action and every kind of work demands ethics, self-knowledge, and being aware of one's helplessness, deficiency, and inadequacy (Çelik, 2010, p. 111).

In the fifty years since the movement began in the late 1960s, Gülen's personal efforts have borne significant results. His followers constitute one of the largest faith-and-dialogue-based movements in the world, which has evolved into a dense web of transnational educational and charitable networks (Agai, 2004; Ergil, 2012) that is now active in more than 170 countries (Çelik et al., 2015). While crossing borders, this movement has been engaged in promoting and advancing intercommunal, intercultural, and interfaith dialogue between all segments of society (Michel, 2005). In Turkey, the cradle of the movement, Gülen's followers successfully established hundreds of schools, colleges, and several universities, organized businesspeople and entrepreneurs around a common platform (*Tüskon*), established Turkey's largest daily newspaper (*Zaman*), television channels like Samanyolu and Dünya, and several magazines like *Sızıntı*, *The Fountain*, *Yeni Ümit*, and *Yağmur*.

However, after the July 15, 2016 coup attempt in Turkey, President Erdoğan and his AKP government immediately accused Gülen of being the brains behind the coup. Schools and universities, charitable institutions, television channels, and media companies associated with his name were all confiscated—if they had not previously been closed. Those thought to be associated with Gülen, including judges and prosecutors, police officers, teachers, academics, and businesspersons, were arrested en masse, fired, or prosecuted as terrorists and traitors for alleged involvement in the coup attempt.[6] The Turkish government under leadership of Erdoğan asked the United States to extradite Gülen. However, the U.S. government demands hard evidence of his involvement. Gülen keeps repeating that he had nothing to do with it. He wants the coup attempt to be investigated by an independent international commission (Gülen, 2016). He says to accept the results of such an investigation immediately and unconditionally. Such a commission of inquiry has not yet been installed.

The movement now seems to be ruined entirely in Turkey, but outside Turkey, the movement, which evolved around the ideas of Fethullah Gülen, continues his activities and projects—though not as intensively as before the attempted coup—and provides an example of a renewal with the potential to impact the relationship between modernity and spirituality in the world and public life (Valkenberg, 2015; Weller & Yilmaz, 2012).

Gülen tirelessly preaches to his people from his residence in Pennsylvania and inspires and encourages his followers to contribute to world peace by building bridges between peoples and cultures, serving humanity just for the sake of God (Alam, 2019; Pahl, 2019).[7] More notably, he frequently emphasizes that his own position is more of an inspirational and guiding thinker, rather than the formal leader of a social movement. In January 1995, the journalist Nuriye Akman of *Sabah* asked Gülen: "Can humility change the reality? Since a group has gathered around your name, don't you automatically become a leader?" Gülen replied as follows:

> I insist on saying "I am not a leader" because I expressed my thoughts for 30 years in the pulpits (of mosques) and people sharing the same feelings and thoughts responded. For example, I said to them: "Establish university preparatory courses. Establish schools." As an expression of their respect for me, they listened to what I said. This might have been a mistake, but they listened and we met at that point. I saw that just as I was saying "schools," I found that a lot of people were saying "schools". They come to ask about other, especially religious, issues as well. Sometimes they even ask about economic matters. I tell them that "such issues require subject-specific expertise," and send them to experts. (Ünal & Williams, 2000, p. 34)

Despite this modesty, it is clear that, for many, Gülen does indeed stand at the head of a vast, transnational movement that has achieved and appears likely to continue to enjoy considerable and repeated successes in its chosen fields. In seeking to identify the immediate causes of this success and his leadership, we examine his approach to leadership from an Islamic perspective, along with his own writings and statements about leadership, education, and dialogue.

LEADERSHIP FROM AN ISLAMIC PERSPECTIVE

Leadership in Islam is based on trust and emphasizes sincerity, integrity, and compassion. It is a psychological contract between a leader and his or her followers, guaranteeing that the leader will do everything possible to guide them, protect them, and treat them justly. Leadership in Islam is rooted in the belief in and a willing submission to the Creator; it centers on serving Him. This means that a Muslim leader acts in accordance with the injunctions of the Creator and His Prophet and must develop a strong Islamic moral character that requires leaders to emphasize the following five key parameters of Islamic behavior: justice, trust, righteousness, the struggle within oneself toward self-improvement, and promise-keeping (Beekun & Badawi, 1999, pp. 25–33).

From a general and historical approach, we can divide leadership types in Islam into three categories: spiritual leaders, opinion leaders, and "application leaders." Spirituality refers to leaders' views regarding Sufism and religiosity, and religious leadership can be classified as part of spiritual leadership. Opinion leaders include Muslim intellectuals and scholars, along with those who mainly contribute to the followers' intellectual development. Application leaders refer primarily to pioneering activists in Islam.

The two primary leadership roles from an Islamic perspective are those of servant-leader and guardian-leader. First, leaders are servants of their followers (*sayyid al qawmi khadimuhum*; Çaldıranlı, 1998). They look out for their welfare and guide them toward what is good. The idea of a leader as a servant has been part of Islam since its beginning and has only recently been further developed by Robert K. Greenleaf (1991). We describe this below while explaining the leadership characteristics of Gülen from the perspective of servant-leadership. A second major role of the Muslim leader is guardian-leader, who strives to protect their community against tyranny and oppression. Guardian-leaders also encourage God-consciousness and *taqwa* (piety) and promote justice, trust, and integrity (Beekun & Badawi, 1999, p. 15); in other words, leaders are considered honest to the extent that there is consistency between word and deed. In the Qur'an (Al-Qasas, 28:26), the Prophet Moses is described as "strong and trustworthy," and the Prophet Yusuf is depicted as truthful (Yusuf, 12:46). It is reported from Sahih Bukhari that Prophet Mohammed said, "all of you are guardians and are responsible for your wards" (Hadith 3.733). Affirmingly, Gülen (1996, pp. 92–124) characterizes the Prophet of Islam as a universal and unique leader and indicates that the Prophet Mohammed has shown the path to Muslim leaders and followers for all time. Successful Muslim leaders endeavor to acquire practical knowledge and the ability to apply it appropriately. People are more likely to follow leaders' directives if they believe that leaders know what they are doing. Additionally, aspiring leaders in Islam are encouraged to emulate attributes like strength of character, patience (*sabr*), humility, magnanimity, self-understanding, the willingness to seek consultation, equity (impartiality), modesty (simplicity), and responsibility (Beekun & Badawi, 1999, pp. 37–47).

SERVANT-LEADERSHIP

In social life, people have a window, or status, through which they see and are seen by others. If the window is built higher than their real stature, people try to make themselves appear taller through vanity and assumed airs. If the window is set lower than their real stature, they must bow in humility in order to look out: to see and be seen. Humility or modesty is thus the measure of greatness, while vanity or conceit is the measure of low character: "The greater one is the one who is the modest one" is a well-known adage in the Islamic tradition (Gülen, 2005b, pp. 297–298). Modesty is a great virtue. To Said Nursi (2008), humility is the most important aspect of leaders' servanthood.

The Prophet Mohammed defines a leader as the servant of the people. Once, when the Prophet was serving his friends, a Bedouin came in and shouted: "Who is the master of these people?" Mohammed answered so as to introduce himself while expressing a significant principle of Islamic leadership and public administration: "The people's master is the one who serves them."[8] Ali, his son-in-law, also reported that Mohammed was one of the people. This community leadership principle was also written down centuries ago on the wall of the old town hall of Den Bosh in The Netherlands: "People can only be led by serving them."

Simply put, the understanding of servant-leadership is founded on serving the people. This sense of leadership is also considered by Gülen and many other Islamic scholars to be an example of the illustrious practices of the Prophet that have been a way of life for and guide to managers and leaders for almost fifteen centuries. If leaders do not sacrifice and serve, then the followers, the people, or the employees will not follow suit; they do not feel loyalty, trust, or fidelity (Çelik & Alan, 2003). In servant-leadership, there is no intention to be a master but to serve the nation. Nevertheless, he or she who serves people is their master. The perspective of servant-leadership is based on the awareness that leadership begins with servanthood.

According to contemporary management criteria, "if administrators or managers participate in a project or team, the system will function better, and the performance, employee engagement, and employee involvement will increase" (cf. Tims, Arnold, & Xanthopoulou, 2011; Vincent-Höper, Muser, & Janneck, 2012; Wedley & Ferrie, 1978). Although the phrasing appears new, this dominant tenet of management is fundamentally the same principle: "The master of a community is the one who serves them." Accordingly, managers who want to gain value from people should sweat, serve, roll up their sleeves, and clean their own desks. But some might have the following question: "Should there be a hierarchy at all?" Indeed, there should not be in this sense. Respect is a matter of decision, not of expectation. Leaders and managers cannot solve anything through domination, whereas modesty and participation in activities help enormously in getting things done. As Gülen puts it, "When people are cooking, and you are expected to blow into the fire, you should do it, and if you are expected to collect wood, you should do it. In the home environment, if necessary, washing the dishes, making soup, cleaning, constantly helping the household is the practice of this conception" (2011, p. 154).

Robert K. Greenleaf (1904–1990) reintroduced this leadership concept during the second half of the twentieth century: "The servant-leader is servant first. It begins with the natural feeling that one wants to serve. Then conscious choice brings one to aspire to lead" (1991, pp. 7–8). Greenleaf (1977/2002) builds on examples found in the New Testament (Sendjaya & Sorras, 2002), proposing that service to followers is the primary responsibility of leaders and the essence of ethical leadership. The servant-leader seeks to involve others in decision-making. His or her philosophy promotes ethical and caring behavior and enhances the personal growth of workers while improving the quality of organizational, intellectual, and spiritual life (Çelik, 2002).

Servant-leaders may or may not hold formal leadership positions. This leadership principle is central to unlocking a dilemma of humanity: is it possible to be virtuous and powerful, to both serve and lead? Synchronous manifestation of opposites can cause a sort of wise and beneficial contest. Opposites transgress each other's bounds, which brings conflict and change into being. The universe is subject to the law of change and transformation and the principles of progress and advancement. The dilemma of opposites opens the door to striving, which is the means of all human progress. Servant-leadership is a dynamic balance that uses dialogue, trust, and sincerity to produce and reproduce knowledge, identity, and culture in a globalized time

(Laub, 1999). Gülen defines servant-leadership as the way of the Prophets, and it has developed in leaders' daily lives since the beginning of Islam.[9] Service reminds servants to be useful to their nations and the whole of humanity.

But servant-leadership still appears contradictory and challenges our traditional beliefs about leadership. Leaders lead and servants follow; that is common sense (Northouse, 2019). How can leadership be both service and influence? How can a person be a leader and a servant at the same time? In different parts of our lives, we are leaders and followers. We can be employees at work but leaders of the family at home. Even when we are managers at work, we are still responsible to a higher authority. One of the most exciting contrasts is servant-leadership, which makes servant and leader coexist, synthesizing the two roles. Servant-leadership offers a unique perspective that encourages everyone to establish a balance between these two roles. In the end, it is expected that simultaneously playing these two roles makes significant contributions to the quality of our institutions and enriches our individual lives. The servant-leader is, above all, a servant. Greenleaf believed that followers of such leaders are inspired to become servant-leaders themselves (Yukl, 2013).

A servant—and thus a leader—is a person who tries to be useful to his or her people and to all humanity. The sense of being a servant comes from a natural sense of helping others. This conscious choice leads a person to leadership, making leaders even out of those who neither sought nor expected that role. The crucial element is service, not leadership, which is but a special case of service.

Servant-leaders put followers first, empower them, and help them develop their full personal capacities. They prefer to serve first and then lead. The most successful leaders are talented, determined, prudent, exceptional personalities who consider themselves servants, working for the joy of humanity in the spirit of dedication. The essence of dedication is to abandon the pleasure of living for the sake of the pleasure of living for others.

Servant-leaders respect those around them and take care of their needs and desires, especially in difficult times. Servant-leaders value everyone's skills and capacity and guide people according to their abilities. They contribute to the development of those around them. The servant-leader does not say, "I do not care," but always acts with a sense of responsibility. Servant-leaders love people, and people love them.

Today, the approach to managing people in the classic, authoritarian, and oppressive style has become outdated. Administrators with that sense of management cannot buy the hearts, minds, and souls of those under their responsibility (Covey, 2013). What they can buy and control in return for a salary is only the time and labor of employees. Servant-leadership is an understanding far from strict control. In the twenty-first century, only companies and institutions that can attract the hearts and energy of employees to the work or the organization will survive.

In the same way, all institutions and organizations that serve society in every field and level will be able to maintain their existence as long as they conquer the hearts of people, ensure their peace, and nurture their motivation. This requires servanthood, sacrifice, and a sincerity of intention. Servant-leadership is an understanding of positive and structural changes that require a long-term transformation of our perspective and business life.

GÜLEN AND THE TEN CHARACTERISTICS OF A SERVANT-LEADER

Larry Spears (1998a,b) has identified ten characteristics of the servant-leader. They are based on Robert Greenleaf's work, are by no means exhaustive, and often occur naturally within individuals. The possession of these characteristics marks the greatest and most prominent leaders in history and in today's world. We applied these characteristics to Gülen to analyze his leadership path and patterns.

Listening

Leaders have traditionally been valued for their dialogue competencies, communication talents, and decision-making skills. Listening, coupled with periods of reflection, is essential to the growth and well-being of the servant-leader. Gülen is experienced as a person and leader with a deep commitment to listening intently to others and seeks to identify the will, perceptions, and intentions of his audience to help clarify their will and views. He listens receptively to what is said and what is unsaid. His listening also encompasses the idea of getting in touch with one's inner voice. Gülen has strong will-power and resolve; all respondents have indicated that they never saw him evince even one moment of hopelessness.

Empathy

People need to be accepted and recognized for their unique spirits. The most successful servant-leaders are those who have become skilled empathetic listeners. According to the respondents, Gülen strives to understand and empathize with others; he is characterized as a person who puts himself in the position of the other and tries to understand that person's perceptions and experiences. The cultivation of empathy gives one the basis for detachment, the ability to stand aside and see oneself in a perspective relative to the context of one's experience.

Healing

The healing of relationships is a powerful force for dialogue, transformation, and integration. One of Gülen's great strengths is his belief in the potential for healing one's self and one's relationships with others. Many people have broken spirits and have suffered from a variety of emotional traumas. Although this is a part of being human, servant-leaders recognize that they have an opportunity to help make people whole. Gülen has dedicated his life to solving social problems, satisfying spiritual needs (2004), healing relations between people, and encouraging interpersonal and intercultural dialogue (2010).

Awareness

General awareness—especially self-awareness—strengthens the servant-leader. Awareness helps one understand issues involving ethics, power, and values. It lends itself to realism and being able to view most situations from a more integrated, holistic position. As Greenleaf observes, "awareness is not a giver of solace; it is just the opposite. It is a disturber and an awakener. Able leaders are usually sharply awake and reasonably alert. They do not seek solace. They have their own inner serenity" (1991, p. 20). Everything should be directed toward perfecting one's awareness of personal responsibility. In no way should one be seduced by the world's charms and life's attractions. Gülen understands the issues and prevailing conditions as they actually are; he is aware of all advantages and disadvantages. His messages and demands do not contradict reality. His students also indicated that he offers intuitive insights about the future when needed and that his doors of perception are open wide.

Persuasion

When making decisions within his community, Gülen relies on persuasion and absolute belief in his message rather than on positional authority. He seeks to convince others instead of coercing compliance, is effective at building consensus within groups, and promotes a genuine dialogue among cultures, religions, and civilizations. Gülen (2010) has stated that the only way to get others to accept your ideas in the modern world is by persuasion. This message comes to the fore in both his sermons and his activities. It originated in Gülen's influential mentor, Said Nursi (1876–1960), whose "victory with civilized persons is won through persuasion" is often cited by Gülen. In this respect, Gülen can be characterized as a highly persuasive person. The respondents emphasized that his conviction has never faltered and that he has never renounced his mission. Persuasion is, according to respondents, also related to Gülen's personal courage. Even if left alone, he has enough courage to persevere and resist all the difficulties he might encounter. Gülen shows high confidence in his followers, is very persuasive, and is very proficient in his use of body and verbal language. He also makes effective use of storytelling, including the use of symbolism and metaphor to motivate his audience. We observe in his speeches and sermons that he frequently uses stories about the Companions of the Prophet Mohammed to motivate his audience.

Conceptualization

Gülen seeks to nurture his abilities to dream great dreams. The ability to look at a problem or a society from a conceptualizing perspective means that one must think beyond day-to-day realities. Gülen stretches his thinking to encompass broader conceptual thinking and seeks a delicate balance between conceptual thinking and a common operational approach. He always takes local conditions and circumstances into account. The respondents also indicated that Gülen pays a great deal of attention to surveying and studying his environment, honing his words and deeds to suit the situation. Gülen's activism and global thinking strongly affirm his capability to conceptualize.

Foresight

Leaders must have a sense of direction and a long-term vision. This characteristic is also closely related to conceptualization and being goal centered. Foresight enables the servant-leader to understand lessons from the past, the realities of the present, and a given decision's likely consequences in the future. According to the respondents, this aspect of Gülen's leadership is deeply rooted in his intuitive mind. Foresight remains a largely unexplored area in leadership studies but comes to the fore as the most notable characteristic of his leadership when we look at his community leadership since the 1960s. All respondents confirmed that Gülen is farsighted and goal centered. He can discern and plan for potential developments, evaluating the past, present, and future to reach a new synthesis.

Stewardship

Peter Block (1993, pp. xx) has defined stewardship as "holding something in trust for another." Gülen views institutions as places where all members play significant roles in holding their institutions in trust for the greater good of society. Servant-leadership, like stewardship, assumes above all a commitment to serving the needs of others. Gülen also emphasizes the use of openness and persuasion rather than control and points out that dialogue, persuasion, and discussion based on evidence are essential for people who seek to serve humanity. According to the respondents, Gülen has a strong character and praiseworthy virtues. He is determined but flexible while carrying out decisions and knows when to be unyielding and when to be relenting and compassionate. He knows when to be earnest and dignified and when to be modest; always, he is upright, truthful, trustworthy, and just.

Commitment to the Growth of People

Servant-leaders believe that people have an intrinsic value beyond their tangible contributions as workers. This means that leaders should have personal knowledge of followers. Leaders should be fully aware of each follower's dispositions, character, competencies, shortcomings, ambitions, and weak points. If they lack this knowledge, how can they fill vacant posts with the appropriate people? Gülen is deeply committed to the growth of every individual within his community. He recognizes the tremendous responsibility to do everything in his power to nurture the spiritual, personal, and professional growth of everyone in that community. From Gülen's perspective, this includes encouraging people to continue serving humanity, involving others in decision-making, and caring for one another.

Building Community

The servant-leader senses that much has been lost in recent human history as a result of the shift from local communities to large institutions as the primary shaper of human lives. This awareness causes the servant-leader to search for means to build a genuine community among those who work within a given institution. Greenleaf puts it this way: "All that is needed to rebuild community as a viable life form for large numbers of people is for enough servant-leaders to show the way, not by mass movements, but by each servant-leader demonstrating his or her unlimited devotion to a quite specific community-related group" (1991, p. 30). The community, which has formed around Gülen, is itself a concrete example of the servant-leadership principle of building community. Most respondents stressed that modesty, and an absence of worldly ambitions and abuse of authority, are the crucial aspects of Gülen's growing community. Leaders should live like the weakest members of their community. They should never discriminate among their subjects; instead, they should strive to love them, prefer them over themselves, and act so that their people will love them sincerely. They should be faithful to their community and secure their community's loyalty and devotion in return. Gülen concentrates on making the community very clear and distinct by separating it from other communities. He constantly attempts to build the image of the community in the hearts and minds of his followers.

Our analysis shows that Gülen possesses a substantial number of the servant-leadership qualities mentioned above. Most respondents believed Gülen to be realistic and felt convinced that the message he conveys to people is true and practicable. He has a courageous nature and strong willpower, remaining buoyant and hopeful despite the tensions of self, life, and community. He is aware of his responsibility (cf. Robinson, 2017) and of possible hindrances and stumbling blocks. Systematically and purposefully, he is working on his activities, projects, and programs. He is farsighted and proactive and has determined his goals well. He knows the members of his community individually and mobilizes them to reach their goals. Furthermore, the respondents describe him as a person who does not cherish worldly ambitions or abuse his authority.

An overwhelming majority of respondents emphasized that Gülen is a servant first, and then a leader. He is not a charismatic leader, who tends to demand blind obedience and dependence from followers. Although Gülen is highly respected by the movement's participants, they see him as a wise and revered person and a generator of opinions, not a charismatic figure. They see Gülen primarily as a religious leader and as a prominent source of inspiration for establishing intercultural dialogue and initiating educational projects and institutions around the world.[10]

According to Karakaş's analysis (2006), Gülen's way of leadership is closer to servant-leadership than charismatic leadership. Fontenot and Fontenot (2009, pp. 147–165) agree, differentiating Gülen from charismatic leaders and identifying him as a transformational leader who can "transform" his followers' attitudes, beliefs, and behaviors[11] to socially engaged and active people. The potential benefits derived from development and empowerment of followers, volunteers, and workers have been widely demonstrated in studies on participative, supportive, and transformational leadership.

We also found examples of this conviction in Gülen's conversations, interviews, sermons, and writings. In 1995, the journalist Nuriye Akman made the following statement to Gülen: "You always emphasize that you're not a sheikh (or the leader of a dervish order), nor do you show any tendency to accept that you are a leader of a religious community." Gülen answered her question from the perspective of a servant—even a "slave"—instead of a leader: "I've never called myself a leader. I'm an ordinary man. A leader is someone with capabilities, genius, charisma, and high performance. I don't have any of those" (Akman, 1995).

Gülen is further typified as a man of deliberate action who never hesitated in putting his plans into action. Respondents indicated that consultation is one of Gülen's eminent practices, demonstrating the decision-making process that defines his leadership style. Furthermore, he has been described as a leader who gains the love and trust of his followers by solving their problems, whether personal or public, whether individual or touching the community as a whole.

Gülen offers hope, caring, and responsibility for future generations to produce and work better. He promotes the value and development of people, the building of community, the practice of authenticity, the providing of leadership for the good of those led, and the sharing of power, knowledge, and status for the common good of each individual and an inclusive society. Gülen's leadership supports people who choose to serve first and then lead as a way of expanding service to individuals, institutions, and societies. His leadership style encourages enthusiasm, synergy, trust, foresight, listening, and the ethical use of power and empowerment.

In addition to the above characteristics, the experts and followers we interviewed pointed out that the Gülen's understanding and praxis of leadership is primarily supported by his faith and thus involves certain theological foundations. The following are some excerpts from our interviews:

Gülen's ultimate aim is to have the consent of God. His understanding of leadership is premised on the belief that there is no aim or reward beyond the approval and love of God. The easiest way to acquire this is obeying the rules explained by the Prophet Mohammed and imitating the Prophet's way of life.

Gülen's purpose is not to be or become a leader; he would rather be a slave and servant. He has so many followers that he does not even have a desire to lead. He regards his "reputation" as a credit from God and uses this to motivate people. One who cannot manage his or her worldly desires cannot rehabilitate someone else.

Gülen never "contaminates" the realities and does not "shade" the facts with any personal interest. Therefore, the messages reflect what is in his mind and heart and what illuminates people.

Gülen always interrogates himself; he never deceives himself. He practices what he preaches. It is this sincere and honest search for reality that has won him millions of global followers. His followers are disciples of sincerity, honesty, and compassion.

In the end, the respondents stressed that Gülen's inspiration comes from religion, and it is his devotion to God that makes people follow him.

CONCLUDING REMARKS

In conclusion, we can say that although Gülen is known as an Islamic scholar and spiritual guide, he is also a leader possessing extraordinary competences like intuition and foresight that extend beyond any one faith. From our analysis, we have concluded that Gülen has led his community intellectually, spiritually, and socially and has transformed a tremendous traditional social movement that emerged in Turkey into a worldwide community in close touch with modernity. Internationally, the Hizmet movement has extended its network of educational and dialogue efforts to all parts of the globe. Some people inside and outside the movement describe him as a charismatic figure. However, rather than having charisma, he describes himself as a servant. He is regarded as a caring community leader with a profound appreciation of the Islamic sciences and contemporary thought and a passionate activist (Sarıtoprak, 2005). Successful leaders represent and express what they hope to attain through their actions and then translate those efforts into words. As Gülen himself puts it, "for us action precedes thought" (1998, p. 91); this is a distinguishing characteristic of his leadership style.

Moreover, we argue that Gülen possesses two essential leadership characteristics. He developed his own philosophy and knew his way very well (demonstrating a *clear vision*), and he is reliable and on a path (indicating *deliberate actions*). The leadership principle that the whole world steps aside for the person who knows where to go is also accompanied by the charm and grace needed to create followers. He can persuade other people to go with him. The Hizmet movement inspired by Gülen counts millions of sympathizers worldwide, and people follow others that they personally admire. Legitimate leaders gather followers through dint of personality and charm not through external power or authority.

Great leaders have different leadership qualities and can be leaders not only in one aspect of life but can—and should—lead their community or organization to success in other areas. Many of the greatest and most influential commanders, politicians, community leaders, religious leaders, and spiritual guides in human history have done just that. And leaders are the servants of the communities they represent; that is, if a leader claims to be the master of a nation, institution, company, society, or community, he or she should devote himself or herself to their service. From these points of view, we can characterize Gülen as a servant-leader of his community, in particular, and of humanity, in general.

In sum, his leadership is based on a deep understanding of the faith and the core values that drive his actions. Effective leadership requires the development of a compelling personal and spiritual vision that engages others by offering meaning, dignity, and purpose. In this respect, Gülen is a living example of a servant-leader, the kind of leader who is necessary to solve the common problems of humanity: ignorance, poverty, and discord.[12] One of the central aims of his leadership is building a golden generation featuring more humane relationships, institutions, and societies. What can be learned from Gülen's example is that effective leaders need to develop the dynamism, harmony, and critical imagination required to embrace individual, organizational, and global change through the use of dialogue, peace, cooperation, hope, and courage. The scope of this study is not enough to analyze all leadership aspects and patterns of Fethullah Gülen. Further research could focus, for example, on his leadership trihelix of intellectual, behavioral, and spiritual aspects.

Finally, looking at our century, we see that there are leaders like Gülen who have embraced the line of servant-leadership and practiced it as a way of life in various parts of the world (cf. Ferch, 2012), with forgiveness, wisdom, love, and legitimate power in an age of chaos. The presence of these leaders is an excellent benevolence for the sake of humanity. They are the ones who cultivate future servant-leaders with the seeds they sow and the troubles they suffer. To understand whether a person is a servant-leader, the best test is to look at those around him or her: "Do those served grow as persons? Do they, while being served, become healthier, wiser, freer, more autonomous, more likely themselves to become servants?" (Greenleaf, 1974, p. 27). This is the heart of the matter.

NOTES

1. This chapter was previously published as Celik, G., & Yusuf, A. (2007). Fethullah Gülen as a servant-leader. *The International Journal of Servant-Leadership.* *3*(1), 247–265.

2. All interviewee names have been anonymized and oral consent was provided for the use of their words in this chapter.

3. This view is also held by leading journalists, academics, TV personalities, politicians, and Turkish and foreign state authorities.

4. The Romanian commission of UNESCO presented Fethullah Gülen with an award for his contributions to tolerance and dialogue and for his efforts toward cooperation and peace between the nations of the world. See www.fgulen.com, his official internet site.

5. Gülen's talk dated 9 January 2013, http://tr.fgulen.com/content/view/21600/11

6. As of 4 March 2019 the figures are as follows: 150,348 people have been sacked, with 6,021 academics and 4,463 judges and prosecutors dismissed; 500,650 people have been detained, and 85,998 have been arrested; 3,003 schools, dormitories, and universities have been closed; 189 media outlets have been shut down; and

319 journalists have been arrested. These figures include state officials, teachers, bureaucrats, members of the security forces, and academics dismissed by government decree since July 15, 2016 (www.turkeypurge.com).

7. See www.herkul.org, the website announcing his weekly speeches.

8. See the hadith in *Ibn Hisham*, 2:137.

9. Unpublished notes from talks of Fethullah Gülen, 21–28 August 2003.

10. The analysis is based on the authors' personal interviews and observations of the Gülen movement.

11. Karen Fontenot and Michael Fontenot analyze Gülen's leadership style and his influence on the movement by using transformational leadership theory. This concept was first introduced by Burns (1978) and further developed by Bass (1985). Based on Bass's four dimensions of transformational leadership—idealized influence, inspirational motivation, individualize consideration, and intellectual stimulation—both scholars demonstrate how Gülen embodies those attributes and identify him as exemplary in transforming the way Islamic thought relates to the imperatives of modern society.

12. Terror, anarchy, and conflict are the three main enemies of humanity and are caused by the combination of ignorance, poverty, and discord—as put by Nursi (2002, p. 81) almost a century ago. According to him, they can only be overcome with the cooperation of knowledge (through education), work capital (through labor), and unification (through dialogue).

REFERENCES

Agai, B. (2004). *Zwischen Netzwerk und Diskurs–Das Bildungsnetzwerk um Fethullah Gülen (geb. 1938): Die flexible Umsetzung modernen islamischen Gedankenguts* [Between network and discourse–The educational network around Fethullah Gülen: The flexible implementation of modern Islamic ideas]. Schenefeld bei Hamburg: Eb-Verlag.

Akman, N. (1995). I feel extremely uncomfortable. I don't have such a principle. *Sabah.*

Alam, A. (2019). *For the sake of Allah: The origin, development and discourse of the Gülen movement.* Clifton, NJ: Blue Dome Press.

Ateş, T., Karakaş, E., & Ortaylı. I. (2005). *Barış Köprüleri: Dünyaya Açılan Türk Okulları* [Bridges for peace: Turkish schools opened to the world]. Istanbul: Ufuk Kitapları (DA Yayınları).

Bass, B. M. (1985). *Leadership and performance Beyond Expectations.* New York, NY: Free Press.

Beekun, R. I., & Badawi, J. (1999). *Leadership: An Islamic perspective.* Beltsville, MD: Amana Publishers.

Block, P. (1993). *Stewardship: Choosing service Over Self-Interest.* San Francisco, CA: Berrett-Koehler.

Bulaç, A. (2005). Fethullah Gülen: An intellectual and religious profile. Paper presented at the conference Islam in the Contemporary World: The Fethullah Gülen

Movement in Thought and Practice, 12–13 November 2005, Rice University, Houston, TX.

Burns, J. M. (1978). *Leadership.* New York, NY: Harper & Row.

Çaldıranlı, S. (1998). Hizmetkar Liderlik [Servant leadership]. *Sızıntı, 239,* 489–493.

Carroll, B. J. (2007). *A dialogue of civilizations: Gülen's Islamic ideals and humanistic discourse.* Somerset, NJ: The Light, Inc. & The Gülen Institute.

Çelik, G. (2010). *The Gülen movement: Building Social Cohesion Through Dialogue and education.* Delft: Eburon.

———. (2011). Peacebuilding through dialogue and education: Lessons from the Gülen movement. *Journal of Peacebuilding and Development, 6*(1), 86–90.

Çelik, G., & Alan, Y. (2003). *Hizmetkar Liderlik* [Servant leadership]. Rotterdam: Libertas Media.

Çelik, G., & Alan, Y. (2012). Modern ideals and Muslim identity: Harmony or contradiction? A text linguistic analysis of the Gülen teaching and movement. In P. Weller & I. Yilmaz (eds.), *European Muslims, civility and Public Life: Perspectives on and from the Gülen movement* (pp. 21–34). London: Continuum.

Çelik, G., & Steenbrink, K. (2015). Ethical priorities of Gülen: The true middle road. In G. Çelik, J. Leman, & K. Steenbrink (eds.), *Gülen-Inspired Hizmet in Europe. The Western journey of a Turkish Muslim movement.* (pp. 85–100). Brussels: Peter Lang.

Çelik, G., Leman, J., & Steenbrink, K. (eds.) (2015). *Gülen-Inspired Hizmet in Europe. The Western journey of a Turkish Muslim movement.* Brussels: Peter Lang.

Çetin, M. (2009). *The Gülen Movement: Civil service without borders.* New York, NY: Blue Dome Press.

Covey, S. R. (2013). *The Seven Habits of Highly Effective People: Powerful lessons in Personal Change* (25th anniversary ed.). New York, NY: Simon & Schuster.

Ebaugh, H. R. (2010). *The Gülen movement: A Sociological Analysis of a Civic Movement Rooted in Moderate Islam.* Dordrecht: Springer.

Ergene, M. E. (2008). *Tradition witnessing the Modern Age: An analysis of the Gülen movement.* Istanbul: The Light, Inc.

Ergil, D. (2012). *Fethullah Gülen and the Gülen movement in 100 questions.* New York, NY: Blue Dome Press.

Esposito, J. L., & Yilmaz, I. (eds.) (2010). *Islam and peacebuilding: The Gülen movement initiatives.* New York, NY: Blue Dome Press.

Ferch, S. R. (2012). *Forgiveness and Power in the Age of Atrocity: Servant Leadership as a Way of Life.* Lanham, MD: Lexington Books.

Fontenot, K. A., & Fontenot, M. J. (2009). M. Fethullah Gülen as a transformational leader: Exemplar for the "Golden Generation." In *Proceedings of Islam in the Age of Global Challenges: Alternative Perspectives of the Gülen Movement* (pp. 149–165), held on 14–15 November 2008 at Georgetown University, Washington, DC: Rumi Forum.

Greenleaf, R. K. (1974). *Trustees as Servants.* Indianapolis, IN: The Greenleaf Center.

———. (1977/2002). *Servant leadership: A journey into the nature of Legitimate Power and greatness.* Mahwah, NJ; Paulist Press.

————. (1991). *The Servant as leader.* Indianapolis, IN: The Robert K. Greenleaf Center.

Gülen, M. F. (1996). *Prophet Muhammad as commander.* London: Truestar.

————. (1998). *İrşad Ekseni* [On Guidance]. Izmir: Nil.

————. (2004). *Key concepts in the practice of Sufism: Emerald hills of the heart.* Vol.1, *The Fountain.* Rutherford, NJ: The Light.

————. (2005a). *The statue of Our Souls: Revival in Islamic thoughts and activism.* Somerset, NJ: The Light, Inc.

————. (2005b). *The Messenger of God Muhammad: An analysis of the Prophet's life.* Somerset, NJ: The Light, Inc.

————. (2010). *Toward a Global Civilization of love and tolerance.* Somerset, NJ: The Light, Inc.

————. (2011). *Ümit Burcu* [The Tower of Hope]. Kırık Testi, vol. 4. İstanbul: Nil Yayınları.

————. (2016). "Fethullah Gülen: "Je demande une enquête internationale sur le putsch raté en Turquie" [Fethullah Gülen: "I demand an international commission for the coup attempt in Turkey], *Le Monde.*

Karakaş, F. (2006). Global peaceful social innovation: The case of Gulen network. In *Proceedings of Second International Conference on Islam in the Contemporary World: The Fethullah Gülen Movement in Thought and Practice*, 4–5 March, Southern Methodist University, Dallas, Texas.

Laub, J. A. (1999). *Assessing the servant organization* (doctoral dissertation). Boca Raton, FL: Florida Atlantic University.

Mercan, F. (2017). *No return from democracy: A survey of interviews with Fethullah Gülen.* Clifton, NJ: Blue Dome Press.

————. (2019). M. *Fethullah Gülen: Allah Yolunda bir Ömür* [A life in the path of Allah]. New Jersey, NJ: Sureyya Yayınları.

Michel, T. (2005). Een anlayse over de vrede [An analysis of the peace]. In. G. Çelik, P. Cobben, J. van Dijk, & P. Valkenberg (Eds.), *Voorlopers in de Vrede* [Forerunners in peace] (pp. 31–44). Budel, The Netherlands: Damon.

Northouse, P. G. (2019). *Leadership: Theory and practice* (8th edition). Los Angeles, CA: Sage.

Nursi, B. S. (2002). *The Damascus Sermon* (2nd edition). Translated by Ş. Vahide. Istanbul: Sözler Publications.

————. (2008). *Letters.* Risale-i Nur Collection. Vol. 2. Somerset, NJ: Tughra Books.

Pahl, J. (2019). *Fethullah Gülen. A life of Hizmet. Why a Muslim Scholar in Pennsylvania matters to the world.* Clifton, NJ: Blue Dome Press.

Robinson, S. (2017). *The spirituality of responsibility: Fethullah Gülen and Islamic thought.* London: Bloomsbury Academic.

Sarıtoprak, Z. (ed.). (2005). Islam in contemporary Turkey: The contributions of Fethullah Gülen. *The Muslim World, 95*(3), 325–471.

Sendjaja, S., & Sarros, J. C. (2002). Servant leadership: Its origin, development, and application in organizations. *Journal of Leadership amd Organizational Studies, 9*(2), 57–64.

Sevindi, N. (2008). *Contemporary Islamic conversations: M. Fethullah Gülen on Turkey, Islam, and the West.* Albany, NY: SUNY Press.

Spears, L. C. (1998a). Creating caring leadership for the 21st century. *The Not-for-Profit CEO Monthly Letter, 5*(9), 1–3.

———. (1998b). *The power of servant-leadership*. Indianapolis, IN: The Greenleaf Center for Servant-Leadership.

Tims, M., Arnold, B. B., & Xanthopoulou, D. (2011). Do transformational leaders enhance their followers' daily work engagement? *The Leadership Quarterly, 22*(1), 121–131.

Ünal, A. (2002). *M. Fethullah Gülen: Bir Portre Denemesi* [A Portrait Attempt]. Istanbul: Nil.

Ünal, A., & Williams, A. (eds.). (2000). *Fethullah Gülen: Advocate of dialogue*. Fairfax, VA: The Fountain.

Valkenberg, P. (2015). *Renewing Islam by service: A Christian view of Fethullah Gülen and the Hizmet movement*. Washington, DC: The Catholic University of America Press.

Vincent-Höper, S., Muser, C., & Janneck, M. (2012). Transformational leadership, work engagement, and occupational success. *Career Development International, 17*(7), 663–682.

Wedley, W., & Ferrie, A. J. (1978). Perceptual differences and effects of managerial participation on project implementation. *Journal of Operational Research Society, 29*(3): 199–204.

Weller, P., & Yilmaz, I. (eds.). (2012). *European Muslims, civility and Public Life: Perspectives on and from the Gülen movement*. London: Continuum.

Yavuz, M. H., & Esposito, J. L. (eds.). (2003). *Turkish Islam and the Secular State: The Gülen movement*. Syracuse, NY: Syracuse University Press.

Yukl, G. (2013). *Leadership in Organizations* (8th edition). Boston, ma: Pearson.

Chapter 14

Learners' Perceptions of Servant-Leadership in Classrooms

Kong Wah Chan

The[1] term "servant-leadership" was coined by Robert Greenleaf (1970) through his collection of essays titled *The Servant as Leader*. His message is that the best leader is first a servant. Beazley (2003) described servant-leadership as an art, a calling, a way of being, and a philosophy of life. Hence, it is not a modern theory of leadership and management technique but rather the process of serving and developing the led that are being served. Omoh (2007) considered that the results of servant-leadership include follower-empowerment, as well as mutual trust and collaboration between the servant-leader and the led. More specifically, Hays (2008) argued that the applications of servant-leadership principles can "make a profound difference on the impact of learning and in the learning experience of both students and teachers" (p. 113).

The researcher agrees with Hays that the belief of servant-leadership is in alignment with the purpose of education in school. The researcher's position is that those teachers who choose to be servant-leaders serve the needs of learners in classrooms, and in partnership with learners, create a learner-centered community operating with servant-leadership principles. This chapter seeks to explore the application of servant-leadership in meeting the cognitive, social, individual, and motivational needs of learners in classrooms of a Hong Kong school.

LITERATURE REVIEW

The imagery of a servant-leader is contradictory to the stereotypical dominating figure of a leader.

> The servant-leader is servant first . . . It begins with the natural feeling that one wants to serve, to serve first. Then conscious choice brings one to aspire to lead . . . The difference manifests itself in the care taken by the servant-first to make sure that other people's highest priority needs are being served. (Greenleaf, 1970, p. 13)

Its essence is hidden in the hyphenation between the words "servant" and "leader." Such punctuation highlights the fluid and hybrid nature of a servant-leader. Trompenaars and Voerman (2009) pointed out that the word *servant* is not a modifier of the word leader. *Servant-leader* is a compound noun. The two roles have equal values and are intrinsically linked. Blanchard (2007) described the blending of these two extremes as such:

> In the visionary role, leaders define the direction. It's their responsibility to communicate what the organization stands for and wants to accomplish . . . Once people are clear on where they are going, the leader's role shifts to a service mindset for the task of implementation. (p. 250)

In summary, a servant-leader casts a vision and supports its implementation. The true test of a servant-leader, as posted by Greenleaf (1970), is that the led "become healthier, wiser, freer, more autonomous, and more likely themselves to become servants" (p. 13).

CHARACTERISTICS OF A SERVANT-LEADER

Spears (2010) distilled Greenleaf's original writings into ten characteristics of servant-leaders. A servant-leader is characterized with the following attributes and desires to develop these traits while serving others. In the latter part of the list, Barbuto and Wheelers' (2002) and Patterson's (2003) work are supplementary to highlight the character development of servant-leaders.

Listening

Listening is more than a technique but an attitude and a desire to understand what is said and not said. A servant-leader listens to others and pays attention to his/her inner voice. "Listening, coupled with periods of reflection, is essential to the growth and well-being of the servant leader" (Spears, 2010, p. 27).

Empathy

A servant-leader is empathetic of others, demonstrating acceptance and understanding. A servant-leader assumes the good intention of others, even when they may not meet expected performance. A servant-leader values and shows respect for the uniqueness, in terms of intrinsic worth, of individuals. "The most successful servant leaders are those who have become skilled empathetic listeners" (Spears, 2010, p. 27).

Healing

A servant-leader assumes responsibility in mending broken relationships and bringing healing to those who are emotionally hurt and broken-spirited. Such restoration sets free one's potential for transformation and further development. A servant-leader inspires the led in a shared search for wholeness. "One of the great strengths of servant leadership is the potential for healing one's self and one's relationship to others" (Spears, 2010, p. 27).

Awareness

A servant-leader evaluates a situation holistically from complementary and contradictory perspectives, aiming to develop insights. Although a servant-leader is not a solace seeker, he/she maintains his/her inner serenity through solitude, which leads to self-awareness. The development of general and self-awareness gives a servant-leader a clear sense of priorities, distinguishing the important from the urgent and achieving optimal results. "Awareness helps one in understanding issues involving ethics, power, and values. It lends itself to being able to view most situations from a more integrated, holistic position" (Spears, 2010, p. 27).

Persuasion

A servant-leader convinces instead of coerces others into compliance. "This particular element offers one of the clearest distinctions between the traditional authoritarian model and that of servant-leadership" (Spears, 2010, p. 28). Greenleaf (1970) illustrated the approach and action of persuasion through the example of John Woolman, an American Quaker who made an influential impact on the members of the Society of Friends (Quaker) on the abandonment of slavery. John Woolman traveled long distances by foot or horseback visiting slaveholders. He did not accuse, but persuaded people one by one with his gentle and non-judgmental arguments. His method of persuasion was proven to be effective, and no Quakers were slave-owners by 1770 after his thirty enduring years of ministry.

Conceptualization

Spears (2010) noted that "servant-leaders are called to seek a delicate balance between conceptual thinking and a day-to-day operational approach" (p. 28). A servant-leader is expected to cultivate conceptual thinking ability. However, it is easy for a leader to be consumed by the day-to-day operational demand and the expectation of meeting short-term goals. If so, a leader may lose sight of the big picture or fail to develop and then articulate the vision of an institute. A servant-leader needs to be a visionary and sharpen his/her vision continually. Conceptual thinking skill can be acquired but it requires a disciplined mind with purposeful practice.

Foresight

Foresight was described by Spears (2010) as "a characteristic that enables the servant-leader to understand the lessons from the past, the realities of the present, and the likely consequence of a decision for the future" (p. 28). Foresight allows a servant-leader to make ethical choices and avoid future failure. The ability of foresight is considered to be embedded in one's own intuition. Greenleaf (1970) argued that foresight is the "lead" element of a leader. Without foresight, a leader is one in name only. Foresight allows the leader to see the unforeseeable and to know the unknowable so that he/she holds more information than others. With foresight, a leader leads others toward the next step. Without foresight, a leader merely responds or reacts to the current situation.

Stewardship

Barbuto and Wheeler (2002) described a steward in the medieval times as one who was assigned to prepare the prince for his reign. The steward was entrusted with valuable assets because of his/her proven dedication and commitment. This implies that a servant-leader, as a steward, is entrusted to prepare others for betterment. In addition, a servant-leader is held accountable for the success of the organization as well as its relationship to, and impact on, society. Stewardship is a great responsibility, moving from individual to societal obligation.

Commitment to the Growth of People

A commitment to the growth of people requires a servant-leader to possess a growth mindset and a belief that people can gain new understanding and reach greater accomplishment. A servant-leader models on-going learning and encourages others to acquire new knowledge and skills. Such commitment compels a servant-leader to find ways to support others' personal, professional, and spiritual development (Barbuto & Wheeler, 2002). Spears (2010) suggested "concrete actions such as making funds available for personal and professional development, taking a personal interest in the ideas and suggestions from everyone, encouraging worker involvement in decision-making" (p. 29). A servant-leader mentors others to become servant-leaders (Patterson, 2003).

Building Community

A servant-leader desires that individuals find their sense of belonging in a community. In a community operating with servant-leadership principles, members value and connect to each other. They can draw support among themselves in their niche. As the size of an organization grows, a servant-leader needs to apply concerted effort to build supportive networks with their led. Greenleaf (1970) and Spears (2010) believed that community building is vital to healthy institutional living and servant-leaders are responsible to nurture people's communal needs.

From the overview of these ten characteristics of servant-leaders, the researcher is interested in its application in the context of classrooms of a Hong Kong school. Herman and Marlower (2005) suggested that servant-leadership shifts "a classroom mindset where adults stress obedience to authority to a community mindset where leaders stress helping others" (p. 175). A learning community operating with servant-leadership principles could be characterized by "a vibrant and loving sense of togetherness and common purpose" (Van Brummelen, 2005, p. 21).

LEARNERS' NEEDS IN CLASSROOMS

The search for servant-leadership in classrooms begins with an understanding of what learners' needs are and how to meet these needs. The participants of this study are learners who are aged eleven to eighteen studying in grades 7–12. The words *learners* and *students* are used interchangeably in this chapter. The following sections describe learners' cognitive, social, individual, and motivational needs.

Cognitive Needs

To stimulate cognitive development, students are excited with meaningful learning tasks, which are contextually relevant (McCombs & Miller, 2009). These practical lessons, in the forms of solving real-world problems, provide opportunities for students to evaluate priorities in life. As a result, they learn to become creative problem solvers.

Christensen, Allworth, and Dillon (2012) argued that students need to "develop the skill to develop better skills, the knowledge to develop deeper knowledge, and the experience to learn from his/her experiences" (p. 73). This implies that students need to be exposed to what to think and how to think, so that they develop capability to visualize and arrive at their own conclusions of what to do. In sum, students need to develop their critical and analytical thinking skills through cognitive challenges of relevant and meaningful learning tasks.

Social Needs

McCombs and Miller (2007) argued that students are social beings who seek connections with their peers, their teachers, their school, and their community. Therefore, a learning atmosphere permeated with mutual respect is favorable for students to cultivate positive social skills (i.e., collaboration and cooperation).

Ridnouer (2006) defined such a learning community as a place where students mature in their social skills to support one another regardless of their social, economic, religious, and achievement differences. Furthermore, Kleiner (2008) argued that students develop their social acumen when they take turns being leaders and followers, thus learning to value responsibility and contribution, regardless of roles. In a learning community, good followers are just as important as good leaders.

Individual Needs

McCombs and Miller (2009) argued that every learner has a unique history, experience, culture, context, interests, strengths, and needs. Individual differences can be results of linguistic, cultural, and social backgrounds. Hence, a teacher cannot assume to use the same stroke for all folks. Hendricks (1987) commented that "how people learn determines how you teach" (p. 129). This means that a teacher needs to know his/her students in order to employ effective strategies for guiding their development.

However, the researcher argues that there are common qualities learners need to acquire, regardless of their individual differences. Teachers leverage different methods to shape students' character. The philosophy of servant-leadership emphasizes that the goal of a servant-leader is to develop the led to "become healthier, wiser, freer, more autonomous, more likely themselves to become servants" (Greenleaf, 1970, p. 13). The researcher implies that a servant-leader teacher works with different students but has the same goal, that they face obstacles in life with resilience, explore and develop their potential, and live their lives to the fullest, with the mindset to benefit beyond themselves to their society.

Motivational Needs

Motivation can be classified as being either extrinsic or intrinsic. Christensen et al. (2012) argued that the opposite of job dissatisfaction is not job satisfaction, but rather an absence of job dissatisfaction. Likewise, extrinsic motivators such as rewards and punishment in classrooms do not lead students to develop a love for learning.

On the contrary, intrinsic motivators promote learning and learners persevere through good and bad times. Intrinsic motivators can be manifested in forms such as "challenging work, recognition, responsibility, and personal growth" (Christensen et al., 2012, p. 21). They all lead to learners' engagement as well as a sense of accomplishment as defined by meaningful and exciting work. These arguments are supported by the American Psychological Association (1997), which noted that intrinsic motivation is triggered when one exercises personal choice, control, and when tasks are relevant to personal interests.

In sum, learners' needs can be categorized into cognitive, social, individual, and motivational domains. The quest of the study in this chapter is to investigate whether teachers, who are characterized as demonstrating these servant-leadership traits, meet these learners' needs.

PURPOSE OF THE STUDY, RESEARCH QUESTIONS, AND CONCEPTUAL FRAMEWORK

The study presented in this chapter aims to explore learners' perceptions of servant-leadership as practiced by teachers in the context of classrooms, in the cultural setting of a Hong Kong school. It is a worthwhile study considering the following rationale.

First, empirical studies of servant-leadership have proven a positive correlation between servant-leadership practices and school climate (Black, 2010), organizational commitment (Cerit, 2010), student achievement (Lambert, 2004), job satisfaction (McKenzie, 2012), and teaching effectiveness (Metzcar, 2008). Parris and Peachey (2013) conducted cultural, cross-cultural, and contextual analysis of thirty-nine empirical studies from twenty-seven different peer-reviewed journals between 2004 and 2011. A majority (44 percent) of these studies were conducted in educational settings. Hence, it is evident that servant-leadership can be a beneficial practice in school settings. The researcher argues that further study can be useful in understanding its application at a classroom level.

Second, the aforementioned studies, along with many others as mentioned by Parris and Peachey (2013), were conducted with adults as participants. The researcher is curious about students' perceptions toward servant-leadership practices.

Lastly, the study of servant-leadership in America has gained momentum in recent years, but the same cannot be said for Hong Kong. It is interesting to examine its cultural relevance in Hong Kong. Therefore, the following research questions are formulated:

1) What are learners' perceptions of servant-leadership as practiced by teachers in classrooms?
2) How does servant-leadership meet the needs of learners in classrooms?
3) How does the practice of servant-leadership build a learning community in the classroom?
4) How relevant is the concept of servant-leadership to classrooms in a Hong Kong school?

Figure 14.1 illustrates the conceptual framework of this study, which graphically presents the variables of interest and their relationship to one another. The main actors in a classroom are the teacher and learners. This research explores (a) the connection between teachers' servant-leadership attributes and learners' needs and (b) the sequential order of servant-leadership actions in building a learner-centered community.

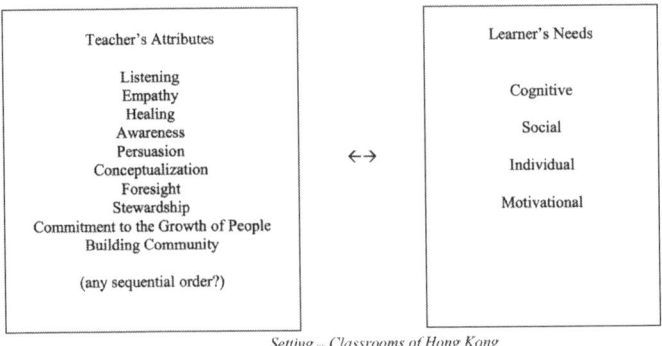

Setting – Classrooms of Hong Kong

Figure 14.1 Graphic presentation of conceptual framework, illustrating servant-leadership characteristics and possible connection with learners' needs. *Source:* Kong Wah Chan.

RESEARCH METHOD

This study is grounded in a pragmatic paradigm, finding the most suitable explanations for the research questions (Powell, 2001). Hence, the researcher adopted a mixed-methods design with three phases, and they were conducted in a sequential manner. It was carried out in a Hong Kong school with context as described below.

Sample

The fieldwork was conducted in a K-12 school located in Hong Kong. It is a private (tuition-based) school, which uses a Canadian-based curriculum and has registration with the Education Bureau of Hong Kong. The school had a student population of 283 in the grades of 7–12 at the time of data collection of this study. They were all invited to participate in phase one of the three-phased research study.

Research Design

For phase one, all students of the Hong Kong school were invited to complete an online survey. The survey tool was a modification of the Teacher Leadership Assessment (TLA), created by Metzcar (2008) for his empirical study of servant-leadership and effective teaching in classrooms. The TLA is a robust and reliable tool with a Cronbach's alpha of 0.9602. Contextualization of the TLA was necessary, via a pilot study, to ensure its suitability for the students of the Hong Kong school, without culturally laden words or phrases. The modified TLA was tested for internal reliability with Cronbach's alpha of 0.9752. Out of 283 survey respondents, the participation rate was 44 percent. The quantitative data were analyzed by general statistics expressed in modes and rank orders.

For phase two, only students who fully completed the survey were considered for stratified purposeful sampling. This sampling method was selected because of its advantage as described by Seale (2012):

> A stratified sample is more accurate, and therefore more representative of the population than a simple random sample, but also more complex. Each member of the population is divided into groups or strata and then a simple random sample is selected for each stratum. (p. 140)

It is crucial to collect students' experiences of the studied Hong Kong school, and not that of any other schools. Thus, prospective participants were further screened with remaining interviewees who had enrolled in the school for at least one academic year. These finalized participants were invited for focus-group interviews. These focus groups were grade-level specific, with the intent that interviewees of the same group had similar teachers and probably learning experiences, so that purposeful discussion could be achieved. These were semi-structured interviews and the questions were piloted before actual data collection. The interviews were audio recorded to create verbatim transcripts for thematic analysis, following Miles and Huberman's (1994) *Qualitative Data Analysis: An Expanded Sourcebook*. Prior to each focus-group interview, written consents were sought from the interviewees and their parents/guardians.[2]

For phase three, a teacher who was highly regarded by the focus-group interviewees, was invited to provide a written reflection of his philosophy of education and approaches to teaching. The reflection was also analyzed thematically against students' verbatim transcripts in phase two. Source triangulation was conducted which compared the teacher's reflection with the students' stories. It addressed the research questions from different perspectives.

RESULTS AND ANALYSES

Descriptive Statistics: Phase One

The contextualized survey, TLA, had sixty-four items, which were categorized into the following seven constructs: "Value Others," "Develop Others," "Build Community," "Display Authenticity," "Provide Leadership," "Share Leadership," and "Role Satisfaction." Each item was written with a Likert-type scale of "never," "rarely," "sometimes," "often," and "almost always." Modes reflected the most selected choices of survey respondents. Out of sixty-four items, there were three modes of "sometimes," forty-nine modes of "often," and twelve modes of "almost always." The practice of servant-leadership was often observed by the learners surveyed in this study.

Survey items were categorized by constructs and the tallies were converted to percentages for ranking. As a result, "Provide Leadership" was the construct most observed by learners in classrooms. Further examination of the items with the highest counts of "often" and "almost always" provided practical examples of their meaning of "Provide Leadership." From the perceptions of these student respondents, their teachers provided leadership in classrooms so that everyone knew what took place in the class and were clear on the key goals of the classroom. The teachers provided support and resources needed to help students meet learning goals.

"Role Satisfaction" and "Value Others" were the constructs least observed by learners in the classrooms. Further examination of the items with the lowest counts of "often" and "almost always" revealed that these student respondents did not often feel appreciated by those in the classes for what they contributed. They did not often receive encouragement and affirmation from others in their classes. The focus of these concerns was not on the teachers only, but involved every member of their class.

The purpose of phase one in this study was to generate an overall understanding, in terms of presence or absence, of servant-leadership practices in classrooms. The survey result showed that students perceived that their teachers often demonstrated actions of servant-leadership in classrooms. The main emphasis was on phases two and three of this study, which unfolded students' stories and compared them with a teacher's reflection.

Thematic Analysis: Phases Two and Three

Qualitative data in the form of transcripts collected through focus-group interviews were analyzed thematically. It consisted of (a) affixing codes, (b) sorting the codes by patterns of commonality and differences, (c) identifying themes, and (d) generalizing key findings.

From particulars to general, eleven themes were identified from the codes. They were (a) conceptualization, (b) awareness, (c) foresight, (d) persuasion, (e) listening and empathy, (f) community building, (g) commitment to the growth of people, (h) healing, (i) stewardship, (j) mindset, and (k) relationship. Quotations were selected among these codes as evidence to support these themes. A reference to a quotation was indicated with the altered name code, such as Jnp1. Lastly, these themes were generalized and categorized into five key findings.

Finding 1: The cognitive needs of students can be met by teachers who are characterized by conceptualization, awareness, and foresight.

Conceptualization

Students were interested to know the reasons for their class activities. They favored teachers who had structured work plans for the lessons and gave clear instructions. Two verbatim quotes are:

> Jnp1: He is more prepared. You will have a schedule. He will assign all the work for the whole month. He has more structure . . .

> Ktp3: I always like teachers to give clear instruction because you know what to do.

Awareness

Awareness of students' prior knowledge and interests helped teachers to adjust their lessons so that students found relevance in the new knowledge to their personal experiences. They were able to relate their learning tasks to their situations. Two verbatim quotes are:

> Ktp6: He describes the context in term of story so that we can relate much. Sometimes it relates to our personal life also so I remember more . . .

> Jsp5b: She has a lot of experiences and she knows how to approach different people and different topics with the right methods.

Foresight

Teachers with foresight were able to explain to students explicitly how they could move forward in their learning path. In cycles of show-and-tell, teachers showed their students how to proceed and students told their teachers about their progress, and more importantly what hindered their progress. It was a regular, on-going feedback loop. Teachers with foresight created opportunities for productive dialogue between the teachers and learners. Two verbatim quotes are:

> Mlp3a: He taught for the first 15 minutes. It was clear and understandable. Then you just work. I think you need to do it in order to understand it . . .

> Lyp1a: During class time, he usually teaches for the first 20 minutes and we have 30 minutes of class work time. During the class work time, we are able to do the questions and he is able to be there to help us.

Finding 2: The social needs of students can be met by teachers who are characterized by persuasion, listening and empathy, and community building.

Persuasion

Students respected teachers who had clear and reasonable rules and guidelines for the classrooms. They valued opportunities to make decisions and freedom to explore and express their individuality. They also supported clear consequences for their actions. Persuasion was modeled when teachers disagreed with students' choices and actions but still expressed care for their students and made an effort to support them. Two verbatim quotes are:

> Atp5: I guess he isn't lenient but he isn't very strict either. He would talk to us about it until we reach agreement. He tells us what he doesn't like and within that boundary we can do whatever we want . . .

> Zep5b: She won't get mad at you when you don't pay attention. When you ask her she would still answer you. She would tell you to pay attention next time.

Listening and Empathy

Students expressed gratitude to teachers who cared for their well-being, showed understanding of their struggles, and ultimately offered support. Two verbatim quotes are:

> Tmp3: I feel like she really wants us to do well and I actually feel that she cares what happened to our class and our grades. She is very understanding of what we are doing and how we feel . . .

> Lyp2a: She helps us a lot. She would actually listen and she understands the situation we are in. Yes, she is willing to help and I am happy about that.

Community Building

The following quotes were taken from grade twelve respondents who had studied together as classmates for years. They shared responsibilities to care for classmates in their community.

> Dmp10a: We have these study groups and it actually boosts my grade a bit. Sometimes I stay afterschool. If I need help I can go to them and it is really helpful . . .

> Jnp10a: We have study group on Friday during lunch and we just talk about life lessons. We would go out to eat. We have Bible study time. The relationship with the teacher and students is really close. Yeah!

Finding 3: The individual needs of students can be met by teachers who are characterized by commitment to the growth of people, healing, and stewardship.

Commitment to the Growth of People

Teachers' commitment to their students was described by students in terms of time and specific feedback for improvement in the areas of performance, formative and summative assessments. Two verbatim quotes are:

> Zep5c: She asks anyone who have questions to come afterschool to get extra help up to whatever time until you understand the concepts and all that . . .

> Jnp10b: She spends time to go over the draft with each one of us. It takes a lot of her time. She really likes to help. She encourages people to stay afterschool. She teaches you the details and slowly shows you.

Healing

An observant teacher was sensitive to a student's verbal and non-verbal cues. As such, the student trusted and respected his teacher, willing to seek advice and ready to accept counsel from the teacher. For example:

> Ptp5: He walks around the class and look at what people are doing, see if anyone needs help. Whenever I have trouble doing something or trouble in social life, he would notice it like I am not happy. I can relate to him and I go to him.

Stewardship

A teacher named Mr. X was commended by all the interviewees who had him as their teacher. He took upon himself the responsibility of supporting all students who came to seek his help. He did not allow students to slack off, but held them accountable for their learning tasks. He was available to his students whenever they needed him, including weekends. These stories from students were examples of Mr. X as a steward. His support for students came in various forms. Two verbatim quotes are:

> Slp3: He is willing to help even during his spare time. During weekend, I sent him three emails with many questions. He takes his time to answer them and actually quickly . . .

> Dmp10b: He doesn't help me in one subject alone. He helps me in different subjects and life, like making good decisions.

The first, second, and third key findings qualified students' perceptions of servant-leadership as practiced by teachers in classrooms. Teachers who exhibit these ten characteristics of servant-leadership can meet students' cognitive, social, and individual needs. Furthermore, the researcher found two other interesting key findings concerning student motivation and teacher–student relationship as described below.

Finding 4: The motivational needs of students can be met by teachers who encourage students to develop a growth mindset, believing in the impact of effort and attitude.

Mindset

During the interviews, students were asked how they handled difficult subjects at school. Two distinct mindsets were observed. Students with optimism were confident that they could turn their setbacks into success. The virtues of perseverance and resilience were determining factors for their current and future results. Two verbatim quotes are:

Gyp2b: I just keep asking him. I am in the same question and he is two questions ahead. I just ask him to go back and answer my question . . .

Jsp4: I attend classes for the purpose of bettering my education. I guess that doesn't take the enjoyment out of it but I think I have a goal that I want to achieve rather than having fun. I do what I need to do. It is not about enjoying.

On the other hand, students who were less hopeful, or perhaps a little hopeless, perceived their performance was a result of their innate abilities. They convinced themselves that there was very little they could do to affect the outcomes of their school experiences. Their comments fit with the lowest ranked survey items under the construct of "Role Satisfaction" as mentioned in the phase one survey result. Two verbatim quotes are:

Nip3: If you give it all and you still get a bad mark for your subject, it is very discouraging. For this subject, I just cannot do it . . .

Atp1: A lot of times our best work is not even adequate for passing marks, which may be a bit stressful. Doing hard work and doing possible work are two different things. We are kind of in the impossible range sometimes.

The difference in mindsets led to positive responses or negative reactions to challenges in learning. The researcher infers that encouraging and supporting students to develop a growth mindset could result in intrinsic motivation for learning. As a result, students' perceptions of "Role Satisfaction" could also be improved.

Finding 5: Building teacher–student relationship could be the primary and most effective way to serve students.

Relationship

It was noteworthy that nine out of twelve students in grades 7 to 9 (75 percent), and eight out of twelve students in grades 10 to 12 (67 percent), described their teachers as meeting their social–relational needs prior to cognitive, motivational, or individual needs. Two verbatim quotes are:

Jnp5: I think that my favorite is Mrs. T. Mrs. T is really down to earth and she is really honest with us. She tries to help each of us. She spends time to go over the personal essay with each one of us . . . She spends a lot of time overlooking a lot of essay.

Msp1e: I really like Mr. X because he is really caring. I asked him for resource and he said sure I will send you my resources. You can come and ask me or after school we can have a class. This is what he said and I think that he is very caring and helpful.

The fourth and fifth key findings suggested two developmental aspects of learners that greatly affected their learning. First, students' mindset affected their motivation toward learning. Thus, it was important for teachers to cultivate a growth mindset and communicate hope to students, especially when they faced hardship. Second, adolescents are emotional and relational beings. Many of them filtered their learning tasks and evaluated their learning experiences through their relational reserves with their teachers. Hence, teachers needed to know their students as people in order to be effective in impacting their education. These findings were supported by evidence from interviewees who spoke highly of an identified teacher, Mr. X.

Subsequently, Mr. X was approached to provide a written reflection of his philosophy of education and approaches to teaching and learning. Phase two of this study was a collection of students' stories through semi-structured focus-group interviews. Phase three of this study was a collection of a teacher's reflection. Source triangulation was conducted to compare and validate the consistency of their realities from the perspectives of students and a teacher.

Mr. X's reflection was analyzed thematically, and six themes were identified. They were: (a) self-awareness, (b) conceptualization, (c) foresight, (d) persuasion, (e) commitment to the growth of people, and (f) stewardship. These were six of the ten servant-leadership traits as identified by Spears (2010). Quotations are listed below as examples:

Self-awareness, Sharing of Philosophy of Education

- "Deep in my heart, I know I have a passion for teaching. A teenager spends most of his time in school and I can see school is a strategic place to reach out to youth."
- "In school, I can reach out to students through academics. I can walk alongside with them with their studies."

Conceptualization, Meeting the Cognitive Need of Students

- "It is natural to me to break down outcomes and concepts into smaller correlated chunks and to identify practical steps in helping students to attain the knowledge."
- "I categorize and summarize, give big pictures and detailed steps as well."
- "It is my strength to explain the complex concepts using different approaches that students can understand."

Foresight, Meeting the Cognitive Need of Students

- "I model how to think and how to reason to solve problems."
- "I usually see the underlying question and am able to help the student with more than what he has asked for."

Persuasion, Meeting the Social Needs of Students

"I encourage students to set personal goals and emphasized the importance to actively think about their own learning."

Commitment to the Growth of People, Meeting the Individual Needs of Students

- "Equips them for the challenge and demand of the world, but more importantly, to prepare them to be faithful steward to serve God and mankind."
- "I strive to provide a diverse environment so that every student can experience learning according to the different needs and ability and learning style."

Stewardship, Meeting the Individual Needs of Students

- "I will find ways to help students to learn, and if one way does not work, I will find another way."
- "I respected their uniqueness because they are all bearer of God's image."
- "Students should be treated fairly but not equally because every student is different."

Table 14.1 provides matches of students' experiences with Mr. X's reflection. This source triangulation supported the conceptual framework of this study, that there were connections between teachers' servant-leadership traits and learners' needs in classrooms. In particular, teachers' practices of servant-leadership met learners' cognitive, social, and individual needs.

Meta-Analysis of Phases One, Two, and Three

Meta-analysis of evidence from the three phases supports a model of a learner-centered community operating with servant-leadership principles. In this model, the ten characteristics of servant-leadership are presented in a sequential order, which can also be summed with three key actions of service, leadership, and community building.

Service

The fifth key finding of this empirical study states that building positive teacher–student relationships could be the primary and most effective way to serve students. From the interpretation of students' stories, which were organized into themes, a teacher began to serve his/her students by listening attentively to understand the other persons' worldviews, opinions, experiences, and interests. This allowed the teacher to know the students so that the teacher could genuinely show empathy and effectively bring healing into the

Table 14.1 Possible Connections between a Servant-Leader's Character Traits and Learner's Needs

Characteristics of a Servant-Leader	Excerpts from Mr. X	Excerpts from Students	Learners' Needs
Conceptualization Awareness Foresight	• It is natural to me to break down outcomes and concepts into smaller correlated chunks and identify practical steps in helping students to attain the knowledge • My classes are structured, well planned, and clear. • Explain the complex concepts using different approaches that students can understand. • I model how to think and how to reason to solve problem.	• I always like teachers to give clear instruction because you know what to do (Ktp3) • He is more a neat and tidy person who writes things out . . . I prefer to learn things in a neat way (Gyp2a) • He gives you samples and tells you what to write. We don't need to guess all the times. He actually explains the problems (Nip9)	Cognitive needs
Persuasion Listening Empathy Community Building	• I encourage students to set personal goals and emphasized the importance to actively think about their own learning.	• He encourages those who don't participate to participate more and he give out prizes (Zep2)	Social needs
Commitment to the Growth of People Healing Stewardship	• I strive to provide a diverse environment so that every student can experience learning according to the different needs and ability and learning style. • I will find ways to help students learn, and if one way does not work, I will find another way. • I want to teach them self-discipline so that they can achieve their own goals in life, not just study.	• We get our tests back and he would talk to us individually (Nip5) • He doesn't help me in one subject alone. He helps me in different subjects and life like making good decisions (Dmp10b)	Individual needs

Source: Kong Wah Chan.

lives of the students. Through serving, the teacher and students established respectful and caring relationships. The teacher might then lead the students with relational authority and referent power.

Leadership

Mr. X's reflection showed that the combination of awareness, persuasion, conceptualization, and foresight led him to (a) set priorities among all demands; (b) influence students with insights and with patience; (c) evaluate the overall needs of the learning process; and (d) mentor the students' growth and development with positive reinforcement and critical feedback. He used different ways to lead the students and meet their needs.

Source triangulation of learners' transcripts and teacher's reflection revealed that Mr. X did not direct the students according to his own agenda, but toward the best interests of the students. He exhibited both serving and leading his students in different contexts. The researcher argues that Mr. X has displayed stewardship and commitment to the growth of people, which can be symbolized by the hyphenation linking the words servant and leader as servant-leader.

Community Building

Finally, the survey result confirms that students of the studied school often observed the practices of servant-leadership. However, "Role Satisfaction" and "Value Others" were the constructs least observed. The researcher's suggestion is that through service to one another, students contribute positively to their classroom community. These experiences could result in improved perceptions of "Role Satisfaction." When students emulate their servant-leader teachers and act as givers in their social interactions with others, they feel valued and desire to value others. As a result, a classroom becomes a training ground for students to develop as servant-leaders who work together in building a service-oriented community. The researcher argues that the philosophy and practices of servant-leadership are applicable to classroom community building. Figure 14.2 presents a model with progressive stages of a teacher (a) serving and (b) leading his/her students toward (c) building a community together. It aims to create a learner-centered classroom governed by servant-leadership attributes.

EVALUATION OF THE RESEARCH QUESTIONS AND CONCLUSION

The study presented in this chapter explored learners' perceptions of servant-leadership in classrooms. The researcher used empirical evidence to address the four research questions below.

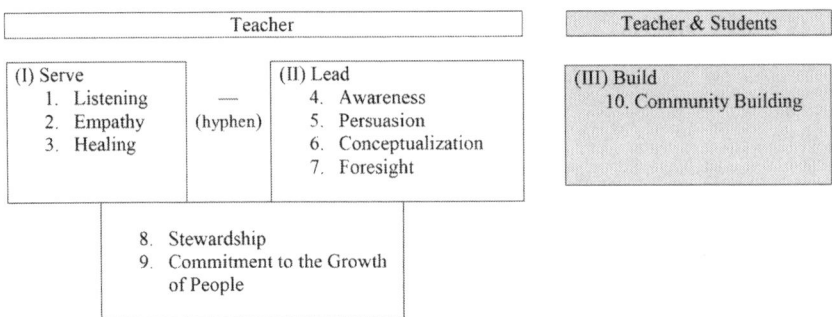

Figure 14.2   Progressive model of a learner-centered classroom operating with servant-leadership principles. *Source*: Kong Wah Chan.

First, survey results show that the practice of servant-leadership in class-rooms was often observed by learners of the studied Hong Kong school. "Provide Leadership" was the construct most observed by learners, while "Role Satisfaction" and "Value Others" were the constructs least observed by learners. The researcher suggests that building a learning community operating with servant-leadership principles can improve learners' perceptions of "Role Satisfaction" and "Value Others."

Second, key findings one, two, and three give evidence that the practices of servant-leadership by teachers meet learners' cognitive, social, and individual needs. Selected quotations from interviewees are examples of students' experiences and teachers' behaviors. Although the researcher is unable to find correlation between servant-leadership traits and learners' motivational needs, her presumption is that learners may likely develop intrinsic motivation when they are appropriately challenged with tasks in a caring environment—where they have freedom to make responsible choices and express their individuality. In other words, learners' motivational needs may be met indirectly when their cognitive, social, and individual needs are satisfied.

Third, a model of classroom learning community is proposed with the ten characteristics of servant-leaders staged in a sequential order. It is featured with three key actions of service, leadership, and community building. Service leads to an establishment of legitimacy for leadership. One of the goals of servant-leadership is to develop the next generation of servant-leaders. Servant-leadership is a blend of imminence with transcendence and it results in building wholeness for both the leader and the led, teacher and students.

Fourth, it is evident that Mr. X has practiced servant-leadership in his classroom. The philosophy of servant-leadership is based on one's desire to serve (Greenleaf, 1970). Hence, teachers and students can choose to be and become servant-leaders in their classrooms. The practice of servant-leadership is relevant and feasible for classrooms of this Hong Kong school.

Overall, the belief and practice of servant-leadership is not about heroic leaders, but about followers and their needs. Greenleaf (1970) argued that it is paradoxical and thought-provoking to consider a servant as a leader and that service can result in leadership. This research contextualizes Greenleaf's belief of servant-leadership within the context of classrooms and the culture of a Hong Kong school. The researcher concludes that the practices of servant-leadership by teachers meet the learners' needs and that it is desirable to build a classroom community operating with servant-leadership principles.

STRENGTHS AND LIMITATIONS

This research used a mixed-methods approach to study the practices of servant-leadership in classrooms of a Hong Kong school. Empirical study of servant-leadership with students as main participants, in the context of classrooms, and in the cultural background of a Hong Kong school, is unique. The model of a learner-centered community operating with servant-leadership principles adds new understanding of the ten characteristics of servant-leaders as described by Spears (2010).

The researcher argues that servant-leadership is favorable and relevant to classrooms of this studied Hong Kong school. However, this study is conducted in one school in Hong Kong. Therefore, findings cannot be generalized as being representative of all schools in Hong Kong. Further studies of servant-leadership application in various types of schools in Hong Kong would provide further insights in this area of scholarship.

SUGGESTIONS FOR FUTURE RESEARCH

A comparative study to explore similarity and difference of servant-leadership practices in classrooms between different types of schools in Hong Kong is worthwhile. This can be conducted between international and local schools, government-funded and private schools, or schools with different religious affiliations. Grounded in an interpretivist paradigm, this comparative study can yield greater understanding of servant-leadership practices in classrooms in Hong Kong.

Another research suggestion is to involve both teachers and students as participants in a servant-leadership classroom study. Metzcar (2008) conducted his study with teachers as the survey respondents. This study was conducted with students as the survey respondents. Metzcar's TLA can be administered to both teachers and students. The differences in perception of the seven constructs can lead to fruitful discussion for improvement. This can be followed up with an action research study.

NOTES

1. This chapter was previously published as Chan, K. W. (2017). Learners' perceptions of servant-leadership in classrooms. *The International Journal of Servant-Leadership, 11*(1). 373–409.

2. All interviewee names have been anonymized and oral consent was provided for the use of their words in this chapter.

REFERENCES

APA Work Group of the Board of Educational Affairs. (1997). *Learner-centered psychological principles: A framework for School Reform and redesign.* Washington, DC: American Psychological Association.

Barbuto, J. E., Jr. & Wheeler, D. W. (2002). Becoming a servant leader: Do you have what it takes? *NebGuide G1481.* Retrieved from http://www.ianrpubs.unl.edu/live/g1481/build/g1481.pdf

Beazley, H. (2003). Forward. In H. Beazley, J. Beggs, & L. C. Spears (eds.), *The servant leadership within: A transformative path.* New York: Paulist Press.

Black, G. L. (2010). A correlational analysis of servant leadership and school climate. *Catholic Education: A Journal of Inquiry and Practice, 13*(4), 437–466.

Blanchard, K. H. (2007). *Leading at a Higher Level: Blanchard on leadership and creating High Performing Organizations.* Upper Saddle River, N.J.: Pearson/Prentice Hall.

Cerit, Y. (2010). The effects of servant leadership on teachers' organizational commitment in primary schools in Turkey. *International Journal of Leadership in Education, 13*(3), 301–317.

Christensen, C. M., Allworth, J., & Dillon, K. (2012). *How Will You Measure Your Life?* New York, N.Y.: Harper Collins.

Greenleaf, R. K. (1970). *The servant as leader.* Indianapolis, IN: Robert K. Greenleaf Center.

Hays, J. M. (2008). Teacher as servant: Applications of Greenleaf's servant leadership in higher education. *Journal of Global Business Issues, 2*(1), 113–134.

Hendricks, H. (1987). *Teaching to Changes Lives.* Colorado Springs, CO: Multnomah Books.

Herman, D. V. & Marlower, M. (2005). Modeling meaning in life: The teacher as servant leader. *Reclaiming Children and Youth, 14*(3), 75–78.

Kleiner, K. (2008). Rethinking leadership and followership: A student's perspective. In R. E. Riggio, I. Chaleff, & J. Lipman-Blumen (eds.), *The art of followership* (pp. 90–93). San Francisco, CA: Jossey-Bass.

Lambert, W.E. (2004). Servant leadership qualities of principals, organizational climate, and student achievement: A correlational study. *Dissertation Abstracts International, 66*(02), 430. (UMI No. 3165799)

McCombs, B. & Miller, L. (2007). *Learner-Centered Classroom Practices and assessments: Maximizing student motivation, learning, and achievement.* Thousand Oaks, CA: Corwin Press.

————. (2009). *The school leader's guide to learner-Centered Education from Complexity to simplicity*. Thousand Oaks, CA: Corwin Press.

McKenzie, R. A. (2012). A correlational study of servant leadership and teacher job satisfaction in a public education institution teaching (Doctoral dissertation). Retrieved from http://pqdtopen.proquest.com/doc/1328169298.html?FMT=AI .(UMI No. 3537800).

Metzcar, A. M. (2008). Servant leadership and effective classroom teaching (Doctoral dissertation). Retrieved from http://pqdtopen.proquest.com/doc/288396317.html ?FMT=AI (UMI No. 3344705).

Miles, M. B. & Huberman, A. W. (1994). *Qualitative Data Analysis: An expanded sourcebook* (2nd edition). London, Sage. Retrieved from http://vivauniversity.files .wordpress.com/2013/11/milesandhuberman199.pdf

Omoh, D. A. O. (2007). Analysis of servant leadership characteristics: A case study of a community college president (Doctoral dissertation). Retrieved from ProQuest Dissertations and Theses database. (UMI 3262849).

Parris, D. & Peachey, J. W. (2013). A systematic literature review of servant leadership theory in organizational contexts. *Journal of Business Ethics, 113*, 377–393. doi: 10.1007/s10551 012-1322-6

Patterson, K. (2003). Servant leadership: A theoretical model (Doctoral dissertation). Retrieved from ProQuest Dissertations and Theses database. (UMI No. 3082719).

Powell, T. C. (2001). Competitive advantage: Logical and philosophical considerations. *Strategic Management Journal, 22*(9), 875–888.

Ridnouer, K. (2006). *Managing Your Classroom with heart: A guide for nurturing Adolescent Learners*. Alexandria, VA: Association for Supervision and Curriculum Development.

Seale, C. (2012). Chapter 9: Sampling. In C. Seale (ed.), *Researching society and culture* (3rd edition, pp. 134–152). Thousand Oaks, CA: Sage.

Spears, L. C. (2010). Character and servant-leadership: Ten characteristics of effective, caring leaders. *The Journal of Virtues and Leadership, 1*(1), 25–30.

Trompenaars, F. & Voerman, E. (2009). *Servant leadership Across Culture: Harnessing the strength of the World's Most Powerful Leadership Philosophy*. Oxford: Infinite Ideas Limited.

Van Brummelen, H.W. (2005). Teachers as servant leaders. *Christian School Education, 8*(3), 20–22.

Chapter 15

Accentuating Servant-Leadership in Singapore Leadership Mentoring

Lim Lee Hean and Low Guat Tin

In[1] the Singapore education system, certain features emerge in leadership concepts pertaining to servant-leadership and leadership mentoring. Greenleaf's notions of foresight as the "central ethic of leadership" and conceptualizing as the "prime leadership talent" (Greenleaf, 1970, pp. 16, 23), as well as the practice of leadership learned through mentoring (Low, 1995; Lim, 2005), have come to the fore in recent years. In our experience, the commensurability of these ideas—foresight, conceptualizing, and mentoring—serve as legitimate means toward the end of a more whole and servant-led educational learning environment.

BACKGROUND ON MOVEMENTS OF LEADERSHIP MENTORING IN SINGAPORE EDUCATION

Accentuating aspects of servant-leadership in leadership mentoring in the context of Singapore education quintessentially necessitates locating main historical roots. Leadership development pertaining to mentoring has surfaced in various forms over the past two-and-a-half decades, ranging from pre-service structured or formal form, to unstructured or informal form, to in-service semi-structured form. The Singapore experience has reflected selected mentoring forms, in their broadest sense, in one way or another. Examples include low-profile, fairly formal strategy (Hennecke, 1983); structured formalized mentoring (Moore, 1982; Phillips-Jones, 1983; Geiger-DuMond & Boyle, 1995); facilitated mentoring (Murray & Owen, 1991); mentoring multiplier (Kaye & Jacobson, 1995); and shared mentorship

(Sweeny, 2002). Nomenclature aside, the adoption of such varying empha-sis on mentoring through the years in Singapore leadership development is elaborated upon below.

Over a period of more than one-and-a-half decades, from 1983 to 2000, leadership mentoring was the prime aspect of a development strategy for aspiring school principals attending the Diploma in Education (DEA) pro-gram in Singapore. The one academic year program integrated an eight-week leadership mentoring school attachment component with formal instruction given by university faculty members. During the school attachment, each DEA participant was paired with a practicing school principal who served as a mentor to the participant protégé. The mentors were carefully selected by the Ministry of Education as worthy role models for aspiring school princi-pals in Singapore. As such, there was a tripartite structure involving the staff as program developers and mentoring facilitators, school principals as men-tors, and participants as protégés.

Thereafter, ad hoc informal and unstructured mentoring was in practice when the innovation model predominated in the subsequent iteration of pro-gramming, called Leaders in Education Programme (LEP), starting in 2001. Even now, the distinctive features of co-creation and synergy with schools through the Ministry of Education (Lim, 2007) permeate the core of both the DEA and the LEP leadership programs for aspiring principals. Two-and-a-half decades of in-service experience in leadership preparatory programs have shown that instead of pervasively discarding the past as obsolete, pro-gram developers can take cognizance of pertinent local distinctive features and capitalize on their strengths, in an attempt to generate the next wave of seascape change in Singapore school leadership development.

Further, in March 2007, a one-year leadership mentoring program for beginning principals was launched. The initiative serves to promote "a cul-ture of school leaders taking responsibility for grooming their peers" (Ho, 2006, p. H6), with "school autonomy," "regular refreshing and recharging," and the "sharing of expertise" the three factors necessary for building a qual-ity school system.

The nature of leadership in the Singapore school system involves a con-stant embrace of change itself. With school heads in Singapore rotated on a regular basis, approximately 40 percent of Singapore schools have had a change of principals in the past half-decade. This approach is deemed positive, as it promotes a communal idea of forming good schools. This is also consistent with local research findings on the systemic impact of DEA-structured leadership mentoring, facilitated by university faculty, that encourages "principals to lead their own learning in collaboration with their peers in the education arena" (Lim, 2005a, p. 92). In this context of change, subsequent evolving forms of mentoring will continue to impact learning, and because of this, further research can be helpful in examining assumptions in program development.

The pertinent developments of mentoring in the Singapore education system also offer an insight into the relevance and significance of relationships that were emphasized in the findings of previous Singapore studies (Lim & Low, 2004). It is evident that "mentoring fosters leadership training in the essential relationship skills" (p. 34). Against the backdrop of leadership mentoring movements in the Singapore education system, the servant-leadership dimension of conceptualizing becomes crucial to leadership mentoring.

BRIDGING CONCEPTUALIZING

The emphasis on conceptualizing was framed by Katz (1975) as increasing in importance as the level of management gets higher. In Greenleaf's elaboration on "conceptualizing—the prime leadership talent" (Greenleaf, 1970, p. 23) it was asserted that "a truly remarkable social, political, and economic transformation, stemmed from one man's conceptual leadership" (p. 25), that of Nikolai Frederik Severin Grundtvig in the nineteenth-century Denmark. Known as the Father of the Danish Folk High Schools, Grundtvig "did not found or operate a Folk High School, although he lectured widely in them" (p. 25). Terms associated with conceptualizing include "love," "dedication," "faith," and motivation as in the arousal of the "spirit":

> What he gave was his love for the peasants, his clear vision of what they must do for themselves, his long articulate dedication—some of it through very barren years, and his passionately communicated faith in the worth of these people and their strength to raise themselves—*if only their spirit could be aroused.* (p. 25)

The elements of "love," "dedication," and "faith" featured in servant-leadership are similarly featured in mentoring. We believe the conceptualization of the core of powerful mentoring depicts "unconditional loving relationships, nurtured and led by the mentor, which feature aspects of altruism, care and faith" (Lim, 2005b, p. 108). Data on mentoring from protégés indicated the surfacing of "unlimited love" (Okawa, 2002, p. 81) as an element offered by mentors, establishing a trust connection based on mutual self-disclosure and sharing. This is consistent with what other writers have maintained (for example, Linehan & Walsh, 1999; Sim, 2002). Altruism, care, and faith appear to emerge as motivational forces that could propel mentors to serve beyond their call of duty (Lim, 2005b, p. 109), with "faith" that the protégé possesses a potential or the potential. Such remarkably similar features in two established leadership paradigms could signify inclusiveness in both.

Closely linked to "faith" in protégés is the element of trust. Research on leadership mentoring in Singapore (Lim, 2005a, p. 40) indicates that protégés learned from their mentors' trusting of subordinates and gave them substantial authority to make decisions in their areas of work, as exemplified by the following quote:

> Middle management would be my heads of department. In empowerment, there must be trust; there must be accountability. So like in areas of their department work, I give them the freedom to come up with their proposals. Sometimes when they want to review, to change certain things, they themselves would discuss it openly with the staff. They would invite suggestions from their department staff, and then they proceed. (Protégé observation, 2007)

As in servant-leadership, mentoring behaviors include faith in the worth of the protégé, and this has to be communicated. Protégés who had the opportunity to experience quality leadership mentoring learned from their mentors the practice of promoting trust. Behaviors showing communication integrity formed a bond of trust and genuineness in relating with people. In Lim's study, trust in leading, exemplified through relating well with people, encompassed congruency in belief, action, and speech, as illustrated below:

> You want to establish trust, you must make sure that you are helping. You have to act what you believe, what you say. Say what you believe, act what you say. Saying is not important, you have to supplement or complement with action. People will say, "Ya! This is what you really are going to do, what you say, and what you believe." All these three must link together. And people from time to time will put these three together, see whether the jigsaw puzzle can match together. If you can't, then you cannot get a complete picture of their trust. (Protégé observation, 2007)

Lim's work revealed that promoting trust also encompassed being "open" in personal and professional matters, with the assurance that revelation of "secrets" or "weaknesses" would not lead to penalties:

> I find that there was openness and trust in the [mentoring] school, and this is something which I am trying very hard to establish here . . . it took time to sink in that this is something I believe in, something I would carry on . . . When I was with the mentoring principal, I shared the same office as her, so she would sit here [laughter] and I, there. So occasionally, teachers with problems would approach her, consult her, and she would give advice, whether professional, even personal—she went to that extent. It was made quite clear to the teachers

that we are all developing together, all improving together; by letting us know the secrets, it would not penalise them in any way. I believe many of us are keeping secrets because we are afraid of making mistakes. And in the [mentoring] school I was in, the teachers realised that by revealing their weaknesses, they were not going to be penalised. I believe my mentoring principal helped people overcome their weaknesses. And here, I am trying very hard to emulate the example [of my mentor]. I think I am successful to some extent. (Protégé observation, 2007)

Similarly, on matters pertaining to choice of mentors, Carruthers (1988) brought forth criteria that included the following: "a person you feel you can trust and who trusts you," "a person you can tell personal and professional problems to without fear of penalty," and "a person you respect and who respects you." The dimension of dedication to service as a feature in Singapore leadership mentoring, congruent with servant-leadership, is presented next.

It was reflected that protégés learned and practiced serving as worthy models in dedication to service (Lim, 2005a). Their personal commitment helped influence others to follow their example. For instance, it necessitated being caring, perceptive, and approachable:

The principal leads by example . . . She also practices care not just for her pupils but for her staff as well. It comes across very well that she is there to help you when you come across any problem, even personal problems. She has been a principal there for many years...so they know her very well. I think also, she is very alert and perceptive. If she sees any teacher who may be having some problems—she will approach the teacher and let the teacher know that she's there, if they want to talk. I think she shared with me how she has helped some of the teachers with their personal problems—she counselled them too . . . We shared a lot. (Protégé observation, 2007)

Sometimes if we go that extra mile, the teacher will go that 99 percent for the students. This particular teacher who had medical problems . . . probably went to tell others in the staff room. In the end she did not get to see her letter of termination [from the Ministry of Education]. I spent three hours going from place to place [for her]. It's worth it. The teacher was very appreciative. (Protégé observation, 2007)

If you are able to show care and concern for the teachers, I think somehow this also rubs off on the teachers, that they must show care and concern to their pupils, you see. It must filter down. So therefore the head must take the lead to do this, so it can filter down or permeate or percolate, so to speak. (Protégé observation, 2007)

BRIDGING FORESIGHT

According to Greenleaf (1970, p. 16), foresight refers to "a better than average guess about *what* is going to happen *when* in the future" and is deemed
"the central ethic of leadership." This is elaborated upon as follows:

> The failure (or refusal) of a leader to foresee may be viewed as an ethical failure;
> because a serious ethical compromise today (when the usual judgment on ethical
> inadequacy is made) is sometimes the result of a failure to make the effort at an
> earlier date to foresee today's events and take the right actions when there was
> freedom for initiative to act. (p. 18)

Can foresight be learned? Literature on management learning reveals the existence of competence-based learning of content (cerebral or cognitive) knowledge and skills (or behavior), as well as meta-competence-based learning which
could incorporate learning from experience. Of relevance is Brown's (1994)
suggestion that distinctions be drawn among managerial processes. Managerial
processes could be competence-based (skills plus their accompanying knowledge for application). There are also those based on meta-competencies (the
higher order abilities which have to do with being able to learn, adapt, anticipate, and create). It was expressed that knowledge merges with experience
at two levels. At the level of competency, management education may equip
participants with specific work-content skills. On the other hand, with reference
to meta-competencies, management education must rely more on learning from
experience. Meta-competencies can be learned but cannot be explicitly taught.
It was further suggested that meta-competencies are a prerequisite for the
development of capacities such as judgment, intuition, and acumen. Foresight
then is aligned with meta-competencies in learning and practice.

Further, with regard to foresight, a practicing leader develops "a high level
of intuitive insight about the whole gamut of events from the indefinite past,
through the present moment, to the indefinite future. One is at once, in every
moment of time, historian, contemporary analyst, and prophet" (Greenleaf,
1970, p. 17). In the Singapore context, it is apt that a focus on foresight at
this time be linked to the background on movements of leadership mentoring
in Singapore education presented at the beginning of this chapter. Knowledge
and understanding of the past facilitates appropriate selective decision-
making for the future. As such, forms may differ, but the core of co-creation
and synergy remains. On a similar note, existing forms deemed inappropriate
for the present or near future could be adopted or modified for value in the
distant future.

Research on leadership mentoring in Singapore provides evidence of
foresight in learning and practice. For instance, on matters of helping staff

develop, the practice of learning from the mentor the ability to foresee probable serious mistakes and take the right actions becomes a part of the process.

> [I learned] how to "move" and mobilise HODs [Heads of Department] into action . . . I see the Heads of Department as being in a transitional stage. They should move on and move up. I moved them out of their comfort zone . . . gave some responsibilities in terms of school management . . . covered duties [for the principal]; but I did it step by step . . . Slowly, they saw that I was handholding them. Until such time that I could see and I could feel they were confident, then I let go...I watch them very closely. But I try not to interfere. If I interfere too much, it stifles them; then you sort of tie their hands and legs and they cannot move . . . They can afford to make mistakes, it's OK. From mistakes, they learn what not to do, if not what to do . . . We are not so wise as to make every good decision all the time . . . No one is perfect. If I see that they are stepping into a big hole [laughter], I will make sure that they don't put their foot in, in the first place. (Lim, 2005a, p. 48)

Foresight and its relevance in mentoring are further elaborated upon here. A review of mentoring literature on the notion of mentor (Lim & Low, 2004, p. 34) reveals that "other than the fairly consistent presentation of the origin of the word 'mentor' itself, it would appear that the word could mean anybody whose presence or contribution, formal or otherwise, is of some positive significance to somebody." But the quality of the dynamic learning relationship between mentor and protégé is often very much dependent on the quality of the mentor. A mentor with the pertinent disposition, experience, and meta-competencies is more likely to facilitate the development of capacities such as intuition and insight. To emphasize the value of mentoring, Noller (1982) adopted a phrase from Samuel Taylor Coleridge's poem "The Friend" (1828), in which Coleridge notes that "a dwarf sees farther than the giant when he has the giant's shoulder to mount on." Similarly, Shea (1992) professed that the word "mentor" could be regarded as synonymous with "trusted adviser" and "wise person"—mentors offer special insight, understanding, and information that are beyond the normal channels or training in an increasingly complex environment.

CONCLUSION

Research on and the practice of leadership mentoring in Singapore have invariably omitted the probable contributions of servant-leadership as an integral component. This chapter explored the dimensions of conceptualizing and foresight as they appear in servant-leadership and leadership mentoring, and reveals connections that support greater agreement than dissension. It is apparent that these leadership approaches—mentoring and servant-leadership—are not mutually exclusive. This relationship may provide the basis for future research related to the explicit incorporation of servant-leadership into leadership mentoring. Future research on leadership mentoring is also needed in order to examine the practice of servant-leadership by effective school leaders who have opportunities to learn from their former mentors in education.

With change as the undeniable constant in life, and change often referred to as synonymous with progress at work, a significant sense of connection with the past becomes vital, as well as connection to the now and to the future on matters pertaining to program development. With foresight and conceptualizing, school leadership program developers at the tertiary level can help to bridge the past and the future in research while maximizing their presence in the present. This can promote the unique and paradoxical notion of wise abandonment with distinct discretion while embracing or creating change itself.

Program facilitators play a substantial role in shaping education in Singapore at the school headship level and are akin to Grundtvig, who did not operate any of the founding schools, but lectured widely in facilitating the transformation from conception to concrete reality. As programs evolve positively, a continual development and retention of committed facilitators occurs, so that whatever retreats we face along the evolutionary scale of program development can eventually lead to genuine advancement in preempting the lament of foresight upon hindsight.

NOTE

1. This chapter was previously published as Lim, L. H., & Low, G. T. (2007). Accentuating servant-leadership in Singapore leadership mentoring. *The International Journal of Servant-Leadership. 3*(1), 177–188. All interviewee names have been anonymized and oral consent was provided for the use of their words in this chapter.

REFERENCES

Brown, R. B. (1994). Reframing the competency debate: Management knowledge and meta-competence in graduate education. *Management Learning, 25*(2), 289–299.

Carruthers, J. (1988). Beginning teachers, mentors and principals. *The Practicing Administrator, 70*(1), 42–44.

Geiger-DuMond, A. H., & Boyle, S. K. (1995). Mentoring: A practitioner's guide. *Training and Development, 49*(3), 51–54.

Greenleaf, R. K. (1970). *The servant as leader.* Indianapolis, IN: The Robert K. Greenleaf Center.

Hennecke, M. J. (1983). Mentors and protégés: How to build relationships that work. *Training 20*(7), 36–41.

Ho, A. L. (2006). Pilot scheme lets rookie principals pick own mentors. *The Straits Times*, p. H6.

Katz, R. L. (1975). Skills of an effective administrator. In *Harvard Business Review— On Management* (pp. 19–38). New York: Harper and Row.

Kaye, B., & Jacobson, B. (1995). Mentoring: A group guide. *Training and Development, 49*(4), 23–27.

Lim, L. H. (2005a). *Leadership mentoring in education.* Singapore: Marshall Cavendish Academic.

———. (2005b). Illuminating the heart of mentoring: Intrinsic value in education. *New Horizons in Education, 51*, 106–110.

———. (2007). Illuminating the core of Singapore school leadership preparation: Two decades of in-service experience.*International Journal of Educational Management, 21(5), 433-439.*

Lim, L. H., & Low, G. T. (2004). Relevance and significance of relationships. *International Studies in Educational Administration, 32*(3), 34–43.

Linehan, M., & Walsh, J. S. (1999). Mentoring relationships and the female managerial career. *Career Development International, 4*(7), 348–352.

Low, G. T. (1995). Mentoring in Singapore: What and how do protégés learn? *International Studies in Educational Administration, 23*(2), 20–26.

Moore, K. (1982). The role of mentors in developing leaders for academe. *Educational Record, 63*(1), 23–28.

Murray, M., & Owen, M. A. (1991). *Beyond the myths and magic of mentoring.* San Francisco, CA: Jossey-Bass.

Noller, R. B. (1982). *Mentoring: A voiced scarf.* New York: Bearly Limited.

Okawa, Gail Y. (2002). Diving for pearls: Mentoring as cultural and activist practice among academics of color. *College Composition and Communication, 53*(3), 507–532.

Phillips-Jones, L. (1983). Establishing a formalized mentoring program. *Training and Development Journal, 37*(2), 38–42.

Shea, G. F. (1992). *Mentoring: A guide to the basics.* London: Kogan Page.

Sim, W. H. (2002). Pao Kun is still alive. In *Kuo Pao Kun* (pp. 172–201). Singapore: Cruxible.

Sweeny, B. (2002). Structures for induction and mentoring programs. In K. Burke (ed.), *Mentoring Guidebook: Starting the journey* (2nd edition, pp. 5–29). Arlington Heights, IL: Pearson Education, Inc.

Chapter 16

Human Rights from Its Origins to the Twenty-First Century

A Journey through Empathy, Love, the Will to Power, and the Will to Meaning

Toni Jiménez Luque

What[1] is servant-leadership? And what is the connection between this philosophy and set of practices with human rights' design, implementation, and defense? According to the Robert K. Greenleaf Center for Servant Leadership website, we are talking about a philosophy and set of practices with the aim of enriching the lives of individuals, building better organizations, and ultimately creating a more just and caring world. With regard to human rights, we have a variety of definitions, but basically we understand them by respect for the individual, the assumption that each person is a moral and rational being who deserves to be treated with dignity. A connection between both terms can be established when the servant-leadership approach tries to enrich the lives of individuals and create a more just and caring world, just as human rights philosophy, which aims to empower every single human being and build a more fair and equal society at a global level.

The concept "servant leadership" was coined by Robert K. Greenleaf in *The Servant as Leader*, an essay that he first published in 1970. Later, Greenleaf would publish several works developing this idea in a deeper way. Thus, he stated the definition of this concept:

> It begins with the natural feeling that one wants to serve, to serve first. Then conscious choice brings one to aspire to lead . . . The best test, and difficult to administer, is: Do those served grow as persons? Do they, while being served become healthier, wiser, freer, more autonomous, more likely themselves to become servants? (1991, pp. 40-41)

In the following sections of this chapter, I will show how these ideas seem very connected with the human rights' ideas of autonomy and dignity ("healthier, wiser, freer, more autonomous" for Greenleaf). In addition, I will provide information proving that these concepts were developed during the enlightenment in the eighteenth century by a group of philosophers, writers, and intellectuals who aspired to lead, foster, and promote these ideas. As Greenleaf (1977) proposed two centuries later, a group of leaders have to show the way and point the direction to other people. Whether by consensus or inspiration, leaders present a goal that inspires others to follow. As we will see in this chapter, a group of people in the eighteenth century had foresight, a visionary goal. But they also had trust and confidence in their cause, and their followers accepted the risk along with the leaders. In other words, and as Greenleaf (1977) summarized brilliantly, "Not much happens without a dream. And for something great to happen, there must be a great dream. Behind every great achievement is a dreamer of great dreams" (p. 16).

Throughout the following sections of this chapter, we will see that in order to develop human rights discourse, the idea of empathy was a key element. About this concept, Greenleaf (1977) argued that people grow taller when their leaders empathize and accept them for who they are, thereby earning trust.

However, throughout my years coordinating the International Cooperation for the Development of Solidarity Foundation at the University of Barcelona, I met people from all around the world feeling or experiencing empathy for the impoverished, the voiceless, and the excluded. Unfortunately, that feeling was not enough to commit them to a cause, to bring them from their "ivory towers" to the field, and that situation has been very frustrating. Perhaps Greenleaf (1977) was warning us about this when he stated that the real danger to individuals and society is natural servants who fail to lead or choose to follow someone other than a servant-leader. As a consequence, I have been wondering for many years about what is the necessary element to translate "theory" into "practice."

As a result of this personal experience, I will explore in this chapter how love was the energy that from empathy made the people of the eighteenth century transform their society. In addition, I will also show how, as soon as empathy and love were limited with the spread of the nihilistic and cynical ideas related with Friedrich Nietzsche's concept of will to power, and above all nationalism—an ideology that was focused on a national and not a universal level—a human rights' crisis was initiated and brought humanity to the two most atrocious wars in history: World War I and World War II. However, nowadays, even if empathy and love still seem limited, I will argue that a human rights movement has been recovered and fulfilled with more meaning as a result of the spread of the will to meaning, a concept based on Viktor Frankl's work. This research, applied to human right's discourse, tries to give a deeper and more holistic approach to its implementation and defense, and especially to human dignity. In this respect, Greenleaf was an excellent visionary when he wrote in 1977 that although he could not predict the future, he was hopeful for a society in which the authentic needs of the less fortunate were identified through patience and listening, rather than having those needs defined by a privileged class. Personally, I believe human rights approaches today are too limited to the juridical and political fields, and with this chapter's description of the origin and evolution of human rights, I will show how the social component of their origins has been forgotten and needs to be recovered. According to my personal experience, in the university system in Western countries, curricula and professors are too focused on juridical aspects and do not embed their classes with a social connotation. Greenleaf (1977) observed that the current university system, based on medieval notions of learning, does little to inspire the creativity of students; an elitist and standardized attitude toward education makes adapting to value shifts in society increasingly difficult.

The purpose of this chapter is to explore the servant-leadership characteristic of empathy—along with the power of love—and their influence in the origins and crisis of human rights, and also to understand the process of recovering the movement today through the will to meaning. In doing so, we will have a better understanding of the necessity of a servant-leadership approach and the perspective of the will to meaning in the human rights curriculum of the university today.

Otherwise, we will continue focusing only on the juridical and political parts of a holistic movement that, in order to be efficient, needs the social approach that both the servant-leader and the will to meaning offer. And as Greenleaf (1977) concluded, if we are to realize a more just and loving society that encourages creativity, "Then the most open course is to raise both the capacity to serve and the very performance as servant of existing major institutions by new regenerative forces operating within them." (p. 49)

Finally, even if some of these ideas regarding human rights as a social movement connected with the will to meaning seem too idealistic, we can embrace Greenleaf's notion that our future progress will be based on a continued determination to achieve the impossible.

EMPATHY AND THE WILL TO LOVE: HUMAN RIGHTS ORIGINS

In the 1760s, the French invented the expression "rights of man" (*Droits de l'Homme*) that became very popular in the country thanks to its use by

Jean-Jacques Rousseau in his *Social Contract* of 1762 (Rousseau, 1987). However, along with that expression, Rousseau also employed other concepts such as "rights of humanity," "rights of citizen," etc., with the aim of expressing a very general idea, but without the political connotations of transformation or change (Hunt, 2007), so the idea of human rights that we understand today was not mature enough. It is not until 1786, when Marquis de Condorcet, influenced by the experience of the American Revolution, wrote his essay *On the Influence of the American Revolution on Europe*, linking the expression "rights of man" with that revolution (Innes & Philp, 2013) and embedding the concept with a political view. For him, the American Declaration of Independence was the exposition of these venerable and buried rights (Hanley & McMahon, 2010) that we needed to recover.

From that moment on, ideas on human rights started to spread around pre-revolutionary France and Great Britain, even if they were lacking a definition of the source of their power. In 1755, the French Enlightenment writer Denis Diderot wrote:

> The use of this term is so familiar that there is almost no one who would not be convinced inside himself that the thing is obviously known to him. This interior feeling is common both to the philosopher and to the man who has not reflected at all. (Wasserstrom, Grandin, Hunt & Young, 2007, p. 8)

Even ambiguous, this was the first definition of the rights of men, and with it, Diderot introduced a key element regarding the power of the concept: the rights of men require an "interior feeling" that everybody can experience, just because the fact of being human, and in spite of social class or educational level. In other words, we were talking about emotions and sentiments in the Age of Reason. We were talking about empathy.

Regarding the term empathy, psychologist Edward B. Titchener (1909) is credited with the invention of the term, and in his *Experimental Psychology of the Thought Processes*, he wrote, "Not only do I see gravity and modesty and pride and courtesy and stateliness, but I feel or act them in the mind's muscle" (Titchener, 1909, p. 21). In other words, we can feel as well as perceive certain emotions. Moreover, he translated the term *Einfühlung* as empathy from the Greek *empatheia*, which means "in" (en) "suffering or passion" (pathos). To him, empathy represented a combination of visual and kinesthetic imagery by which certain types of experiences were possible. Also, he described it as a feeling or projecting of one's self onto an object. Eventually, in his later writings, Titchener (1915) gave empathy a more social implication when he stated that it was a way to make our communities more human.

In connection with servant-leadership, empathy is one of the ten character-istics that Larry Spears presented (Spears & Lawrence, 2004) and according to him:

> The servant-leader strives to understand and empathize with others. People need to be accepted and recognized for their special and unique spirits. One assumes the good intentions of co-workers and colleagues and does not reject them as people, even when one may be forced to refuse to accept certain behaviors or performance. The most successful servant leaders are those who have become skilled empathetic listeners. (Spears, 2010, p. 3)

However, do all human beings feel empathy? Do some feel it more than others? And the key question, can empathy be taught? (Hatcher, Nadeau, Walsh, Reynolds, Gales, & Marz, 1994). Although biology may provide an essential predisposition, each culture shapes the expression of empathy in its own particular way because empathy is developed through a process of social interaction. In the eighteenth century, those who read novels learned to work on empathy through established social boundaries in terms of class or gender. As a result, they started to see people they did not know like themselves as a consequence of having similar inner emotions (Hunt, 2007, p. 39). In other words, the characteristic or ability of empathy is something that we can learn and work on. And that was just what the people of the eighteenth century decided to do.

One of the most important novels of that time was Jean Jacques Rousseau's *Julie et la nouvelle Heloise* (1761), which became a best-seller. The story portrays the life of two separated lovers who exchange intimate letters, show-ing their feelings of suffering, sadness and love; the novel's power lays in the fact that the readers could identify their own feelings with those of the characters. As Lynn Hunt (2007) explains:

> Courtiers, clergy, military officers, and all manner of ordinary people wrote to Rousseau to describe their feelings of a "devouring fire," their "emotions upon emotions, upheavals upon upheavals." One recounted that he had not cried over Julie's death, but rather was "shrieking, howling like an animal." As one twentieth- century commentator on these letters to Rousseau remarked, eighteenth-century readers of the novel did not read it with pleasure but rather with "passion, delirium, spasms and sobs." (p. 36)

Some years before, Samuel Richardson had written in England *Pamela* (1740) and *Clarissa* (1747–48) with similar effects among the readers, and in Germany, Johann Goethe wrote in 1774 *The Sorrows of Young Werther*, a novel that is thought to be one of the starting points of Romanticism and a psychological revolution in its time in terms of empathy. In the novel, the hero shoots himself after an ill-fated love; shortly after its publication, there were many reports of young men using the same method to commit suicide and lots of them were dressed like him—blue blazer and yellow vest (Coleman, 2004).

As we can see, the performativity and power of the text is huge and impacted readers in the eighteenth century who started to identify themselves with ordinary characters who were before invisible to them, but were now present in novels, poems, and paintings (Bermingham & Brewer, 1995). As a result of this process that constructed this new psychology based in empathy, the established social and political order was destined to change because thousands of people that did not "exist" before in terms of social and political consideration suddenly "appeared" in different cities of Europe (Bray, 2003). In other words, we are referring to the inflection point that allowed them to go one step further from empathy to action: the origin of the construction of human rights.

In 1771, Thomas Jefferson declared that when reading these works, he experienced a "strong desire in ourselves of doing charitable and grateful acts" and at the same time he felt disgusted by evil and immoral actions and behaviors. According to Jefferson, reading fiction was even more effective than reading history in order to produce the desire for moral emulation (as cited in Boyd, 1950, pp. 76–81).

Now empathy had made visible the invisible and given voice to the voiceless, but what was that force or "strong desire in ourselves" that pushed people like Jefferson to do "charitable and grateful acts?" As a consequence of that feeling, they could not accept anymore a political, juridical, and social community where huge sectors of the population were oppressed. In other words, they realized through empathy that their social status and amount of power needed to be legitimized, but how? According to bell hooks: "To begin by always thinking of love as an action rather than a feeling is one way in which anyone using the word in this manner automatically assumes accountability and responsibility" (hooks, 1999, p. 13). Moreover, it was not a coincidence that after the "golden ages" of the Epistolary Novel (1760–1780), which helped to construct empathy, Romanticism held sway from the end of eighteenth century to the first half of the nineteenth century. In other words, there was a process from the internal feeling (empathy) to action, and the energy that made possible that transition was love (as action, rather than as feeling, as hooks proposes); and with empathy and love came the evolution of human rights discourse and its gradual application (White, 2005).

About love: "We do not have to love. We choose to love" (Peck, 1978, p. 83), and people from the Age of Reason chose to feel empathy for the excluded, but also leave their comfortable positions and act thanks to the energy of love. As a result they created hundreds of societies to defend the rights of minorities and to advocate for the abolition of torture and slavery in different countries in the world (Bales, 2007). However, even if all these processes were very complicated and not always achieved, what can be considered a success is the fact that, for the very first time in history at a global scale, the voiceless and the invisibilized had a voice and were visible thanks to the different human rights declarations that empowered them to be agents of their own destiny (Harris, 2007). The social elites that initiated that movement of empathy and love were aware that they, as we are doing today in our "liquid" times (Bauman, 2006), were living in a "transitional" period in history from the Ancient Regime to Modernity, and they decided to define and establish that paradigm shift through a set of declarations of the rights of men and citizens.

That process was very similar to the proposal that Margaret J. Wheatley suggests when she states:

> A few phrases come to mind from a wonderful gospel song: 'We are the ones we've been waiting for.' This is the time for which we have been preparing, and so there is a deep sense of call. Servant-leadership is not just an interesting idea, but something fundamental and viral for the world, and now the world that truly needs it. (as cited in Ferch, 2012, p. 119)

And that was precisely what the people of eighteenth century did; they started a movement to defend human rights initiated through empathy and love, with the aim of changing the world. In order to accomplish that goal, they acted as leaders with great foresight and awareness, serving their followers to transform them as leaders. They had initiated their servant-leader movement along with human rights discourse.

NATIONALISM, THE WILL TO POWER AND LACK OF EMPATHY: HUMANS RIGHTS IN CRISIS

In 1789, we see first the French Revolution and the rise of Napoleon Bonaparte's empire later. Napoleon's era represented a continuation of the struggle between human rights and the despotic monarchies in Europe that responded to revolutions in America and France (Englund, 2005), though with many differences and nuances. However, as soon as the French Empire disappeared, a national sentiment arose contrary to the former centralist conception of Napoleon. All around Europe and the Latin American colonies, nationalist ideas gave origin to the Age of Nationalism throughout the nineteenth and the twentieth centuries (Pilbeam, 1995).

Notably, the first half of the nineteenth century was embedded with Romanticism's ideas that influenced to a high degree the development of the first national movements such as the Greek War of Independence in 1823 (in which Lord Byron, one of the most well-known romantic writers, went to fight) and the European Revolutions of 1848 (Broers, 1996). In other words, the discourse of human rights (along with empathy and love), which had been developed at the end of the eighteenth and the beginning of the nineteenth centuries, was still a key element in creating the conditions that inspired those revolutions.

Nevertheless, the nationalist movements that initiated their journey, along with the discourse of human rights and Romanticism, gradually became more conservative, and from their universal point of view in the defense and protection of human rights, started to adopt more particularistic approaches (Hunt, 2007, p. 183). As a consequence of this, they continued forwarding the discourse of human rights, but now considered their nationals "more human" than other nationals, starting what Hobsbawm (1986) called the Age of Empires, a historical period that saw the Western world attempt to conquer the whole world (Imperialism). As a consequence of these nationalist movements, empathy was limited from a global level to a specific nation, and the same happened with the idea of love. As Greenleaf (1977) stated regarding the concept of love, this is a term difficult to define, with complex and deep manifestations. He believed it was conditioned on "unlimited liability! As soon as one's liability for another is qualified to any degree, love is diminished by that much" (p. 38). Unfortunately, nationalist movements limited love's liability and with it, its energy to transform internal feeling (empathy) into action.

On the other hand, it is not a coincidence that the period that I call "the crisis of human rights," which goes from the end of the nineteenth century to the half of the twentieth century, is the time when the philosopher Friedrich Nietzsche wrote his works (1870 and 1890), and especially *The Will to Power*, published after his death during the first decade of the twentieth century (Safranski, 2003). According Nietzsche's *The Will to Power*, the goal of every person is to take power and to concentrate it. This is something completely different from a human rights perspective, which tends to give legitimate power to every person in order to transcend the negative, destructive, and illegitimate concentration of power the philosopher advocated (Nietzsche, 2011, p. 375).

Gradually, these ideas started to embed in nationalist movements that became more and more conservative. As Nietzsche (2011) stated:

The whole of "altruism" reveals itself as the prudence of the private man: societies are not "altruistic" towards one another—the commandment to love one's neighbor has never yet been extended to include one's actual neighbor. That relationship is still governed by the words of Manu: "We must consider all countries that have common borders with us, and their allies, too, as our enemies. For the same reason, we must count all their neighbors as being well-disposed toward us." (p. 382)

This nationalism, based partly in its racist conception of a superior culture, tended to make nations homogeneous in terms of culture (One Nation, One State) and did not hesitate to destroy other cultures both in a physical and symbolical way, inside and outside borders. In other words, nationalism created homogeneous nations imposing a "superior" culture in a national society where there were before different primary cultures (Gellner, 2009).

With the mentality of nationalism came an emphasis on the will to power. During the second half of the nineteenth century, people experienced the rise of xenophobia, the control of immigration, and the consolidation of racism as the dominant ideology (Fredrickson, 2003). Again, and within this new context, what happened with respect to the protection of human rights? The answer was easy: on the eve of World War I, all the countries embedded by this new ideology were still defending human rights discourse, but their vision of human rights was not a global vision for mankind as it was for the people of the end of the eighteenth century. Now they cared only about the rights of their nationals, and other countries were considered inferior and not deserving of their rights to be protected and guaranteed (Hunt, 2007, p. 186).

Moreover, if necessary, they considered themselves "legitimized" to attack when their "superior" nation was threatened. Nietzsche (2011) summarized this new mindset when he wrote: "A declaration of war on the masses by *higher men* is needed! Everywhere the mediocre are combining in order to make themselves master!" (p. 458). This process brought the world some years later to the two most atrocious and terrible wars of history: World War I and World War II, which resulted in the death of millions of people, the destruction of hundreds of cities and towns, and in the end, a lack of hope and trust in mankind (Hobsbawm, 1996).

To exemplify how much influence *The Will to Power* had in this process, it is interesting to compare the declarations of the Nazi War Criminal during World War II, Adolf Eichmann, and the particular vision that Nietzsche had some decades before on similar issues. According to Hannah Arendt, who followed Eichmann's trial in Jerusalem in 1961, he was a very ordinary man in appearance with a flat affect. In his testimony throughout the trial, he insisted he had no choice but to follow orders, as he was bound by an oath of loyalty—the same superior orders defense used by some defendants in the 1945–1946 Nuremberg Trials (Arendt, 2006). Thus, it is surprising to realize that Eichmann's declaration is almost exactly what the German philosopher had written some decades before:

> None of you has the courage to kill a man, or even to whip him, or even to—but the tremendous machine of the state overpowers the individual, so he repudiates responsibility for what he does (obedience, oath, etc.) Everything a man does in the service of the state is contrary to his nature. In the same way, everything he learns with a view to future state service is contrary to his nature. This is achieved through division of labor (so that no one any longer possesses the full responsibility): The lawgiver—and he who enacts the law; The teacher of discipline—and those who have grown hard and severe under discipline. (Nietzsche, 2011, p. 383)

Today, there is controversy whether Nietzsche was using the concept of will to power to propose a new society based on it, or whether he was just trying to anticipate the risks toward where European society was going. Whatever the philosopher's idea, the final result was that the ethos of *The Will to Power* had become embedded in the minds of the imperialist nations and Nazi criminals used Nietzsche's work in order to legitimize and justify their crimes.

A "MAGIC TRIANGLE" WITH THE
WILL TO MEANING: HUMAN RIGHTS
EMERGING AS A SOCIAL MOVEMENT

After two world wars, the international community decided to recover the idea of human rights from a global point of view after the particularistic approach where nationalism embedded the fundamental rights of the people. Here the idea was to control and to limit the power of the State as a consequence of atrocities committed in its name (Donnelly, 1997). As a result of this, on December 10th, 1948, the General Assembly of the United Nations approved the "Universal Declaration of Human Rights" (UDHR) and its Preamble recognized how the discourse of human rights had been forgotten and how necessary it was to recover:

> Whereas recognition of the inherent dignity and of the equal and inalienable rights of all members of the human family is the foundation of freedom, justice and peace in the world; whereas disregard and contempt for human rights have resulted in barbarous acts which have outraged the conscience of mankind, and the advent of a world in which human beings shall enjoy freedom of speech and belief and freedom from fear and want has been proclaimed as the highest aspiration of the common people.

Even if the UDHR was the expression of a set of aspirations more than a reality that could be reached in the context of the Cold War, it represented a group of moral obligations for the international community similar to the declarations at the end of eighteenth century (Hunt, 2007, p. 213). Notwithstanding, a key question arose again after the creation of the United Nations and its organs and instruments of protection of the international system of human rights: What happened to acting with empathy and love? It seems clear that after the atrocities committed during World War II, it was not very difficult (as human beings) to feel empathy for victims, and just the fact of acting and creating such a developed system in an international sphere was also a proof of certain love (again, from the internal feeling to action). However, in the context of the Cold War, where the world was divided into capitalist and communist blocs, it was necessary for a new element to be added in order to really enjoy the fulfillment of those rights in a global way, not repeating the same mistake of particularism (now not in the name of a limiting nation but of a limiting bloc) that some decades before brought humanity to two world wars (Website of the *Center on Law and Globalization*).

However, several decades later, the Communist Bloc disappeared and with it the limitations for a global discourse on human rights. Thus, a process called globalization—the globalization of the "Western world localization"—was initiated. Unfortunately, this process did not have the aim of spreading the human rights' movement, but only its economic system, neoliberalism, which was imposed almost all around the world (Lash & Featherstone, 1999). This economic system, which has the capacity to affect all different aspects of life (politics, culture, etc.),exploits a big part of humanity as means and not as ends, and concentrates on materialistic issues more than on spiritual ones (Santos, 2005). As a result of that worldview, the number of people experiencing an existential vacuum, confusing the material and superficial life with happiness and personal realization, has arisen throughout the world.

I believe this lack of connection with other human beings, nature, and the universe must be fixed in order to avoid the return of the will to power and particularism. Moreover, I consider it is essential to fulfill the lives of millions of people embedded with cynicism, hypocrisy, and nihilism (especially in Western countries) with meaning and commitment to a cause or to the whole of humanity. According to Viktor Frankl (2014), the human being must strive to transcend and reach out for something other than itself (p. 55). That is why in order to transcend what could be seen as a discourse originated from above during the Cold War (human rights designed by the victors of World War II), it has become a social and global movement from below, and human rights have been there to show the way. Referring to Logotherapy, Frankl (2014) wrote: "If there is, as some authors contend anything such as a

'logotherapeutic movement,' it certainly belongs to the human rights movement. It focuses on the human right to a life as meaningful as possible" (p.
168).

For example, in connection with this idea, Article 3 of the UDHR affirms:
"Everyone has the right to life, liberty and security of person." But what did
the countries that prepared the Declaration in 1948 mean by the human right
to life? For them, the conception of life was only a biological perspective.
In other words, their idea was that life is just the fact of being alive and
breathing and, besides, the human being is separated from nature (Santos,
1995). However, as soon as social movements decided to appropriate the
term of human rights and to defend their cause, they decided to change that
reductionist and limited biological vision of life and enhance it through a
deeper meaning of the right to life, advocating for the right to a dignified
and meaningful life where the human being is connected with nature (Saura,
2009). In doing so, they started a new social movement from below that until
today tries to connect the discourse of human rights with the voiceless and
the excluded; the process that happened at the end of the eighteenth century
can be seen as a consequence of the development of empathy and love,
interior feeling, and action. However, this social movement appears today
in a deeper and more intense process of globalization, and in order to act,
it is necessary to be aware of a global community. According to Greenleaf
(1977):

> Where there is not community, trust, respect, and ethical behavior are difficult
> for the young to learn and for the old to maintain. Living in community as one's
> basic involvement will generate an exportable surplus of love which the indi-
> vidual may carry into his many involvements with institutions which are usually
> not communities: businesses, churches, governments, schools. (p. 39)

Again, empathy and love can be seen as essential elements, but I believe they
need to add one more element to their group in order to be effective in a world
that has changed as a result of globalization and the neoliberalist system. I
call it the "Magic Triangle": empathy, love, and meaning. And what really
makes this "Triangle" "Magic" and unique is that from a top-down process
with a passive perception of people—we need to feel empathy and to love
them—we go to a bottom-up movement with an active proposal where they
are agents who decide their meaning and purpose in life. It is not only about
leaders who through empathy and love improve the lives of the followers.
Now we are talking about followers that have become leaders through meaning and purpose in their lives; oppressed people in a global dimension that
have been empowered through empathy, love and, above all, with the creation
of elements for them to develop their own capability, in order to define their

meaning and purpose in the world. As a result of linking this magic triangle with human rights in the twenty-first century, we have the fourth generation of human rights, or emerging human rights, which consists of civil society's legitimate claim for the formulation of new or updated human rights (Palop, 2010). In other words, today the key element in that journey of human rights is to see people finding meaning and purpose in their lives through empathy and love, without any limits imposed from above by a nation or political bloc. Frankl (2000) argued that meaning was "down to earth." But he also recognized that some kind of meaning could be "up to heaven" as it were; some sort of ultimate meaning, that is; a meaning of the whole, of the 'universe,' or at least a meaning of one's life as a whole; at any rate, a long-rage meaning" (p. 143).

I believe emerging human rights is a matter of justice, dignity, empathy, and love. They give meaning to our lives and make us transcend ourselves in a relativist, but also global way that could be the answer we are waiting for. In other words, a comprehensive approach from below that unites all different elements, and a global and active way of viewing the world and thinking, conversely to the narrower design elaborated from above by the victors of World War II. Moreover, this new perspective seeks to avoid the separated way that human rights were built in 1948 and is a process of reconnecting mankind, nature, universe, and divinity.

CONCLUSION

A servant-leadership approach aims to transform followers into leaders. This is where the legitimacy of its power remains, which the people of the eighteenth century realized as they sought their goal of constructing a fairer and more equal society. They were aware of the paradigm shift of their time and formulated a beginning to the process of human rights through empathy and love. In other words, they showed the way and pointed the direction: "By clearly stating the goal, the leader gives certainty and purpose to others who may have difficulty in achieving it for themselves" (Greenleaf, 1977, p. 15). Unfortunately, it was not enough, and what seemed like an unstoppable movement apparently found its nemesis in another one: the will to power that embedded the nationalist movements at the end of nineteenth century and the beginning of the twentieth century. Its cynicism, hypocrisy, and nihilism brought the world the most atrocious wars in history and led an existential vacuum in the lives of millions of people.

Today, after trying to recover human rights discourse through the design of a very sophisticated system for the protection of human rights, the world is still suffering from the strong influence of cynicism, hypocrisy, and nihilism.

In order to fight against these anti-values, empathy and love seem insufficient. At the moment, more than ever, it is essential to add the *will to meaning* to our lives, consolidating a "Magic Triangle" that may be able to overcome the shadows of the *will to power*. Moreover, the will to meaning can also be seen as a tool to empower the oppressed and to transform them into leaders. Through meaning and purpose they decide what they want to do with their lives in an active exercise that goes beyond the passive situation where they were settled before, even if they were enjoying empathy and love.

Today, we are living in a global economic system where human beings are used as means and not as ends, and where we confuse money with happiness. That is why it is so important to recover the dignity of human beings through meaning and purpose. Every human life is meaningful and every single person has a purpose in life that can be developed through love for others or commitment to a cause. That is why we need to have a long-term vision and global mindset; otherwise, we will be only concerned with accumulating money and/or power but not considering the key element of the long term and foresight. According to Greenleaf (1977), foresight provides the "lead" for the servant-leader. Without foresight, there is no authentic leadership, but a series of reactions to situations and events. And here arises the following question: Are our leaders today aware of the need for foresight and vision? Personally, I think they are more concerned with winning elections every two or four years—or in winning money and power—than in designing a vision for the long term, concerned about how to foster and help develop purpose in life for the people they lead. As Greenleaf (1977) stated regarding two types of power in our present times, it can be a matter of persuasion or of coercive power that dominates. In the former, leaders utilize power to create opportunities and choices that lead to greater freedom, while in the latter, individuals are forced into a preset path.

So can we teach our young generations to have empathy, to love, and to have meaningful lives? This is a key question, but also a tough one, especially in the global and neoliberal context of today. However, even if we do not have the answer, I believe we can be congruent and teach empathy and love, giving meaning and purpose to their lives through love to others or commitment to a cause. It is our personal contribution, maybe a water drop into the ocean, but it will be our water drop. As Greenleaf argued (1977), even if there were a better system than the one we have now, without the presence of servant-leaders, that alone is no guarantee of a better society. It is clear that in terms of teaching human rights, a servant-leadership approach that encompasses empathy and love, committed to the growth of people in order to build community and to develop meaningful lives, seems more essential than ever.

I see empathy as my personal strength, but unconditional and sustainable love (or energy to action) I see as my weakness. However, knowing one's self is the first step to improve one's quality as a human being as an end—and in my case, teaching at the university, I aim to be a better professor as a means to make those around me become more wise, more free, more autonomous, more healthy, and better able themselves to become servants (Greenleaf, 1977, p. 14): servants of the cause of human rights and social justice.

However, as a human being, the shadows of cynicism, hypocrisy, and nihilism are present in me and the strength of our materialistic world is very strong. I believe it is the "Magic Triangle" which gives us the courage and the energy to embrace our shadows and to serve as "sustainable" leaders in the human rights field in particular, and life in general. I know it is difficult, and I am sure it is going to be even more difficult in the future, but as Antonio Gramsci (2011) said in *Letters from Prison*: "I'm a pessimist because of intelligence, but an optimist because of will" (p. 299).

NOTE

1. This chapter was previously published as Luque, T. J. (2017). Human rights from its origins to the twenty-first century: A journey through empathy, love, the will to power, and the will to meaning. *The International Journal of Servant-Leadership.* *11*(1), 71–100.

REFERENCES

Arendt, H. (2006). *Eichmann in Jerusalem. A report on the banality of evil.* London, UK: Penguin Classics.

Bales, K. (2007). *Ending slavery: How we free today's slaves.* Oakland, CA: University of California Press.

Bauman, Z. (2006). *Liquid times: living in an age of uncertainty.* Cambridge, UK: Polity Press.

Bermingham, A., & Brewer, J. (ed.). (1995). *The consumption of culture, 1600–1800: Image, object, text.* New York, NY: Routledge.

Boyd, J. (Ed.). (1950). *The papers of Thomas Jefferson,* 30 vols. Princeton, NJ: Princeton University Press.

Bray, J. (2003). *Epistolary' novel: Representations of consciousness.* New York, NY: Routledge.

Broers, M. (1996). *Europe after Napoleon: Revolution, reaction and romanticism, 1814–1848.* Manchester, UK: Manchester University Press.

Coleman, L. (2004). *The copycat effect: How the media and popular culture trigger the mayhem in tomorrow's headlines.* New York, NY: Simon and Schuster.

Donnelly, J. (1997). *International Human Rights: Dilemmas in World Politics.* Boulder, CO: Westview Press.

Englund, S. (2005). *Napoleon: A Political Life.* Cambridge, MA: Harvard University Press.

Ferch, S. (2011). *Forgiveness and power in the age of atrocity: Servant leadership as a way of life*. New York, NY: Lexington books.

Frankl, V. (2000). *Man's search for ultimate meaning*. New York, NY: Basic Books.

———. (2014). *The will to meaning. Foundations and applications of logotherapy*. New York, NY: Plume.

Fredrickson, G. M. (2003). *Racism: A short history*. New Jersey, NJ: Princeton University Press.

Gellner, E. (2009). *Nation and nationalism*. New York, NY: Cornell University Press.

Greenleaf, R. K. (1977). *Servant leadership: A journey into the nature of legitimate power and greatness*. New Jersey, NJ: Paulist Press.

———. (1991). *The Servant as leader*. Indianapolis, IN: The Robert K. Greenleaf Center.

Hanley, P. R., & McMahon, D. (2010). *The Enlightenment: Revolutions*. New York, NY: Routledge.

Hatcher, S., Nadeau, M., Walsh, L., Reynolds, M., Gales, J., & Marz, K. (1994). The teaching of empathy for high school and college students: Testing Rogerian methods with the interpersonal reactivity index. *Adolescence, (29)*116, 961–974.

Harris, P. (2007). *The right to demonstrate*. London, UK: Rights Press.

Hobsbawm, E. (1986). *The age of empires: 1875–1914*. Vancouver, BC: Vintage.

———. (1996). *The age of extremes: 1914–1991*. Vancouver, BC: Vintage.

hooks, b. (1999). *All about love: New visions*. New York, NY: HarperCollins.

Hunt, L. (2007). *Inventing Human Rights*. New York, NY: W.W. Norton & Company.

Innes, J., & Philp, M. (2013). *Re-imagining democracy in the age of revolutions: America, France, Britain, Ireland 1750–1850*. Oxford, UK: Oxford University Press.

Lash, S., & Featherstone, M. (1999). *Spaces of culture*. London, UK: Sage.

Nietzsche, F. (2011). *The will to power*. New York, NY: Knopf Doubleday Publishing Group.

Palop, M. E. (2010). *La nueva generación de derechos humanos. Origen y jsutificación* [The new generation of human rights. Origin and justification]. Madrid, SP: Dykinson, S.L.

Peck, S. (1978). *The Road Less Traveled: A New Psychology of Love, Traditional Values and Spiritual Growth*. New York, NY: Simon & Schuster.

Pilbeam, P. (ed.). (1995). *Themes in modern European history 1780–1830*. New York, NY: Routledge.

Rosengarten, F. (2011). *Letters from prison: Antonio Gramsci*. New York, NY: Columbia University Press.

Rousseau, J. J. (1987). *On the Social Contract*. (Cress, D. A. Trans.). Indiana, IN: Hackett Publishing Company.

Safranski, R. (2003). *Nietzsche: A Philosophical Biography*. New York, NY: W. W. Norton & Company.

Santos, B. (2005). *Democratizing democracy. Beyond the Liberal Democratic Canon*. London, UK: Verso.

———. (1995). *Towards a New Common Sense: Law, science, and politics in the Paradigmatic Transition*. New York, NY: Routledge.

Saura Estapa, J. (2009). Noción, fundamento y viabilidad de los derechos humanos emergentes: Una aproximación desde el derecho internacional [Notion, justification and viability of emerging human rights: An approach from international law], in *Derecho Internacionaly comunitario ante los retos de nuestro tiempo. Homenaje a la profesora Victoria Abellán Honrubia [International and comunitarian law facing challenges of today. Tribute to professor Victoria Abellán Honrubia].* Barcelona-Madrid, SP: Marcial Pons.

Spears, L. C. (2010). Character and servant leadership: Ten characteristics of effective, caring leaders. *The Journal of Virtues and Leadership, (1)*1, 25–30.

Spears, L. C & Lawrence, M. (2004). *Practicing Servant-Leadership: Succeeding through trust, bravery, and forgiveness.* San Francisco, CA: Jossey-Bass.

Titchener, E. (1909). *Experimental psychology of the thought processes.* New York, NY: Macmillan.

Titchener, E. (1915). A *Beginner's Psychology.* New York, NY: Macmillan.

United Nations. (1948). Universal declaration of human rights. Retrieved from http://www.un.org/en/universal-declaration-human-rights/

Wasserstrom, J., Grandin, G., Hunt, L., & Young, M. (2007). *Human rights and revolutions.* Lanham, MD: Rowman & Littlefield Publishers, Inc.

White, R. S. (2005). *Natural rights and the birth of romanticism in the 1790s.* London, UK: Palgrave McMillan.

Chapter 17

Servant-Leadership in Higher Education in Saudi Arabia

Areej Abdullah Shafai

Saudi Arabia[1] is seeking to create more effective leaders who meet the highest needs of individuals without using their authority to complete tasks. When looking deeply at servant-leadership approaches in higher education in Saudi Arabia, no known studies reflect what is really happening in practice with Saudi higher educational leaders in terms of defining and providing service. To better understand their leadership methods, it is important to explore their ways of employing authority in day-to-day operations since power is tightly linked to leadership. The purpose of this chapter is to provide an analysis of servant-leadership as it applies to higher education in Saudi Arabia. It also aims to analyze the authority practiced by higher educational leaders as a significant pillar of servant-leadership.

The chapter is organized around five main sections that cover the major aspects of servant-leadership in higher education in Saudi Arabia. The first section presents the background of servant-leadership, followed by the second section that provides a deep look at servant-leadership across cultures. The third section focuses on the notion of servant-leadership in higher education in Saudi Arabia. In addition, an analysis of authority and power is discussed in the fourth section. The last section sheds light on some recommendations for further studies.

BACKGROUND OF SERVANT-LEADERSHIP

Greenleaf (1977–2002) established servant-leadership in 1970 and gave birth to this term as a leadership method. The statement of servant-leadership centered on how Greenleaf lived life, what the author learned from experiences, and more importantly, what the world needs in order to be a better place in which to live (Valeri, 2007). Greenleaf strongly opposed relying on authority and power in leadership, especially coercive power, believing that leaders should shift authority to those who are being led (Northouse, 2016). Greenleaf realized that the need of humanity in the twenty-first century is servant-leadership because inequality and social injustice exist in many institutions and servant-leaders advocate for those who are less privileged (Northouse, 2016).

Sendjaya and Sarros (2002) enriched the term servant-leadership, purifying the inferior and weak meaning that some leaders or scholars might hold:

> It is important to note that the servant-leader's deliberate choice to serve and be a servant should not be associated with any forms of low self-concept or self-image, the same way as choosing to forgive should not be viewed as a sign of weakness. Instead, it would take a leader with an accurate understanding of his or her self-image, moral conviction and emotional stability to make such a choice. (p. 33)

The business book *Good to Great: Why Some Companies Make the Leap and Others Don't* provides an excellent example of some leadership scholars who wrestled with the paradox in leadership and service concepts, as many objected to the term due to its weakness and servitude. Service and leadership are two concepts with seemingly opposite meanings, and this is where the challenge of servant-leadership lies. Northouse (2016) talked about the criticism of the title of servant-leadership, because the name seems contradictory and creates a noisy sound that diminishes the true value of the approach. Furthermore, the name servant-leadership suggests the concept of following, and following is completely contrary to the concept of leadership. These limitations are partly logical for some thinkers, as Saudi leaders may possibly tend to this mindset, but the tenet behind servant-leadership is that it combines leadership and service, power and influence, and decisions and participation, enabling leaders to be effective servants.

In a traditional concept of leadership, a person lower on the chain of command is expected to serve. In servant-leadership, however, "the paradoxical concept of serving from a leadership role seems just the natural way it should work. Servant-leaders often feel they are called to serve" (Tureman, 2013, p. 9). Many leaders enjoy a sense of authority over others, as it is one of the perquisites of a leadership position. Such leaders naturally put themselves first because this is part of human nature. In servant-leadership, the natural desire brings one to serve, to serve first, then to lead, especially for those who are in lower levels of performance (Tureman, 2013). Servant-leaders no longer act as the "headmaster," rather, they serve as "head learner" (Grogan, 2013, p. 377), engaging in the enterprise of the organization by modeling, celebrating, displaying, and serving to make sure individual's needs are met.

Servant-leadership, most of the time, calls for bringing about change. Keeping old ways of performing one's work is enough to stifle innovation and creativity in the workplace:

> Leading as usual with traditional tyrannical styles is not only anachronistic it is also potentially dysfunctional, given the fast pace of globalization, the complexity of transnational corporations, the addition of global educational entities, and the demographical changes in the workplace. (Whitfield, 2014, p. 50)

Servant-leaders bring desired change to organizations by shaping the culture, behaviors, values, relationships, and results of the organization. Furthermore, leading change while being a servant to all is incalculably demanding.

SERVANT-LEADERSHIP ACROSS CULTURES

Culture shapes the practice of leadership and has a marked impact on how leaders are expected to behave (Austell, 2010; Hofstede, 2001; House, Hanges, Javidan, Dorfman, & Gupta, 2004; Shahin & Wright, 2004). The body of research (Carroll & Patterson, 2014; Hofstede, 2001; Shahin & Wright, 2004) reported that culture does not derive from one's genes, but derives from one's social environment. Culture is "all of a collective society's normative behaviors and traditions" (Carroll & Patterson, 2014, p. 20). Culture could also be defined as the interactive aggregate of common characteristics that influence a human group's response to its environment.

"Culture determines the uniqueness of a human group in the same way personality determines the uniqueness of an individual" (Hofstede, 2001, pp. 550–551). Culture clearly affects leadership. Leaders need to understand how cultural differences affect leadership and life in and across organizations (Whitfield, 2014). Embracing servant-leadership characteristics and cultural dimensions is a smart strategy that creates successful servant-leaders who can effectively better serve employees and organizations.

Servant-leadership is a model of leadership employed globally. Considering the perspectives of servant-leadership cross-culturally provides a broader understanding of how different cultures can shape servant-leadership more naturally than others, and how others' values, behaviors, and traditions impact the creation of effective servant-leaders. Shahin and Wright (2004) analyzed the concept of leadership in the context of culture. They stated that understanding and research on leadership itself is a "tricky endeavor, adding a cross-cultural component to the mix in leadership research makes the whole process even more complex" (p. 731). However, Spears (1998) discovered, considering servant-leadership with global eyes, throughout history, organizations that are more successful, viable, and more caring about their employees and their professional growth employ servant-leadership. Although servant-leadership was developed by Greenleaf in the United States, this model is applicable to leaders worldwide. Servant-leadership is suited to all leaders from varieties of cultures and workplaces.

Carroll and Patterson (2014) compared Patterson's model of servant-leadership across two cultures: India and the United States. This model consists of seven characteristics: love, trust, vision, humility, altruism, empowerment, and service. India has more than one billion citizens and exceeds developed countries politically, economically, and socially, containing immense resources and a highly educated workforce. The researchers used the same method to collect data from Indians and Americans to examine the level of leaders practicing the seven characteristics of Patterson's model of servant-leadership. Study findings revealed that this model is appropriate for both cultures and no significant difference emerged among the two cultural samples in perceptions of servant-leadership, except for the characteristic of vision. Visionary leaders are those who focus on the future of organizations and followers, and create imagination and insights for the future. Indians practice vision differently from Americans, perhaps due to a difference in philosophies between the two cultures and the cultural dimension of future orientation.

Another study that showed servant-leadership from a global perspective was Winston and Ryan's (2008) work, as they revealed servant-leadership as a global rather than a Western model. The authors used the Global Leadership and Organizational Behavior Effectiveness Research Program (GLOBE), which constructs human orientation and cultural concepts from Africa, East Asia, the Mediterranean, and India. GLOBE attends to specific characteristics of leaders that are part of the servant-leadership concept: humility, concern, altruism, service, care, fairness, and friendship. By analyzing the relationship between the GLOBE study and servant-leadership, the general score of valuing human orientation is factually higher than practicing human-oriented behaviors. This implies that the practical model of leading with human orientation is lacking, and employing a servant-leadership model may help leaders be more human-oriented leaders. More importantly, Winston and Ryan's study of GLOBE showed that the regions that scored the highest in human orientation were South Asia, Sub-Saharan Africa, and the Anglo regions; the middle scoring regions were Confucian Asia, Latin America, the Middle East, Eastern Europe, and Germanic Europe; the lowest scoring regions were Latin Europe and Nordic Europe. Thus, "overlap between servant-leadership and the global acceptance of the humane orientation is evidence that servant-leadership can be presented as a global rather than a Western concept" (p. 220). Nelson's (2003) study focused on Black South African leaders and Serrano (2005) looked at Latin American leaders. The practices of both cultures supported the viability of servant-leadership in various global cultures, as it is an appropriate style that should be practiced and learned more in Africa, Asia, and the Mediterranean (Winston & Ryan, 2008).

Hannay (2009) studied the application of servant-leadership in a cross-cultural context using Hofstede's (1993) five cultural dimensions as a framework to identify differences and similarities across cultures: power distance, individualism, masculinity, uncertainly avoidance, and long-term orientation. Hannay (2009) identified the best cultural fit for a servant-leadership concept. As a result of the study, Hannay discerned that servant-leadership is best applied in a culture with low power distance, low to moderate individualism, low to moderate masculinity, low uncertainty avoidance, and a moderate-to-high long-term orientation. According to Hannay's study, power distance and uncertainty avoidance seemed to be the most important to the success of servant-leadership. Hofstede (1993) evaluated the United States, Germany, Japan, France, the Netherlands, Hong Kong, Indonesia, West Africa, Russia, and China, researching the manifestation of these five dimensions in their cultures. Chhokar, Brodbeck, and House (2008) defined power distance as "the degree to which members of an organization and society encourage and reward unequal distribution of power with greater power at higher levels" (p. 4). Uncertainty avoidance appears to be consistent with the servant-leadership characteristic of *conceptualization*. Scholars defined uncertainty avoidance as "relying on established social norms, rituals, and bureaucratic practices to decrease the probability of unpredictable future events that can adversely affect the operation of an organization or society" (p. 4).

One significant finding of Hannay's (2009) study was that none of these ten countries provided a good environmental fit for the application of servant-leadership theory. In addition, the United States was the only country of these ten that ranked low on power distance and uncertainty avoidance. Germany, the Netherlands, and the United States ranked high on individualism. The United States and Germany ranked high on masculinity, whereas the Netherlands ranked low on this factor. Also, both Germany and the Netherlands ranked in the moderate category on the long-term orientation factor, whereas the United States ranked lowest.

However, considering the application of servant-leadership in one country is clearly a limiting factor that diminishes the value of the servant-leadership model and its impact on an organization as a whole. The culture of a country influences leadership and the broader culture in an organization. Research (Austell, 2010; Carroll & Patterson, 2014; Hannay, 2009; Hofstede, 2001; Shahin & Wright, 2004; Spears, 1998; Whitfield, 2014; Winston & Ryan,

2008) indicates an obvious correlation between cultural characteristics and the probability of the successful adoption of servant-leadership in the workplace. Scholars need to pay closer attention to "increase intercultural leader capacity to lead in culturally mixed organizations, be they domestic or international, which resulting in minimizing or avoiding institutional or organizational failure" (Whitfield, 2014, p. 48). Servant-leaders can effectively navigate cultural differences and similarities and move around the major attitudes of servant-leaders to be a good fit with the nature of different cultures.

THE NOTION OF SERVANT-LEADERSHIP IN HIGHER EDUCATION IN SAUDI ARABIA

To better analyze servant-leadership as it applies to Saudi higher education, it is important to present some basic features of higher education in Saudi Arabia and some studies conducted about servant-leadership in higher education. Additionally, the discussion of servant-leadership and the use of authority in Saudi higher education are displayed as well.

Background on Higher Education in Saudi Arabia

The general goal of education in Saudi Arabia is for students to understand the true Islam, the dominant religion of Saudi Arabia, and follow it in a comprehensive manner, to provide students with necessary skills and knowledge, and to prepare them to develop their behaviors as individuals and improve their communities (United Nations Educational, Scientific and Cultural Organization, 2011). Education at all levels in Saudi Arabia rests on the Islamic code of ethics, the essential ideology that shapes the lifestyle in the Kingdom of Saudi Arabia (Gonaim, 2017). Education in Saudi Arabia is segregated by gender, including general education for boys, general education for girls, and traditional Islamic education. Both genders follow the same curriculum and take the same annual examinations (Sedgwick, 2001). The Ministry of Education in Saudi Arabia, established in 1952, created a clear vision of education, which summarizes that education is an investment aiming not only to meet societies' demands, but also provide Muslim individuals better quality, creativity, and success for their lives. Saudi Arabia invested approximately $160 billion in its education budget (Smith & Abouammoh, 2013).

The Ministry of Higher Education existed under the general Ministry of Education. Due to tremendous growth in the number of universities and colleges in the last decade in Saudi Arabia, many considered it necessary to establish the Ministry of Higher Education to address issues related to higher education (Alamri, 2011). Higher education institutions provide a wide range of programs and specialists in many fields. The number of universities and colleges increased significantly and enrollment in universities doubled between 2010 and 2014 (Clark, 2014). The system of higher education witnessed marked development in expanding higher education institutions in Saudi Arabia, including twenty-three public universities, eighteen primary teacher's colleges for men, eighty primary teacher's colleges for women, thirty-seven colleges and institutes for health, twelve technical colleges, and thirty-three private universities and colleges (Alamri, 2011). Education is free at all levels for Saudi students, except for those who choose to attend private institutions. According to Ministry of Higher Education (2017) statistics, 1,527,769 students enrolled in higher education institutions during the 2014–2015 academic year.

The Ministry of Higher Education is responsible for funding, development of curriculum and systems, recruitment of faculties, and improvement of the higher education sector at all levels (Clark, 2014). The Ministry of Higher Education is committed to preparing teachers and faculties to best serve universities and students. According to the United Nations Educational, Scientific, and Cultural Organization (2011), the full role of the higher education system is to "prepare and graduate qualified staff; upgrade the educational and professional standards of the current general education teachers, principals and administrators by offering various training courses in cooperation with the Ministry of Education" (p. 13).

Servant-Leadership in Higher Education

Research studies lack knowledge of servant-leadership in higher education institutions (Keith, 2010). After working in various universities and colleges after retiring from AT&T, Greenleaf realized the needs of campuses and students to achieve a high level of performance. It is unsurprising that Greenleaf cared about the growth of students, universities, and colleges (Greenleaf, 1977/2002). Greenleaf found that colleges and universities were not preparing young people to lead. To best prepare young people to lead, colleges must have faculty members and leaders who devote themselves to serve others. In *Teacher as Servant*, Greenleaf wrote about an environment called "Jefferson House." This was a residence for students who were committed to service and who grew through conducting service projects and engaging in internships (Greenleaf, 1977/2002). Greenleaf called upon university and college leaders to build campuses that value service and make it a core mission to be achieved.

Higher education in an academic setting seeks to be more effective in preparing students to have better lives in the future. Satyapuitra (2013) reviewed the work of Wheeler (2011) that speaks about servant-leadership in higher education. Wheeler (2011) observed that most current leadership models in higher education are unsuccessful, unsuitable, and short-term models. Without an intensive effort to adopt proper leadership models in higher education, colleges and universities will face heavy burdens and potential obstacles that prevent them from fulfilling their desired goals. Wheeler (2011) recognized that the primary aim in higher education is to provide service to others and averred that servant-leadership is the best model to enhance the culture of service in higher education. Higher education institutions will function in a more powerful way by embodying a servant-leadership model that brings a long-term commitment to organizational effectiveness, because it is a way of living and leading that creates servant-leaders who care about thriving people and organizations (Satyapuitra, 2013; Wheeler, 2011).

Scardino (2013) examined the extent to which full-time professors at three Franciscan institutions of higher education exhibited servant-leadership qualities and whether their practice of servant-leadership impacted student engagement. The author used two types of surveys to gather the required data. Full-time professors at three institutions of higher education completed the Servant-Leadership Questionnaire, which measures their levels of embodying servant-leadership characteristics. Also, Scardino used the Faculty Survey of Student Engagement to measure the engagement of students with faculty. The results of the study revealed a direct correlation between servant-leadership and deep approaches to learning. Those deep approaches to learning were explained by the linear combination of altruistic calling, emotional healing, wisdom, persuasive mapping, and organizational stewardship. The most significant finding was that only emotional healing contributed significantly to the model. Thus, emotional healing was considered a vital characteristic of full-time professors at Franciscan institutions of higher education and these types of learning environments. Emotional healing helps students at higher education institutions maximize their learning process.

Erkutlu and Chafra (2015b) investigated the relationship between servant-leadership and voice behavior by testing the role of psychological safety and psychological empowerment as two essential scales that measure how servant-leadership affects voice behavior. The authors recognized that the study of how the mechanisms of servant-leadership impact voice behavior has been lacking. They focused on the psychological safety of employees in speaking up and discussing issues openly. Erkutlu and Chaff (2015a) used the Psychological Empowerment Scale, which measured meaning, competence, impact, and self-determination. To examine how servant-leadership affects employees' voice behaviors, 793 faculty members from ten state universities in Turkey completed the voice-behavior, psychological-empowerment, and psychological-safety scales. Of those faculty members, sixty-four deans were asked to complete the servant-leadership scale. Results revealed a significant relationship between servant-leadership and voice behaviors. Servant-leadership of faculty deans positively related to the psychological safety and psychological empowerment of faculty members. This implies that "given the risks associated with employees' voice and due to the power that leaders hold over employees' resources and outcomes, trust in leader may play an important role in employees' decisions to voice their opinions" (Erkutlu & Chafra, 2015b, p. 31).

Jordan (2006) studied the impact of servant-leader professors on student learning and success on campus. The researcher hoped to contribute to preliminary discussions of servant-leadership as an educational-leadership paradigm for faculty in higher education in the twenty-first century. Jordan recognized that "teacher quality is one of the most powerful determinants of student achievement and virtually every category of educational outcomes" (pp. 16-17) and, specifically faculty members were one of the most powerful educational forces. Faculty members not only play a significant role in the academic paths of the students they teach, but also in the universities they serve and the community at large. To investigate this issue, Jordan conducted a qualitative case study of selected self-identified servant-professors who could provide information about a real-life higher education classroom situation regarding servant-leadership. Several themes emerged from the faculty members' participation: (a) integrity of belief and practice; (b) a commitment to student-centered learning; (c) a commitment to the development of learning communities; (d) a commitment to personal growth; (e) a commitment to the greater common good; (f) courageously pursuing innovation; (g) displaying a passionate dedication to their students; and (h) establishing equality and justice.

Clearly, results from the Jordan (2006) study lay in reporting answers to the three research questions. The first question was, "What is the praxis of servant professors?" Findings showed that the perspectives of servant-professors about servant-leadership in classrooms summarized "a process in which a collaborative community of learners learned with passion and excellence" (p. 197). The second question was, "How does a higher education servant-professor define servant-leadership?" The characteristics of the three servant-professors are the same ten characteristics of servant-leadership created by Spears. Those qualities include listening, empathy, healing, awareness, persuasion, conceptualization, foresight, stewardship, building community, and commitment to the growth of people. The last question was, "How does a servant professor apply servant-leadership in her or his classroom?" The three faculty participants agreed that balancing leadership, learning, and service is important to ensure the success of the application of the servant-leadership model in higher education classrooms. Furthermore, empowering each individual to become a leader and a follower—a teacher and a student at the same time—is a critical practice of servant-leadership. Jordan concluded that "educators, as leaders, impact and influence the students entrusted to them in a powerful way, whether for good or evil. Teachers can inspire and empower students or devalue, ridicule, and stunt intellectual, social, and emotional growth" (p. 7).

Servant-Leadership and the Use of Authority in Saudi Higher Education

There is a cultural and perceptual paradox when practicing servant-leadership because each culture has its own beliefs about leadership and authority, even if those beliefs are outmoded and not compatible with reality. Saudi Arabia has its unique cultural understanding of the word "servant" as it can be perceived negatively. Saudis believe that servants are those who do the common good for society without being privileged. When it comes to the term "servant-leadership," Saudi Arabians faced difficulties processing the word "servant" and linking it to the word "leadership." Austell (2010) looked at servant-leadership in an international context. He discussed the method of servant-leadership with a Saudi doctoral student. After hearing a brief definition about servant-leadership, the Saudi student stated: "I will never be what you call a servant-leader" (p. 14), believing that a leader should be the one who is being served not the one who serves others. This sensitivity is derived from the belief that leadership means authority and has nothing to do with being a servant.

Saudi Arabia faces major challenges in practicing leadership in higher education. Wilson (2011) revealed that "there is a remarkable scarcity of solid studies on leadership theory and practices in Saudi Arabia" (p. 180). Although it is a time when service is mostly needed, not enough attention and support is giving to the value of service in Saudi Arabia, as it diminishes and ignores the servant-leadership method, because no definition or determination of its use as a practical leadership style exists (Al-Yousef, 2012).

In their study, Shmailan and Wirbaa (2015) revealed that the majority of educational leaders in Saudi Arabian universities are transformational leaders and transactional leaders, while fewer are laissez-faire leaders. The general concept of servant-leadership remains undefined as a practical leadership model in Saudi Arabia (Al-Yousef, 2012; Shmailan & Wirbaa, 2015).

Salameh, Al-Wyzinany, and Al-Omari (2012) determined the absence of important servant-leadership principles among academic administrators in Jordan and Saudi Arabia. Researchers found a lack of research in the area of servant-leadership not only in Jordan and Saudi Arabia, but also in the research world in general (Russell & Stone, 2002). In addition, the number of years of teaching experience one achieved identified to what extent one practiced the principles of servant-leadership. Faculty with more experience perceived the level of practice of "developing others" and "building community" higher than those with less experience (Salameh et al., 2012). Previous studies (Al-Yousef, 2012; Salameh et al., 2012; Shmailan & Wirbaa, 2015) concluded that servant-leadership needs more attention in the area of research across countries generally, and in Saudi Arabia specifically.

Gonaim (2017) investigated leadership characteristics and behaviors of department chairs in higher education in Saudi Arabia. Very few studies measured leadership approaches used by higher educational leaders in general, and in Saudi Arabia in particular. "The academic department is a fundamental unit for transforming the university's visions and goals into reality" (p. 1). The findings demonstrated that department chairs are distinguished by their attitudes such as appreciation, respect, and trust, in addition to their knowledge and skills such as clear communication, listening, convincing, problem solving, time management, and adopting change. More importantly, according to department chairs' perspectives in Saudi Arabia, a tendency exists to call for more collaborative leadership approaches that urge common effort, shared authority, ethics, and collective interest (Gonaim, 2017).

Higher education leaders in Saudi Arabia still practice the oldest forms of leadership that focus on the performance of workers, not the workers themselves (Alamri, 2011). Although the majority of Saudi higher education leaders (e.g., deans) received their education internationally, they tend to use bureaucratic leadership styles that heavily rely on formal authority. Bureaucracy is still the major challenge for the higher education system in Saudi Arabia (Alamri, 2011).

In addition, researchers conducted very few studies that examined leadership styles of staff in universities in Saudi Arabia (Shmailan & Wirbaa, 2015). The researchers found that significantly more leadership development and training for managers and staff was taking place in universities in Saudi Arabia because increasing demands of higher education in Saudi Arabia require successful educational leadership that brings positive change to organizations. The Ministry of Education in Saudi Arabia revealed that Saudi leaders suffer from unfamiliarity with leadership education. They receive no leadership education before they receive leadership positions (Mathis, 2010). When educators become eligible to advance their careers to be educational leaders, they get their new leadership positions without prior engagement in any professional-development activities that prepare them professionally to be successful leaders (Mathis, 2010).

Because servant-leadership is not yet known and practiced by some leaders in Saudi Arabia, no known studies assessed the nature of the authority used by Saudi higher education leaders. For instance, some Saudi leaders may embody the characteristics of servant-leadership, but do not think of themselves as servant-leaders. Their potential lack of knowledge about servant-leadership may cause a failure to recognize themselves as servant-leaders. The type of authority of those leaders who are servant-leaders still needs to be defined. Currently, it appears that no study has explored servant-leadership in higher education in Saudi Arabia. Researchers need to determine the level of the use of moral authority by Saudi higher educational leaders as an essential pillar of servant-leadership. Their ways of employing authority will clearly define whether they are real servant-leaders.

ANALYSIS OF SERVANT-LEADERSHIP, POWER, AND AUTHORITY

Authority is a main pillar of servant-leadership as a servant-leader is careful when choosing the right type of authority that does not hurt others. Three essential issues show the link between authority and servant-leadership, which include understanding the authority and power in servant-leadership, shifting from "formal authority" to "moral authority," and the relationship between the five bases of power and servant-leadership.

Authority and Power in Servant-Leadership

Some people want power to live a better life, make money, or create a good reputation and image in other people's eyes. San Juan (2005) illustrated how power is one of the most studied topics in the world; that's because every individual to some extent desires power. In a workplace environment, leaders and employees seek to gain power: leaders need power to run an organization and its employees, and employees desire power to gain the ear of their bosses to, for example, change some of their daily work life (Fuqua, Payne & Cangemi, 2000). Of consequence is how leaders use their power without hurting the organization and its members.

   To better understand how servant-leaders should use power, it is helpful first to understand the concept of power because "power is a compelling aspect of leadership" (San Juan, 2005, p. 187). Scholars hold different definitions of power based on their perspectives and perceptions. They defined power as a relationship between people, control over people, use of resources, and access of information. Van Der Toom et al. (2014) stated, "power is typically defined as asymmetric control over valued resources in the context of social relations" (p. 2). Cangemi (1992) asserted, "power is the individual's capacity to move others, to entice others, to persuade and encourage others to attain specific goals or to engage in specific behavior; it is the capacity to influence and motivate others" (p. 2). Still other researchers defined power as the "ability to influence the actions of others, individuals or groups. It is understood as the leader's influence potential" (Krausz, 1986, p. 69). Despite these different dimensions of power, scholars agreed that power is the ability to influence others toward better accomplishments of organizations. Power can be understood as *power over* and *power to*, as Grogan (2013) described. *Power over* emphasizes controlling people and outcomes, such as what, when, or how people do things. *Power to* is goal-bound, viewed as a resource of energy for achieving shared purpose and goals.

Authority and power seem similar, but each one provides certain resources and foci. Power is the ability to influence others to achieve an organization's goals (Christman, 2007). Authority is not ability; rather, it is the right given to the manager to accomplish certain tasks (Serrat, 2014). Every leader holds authority to give orders to accomplish tasks, but any individual—not necessarily leaders—can hold power when they are able to influence others to do, avoid, or change things (Mooney, 1985). The major difference between power and authority rests in the notion that authority aligns with social position, whereas power ties to personal characteristics. Power is a factual relation, whereas authority is a legitimate relation (Coleman, 2013).

As authority is one of the perquisites of leadership, Serrat (2014) wrote about authority and power in terms of function, application, and comparison. Formal authority is a type of authority used by leaders to control and change certain objects.

> Formal authority—the power to direct—is the defining characteristic of societal and organizational hierarchy. Charting a chain of command, one eventually locates somebody, or some group, who administers an organization's collective decision rights, and enjoys the perquisites ascribed to the function. (p. 10)

Serrat (2014) argued that formal authority is best described as power held because of one's position. Although the twenty-first century needs to expand this type of authority by leveraging mutual influence, "the power of formal authority is eroding as its utility becomes less evident" (p. 10). Greenleaf turned down many promotions because of a fear that formal authority would interfere with the moral authority that Greenleaf admired (Sipe & Frick, 2015). Legitimate and moral authority need to be practiced and inherited in today's organizations (Sipe & Frick, 2015).

A majority of leadership writers acknowledge leadership as a position, not as a function, whereas position does not mean leadership. Servant-leadership recognizes that leadership is a function and mindset that shapes an organization and its people. Servant-leaders cherish the resulting behaviors and ethics, carefully using the position to allow this paradigm and its values to be realized, then practiced (Christman, 2007). One requires position to easily and quickly accomplish tasks, but position is not necessarily required to lead (Christman, 2007). Northouse (2016) stated: "people have power when they have the ability to affect others' beliefs, attitudes, and courses of action" (p. 6). Robbins (1998) added that position is not a prerequisite for power. Some people prove their abilities and power to change others' behaviors, but they do not hold a position that allows them to control others.

Christman (2007) argued that power is often perceived as a negative force and Karp (1996) listed three perspectives of power: good, evil, and natural. Christman (2007) stated: "power isn't good and it isn't bad; it simply is, just as electricity isn't intrinsically good or bad, it just is. It is how it is used that makes a difference" (p. 13). Robbins (1998) enhanced the understanding of power by stating, "Power refers to a capacity that A has to influence the behavior of B, so that B acts in accordance with A's wishes" (p. 396). Leaders need to realize that personal power is an optimal source for the development of a servant culture and authority is autonomous from providing service. Effective leaders grow their personal power by actually growing and empowering others in the organization. As Fuqua et al. (2000) illustrated, leaders who exercise authority over others most of the time are seen as untrustworthy because their employees feel the need to avoid arguing, dominating, and engaging in any informal conversation with them.

In contrast, servant-leaders do not rely on their position, but rather rely on their legitimacy and ethics in addressing followers and meeting their needs (Spears, 2010; Spears & Lawrence, 2004). Greenleaf strongly opposed relying on authority and power in leadership, especially coercive power, believing that leaders should shift authority to those being led (Northouse, 2016). "The more that power is concentrated in the office of a leader, the more inevitability that later will become isolated" (Mooney, 1985. p. 82). Further, Russell and Stone (2002) demonstrated the danger of viewing leadership as authority or power and diminished the value of the service-in-leadership concept. They stated,

> as long as power dominates our thinking about leadership, we cannot move toward a higher standard of leadership. We must place service at the core; for even though power will always be associated with leadership, it has only one legitimate use: service. (p. 145)

Leaders can only practice servant-leadership by modeling moral authority. To establish moral authority, one's authority must be viewed as legitimate (Grogan, 2013). Christman (2007) reported some types of power servant-leaders could practice. One of these types is rooted in followers viewing their leaders as legitimate, dubbed *legitimate power*. Legitimate power is the type of power viewed as fair. People do what they are asked to do under a sense of volunteering, because they see their leaders' behaviors and decisions as legitimate. Leaders never receive obligation if their power is seen as illegitimate (Tyler, 2006).

Shifting from "Formal Authority" to "Moral Authority"

Ethics is the core value of the development of leadership. Leadership scholars realize that although servant-leadership and other leadership theories—transformational, cultural, and ethical—emphasize ethical behaviors and values, "the world is full of the selfish, non-transparent and greedy leaders" (Dambe & Moorad, 2008, p. 585). Thus, embracing leadership ethics, modeling ethical behaviors, and shifting leaders' practices of authority from formal authority to more moral authority is critical in today's workplace.

An effective leadership style does not depend on formal authority. Often, leaders who avoid relying on their authority create it into a seeming necessity (Serrat, 2014). Leaders who heavily use their authority and power seek to get conformity without acceptance and to issue a chain of commands without influence, giving them a feeling of clutching the reigns and controlling others' performance (Serrat, 2014). Servant-leaders do not use formal authority. They recognize that formal authority may prevent them from providing service that is the core element of servant-leadership (Greenleaf, 1977/2002). Moral authority consists of character strengths that are considered a primary greatness, whereas formal authority is a secondary greatness that can be defined as wealth, reputation, and position (Covey, 2006). When people with formal authority or a position of power (secondary greatness) use their authority or power as a last resort, their moral authority tends to increase, because they use persuasion, empathy, reasoning, and trust instead of subordinating their ego.

Leaders with moral authority act as servant-leaders (Sipe & Frick, 2015). Sipe and Frick (2015) detailed that moral authority does not come automatically with position. Earning moral authority depends on following the six pillars of servant-leadership because those pillars represent the essential moralities that align with servant-leadership attributes. The six pillars are (a) leaders need to act as people of character with integrity, humility, and spirituality; (b) putting people first through serving, caring, concerning, and mentoring; (c) being skillful, empathetic communicators who appreciate feedback; (d) collaborating compassionately and building diverse teams; (e) exercising foresight and inspiring and supporting an audacious vision; and (f) being a systems thinker, who considers the greater good and effectively engages in a complex environment (Sipe & Frick, 2015). Greenleaf (1977/2002) wrote the following famous passage summarizing the moral authority in servant-leadership:

> A new moral principle is emerging, which holds that the only authority deserving one's allegiance is that which is freely and knowingly granted by the led to the leader in response to, and in proportion to, the clearly evident servant nature of the leader. Those who choose to follow this principle will not casually accept the authority of existing institutions. Rather, they will freely respond only to individuals who are chosen as leaders because they are proven and trusted as servants. (pp. 23–24)

The significance of moral authority goes beyond the advantage it brings to an organization and its people. It can be considered a survival tactic or the demise of an entire organization (Sipe & Frick, 2015). Every institution should adopt enduring moral principles rather than rules, because moral principles are the critical indicators of the health of the environment that ensure continuity and productivity. Moral authority leads to formal authority. Leaders who use moral authority earn the power and freedom that are given by people to expand their voices. When they become advocates for their people, they naturally gain formal authority that enables leaders and followers to share a common vision. Exercising formal authority leads to the accomplishment of the required tasks, but by exercising moral authority and leading by example, leaders strengthen their power and see followers' potential and worth.

The Relationship between the Five Bases of Power and Servant-Leadership

Processes of power are varying and complex in our society. The five bases of social or organizational power and influence comprise a theory developed by French and Raven in 1959. Those bases started from the premise that power and influence involve relations between at least two parties; these bases of power include legitimate, reward, coercive, expert, and referent.

Legitimate Power

To enrich legitimate power and fully understand it, it is critical to be familiar with the dimensions of the word *legitimacy*. Tyler (2006) defined the term legitimacy as "psychological property of an authority, institution, or social arrangement that leads those connected to it to believe that it is appropriate, proper, and just" (p. 375). Because of legitimacy, people feel they can follow rules, obey orders, agree with decisions, and do what they are asked to do in a satisfactory manner, without fear of punishment or anticipation of rewards, but rather under the feeling of obligation and through volunteering. Fuqua et al., (2000) revealed, "people with legitimate power fail to recognize they have it, and then they may begin to notice others going around them to accomplish their goals" (p. 2).

Reward Power

Reward power comes from individuals who have the ability to reward and compensate, and mediate the reward, as perceived by others (French & Raven, 1959). Reward power is the ability to give either positive conse-quences or remove negative consequences for doing what is wanted and expected. Powerful leaders can provide tangible and intangible rewards to employees to keep them influenced. Tangible rewards are physical items such as salary increases, bonuses, and certificates. Intangible rewards are moral rewards such as recognition, positive feedback, and praise (Petress, 2013).

Coercive Power

Coercive power is an inappropriate tool in addressing others because it results in distrust, fear, lack of loyalty, and satisfaction toward the powerful (Petress, 2013). Leaders use coercive power when they force or threaten others for noncompliance. Force includes emotional, social, and political force. Leaders who use this power punish others, because they do not conform to the leader's ideas and demands.

Expert Power

Expert power is the faith that a person is more knowledgeable and has more insights and expertise in certain ways (French & Raven, 1959). Expert power is very similar to informational power, which was added five years after devel-oping the five bases of power by French and Raven in 1959. Informational power implies the control of information and knowledge needed by others to reach specific goals (French & Raven, 1959).

Referent Power

Raven (2008) described referent power as a basis of identification of a person with others:

> Referent power stems from the target identifying with the agent, or seeing the agent as a model that the target would want to emulate. ("I really admire my supervisor and wish to be like him/her. Doing things the way she believes they should be done gives me some special satisfaction.") (p. 3)

Referent power is the ability to cultivate the admiration and respect of followers so leaders can influence others because of others' friendship, admiration, and loyalty (French & Raven, 1959). Only people who create a strong interpersonal relationship with others can gain referent power because it heavily relies on the mutual perspectives between people and power (Raven, 2008).

In this taxonomy, Christman (2007) defined the types of power used by servant-leaders through the lens of the two major categories of power: positional power and personal power. Positional power is the authority bestowed by a position to whoever is occupying this position. The individual who has positional power is using their rights to exert power in the scope of a particular position, which means this category of power is limited to the boundaries of the title or position and its advantages do not go beyond this exact position (Greenberg & Baron, 2003). Positional power emerges in the form of a CEO or vice president who takes their role seriously and uses their given rights to create a safe, growth-oriented environment, so employees and stakeholders can be served better. Greenberg and Baron divided positional power into four possible subcomponents, originally classified by French and Raven in 1959. These four types of power are legitimate, coercive, reward, and information power, as described in previous paragraphs.

The second main category of power is personal power. Personal power is the power one has based on the ability to influence. Effective leaders are those who rely on their personal power more than their positional power (Christman, 2007). Personal power is what "one derives because of his or her individual qualities or characteristics" (Greenberg & Baron, 2003, p. 445). Those qualities are the predominant source of influence. One realizes personal power by establishing deep relationships with others that in turn creates a bond of trust, honesty, ethics, and collaboration. Leaders who use their personal power tend not to use their title or position to influence others to encourage them to do their work; instead, they seek to build trusting and long-lasting relationships that make followers feel secure and engaged. Personal power can be actualized by a position-holder by practicing the last two types of power defined by French and Raven (1959): expert power and referent power (Greenberg & Baron, 2003).

Servant-leadership can only be practiced by those leaders who consider personal power as an optimal resource for the creation of a servant culture in an organization (Christman, 2007). Positional power is not an optimal platform for the development of servant-leadership, because it may be a deterrent to its actualization. Not all who use personal power are servant-leaders, but all who are servant-leaders use their personal power.

Personal power, utilized by a position-holder within an organization, simply becomes an optimal platform for actualizing servant-leadership. In some respects, positions, like power, are a neutral value, neither positive nor negative. It simply becomes a vehicle of opportunity for a servant-leader. (p. 12)

CONCLUSIONS AND RECOMMENDATIONS

There is a remarkable scarcity in the area of servant-leadership research in Saudi Arabia. The phrase servant-leadership might be confusing for some leaders because of the assumption that leaders are the ones who are being served. Changing this mindset could be a challenge, especially for those leaders who rely on authority and believe in it as an essential factor in leadership. Shifting from a traditional leadership style to servant-leadership can be misunderstood as a weakness of a leader that she/he is no longer able to control things. Saudi higher educational leaders need to be educated in some of the bases and foundations of leadership, which are critical in reforming and developing higher education and its system in Saudi Arabia.

Saudi educational leaders need to engage in continuous professional development and need to be given more accessible and available opportunities and programs designed by the Ministry of Higher Education. Shafai (2014) viewed the need of the Ministry of Education in Saudi Arabia to respond to the current challenges in education institutions. She reported:

In terms of the introduction of new approaches in the educational process, the need for changing the traditional pattern in the education process, and the discovery of alternative techniques of teaching, strategies, and methods of modern education, professional development is essential. (pp. 4–5)

Shifting from the traditional method to servant-leadership method needs to be done gradually and smoothly to reduce the potential risks and challenges that can occur.

This chapter focused on an analysis of servant-leadership in higher education in Saudi Arabia. Future mixed-method studies might focus on experiences of male and female leaders separately and whether they have different perspective on servant-leadership and the use of power. Additionally, exploring and comparing higher educational leaders from different regions in Saudi Arabia will be helpful and can provide a deeper understanding of the impact of an educational environment in practicing servant-leadership and authority.

NOTE

1. This chapter was previously published as Shafai, A. A. (2018). Servant-leadership in higher education in Saudi Arabia. *The International Journal of Servant-Leadership. 12*(1), 297–335.

REFERENCES

Alamri. (2011). Higher education in Saudi Arabia. *Journal of Higher Education Theory and Practice, 11*(4), 88–91.

Al-Yousef, B. (2012). Servant leadership perception and job satisfaction among SFDA employees in Saudi Arabia—A correlational study. Retrieved from http://www.slideshare.net/abaleegh/servant leadership-perception-and-job-satisfaction among sfda-employees-a- correlational-study-baleegh-al-yousef-2012

Austell, D. B. (2010). Servant leadership in International education. *Journal of Global Initiatives: Policy, Pedagogy, Perspective, 4*(1), 1–16.

Cangemi, J. (1992). Some observations of successful leaders, and their use of power and authority. *Education, 112,* 499–505.

Carroll, B. C., & Patterson, K. (2014). Servant leadership: A cross-cultural study between India and the United States. *Servant Leadership: Theory and practice, 1*(1), 16–45.

Chhokar, J. S., Brodbeck, F. C., & House, R. J. (eds.). (2008). *Culture and leadership across the world: The GLOBE book of in-depth studies of 25 societies.* Mahwah, NJ: Lawrence Erlbaum.

Christman, R. (2007). Research roundtable presentation: Servant leadership and power in positional-led organizations. Regent University School of Global Leadership & Entrepreneurship. Retrieved from https://www.regent.edu/acad/global/publications/s_proceedings/ 2007/christman.pdf

Clark, N. (2014, November 3). Higher education in Saudi Arabia. Retrieved from https://wenr.wes.org/2014/11/higher-education-in-saudi-arabia

Coleman, J. A. (2013). Authority, power, leadership: Sociological understandings. *New Theology Review, 10*(3), 31–44.

Covey, S. R. (2006). Servant leadership. *Leadership Excellence, 23*(12), 5–6.

Dambe, M., & Moorad, F. (2008). From power to empowerment: A paradigm shift in leadership. *South African Journal of Higher Education, 22,* 575–587. doi:10.4314/sajhe.v22i3.25803

Erkutlu, H., & Chafra, J. (2015a). The mediating roles of psychological safety and employee voice on the relationship between conflict management styles and organizational identification. *American Journal of Business, 30*(1), 72–91. doi:10.1108/AJB-06-2013-0040

Erkutlu, H., & Chafra, J. (2015b). Servant leadership and voice behavior in higher education. *H. U. Journal of Education, 30*(4), 29–41. Retrieved from http://yoksis.bilkent.edu.tr/pdf/files/l 1798.pdf

French, J. R. P., Jr., & Raven, B. H. (1959). The bases of social power. In D. Cartwright (ed.), *Studies in Social Power* (pp. 150–167). Ann Arbor, MI: Institute for Social Research.

Fuqua, H. E., Payne, K. E., & Cangemi, J. P. (2000). Leadership and the effective use of power. *National Forum of Educational Administration and Supervision Journal E, 17*, 1–6.

Gonaim, F. (2017). Delegation: A power tool for department chairs in Saudi universities. *International Journal of Social Sciences and Humanities Invention, 4*, 3515–3520. doi:10.18535/ijsshi/v4i5.08

Greenberg, J., & Baron, R. A. (2003). *Behavior in organizations* (8th edition). Upper Saddle River, NJ: Prentice Hall.

Greenleaf, R. K. (2002). *Servant-leadership: A journey into the nature of Legitimate Power and greatness*. Mahwah, NJ: Paulist. (Original work published 1977).

Grogan, M. (2013). *The Jossey-Bass reader on educational leadership*. San Francisco, CA: Jossey-Bass, Wiley.

Hannay, M. (2009). The cross-cultural leader: The application of servant leadership theory in the international context. *Journal of International Business and Cultural Studies, 1*, 1–12. Retrieved from http://www.aabri.com/manuscripts/08108.pdf

Hofstede, G. (1993). Cultural constraints in management theories. *Academy of Management Executive, 7*(1), 81–94. doi:10.2307/4165110

Hofstede, G. (2001). *Culture's consequences: Comparing values, behaviors, institutions, and organizations Across Nations* (2nd edition). Newbury Park, CA: Sage.

House, R. J., Hanges, P. J., Javidan, M., Dorfman, P. W., & Gupta, V. (eds.). (2004). *Culture, leadership, and organizations: The GLOBE study of 62 societies*. Thousand Oaks, CA: Sage.

Jordan, L. (2006). Leading and learning in higher education: Servant professors in the 21st century (Unpublished doctoral dissertation). University of Colorado, Denver.

Keith, K. M. (2010). *Servant leadership in Higher Education: Issues and concerns*. Palm Beach, FL: Atlantic University.

Krausz, R. (1986). Power and leadership in organizations. *Transactional Analysis Journal, 16*, 85–94. doi:10.1177/036215378601600202

Mathis, B. K. (2010). Educational leadership: A description of Saudi female principals in the eastern province of Saudi Arabia (Unpublished doctoral dissertation). Oklahoma State University, Stillwater. Retrieved from https://shareok.org/bitstream/handle/11244/7500/School%20of%20 eaching%20and%20CiuTiculum %20Leadership_12.pdf?sequence=1

Ministry of Higher Education. (2017). Higher education statistics. Retrieved from http://departments.moe.gov.sa/planninginformatio/relateddepartments/educati onstatisticscenter/eductiondetailedreports/Pages/default.aspx

Mooney, L. F. (1985). *Legitimation deficit in Higher Education Leadership: A World Always at risk* (Doctoral dissertation). University of San Francisco, San Francisco, CA.

Nelson, L. (2003). An exploratory' study of the application and acceptance of servant-leadership theory among Black leaders in South Africa (Unpublished doctoral dissertation). Regent University, Virginia Beach, VA.

Northouse, P. G. (2016). *Leadership: Theory and practice* (7th edition). Los Angeles, CA: Sage.

Petress, K. (2013). *Power: Definition, typology, description, examples, and implications*. Retrieved from http://uthscsa.edu/gme/documents/powerdefmitiostypology examples.pdf

Raven, B. H. (2008). The bases of power and the power/interaction model of interpersonal influence. *Analyses of Social Issues and Public Policy, 5*(1), 1–22. doi:10.1111/j. 1530-2415.2008.00159.x

Robbins, S. P. (1998). *Organizational behavior* (8th edition). Upper Saddle River, NJ: Prentice Hall.

Russell, R. F., & Stone, A. (2002). A review of servant leadership attributes: Developing a practical model. *Leadership and Organization Development Journal, 23*, 145–157. doi:10.1108/01437730210424

Salameh, K., Al-Wyzinany, M., & Al-Omari, A. (2012). Servant leadership practices among academic administrators in two universities in Jordan and Saudi Arabia as perceived by faculty members. *International Journal of Educational Administration, 4*(1), 1–18.

San Juan, K. S. (2005). Re-imagining power in leadership: Reflection, integration, and servant leadership. *International Journal of Servant-Leadership, 7*(1), 187–209.

Satyapuitra, A.G. (2013). [Review of the book Servant leadership for higher education, by D. Wheeler, Colorado Springs, CO: Jossey-Bass.] *Christian Education Journal, 10*(2), 483–486.

Scardino, A. J. (2013). Servant leadership in higher education: The influence of servant-led faculty on student engagement (Unpublished doctoral dissertation). Antioch University, Los Angeles, CA.

Sedgwick, R. (ed.). (2001). Education in Saudi Arabia. *World Education News and Reviews*. Retrieved from http://wenr.wes.org/2001/ll/wenr-nov-dec2001-educa tion-in-saudi-arabia

Sendjaya, S., & Sarros, J. C. (2002). Servant leadership: Its origin, development, and application in organizations. *Journal of Leadership and Organizational Studies, 9*, 57–64. doi:10.1177/107179190200900205

Serrano, M. (2005). Servant leadership: A viable model for the Latin American context? (Unpublished doctoral dissertation). Regent University, Virginia Beach, VA.

Serrat, O. (2014). *Informal authority and the enduring appeal of Servant Leaders*. Manila, Philippines: Asian Development Bank.

Shafai, A. (2014). Teachers and administrators perceptions of using collaborative learning as a professional development method in Saudi Arabia (Master thesis). Retrieved from https://scholarworks.csustan.edu/bitstream/handle011235813/834/ShafaiA.spring2015.p f?sequen=l

Shahin, A., & Wright, P. (2004). Leadership in the context of culture—An Egyptian perspective. *Leadership and Organization Development Journal, 25*, 499–511. doi:10.1108/01437730410556743

Shmailan, A., & Wirbaa, V.A. (2015). Leadership style of managers in universities in Saudi Arabia. Retrieved from http://www.meritresearchjournals.org/er/index.htm

Sipe, J. W., & Frick, D. M. (2015). *Seven pillars of Servant Leadership: Practicing the wisdom of leading by serving.* New York, NY: Paulist Press.

Smith, L., & Abouammoh, A. (eds.). (2013). *Higher education in Saudi Arabia: Achievements, challenges and opportunities.* London: Springer.

Spears, L. C. (ed). (1998). *Insights on leadership: Service, stewardship, spirit, and servant leadership.* New York, NY: John Wiley & Sons

Spears, L. C. (2010). Character and servant leadership: Ten characteristics of effective, caring leaders. *Journal of Virtues and Leadership, 1*(1), 25–30. Retrieved from https://www.regent.edU/acad/global/publications/vEvoll_issl/Spears_Final.pdf

Spears, L. C., & Lawrence, M. (eds.). (2004). *Practicing Servant-Leadership: Succeeding through trust, bravery, and forgiveness.* San Francisco, CA: Jossey-Bass.

Tureman, D. R. (2013). The effectiveness of servant leadership in bringing about change (Senior Honors Thesis). Retrieved from https://digitalcommons.liberty.edu/cgi/viewcontent.cgi?article=l381&context=honors

Tyler, T. R. (2006). Psychological perspectives on legitimacy and legitimation. *Annual Review of Psychology, 57*, 375–400. doi:10.1146/annurev.psych.57.102904.190038

United Nations Educational, Scientific and Cultural Organization. (2011). World data on education. Retrieved from http://www.ibe.unesco.org/sites/default/files/Saudi_Arabia.pdf

Valeri, D. P. (2007). The origins of servant leadership (Unpublished doctoral dissertation). Greenleaf University, St. Louis, MO. Retrieved from http://www.greenleaf.edu/pdf/donald_valeri.pdf

Van Der Toorn, J., Feinberg, M., Jost, J. T., Kay, A. C.,Tyler, T. R., Willer, R,, & Wilmuth, C. (2014). A sense of powerlessness fosters system justification: Implications for the legitimation of authority, hierarchy, and government. *International Society of Political Psychology, 36*(1), 93–106. doi:10.1111/pops.12183

Wheeler, D. W. (2011). *Servant leadership for Higher Education: Principles and practices.* Somerset, NJ: John Wiley & Sons.

Wilson, R. (2011). Globalization, governance and leadership development in the Middle East. In B. Metcalf & F. Mimouni. (eds.), *Leadership development in the Middle East* (pp. 61–86). Northampton, MA: Edward Elgar.

Whitfield, D. (2014). Servant-Leadership with cultural dimensions in cross-cultural settings. In R. Selladurai & S. Carraher (eds.), *Servant leadership: Research and practice* (pp. 48–70). Hershey, PA: IGI Global.

Winston, B. E., & Ryan, B. (2008). Servant leadership as a humane orientation: Using the GLOBE study construct of humane orientation to show that servant leadership is more global than Western. *International Journal of Leadership Studies, 3*, 212–222.

Chapter 18

The Servant-Leader as Persuader

*Sardar Vallabhbhai Patel and
the Integration of India*

Philip Mathew

A global study around the question, "What does it take to be an effective international manager?" identified three competencies essential for managerial success: (1) leadership skills, (2) skills of influence and persuasion, and (3) the ability to engage others with a non-authoritarian style (Frazee, 1998). A number of studies, across a variety of industries, support the notion that relational and influence skills are essential to leading effectively in a global and multicultural workplace (Cseh, Davis, & Khilji, 2013; Lobel, 1990; Rao, 2013; Thomas & Inkson, 2017).

Leadership is about influencing a group of individuals toward purposeful outcomes (Daft, 2015; Northouse, 2010; Rost, 1997; Yukl, 2010). A primary means of influence is persuasion, which is also a defining characteristic of servant-leadership (Greenleaf, 1977; Keith, 2016; Spears, 2011). Rather than employ autocratic and hierarchical methods to achieve outcomes, the servant-leader utilizes persuasion to build consensus, exercise legitimate power, and influence followers to work together in pursuit of the greater good. Kanter (1979) noted that power evolves from two capacities: (1) access to the resources, information, and support necessary to carry out a task and (2) the ability to engender cooperation in doing what is necessary.

In this chapter, I explore the use of persuasion in the leadership of Indian freedom fighter Sardar Vallabhbhai Patel. Patel's leadership offers a fascinating study in the exercise of persuasion and power amidst the complex historical, social, and political landscape of post-independence India. When India gained independence on August 15, 1947, the country was anything but a unified entity. The Indian union consisted of a variety of colonial territories and nearly 600 "princely states" each ruled by independent sovereigns and loosely held together by the British political and administrative system. When the British left India in 1947, the status of these states remained unresolved and undefined. Politically, they belonged to neither India nor Pakistan—but neither were they designated as independent.

The daunting task of integrating these 600 states into a union was given to Sardar Patel. It would prove to be a challenge that he would meet in a strategic and bloodless fashion, largely through the principle and practice of persuasion. I will explore how Patel used persuasion to build bridges, cross boundaries, and span India's deep cultural, religious, ideological, and political divides to avoid a civil war and forge a nation.

SARDAR PATEL'S PATH TO LEADERSHIP

Sardar Patel was one-third of the triumvirate that helped India achieve independence and national integration. The contributions of Mahatma Gandhi, the "father of the nation", and Pandit Jawaharlal Nehru, India's first prime minister, in the Indian freedom struggle are well known and have been recounted frequently. The leadership of Sardar Patel, however, remains less explored, though he played a pivotal role as the unifier of post-independence India. Nehru described Patel as the "Builder and Consolidator of New India" (Krishna, 2007). Gandhi, acknowledging Patel's service to the nation, honored him with the title *Sardar*, meaning "leader" or "chief." The influential *Manchester Guardian* highlighted Patel's leadership as well, asserting that, "Gandhi's ideas would have less practical influence and Nehru's idealism less scope. Patel was not only the organiser of the fight for freedom, but also the architect of the new state when the fight was over" (as cited in Krishna, 2007, p. 2).

Patel's early life was characterized by a love for learning and a willingness to challenge the status quo. Biographers describe him as a bold and outspoken student who was willing to stand up for his classmates; in the sixth grade, he staged a walkout when he observed a teacher treating students harshly (Krishna, 2007; Saggi, n.d.). Patel aspired to become a lawyer, a respectable, but expensive and difficult proposition for the son of an impoverished Gujarati farmer. Through disciplined self-study, however, he passed a district law exam, and with an entrepreneurial spirit, managed to set up his own law practice. In 1910, he traveled to England, passed the bar, and returned to India to become one of his city's most successful attorneys.

A turning point in Patel's life occurred when he attended a freedom rally organized by national activist, and fellow Gujarati attorney, Mohandas K.

Gandhi in 1917. Inspired by Gandhi's vision of a free India, Patel joined the Indian National Congress and played a key role in the fledgling Indian independence movement. He participated in a number of Gandhi's non-violent resistance campaigns (*satyagrahas*), including the famous Dandi Salt March, and was arrested and imprisoned at various times throughout the freedom struggle.

Due to his political rhetorical, administrative, and organizational skills, Patel helped the Congress Party negotiate arrangements with a variety of stakeholders, including the British and the Muslim League. In 1931, Patel was elected President of the Indian National Congress and served as the country's first Home Minister. Another significant milestone occurred when he founded India's massive and respected civil service organization, the Indian Administrative Services.

Patel's greatest leadership achievement, however, was his use of persuasion to unify a diverse and divided group of post-independence princely states to form and unify the nation of India. We turn now to an exploration of persuasion-based leadership frameworks that will be used to analyze Patel's use of this servant-leadership skill.

APPROACHES TO PERSUASION

O'Keefe (2002) defined persuasion as a "successful intentional effort at influencing another's mental state through communication in a circumstance in which the persuadee has some measure of freedom" (p. 17). According to Spears (as cited in Keith, 2016), "Servant-leaders rely on persuasion, rather than using one's positional authority, in making decisions within an organization. The servant-leader seeks to convince others, rather than coerce compliance" (2016, p. 83). Ferch (2012) asserted that persuasion is the means by which leaders exercise legitimate power and that leaders who use persuasion are far more effective than those who resort coercion and fear to achieve their goals,

> At our worst, when trying to get our way, we often resort to the use of manipulation, pressure, and violence. But in a life attuned to beauty and healing, persuasion achieves mutual respect and healthy results without coercion. The life led by persuasion and example is true. In like fashion, the true life is intrinsically persuasive and legitimately powerful. (Ferch, 2012, p. 147)

Greenleaf (1977) illustrated the power of persuasion through the life of John Woolman, an abolitionist in the Quaker faith tradition. Greenleaf described Woolman as a quiet persuader who shared his message of freedom one person at a time. By employing listening, introspection, and questioning, Woolman effected change in the minds and hearts of the enslavers. Specifically, he challenged them to consider how the act of slavery impacted them as individuals and what kind of legacy they would leave to their children. Greenleaf (1977) believed that trying to convince through coercion violates the integrity of the person one is seeking to persuade. He believed that persuasion should happen naturally as the person arrives at a "feeling of rightness about a belief or action through one's own intuitive sense." (p. 139). The litmus test is that the change be "truly voluntary" (p. 140). According to Morgan (2010), "Persuasion means changing someone's mind. If the mind isn't changed, the person hasn't been persuaded . . . Persuasion lies squarely at the center of leadership" (para. 2).

Greenleaf (1977) believed that integral to persuasion is the process of consensus building, which he described as a meeting of the minds without any pressure or constraint. He described four strategic principles that leaders can use to build consensus and mobilize a group of disparate individuals. First, the leader must possess a deep understanding of the issues at hand. This requires patience and personal engagement, especially with individuals who display resistance. Second, the leader should demonstrate and model active listening. The aim of active listening is to achieve understanding by recognizing a variety of viewpoints; the servant-leader then paraphrases so that everyone understands the issues at hand. Third, the leader is encouraged to take the pulse of the group and discern the appropriate time to reach consensus by exploring whether the proposal is a workable solution (Greenleaf, 1977). Finally, if consensus is reached, the leader should remain sensitive to minority opinions and engage in private dialogue with out-group members in a psychologically safe, sensitive, and loving way. Through an iterative process of listening and consensus building, the servant-leader persuades a group to work together in service of a broader vision, mission, or purpose.

Leadership That Persuades

In his mission to unite a diverse and disorganized group of "princely states" to form the nation of India, Patel faced what Heifetz (2009) described as an *adaptive leadership challenge*. According to Heifetz, adaptive leadership is required when organizations or communities face problems that cannot be solved through prevailing knowledge and standard operating procedures. Indeed, the very nature of the challenge is a signal that solutions lie outside existing paradigms and beyond any technical fixes available through routine management approaches. Much like the consensus-building process described by Greenleaf (1977), adaptive leadership requires "orchestrating conflict and discovery across group boundaries, regulating the disequilibrium those differences generate, and holding the parties through a sustained period of stress" (Heifetz, 2009, p. 131).

Heifetz (2009) proposed a two-phase model of adaptive leadership that has much in common with Greenleaf's persuasion and consensus-building process. In the first phase of Heifetz's model, the leader forms a *working group* comprised of subgroup members who are willing to stretch beyond intra-group loyalties and reach across boundaries to seek a solution. In this step, the leader's task is to stimulate a conversation around which persons and issues to include as the leader strives to ensure the presence of diverse perspectives.

In the second phase, the more difficult of the two, members of the *working group* return to their respective subgroups to advocate for and share a collective vision of the adaptive work. Heifetz (2009) observed that the majority of adaptive intergroup processes fail during this challenging phase because "each 'representative' member must lead her own constituents in incorporating and refining the results of the group process, or else the deal unravels" (p. 135). Representatives often face the charge of having "sold out" to the other groups and feel pressure to return to the status quo. In the midst of this process, the leader continues to forge strong relationships with each representative to hold the group together. It is important to note that in the adaptive leadership model, while the leader orchestrates the adaptive work, she places the challenge back in the hands of the parties involved (Heifetz, 2002).

A second model, developed by Kanter (2009), also finds similarities with Greenleaf's (1977) persuasion strategy, particularly with regard to the ethic of respect for the individual. Kanter's framework, summarized below, involves the following six propositions by which leaders make productive use of differences to build consensus:

(1) *Convening Power.* In this step, the leader brings different subgroups together to initiate structured conversations around the issue to find common ground and build energy through a clash of ideas.
(2) *Transcendent Values*: Here, the leader identifies core values that serve as a framework from which to work together. The leader identifies a shared goal or a collective definition of success to serve as a motivating force.
(3) *Future Orientation*: The leader builds a new, forward-looking identity while honoring personal histories. The leader's task is to create a foundation for the building of a transcendent identity through a future-forward focus.
(4) *Important Interdependent Tasks*: In this step, the leader identifies challenging tasks that present an opportunity for shared participation, thus strengthening ownership and intergroup relations.
(5) *Interpersonal Norms and Emotional Integration*: The leader engages in conversations around group norms and codes of conduct. Ground rules

are established, such as mutual respect, avoidance of blame-oriented language, and taking a proactive stance toward problems, all of which serve
to fortify emotional bonds.
(6) *Inclusiveness and Evenhandedness*: Here, the leader emphasizes and
demonstrates inclusiveness—often through a significant investment in
material resources that benefit everyone. This final step involves a degree
of risk as leaders may face criticism from their own subgroup for bound-
ary-spanning gestures. Through these overt acts of generosity, however,
the leader sends a message that everyone is valued.

With these models of persuasion in mind, I explore Patel's use of persuasion
to cross divides and span boundaries to integrate a nation.

THE PROBLEM OF THE PRINCELY STATES

The difficulty of Patel's challenge in uniting the 600 princely states cannot
be overstated. They varied widely in terms of region, religion, ethnicity,
language, and ideology; each possessed a unique cultural, social, and psychological identity. The sheer diversity of the Indian subcontinent, combined
with the undefined status of each kingdom, quickly complicated the political
and social situation, particularly in the bloody aftermath of Partition. For
example, some kingdoms, such as Kathiawar, contained 222 individual states.
One kingdom contained 206 people, while another was less than two square
miles in length; the kingdom of Hyderabad was 80,000 square miles with a
population of 17 million people (Krishna, 2007). Furthermore, each princely
state contained its own people-group with a distinct language and culture.

The political situation in India added another layer of difficulty to Patel's
challenge. As part of their exit strategy, the British proposed a plan whereby
the princely states would become independent units free to negotiate their
status, leaving them with the option of remaining independent, joining India,
or becoming a part of the newly created nation of Pakistan.

The Congress Party believed the British proposal threatened the stability
of the entire region and rejected the plan. In their view, the plan would leave
issues such as interstate water rights, tariffs, trade, railways, and telegraphs
unaddressed—each entity would potentially be required to seek permission
from another to transport goods and even water (Krishna, 2007; Menon,
1955). If war were to ensue, the allegiance of these independent kingdoms
would be in question, and there existed a real potential for "these 600 states
[to be] 600 sores in the body of India" (Shivaramu, n.d., para. 2).

Another challenge for Patel was the lack of unity among the princes themselves. Some of the smaller states felt a keen distrust toward the larger states;

others were split between constituencies that favored joining India, while their ruler preferred Pakistan. Furthermore, some of the princes harbored personal political ambitions (Krishna, 2007).

As the new government struggled to formulate a response to this situation, they turned to Patel for leadership. His fair, flexible, and efficient work, on the Partition Council for example, won him the respect of fellow party workers, the British government, and the Muslim League. In light of this confidence, Lord Mountbatten, the last Viceroy of India, appointed Patel as the first Home Minister of the country, a move that met with the full endorsement of key leaders including Gandhi and Nehru (Krishna, 2007; Menon, 1955). The British made a significant concession to Patel upon their exit when they agreed to leave the question of the Indian states in his hands as Home Minister, vowing not to interfere with the process (2007).

This critical agreement provided Patel an opportunity to negotiate and work to unify the country. We turn now to an exploration of how Patel navigated this complex situation through persuasion.

SARDAR PATEL AS PERSUADER

The first step Patel took in this arduous task was to meet with the princes as a group, something that he did soon after his inauguration as Home Minister. This decision paralleled Kanter's (2009) first proposition of *Convening Power*, as well as the initial steps described by Greenleaf (1977) and Heifetz (2002, 2009), all of which involve bringing subgroups together for dialogue. As a prelude to their meeting, Patel made an appeal to the princes, communicating his vision for the nation, thus acknowledging and allaying fears regarding their place in the nation (Krishna, 2007; Menon, 1955),

> Our mutual conflicts and internecine quarrels and jealousies have, in the past, been the cause of our downfall . . . We cannot afford to fall into those errors or traps again . . . The safety and preservation of the States, as well as India, demand unity and mutual cooperation between its different parts. (2007, p. 91)

Patel followed up his address with a personal meeting with the princes in December 1947. Though he initially encountered resistance from several of the leaders, he remained diplomatic and direct. Patel made it clear that the path forward must include compromise by all parties, thus acknowledging the loss that Heifetz (2002) described as part of adaptive work. He also assured the group of his personal investment in the process, "I have come . . .not as a representative of the old Paramountcy or of any foreign power, but as a member of a family trying to solve a family problem" (Krishna, 2007, p. 95).

The first meeting with the working group turned out to be one of many conversations regarding their future and the future of India. Patel organized a number of informal social gatherings and luncheons at his home in Delhi over a period of months. In these meetings, loyalties were refashioned, boundaries spanned, and divides crossed in search of solutions. Though at times he encountered delay tactics, fierce resistance, and political brinksmanship, Patel persisted in meeting with the rulers at various times and places throughout the country. His open dialogue, consistent calls for unity, and persistence in utilizing persuasion was eventually rewarded, as many of the rulers agreed to join India.

Kanter's (2009) second proposition, *An Appeal to Transcendent Values,* was another critical element in Patel's leadership strategy. In a 1947 address, he spoke to the working group, recalling the noble history of the princes and the patriotism of their ancestors. Early in the process he told the group,

> This country with its institutions is the proud heritage of the people who inhabit it. It is an accident that some live in the States and some in British India, but all alike partake of its culture and character. We are all knit together by bonds of blood and feeling no less than of self-interest. (Menon, 1955, p. 69)

Patel appealed to other core values including the duty of princely rulers to care for their people, patriotism, the responsibility of self-rule, and the legacy the princes would leave to future generations (Krishna, 2007, p. 97). On the whole, this values-based appeal would influence and persuade the majority of the group to join India. Patel's appeal to values illustrates Bennis' (1997) idea of *value power*, in which leaders serve as change agents who represent and transmit admirable values (as cited in Russell & Stone, 2002, p. 151).

Kanter's (2009) third proposition, *A Future Orientation,* was another significant element in Patel's approach. Barbuto & Wheeler (2006) labeled this as persuasive mapping, defining it as the ability to use mental models and sound reasoning to visualize the future. Patel reminded the rulers of the groundbreaking nature of their collective work, encouraging them to take heed to the winds of democracy blowing across the subcontinent. He helped them envision greater possibilities and dream great dreams (Greenleaf, 1977). This future-oriented approach was not without its risks, however, as the idea of democracy threatened the foundations of monarchy. Recognizing this, Patel reminded the working group of a newfound strength their people would find by participating in the Indian freedom struggle. Patel bluntly stated in one of his meetings,

I have met some Rulers today, and I have told them that they cannot carry on in the manner they did in the past. They must transfer their power to the people . . . They must move with the times. Let them cease to be like frogs in the well. These are the days of democracy, and the rulers too must trust in their people. (Krishna, 2007, p. 95)

Kanter's (2009) fourth element, *Important Interdependent Tasks*, was also present in Patel's leadership strategy. Similarly, a central task of adaptive leadership is to turn the work over to the people (Heifetz, 2002). Patel provided the working group opportunities to unite around a greater, overarching cause—leadership in service of the nation. This turned out to be a particularly strategic decision, as many of the princes felt uncertain about their future role. Patel addressed these doubts by providing the rulers an opportunity to work with him toward a larger purpose.

After a brief standoff with the Maharaja of Jodhpur, for example, Patel won the vote of the ruler; he offered him a position as an ambassador who would share the idea of integration throughout the country. The Maharaja conveyed Patel's message with enthusiasm and purpose (Krishna, 2007). Patel's strategy was also evident after the resistance and accession of the Nizam of Hyderabad to whom he wrote, "It is the duty of human beings to contribute their share to this process by sincere repentance and by employing the period that is left in discharging their duties to their people and to their God" (2007, p. 146).

Kanter's (2009) fifth proposition, *Interpersonal and Emotional Integration*, was demonstrated in Patel's acknowledgment of the emotional factors involved in change initiatives. Patel understood that logic alone fails to bring enduring change. According to Heifetz (2009), adaptive work entails acknowledging losses that take a variety of forms including "direct losses of goods such as wealth, status, authority, influence, security, and health to indirect losses such as competence and loyal affiliation . . . People do not resist change per se; they resist loss" (p. 131). Patel acknowledged the loss the princes feared in acceding to India. Choosing not to take a heavy hand in this matter, Patel allowed the rulers to reside in their palaces and enjoy many aspects of their lifestyle. He gave a directive to his aides, "Do not question the extent of the personal wealth claimed by them, and never ever confront the ladies of the household. I want their states, not their wealth" (Krishna, 2007, p. 149).

Patel's commitment to Kanter's (2009) fifth proposition was also evident in how he persuaded rulers who were particularly resistant. For example, when faced with fierce opposition from the Maharaja of Travancore, who was feeling increasingly isolated, he wrote a personal note, "It is in my nature to be a friend of the friendless. You have become one by choice, I shall be glad if you will come and have lunch with me tomorrow at 1:00 p.m." (2007, p. 99). Patel helped facilitate the emotional integration of the rulers by acknowledging their perception of loss; he discerned the emotional undercurrents involved in such a radical call to change and forged interpersonal relationships to strengthen their commitment.

Kanter's (2009) sixth proposition, *Inclusiveness and Evenhandedness*, was also evident in Patel's dealings with princes who summarily rejected any possibility of joining India. While Patel was able to win a majority of the states over in a relatively short amount of time, there were at least three states that maintained an active resistance.

The southern Kingdom of Travancore was the first to resist. As noted in the discussion of the fifth proposition, Patel appealed to the ruler by sending him a personal letter inviting him to a meeting to discuss the issue. The Maharaja initially rebuffed the offer and declared that he was preparing to open up diplomatic relations with other countries. In spite of this threat, Patel refused to give up; he convinced the prince to join the Union after several blunt discussions. Patel acknowledged the king's leadership and encouraged him to use his talents for the greater good.

In Junagadh, a state with a 96 percent Hindu majority and a Muslim ruler, Patel discovered that their leader had been engaging in secret negotiations to join Pakistan. After several failed attempts at diplomacy, Patel sent the Indian army to the state's border, spurring the *Nawab* to flee to Karachi. Ultimately, India and Pakistan agreed to hold a referendum on the issue. The majority of the people overwhelmingly voted to join India. In this situation, Patel was lauded for his firm yet evenhanded approach; he avoided communal strife and achieved "a unique victory over Junagadh without causing loss of life and property . . . preserving [it's] integrity and unity" (Krishna, 2007, p. 128).

Another example of Patel's leadership is his reconciliation with the ruler of Hyderabad, despite the leader's maneuverings against the central government. In this case, the *Nizam* covertly backed rebels and sent millions of rupees to Pakistan, while harassing the local Hindu population. After months of negotiation, Patel sent the Indian Army into the state to reestablish law and order. Within five days, the *Nizam* surrendered, order was restored, and Hyderabad became a part of India "with scarcely a shot being fired" (Tharoor, 2007, p. 179). Patel made a visit to Hyderabad in February 1949 to personally reconcile with the Nizam and offer an opportunity to help with national integration, "Your great personality is a valuable asset for India at this critical period when the whole world is in turmoil" (Krishna, 2007, p. 146).

Through the patient and strategic exercise of persuasive servant-leadership, Patel proved to be a leader who crossed political, cultural, ideological, and religious divides. Through the use of legitimate power and a consensus-seeking orientation, he brought diverse and divided parties to the table, appealed to shared values, oriented them toward the future, turned the work over to those affected by the change, acknowledged the importance of inter-personal and emotional integration, and maintained an inclusive and even-handed approach. Patel's leadership through persuasion, use of soft power, active listening, and two-way dialogue provides a compelling example of a servant-leadership approach essential for success in the twenty-first century (Greenleaf, 1977; Heifetz, 2009; Nye, 2004).

Nehru (1964) once described India as "a bundle of contradictions, held together by strong but invisible threads" (p. 563). Through persuasion, Patel unified these threads and integrated the nation of India within 18 months. World leaders have recognized Patel's leadership in this matter. Lord Mountbatten described Patel's contribution as "the most important achievement of the present Government" and told Patel, "had you failed, the results would have been disastrous" (2007, p. 149). Soviet statesman Nikita Kruschev remarked, "You Indians are an amazing people! How on earth did you manage to liquidate the princely rule without liquidating the princes?" (2007, p. 149).

It is important to note that amidst his success, Patel occasionally faced criticism from his own party. At times he clashed with Gandhi and Nehru as the three struggled to carve a path forward. Through the use of persuasion, however, Patel avoided what could have been another violent and bloody chapter in world history as he sought to reconcile, create, and unify a nation.

CONCLUSION

Servant-leaders approach problems in ways that differ from traditional "leader-first" models (Russell & Stone, 2002). These include modeling a singular devotion to persuasion, building relationships based on personhood and autonomy, and acknowledging influence as reciprocal (Greenleaf, 1996). Greenleaf described persuasion was a "prime moving force" (p. 147). In a world and workplace oriented toward positional authority, servant-leaders can effectively facilitate change through persuasion, rather than through control, coercion, and manipulation (Spears, 1998, 2002; Ferch, Spears, McFarland, & Carey, 2015).

As described in this chapter, Patel's practice of persuasion, consensus building, and inspirational appeal aligned with Greenleaf's conviction that persuasion is a critical element of servant-leadership. Indeed, as seen in Patel's leadership, one can be dedicated to the "exclusive use of persuasion as a means of social change" thus enabling others to become wiser, freer, healthier, more autonomous, and the least privileged among us benefited, or at least not further deprived (p. 143).

REFERENCES

Barbuto, J. E., Jr., & Wheeler, D. W. (2006). Scale development and construct clarification of servant leadership. *Group and Organization Management, 31*(3), 300–326.

Cseh, M., Davis, E. B., & Khilji S. E. (2013). Developing a global mindset: learning of global leaders. *European Journal of Training and Development 37*(5), 489–499. doi:10.1108/03090591311327303

Daft, R. L. (2015). *The Leadership Experience* (5th edition). Mason, OH: Cengage.

Ferch, S. R., Spears, L. C., McFarland, M., & Carey, M. R. (eds.) (2015). *Conversations on Servant-Leadership: Insights on Human Courage in life and work.* Albany, NY: State University of New York Press.

Ferch, S. R., & Spears, L. C. (eds.) (2011). *The spirit of Servant-Leadership.* New York: Paulist Press.

Ferch, S. R. (2012). *Forgiveness and power in the age of atrocity: servant leadership as a way of life.* Lanham, MD: Lexington Books.

Forster, B. (2009). Intergroup leadership. *Leadership Review, 9* (Fall), 93–94.

Frazee, V. (1998). What does it take to be a successful international manager? *Workforce 77*(9). Retrieved from https://ezproxy.olympic.edu/login?url=http://search.ebscohost.com/login.aspx?di ect=true&db=f5h&AN=103848&site=ehost-live

Greenleaf, R. K. (1977). *Servant leadership: A journey into the nature of legitimate power and greatness.* New York: Paulist Press.

Heifetz, R. (2002). *Leadership on the line.* Boston, MA: Harvard Business School Press.

———. (2009). Operating across boundaries: Leading adaptive change. In T. L. Pittinsky, *Crossing the divide: Intergroup leadership in a world of difference* (pp. 127–139). Boston, MA: Harvard Business Press.

Kanter, R. (ed.) (1979). Power failure in management circuits. *Harvard Business Review, 57,* 65–75.

Kanter, R. M. (2009). Creating common ground: Propositions about effective intergroup leadership. In T. L. Pittinsky, *Crossing the divide: Intergroup leadership in a world of difference* (pp. 73–85). Boston, MA: Harvard Business Press.

Keith, Kent (ed.). (2016). The contemporary servant as leader [Kindle version]. Retrieved from Amazon.com

Krishna, B. (2007). *India's bismarck: Sardar Vallabhbhai Patel.* Mumbai: Indus Source Books.

Lobel, S. A. (1990). Global leadership competencies: Managing to a different drumbeat. *Human Resource Management, 29.* 39–47.

Menon, V. (1955). *The story of the integration of the Indian states.* London: Longmans, Green, and Co.

Nehru, J. (1946). *The discovery of India.* New York: John Day.

Morgan, Nick (2010). Leadership is all about persuasion. *Forbes.com.* https://www.forbes.com/2010/02/02/communicatiemotionalpersuasionleadershipmanagingspeaking.htm#1d42048d122d

Nye, J. S. (2004). *Soft power: The means to success in World Politics.* New York: Public Affairs.

Northouse, P. G. (2010). *Leadership: Theory and practice* (5th edition). Thousand Oaks, CA: Sage Publications.

O'Keefe, D. J. (2002). *Persuasion: Theory & research.* Thousand Oaks, CA: Sage Publications.

Rao, M. S. (2013). Soft leadership: a new direction to leadership. *Industrial and Commercial Training,* 45(3), 143–149. doi:10.1108/00197851311320559

Russell, R. F., & Stone, A. G. (2002). A review of servant leadership attributes: Developing a practical model. *Leadership and Organization Development Journal, 23*(3), 145–157.

Saggi, P. D. (1953). *A nation's homage: Life and work of Sardar Vallabhbhai Patel.* Bombay: Bombay Overseas Publishing House.

Shivaramu. (n.d.). The architect of integrity. Retrieved September 2012, from Free India: http://www.freeindia.org/biographies/freedomfighters/sardarpatel/pagel5.htm

Spears, L. C. (ed.). (1998). *Insights on leadership: Service, stewardship, spirit and servant leadership.* New York: John Wiley & Sons.

———. (ed.). (2002). *Focus on leadership: Servant-leadership for the 21ˢᵗ century.* New York: John Wiley & Sons.

Tharoor, S. (2007). *The elephant, the tiger, and the Cell Phone: Reflections on India the emerging 21ˢᵗ Century Power.* New York: Arcade.

Thomas, D. C., & Inkson, K. C. (2017). *Cultural intelligence: Surviving and thriving in the Global Village* (3rd edition). Oakland, CA: Berrett-Koehler Publishers.

Yukl, G. (2010). *Leadership in organizations* (7th edition). Upper Saddle River, NJ: Prentice Hall.

Index

accountability, 13, 103–4, 228

Africa: Democratic Republic of Congo (Kabare), 165; East Africa, 85, 101, 157; Hadzabe, 83; Kenya, 85, 111, 151; servant-leadership, 113–16, 119–29, 132, 151; South Africa, 85, 114–16, 167, 169; Tanzania, 83, 92; Xhosa, 85, 167, 169. *See also harambee*; Kenyatta, Jomo; Maathai, Wangari Muta; Mandela, Nelson; Nyerere, Julius Mwalimu; Tutu, Desmond; *ubuntu; Ujamaa*

art, 51, 59–60, 87

awareness, xvii, xviii, 12–15, 19, 21, 23, 40, 43–44, 58, 60, 77, 79, 93, 99, 101, 141, 144, 167, 190, 203, 216; change, 14; questions for self-reflection, 60, 89

Brazil, 67; Cardoso, Fernando H., 74; Freire, Paolo, 69; historical-cultural perspective on servant-leadership, 68; religious culture, 68; Santos, Edival, 76; servant-leadership in corporations, 75–79

Burns, James MacGregor, 5

Canada, 19, 25; Canadian Indian Residential School System, 32; Manitoba, 19, 25, 27; Quebec, 32

change, 2, 14, 22, 24, 28, 37, 77, 79, 91, 168, 255, 280, 285

Chávez, César, 57

China: cultural revolution, 144–45; Lao Tzu, xxi, xxii–xxiii; public servants, xxi; servant-leadership, xxi; Sun Yat-sen, xxi, 143. *See also* Li, Florence

Christianity, 56, 94–95, 139, 168, 171–72, 187

coercion, 6; contrasted with persuasion, xviii, 23, 145, 170, 248, 279–80

commitment to the growth of people, xix, xxii, 24, 97, 141, 146, 192, 205, 213, 217

communication, 22, 39, 42, 79, 103, 228, 284

community building, xix, 24, 31, 37, 41, 43–44, 57, 60, 85, 89, 92, 114–15, 118, 130, 147, 153, 161, 168, 192, 205, 219, 263; art, 60–61; belonging, 31; communication, 39–40, 46; Ktunaxa, 41

conceptualization, xviii, 23, 141, 145, 191, 204, 211, 225, 227, 257

About the Contributors

Philip Mathew, PhD is Professor of Organizational Leadership and Resource Management at Olympic College. He is the founding and lead faculty for Olympic College's Bachelor of Applied Science in Organizational Leadership and Technical Management. He earned his doctorate in leadership studies from Gonzaga University. His dissertation, which is in the United States Holocaust Memorial Museum, investigated psychological resilience and leadership in the life of Holocaust survivor Dr. Viktor Frankl. He holds masters degrees in counseling and divinity, and a certificate in leadership and negotiation from Harvard Law School's Program on Negotiation. Prior to his position at Olympic College, Dr. Mathew was a lecturer in Whitworth University's bachelor's program in psychology, master's program in counseling, and worked as a licensed mental health therapist. Dr. Mathew also served with Jesuit Commons: Higher Education at the Margins as an online volunteer faculty in psychology for students living in refugee camps, including Malawi, Kenya, and Jordan. He is a member of the editorial review board for the *International Journal of Servant-Leadership*, the *Journal of Leadership Studies*, and regularly speaks at conferences and workshops.

Jiying Song, PhD, PMP, is an assistant professor of business and economics at Northwestern College and the associate editor of *The International Journal of Servant-Leadership*. After receiving her master of engineering in China and working in the field of IT for fourteen years, she came to the United States and earned her master of divinity from George Fox University and PhD in leadership studies from Gonzaga University.

Poet and prose writer **Shann Ray Ferch, PhD** is a forgiveness researcher and the author of a work on leadership and political theory, *Forgiveness* *and Power in the Age of Atrocity: Servant Leadership as a Way of Life*, and co-editor of *Conversations on Servant Leadership*, and *The Spirit of Servant Leadership*. In his role as professor of leadership studies with the internationally renowned PhD program in Leadership Studies at Gonzaga University, Dr. Ferch has served as a visiting scholar in Africa, Asia, Europe, South America, and North America. His novel, *American Copper*, is a love song to America revealing the radiant and profound life of Evelynne Lowry, a woman who transcends the national myth of regeneration through violence. The novel won the Foreword Book of the Year Readers' Choice Award and the Western Writers of America Spur Award, and was a finalist for the Washington State Book Award, the High Plains Book Award, and the Foreword Book of the Year Award for Literary Fiction. A former professional basketball player, his collection of stories *American Masculine* was named a "3 Books Every Man Should Read" selection by *Esquire*, and won the American Book Award, the Bakeless Prize, and two High Plains Book Awards, for Best Story Collection and Best First Book. A finalist with Ted Kooser's Splitting an Order and Erin Belieu's Slant Six, his book of poems, *Balefire*, won the High Plains Book Award for Poetry. Having served as a National Endowment for the Arts creative writing fellow and a research psychologist for the Centers for Disease Control and Prevention, his books also include *Sweetclover, Blood Fire Vapor Smoke, Servant-Leadership and Forgiveness* (edited with Jiying Song), and *Atomic Theory 7: Poems to my Wife and God*. He is the editor of *The International Journal of Servant-Leadership*. Because of his wife and three daughters, he believes in love.

Larry C. Spears is president and CEO of the Spears Center for Servant-Leadership, Inc. (Indianapolis). Larry is also servant-leadership scholar at Gonzaga University (Spokane), where he teaches graduate courses in servant-leadership. He serves as senior advisory editor of *The International Journal of Servant-Leadership*, founded in 2005. From 1990 to 2007, Larry served as president and CEO with the Greenleaf Center. Spears is the co-editor of five books of Robert Greenleaf's writings: *On Becoming a Servant-Leader, Seeker and Servant, The Power of Servant-Leadership, Servant-Leadership: The 25th Anniversary Edition*, and *The Servant-Leader Within*, and the editor or co-editor of a series of seven servant-leadership anthologies.

Yusuf Alan is a freelance editor and translator and gives weekly lectures on universal values, general principles, and personal development. He coaches people to make them excel in their growth ambitions. His books include *Lisan ve İnsan* [Language and human] (1994), *Aktif Düşünme ve Yenilenme* [Active thinking and self-renewal] (2001), and *Sözün Gücü* [The power of discourse] (2003).

Josmar Arrais, PhD is the CEO of Aspectum Brazil and of VitalSmarts Brazil. He is an adjunct professor at Andrews University in Michigan, USA. He previously worked as the academic vice-president of University of Santo Amaro in São Paulo, Brazil, and as a business consultant in leadership and organizational development. Dr. Arrais earned his doctorate in leadership from Andrews University.

Gürkan Çelik, PhD completed his doctorate at Tilburg University, the Netherlands, with a thesis entitled "The Gülen movement: Building social cohesion through dialogue and education" (2008). His recent co-edited volumes are Gülen-Inspired Hizmet in Europe: The Western Journey of a Turkish Muslim Movement (2015) and Turkey in Transition: The Dynamics of Domestic and Foreign Politics (2020). Dr. Çelik was knighted in the Order of Orange-Nassau in 2016 for his service to Dutch society.

Kong Wah Chan, EdD (a.k.a. Cora HUI) obtained her Doctor of Education with University of Bristol, UK. Her dissertation focused on learners' perceptions of servant leadership as practiced by teachers in classrooms of a Hong Kong school. Her published research papers include "Servant Leadership Cultivates Grit and Growth Mindset in Learners" (2016), "Learners' Perceptions of Servant-Leadership in Classrooms" (2017), "Cultivating Servant Leaders in Secondary Schooling" (2017), and "Servant Leadership Supports Wellness Development in Adolescents" (2019). Currently, Cora is the head of school at an international school in Hong Kong. The school mission is to develop servant leaders who set examples in speech and behavior, in love, faith, and purity. The philosophy of servant leadership as coined by Greenleaf (1970), and the ten characteristics of servant leaders as stated by Spears (2010) are the cornerstones of the school's character development and holistic education approaches.

Carolyn Crippen, PhD is associate professor of leadership studies at the University of Victoria, British Columbia, Canada. Carolyn has been involved in the philosophy of servant-leadership for over forty years. Carolyn has written and published internationally and works with doctoral students in servant-leader research, particularly in areas such as policing, early childhood, schools, and administration. Leading through service, compassion, and humility are keys to a better society. Carolyn has designed several graduate courses directed toward servant-leadership and begins all her classes with silent reflection.

A/P **Lim Lee Hean, PhD** is with the Policy and Leadership Studies Academic Group at the National Institute of Education of the Nanyang

Technological University in Singapore. She is currently involved in the development and delivery of courses for the professional development of in-service educators and post-graduate students. She has previous training and experiences in the creation, implementation, and reviewing of curriculum materials. Her research interests include management and leadership, leadership mentoring in education, as well as gender issues. Her writings focus on aspects pertaining to research and practice in education, both locally and internationally.

Christopher Horsethief, PhD is an educator and organizational theorist specializing in complex systems and social processes, collectively intelligent problem-solving systems and post-traumatic community resilience. For twenty-five years, Christopher has been facilitating field analysis of the relationship between culture and communication, documenting the dynamics that pose challenges to indigenous leaders and organizational resilience that drives language revitalization. His research interests include social network architectures, cultural entropy and their role in post-crisis cultural network fragmentation and alignment processes. Christopher's instructional experience includes terms as the indigenous scholar in Residence at College of the Rockies and Gonzaga University's MBA-American Indian Entrepreneurship Program. He is a member of the ʔakisq̓nuk First Nation of the Ktunaxa People.

Jeremiah Ole Koshal, PhD is an assistant professor of Leadership at Chandaria School of Business, United States International University—Africa, Nairobi, Kenya. He holds a doctorate in organizational leadership and an MBA in management from Regent University, USA, and a bachelor of commerce from Daystar University, Kenya. Dr. Koshal teaches in the area of management along with leadership and governance. Dr. Koshal also supervises both MBA and Doctor of Business Administration (DBA) students. Dr. Koshal has presented at international conferences as well as offering consulting services in strategy development, change management, and leadership development.

Richard Leider is founder of Inventure – The Purpose Company, where the mission is to help people to "unlock the power of purpose." Richard has written ten books, including three best sellers, which have sold over one million copies. *The Power of Purpose* and *Repacking Your Bags* are considered classics in the personal growth field. Widely viewed as a global thought leader of the purpose movement, his work is featured regularly in many media sources, and his PBS Special—*The Power of Purpose*—was viewed by millions of people. He has taken his purpose message to five continents and advised everyone from AARP to the National Football League and the U.S. State Department.

Peter L. Lim, PhD is the chair of the diversity council at Fuller Theological Seminary in Pasadena, California, and the Headington Chair of Global Leadership Development at its School of Intercultural Studies. He was the acting dean of the school before stepping off to begin his sabbatical on July 1, 2019. His most recent chapter co-written with renowned historian Scott W. Sunquist, focusing on leadership development efforts in Asia, appears in the Oxford Handbook of Presbyterianism published in 2019. He is working on another book, *Conflict Management in Intercultural Partnerships: A Leadership Perspective*, during his nine-month sabbatical. He is married to Stephanie and they have four adult children serving in four different professions.

Toni Jimenez-Luque, PhD was the coordinator for the International Cooperation for Development at the University of Barcelona Solidarity Foundation from 2004 to 2013 and worked with universities, grassroots organizations, and social movements in Latin America, Africa, and Asia. In 2014, Dr. Jimenez-Luque moved to the United States to work at Gonzaga University for the associate vice president for equity, diversity, and inclusion as intercultural research associate, and taught a variety of classes including Leading Across Cultures and Democracy and Human Rights. Since 2018, he is teaching leadership theories at the University of San Diego and developing his research agenda on issues of leadership and social justice from a critical, global, and intercultural perspective.

Robson Marinho, PhD is a professor, leadership researcher, and the associate director of the Andrews University Leadership Center in Michigan, USA. He teaches leadership development, and adult learning, and has published books and articles in English and Portuguese on these subjects. Dr. Marinho holds a doctorate in higher education administration from Indiana University, in Bloomington, Indiana, USA.

Margaret Muchiri, PhD is a renowned educator and social justice activist in Kenya. Her work on helping women become servant-leaders who transcend cultural and interpersonal difficulties and chaos in order to bring healing to others is an important part of Kenyan development and contributes to a deeper understanding of community and culture throughout the world.

Serving his community, **Peter Mulinge, PhD** is the founder and president of Africa Servant Leadership Development initiative (ASLEAD) in the United

States and in Kenya–Africa. He holds doctor of ministries degree (DMin) and a doctorate in leadership studies from Gonzaga University, Washington State in the United States. Dr. Mulinge is an ever invited speaker for leadership seminars and workshops. Dr. Mulinge recently developed a servant-leadership development model entitled MODEL HOUSE. He has published two manuscripts, The Anchor of Servant-Leadership: Julius Nyerere and Virtue of Humility and Altruism and Altruistic Love: Intrinsic Motivation for Servant-leadership. Currently, he is an adjunct lecturer at Northwest University and developing community servant-leaders in rural Kenya.

Kathleen Patterson, PhD serves as professor and the director of the Doctor of Strategic Leadership program at Regent University, where she has been since 1999. Dr. Patterson is noted as an expert on servant-leadership and has coordinated three global roundtables, in the Netherlands, Australia, and Iceland. Additionally, she is involved in numerous consulting projects nationally and abroad and sits on the board of the Larry C. Spears Center, CareNet, and Millennials for Marriage.

Karel San Juan, SJ, PhD is president of Ateneo de Zamboanga University, the Jesuit university in Zamboanga City in southern Philippines. He has a doctorate in leadership studies from Gonzaga University in Spokane, Washington, USA. His talks, seminars, and papers have revolved around the themes of leadership and spirituality, power, organizational development, and management. He represented the Philippine Jesuits in the General Congregation of the Society of Jesus in Rome in October 2016.

Areej Abdullah Shafai, PhD is an assistant professor at the University of Business and Technology (UBT) in Jeddah. She also works as an assistant director general of UBT executive education, in charge of research, development and training. Dr. Shafai is a graduate of the University of San Francisco, where she earned her doctoral degree in organization and leadership.

Mary C. Sobralske, EdD received her doctoral degree in educational leadership from Gonzaga University. She is a family nurse practitioner and a certified transcultural nurse. Her research interests focus on how culture affects health and social issues, community leadership, and public health policy. She believes that leadership can positively influence how health care is delivered and received among the most vulnerable populations served and is crucial to positive health outcomes. Dr. Sobralske is currently working as an advanced registered nurse practitioner for the Spokane Community Colleges Student Health Center, Washington State University, College of Nursing.

Low Guat Tin, EdD is a former staff member in the Policy and Leadership Studies Academic Group, at the National Institute of Education of the Nanyang Technological University in Singapore. Her basic training was in school psychology and she moved on to study educational management at the University of Michigan. She has conducted workshops and seminars in various countries. She has written a number of books and articles in various areas, including management and living creatively.

Patricia Valdés, PhD earned her doctorate in leadership studies at Gonzaga University where her research included servant leadership, non-traditional roles of leadership among Latina students, and the use of stories and art as conduits for healing. She is supervisor of the bereavement department at Hospice of Spokane and participates in an environment that promotes the spirit of servant leadership. Dr. Valdés provides grief counseling where she incorporates stories and art in her practice with individuals and groups. Additionally, she provides outreach to the community and oversees a grief camp for youth. Dr. Valdés previously worked in the School of Social work as a lecturer and administrator at Eastern Washington University and as a bicultural consultant and interim multicultural program supervisor at Spokane Mental Health Center.

Muzabel Welongo is a social entrepreneur and development professional whose work focuses on education, financial inclusion, and youth workforce development. He holds a Master of Global Human Development from Georgetown University, School of Foreign Service. Muzabel moved to the United States in 2017, after twenty-one years of living in refugee camps in Tanzania and Kenya. He is the founder of Resilience Action International, a refugee-run organization that promotes education and economic self-reliance among refugees. Muzabel's work among refugees has been instrumental in promoting education for all, while helping create greater spaces for integration of refugee youth in education and employment. Muzabel speaks English, French, and Swahili fluently.